THEORIES OF COUNSELING

THIRD EDITION

SAMUEL T. GLADDING

WAKE FOREST UNIVERSITY

ROWMAN & LITTLEFIELD

LANHAM • BOULDER • NEW YORK • LONDON

Acquisitions Editor: Mark Kerr
Acquisitions Assistant: Courtney Packard
Sales and Marketing Inquiries: textbooks@rowman.com

Credits and acknowledgments for material borrowed from other sources, and reproduced with
permission, appear on the appropriate pages within the text.

Published by Rowman & Littlefield
An imprint of The Rowman & Littlefield Publishing Group, Inc.
4501 Forbes Boulevard, Suite 200, Lanham, Maryland 20706
www.rowman.com

86–90 Paul Street, London EC2A 4NE

British Library Cataloguing in Publication Information Available

Library of Congress Cataloging-in-Publication Data
Names: Gladding, Samuel T., author.
Title: Theories of counseling / Samuel T. Gladding, Wake Forest University.
Description: Third edition. | Lanham : Rowman & Littlefield, [2022] | Includes bibliographical
    references and index.
Identifiers: LCCN 2021009166 (print) | LCCN 2021009167 (ebook) | ISBN 9781538141076
    (cloth) | ISBN 9781538141083 (paperback) | ISBN 9781538141090 (epub) Subjects: LCSH:
Counseling. | Counseling psychology.
Classification: LCC BF636.6 .G627 2022 (print) | LCC BF636.6 (ebook) | DDC 158.3—dc23
LC record available at https://lccn.loc.gov/2021009166
LC ebook record available at https://lccn.loc.gov/2021009167

To "Pal,"
aka Inez Barnes Templeman,
my maternal grandmother,
a positive and dynamic influence
who accepted me unconditionally,
taught me by example kindness, civility, and generosity,
and showed me how to love others who are "different"

Brief Contents

■ ■ ■

Contents

■ ■ ■

Preface

■ ■ ■

Theories are guiding lights. They give us some direction when we are with clients who have come to us in pain and with problems or concerns they do not know how to handle. Like light, theories can and do change. Some become brighter with time, others shift their focus, and still others fade because they either lack a solid foundation or lose their relevance for the populations we serve. Wondrously new theories, like emerging lights, are generated as insightful clinicians and academics construct them out of the context in which people live.

Because this book is about counseling theories that are most prevalent at the beginning of the 21st century, it should be read in the light of its time. Some of the material covered here will shine brighter in the future whereas other ideas will fade. In addition, some theories explained here may change their emphases. New ways of working with client populations will be created as practitioners discover new means of helping individuals in mental distress. Thus the knowledge gained from this text will be finite. To keep growing as a practitioner, you will have to study and read continuously about the latest developments in counseling and how theories intersect with practice.

So why should you study these theories at this time? It is simple. They are the best and most complete ways of working with others that we have at our disposal. Furthermore, they provide ways of conceptualizing the words and actions of individuals and working constructively with them. Theories, if employed judiciously, will shed light on your work and give you direction as to what helping professionals at other levels and specialties do. Without such a basis for making plans and decisions, you and others who provide counseling services would have to rely on trial and error or on intuition, neither of which is as efficient or effective.

This book is laid out developmentally. The order is chronological starting with a chapter on theories and therapies, then covering 15 widely used theories and ending with chapters on crisis counseling and ethics. Each of the theories covered in this book is distinct as are the branches of a tree. Yet, like branches, they are connected to the trunk of the tree. Conceptually and literally each influences and gives life to the others (see Figure 0.1).

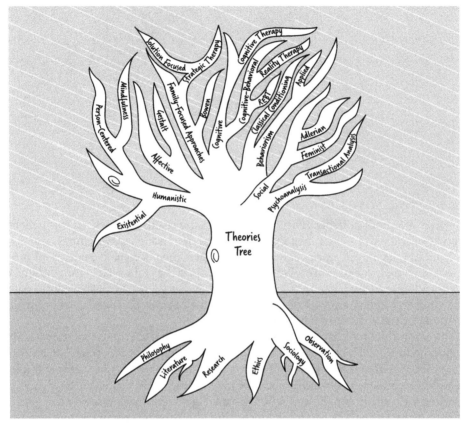

Figure 0.1 Theories tree

Shiri Esh'har for Zebra on Wheels

After chapter 1 of this book, with an exploration of what theories are, the next 15 chapters on theories follow a uniform outline:

- Chapter Overview
- Major Theorist(s)
- View of Human Nature/Personality
- Role of the Counselor
- Goals
- Process and Techniques
- Diversity and Multicultural Issues
- Evaluation of the Theory
- Treating Linda: A case showing how a client would be treated with the chapter theory
- Summing Up
- Chapter Recap
- Learning More
- Classroom Activities

The final two chapters of the book cover ethical issues in counseling and crisis counseling.

NEW FEATURES OF THE THIRD EDITION

This third edition of *Theories of Counseling* is geared toward counselors and those who aspire to be counselors. You will find several new features helpful.

The first new feature in this edition is that each chapter begins with an overview of what the chapter will focus on. In this way, you as the reader get an idea of some of the most important points that will be covered. Parallel to this beginning is an even more extensive ending entitled "Chapter Recap" at the "Summing Up" of the chapters where crucial material covered in the chapters is outlined. Thus as a reader you are exposed to both an expectation and a summarization of the chapter contents.

The second new feature is the inclusion of five reflective questions in each chapter. They are included to help you think more about the theory you are reading about and to personalize concepts. These reflections ask you as a reader to think about your life experiences and the concepts covered. They are meant to make the material in each chapter more personal.

The third new feature of this edition is that more than 125 new references have been added while keeping older classical ones. Consulting both will help you as a reader find pertinent information from sources you may want to follow up on.

The fourth new feature of this edition is a chapter on psychodrama. This theory is more group oriented than the other theories addressed in the book. It is an important way to work with clients who have interpersonal difficulties.

The fifth new feature of this book is it returns to the first edition of this text in that its focus is on counseling rather than human services. This renewed emphasis makes this book more versatile and appropriate for counselors at all experience levels as well as for other mental health professionals who wish to learn more about therapeutic approaches.

Finally, this edition of *Theories of Counseling* has all the references listed in a reference section in the back of the book as opposed to previous editions where the references were listed at the end of each chapter.

As with previous editions of this text, the writing style is engaging, and with tables, figures, charts, and a uniform chapter organization, your ability to see practical applications of theoretical concepts should be enhanced.

I sincerely hope you enjoy this book! Helping others in need is an adventure, privilege, and challenge, as is uncovering the world of counseling theories and discovering their pragmatic aspects.

Acknowledgments

■ ■ ■

I would like to thank my colleagues both past and present for the many contributions they have made to my understanding of theories and the therapeutic process. My work and interactions with fellow clinicians in public mental health centers, private practice, and academic settings have allowed me to gain firsthand experience as a practicing counselor using major theories. My observations of and collaboration with counselor practitioners in the field after natural disasters, in meeting needs in domestic situations, and in providing psychoeducational programs has given me a great appreciation for what we in this specialty do.

I would also like to thank my previous editors, especially Kevin Davis, at Pearson Education for their support, encouragement, and hard work on my behalf. In addition, I want to express my sincere thanks and deep appreciation to Mark Kerr, Courtney Packard, and Rowman & Littlefield for all they have done for me in writing this third edition of *Theories of Counseling*. They have been wonderful to work with.

Finally, I wish to express my gratitude for the support and love my family, particularly my wife, Claire, has shown me throughout this writing project. Without a lot of understanding and some quiet moments, I could not have completed it in a timely way.

I hope you will benefit from reading this book. In the writing process, I have grown to appreciate even more the light and guidance that theories provide. Such may be the case for you as you reflect on the thoughts of the individuals who have provided the foundation for all we do in counseling.

1

Counseling Theories:
An Overview

■ ■ ■

He follows her words
to the end of her thoughts
and hears the deep pain in her voice.
Sensitively, he tries to respond
structuring what he says
through a theory
that slowly unfolds like a story in a book.
The session has begun!

"The Session" © S. T. Gladding

CHAPTER OVERVIEW

From reading this chapter you will learn about

■ What a theory is and specifically why theories are important.
■ Characteristics of thorough theories.
■ The pragmatic nature of theories and how they evolve over time.

As you read, consider

■ What formal or informal theories of people you hold and how they affect your interactions with others.
■ The strengths and limitations of theories in working with others.
■ How theories of others in your world have changed or remained the same.

The Osgood family has been shaken to the core. A category 3 tornado has just destroyed their house. They are wandering around in the rain outside the foundation of the white wooden structure where they have lived for 10 years as they begin realizing everything they owned and valued, outside human life, is gone. They are disoriented, shivering, and having different reactions. The mother, Cynthia, is sitting down crying and has noticeable cuts on her face. The father, Harold, is walking around in a daze with his shirt torn almost in shreds. Earl, their 16-year-old son, is scurrying about in a panic trying to find the family's dog that was outside when the tornado hit. Meanwhile, Janet, age 11, is looking through the debris of what was once a two-story dwelling shaking her head, picking up boards, and repeatedly saying: "Oh no, oh no, oh no!" That is the scene when you and others on your team of mental health practitioners arrive.

While the scene from the Osgood crisis is extreme in its intensity and limited in scope, the dynamics that are a part of it are all too real. Both in times of crisis and in calm people from all lifestyles need help in multiple ways every day. That is where counselors come in. Counseling as defined by the American Counseling Association is "a professional relationship that empowers diverse individuals, families, and groups to accomplish mental health, wellness, education, and career goals" (Kaplan et al., 2014, p. 366).

People helped by counselors range from children to geriatrics. They vary from victims of natural disasters, such as earthquakes, floods, and wildfires, to those who suffer from societal ills such as discrimination, poverty, abuse, and unemployment (Burger, 2018). Counselors focus on individuals, groups, families, and organizations to promote growth, learning, and remediation. The profession is altruistically based and caring.

Reflective Question

What might happen to people in need of mental health services if counselors were not available?

Theories guide counselors in their work (Jones-Smith, 2021). Such knowledge gives them insight into the practices of helping. It also gives them more awareness of how they can be supportive and effective when assisting individuals, couples, families, or groups, especially those struggling with personal and interpersonal relationships. Understanding counseling theories is paramount for counselors providing help for those in need. Theoretical knowledge frees those who work as counselors to operate in ethical, legal, and productive ways. It also gives them knowledge of how those with more or specialized degrees work and how they may work best with these professionals.

This chapter explores what a theory is, what qualities characterize valid theories, why theories are important, how theoretical points of view have developed, and how human professionals use theories singularly, eclectically, and cooperatively in their practices. The emphasis here is not just on theories but on counseling theories that practitioners will find useful and essential.

WHAT IS A THEORY?

In general terms a **theory** is a group of related laws or relationships that provide explanations within a discipline (Sharf, 2016). In counseling and therapy circles, a theory is thought of as "a set of principles used to explain human thought and behavior, including what causes people to change. In practice, a theory creates the goals of therapy and specifies how to pursue them" (Carlson & Engler-Carlson, 2011, p. viii). Thus, a theory is a model or template that gives a practitioner direction and guidance in working with others. Most counseling theories have been developed by exceptional practitioners and academicians, who have formulated their ideas about human nature and ways of working productively with people on the basis of collective and evidence-based experiences, research, and observations.

Practitioners employ counseling theories to address problems individuals, groups, and families develop and to provide possible solutions to their concerns. Most theories are affective, behavioral, cognitive, or systemic in nature. Based on their educational background, philosophy, and interests, as well as the needs of clients, effective helpers decide which theory or theories to apply to a situation. Not all approaches are appropriate. Indeed, one theory may not be adequate for the same client over an extended period of time. For example, a client may need to begin thinking rationally before behaving that way. Thus, a clinician might start out focused on correcting cognitive thoughts before changing to a more behaviorally based theory. Therefore, mental health practitioners must not only choose their theoretical positions carefully but also regularly reassess them for effectiveness.

Reflective Question

What formal or informal theory or theories do you hold of others in your environment? For instance, do you see people as good, somewhat deceptive, or a mixture of many qualities? How do you think most of your friends view those with whom they interact?

CHARACTERISTICS OF THOROUGH THEORIES

Some theoretical models are more thorough and versatile than others. Because of these characteristics these theories are probably used often. According to Hansen et al. (1986), a thorough theory is:

- **Clear, easily understood, and communicable.** It should make sense and be explainable.
- **Comprehensive.** A good theory encompasses explanations for a wide variety of phenomena in human development.
- **Explicit and heuristic.** A thorough theory is didactic in laying out its major tenets. It also generates research because of its design, inviting others to explore its uses.
- **Specific** in relating means to desired outcomes. A well-crafted theory includes a way of achieving a desired end product. It contains guidelines others can follow to obtain similar results.
- **Useful** to its intended practitioners. A complete theory is practical and provides strategies its followers may use under certain conditions or with specific populations.

In addition to these five qualities, a thorough theory matches a practitioner's personal philosophy of helping. It fits like a good suit of clothes. Some theories, like some suits, need tailoring; therefore, effective clinicians realize the importance of alterations. Those who wish to be versatile and effective should learn a wide variety of counseling theories and know how to apply each without violating the theory's internal consistencies (Auvenshine & Noffsinger, 1984). Competent helping specialists are not limited to a few pet theories (see Figure 1.1).

Figure 1.1 "I like my pet theories"
Shiri Esh'har for Zebra on Wheels

Reflective Question

What do you think a counselor should do in order to learn a wide variety of theories and find one or more that fit?

THE PRAGMATIC VALUE OF THEORIES

The practical value of solidly formulated theories cannot be overstressed (Brammer et al., 1993). "A theory guides action toward successful outcomes while generating hope in the therapist and the client that recovery is possible" (Carlson & Englar-Carlson, 2011, p. viii). Theories thus help explain what happens in relationships and assist helpers in predicting, evaluating, and improving results. Furthermore, counseling theories provide a framework for scientific and accurate observations. Theorizing encourages a coherence of ideas and the production of new ideas (Gladding, 1990). It helps make sense out of observations. As Prochaska and Norcross

(2018) put it, "Without a guiding theory ... clinicians would be vulnerable, directionless creatures bombarded with literally hundreds of impressions and pieces of information in a single session" (p. 4) or extended encounter.

Boy and Pine (1983) elaborate even further on the practical value of theories by suggesting that theories are the why behind the how of helping, providing a framework within which helpers can operate. For instance, counselors guided by theories can meet the demands of their roles because they have reasons for what they do with others. Boy and Pine point out six practical functions of theories:

- Theories help practitioners find unity and relatedness within their diversity of experience.
- Theories compel helpers to examine relationships they would otherwise overlook.
- Theories give practitioners operational guidelines by which to work and help them evaluate their development as specialists.
- Theories assist helpers in focusing on relevant data.
- Theories enable practitioners to assist clients in making effective behavior modifications when appropriate.
- Theories assist helpers in evaluating old approaches and constructing new ones to the processes they are using.

"The ultimate criterion for all ... theories is how well they provide explanations of what occurs" (Kelly, 1988, pp. 212–213). The value of theories as ways of organizing information "hinges on the degree to which they are grounded in the reality of people's lives" (Young, 1988, p. 336).

THE EVOLUTION OF THEORIES

Theories, including those in counseling, have evolved over time. In today's world, there are theories that are antiquated and unproven as well as those that are effective and that are supported by research.

Antiquated Theories

Even before recorded time there are indications that people had theories about human functioning and mental disorders. Archeological records show that a practice known as **trephining,** the drilling of holes in the skull of the person being treated, occurred in some prehistoric societies. Ancient people believed that evil spirits possessed individuals who were mentally disturbed. The holes were drilled to let the wicked spirits out or to relieve pressure on the brain. In almost all cases, the treatment was worse than the disorder.

In medieval Europe the same physically-based type of theory for treating psychological stress and disorders continued, resulting in the practice of exorcism, meant to drive out evil spirits and restore mentally deranged individuals to health. Members of the clergy, mainly in monasteries, initially performed exorcisms. They also used techniques such as the laying on of hands and insulting the possessing demon(s) with obscene epithets.

As beliefs about the physical nature of evil spirit possession became more fully accepted, additional unpleasant means were used to drive out demons, such as flogging, starving, using chains, immersing in hot water, and even burning. The idea behind the treatment was that the possessing spirit(s) would leave an inhospitable host. Unfortunately, these remedies resulted in the demise of many persons who were mentally disturbed (Butcher et al., 2013).

In Western societies subsequent treatment of people with mental conditions was eventually replaced because the theory of demon possession was discredited, but not before tragic events such as the infamous Salem Witch Trials in the American colonies of the 1600s. Instead of being tortured to death, individuals with psychological troubles or "abnormal/strange behaviors" were locked up in institutions and "cared for." Sometimes they were given humane treatment whereas at other times they were harshly treated. There was almost no treatment besides physical restraint because no theoretical construct existed as to what should be done. Psychiatric patients were sometimes placed on display for public amusement, and chaos reigned inside their facilities. The now-common term **bedlam** (describing madness or chaos) originated from the Bethlem Royal Hospital in London, which was the first to specialize in treating the mentally ill. It was renowned for its disarray and turmoil.

Modern Theories

Not until the 18th century was a new theory of treatment formulated for working with individuals experiencing emotional problems. That development occurred almost simultaneously in Europe and the American colonies. Benjamin Rust in North America, Phillip Pinel in France, and William Tuke in England led this movement. The **humane theory** proposed that those with mental disorders be unchained and receive better treatment, such as time outdoors each day, a more nutritious diet, and communication with others. The idea was that people would get better when they received sunlight, good food, and kind attention (Ziff, 2012).

This reform had varied success. It gave rise to **talk therapies,** even before Sigmund Freud. Two early examples were initiated by Paul Dubois (1848–1918), a Swiss physician, and Pierre Janet (1859–1947), a French physician. Both practitioners spoke to and with their mentally disturbed patients in a reasonable and logical manner. Those who suffered physical troubles, such as having been in a natural disaster, were not as fortunate in what happened to them unless they lived in a community that was altruistic in nature or had caring neighbors who would assist them.

In recent times, theories of helping have emerged based on a variety of concepts from free will and determinism (Wilks, 2003). For instance, psychodynamic and behavioral theory, both covered in this text, grew out of biologic/psychic determinism and environmental determinism, respectively. More humanistic theories—such as existential, Adlerian, person-centered, and reality therapy, also covered in this book—are grounded in the idea that people have a degree of free will.

Regardless of their base, theories of helping that influence counseling professionals have developed almost exponentially since the 1950s. For instance, in the field of therapy only 36 systems of psychotherapy had been identified in the late 1950s (Harper, 1959). By 1976, Parloff had discovered more than 130 therapeutic approaches, some of which were quite questionable. Only 3 years later, in 1979, *Time* reported that more than 200 therapies had been formulated (Prochaska & Norcross, 2018), and early in the 21st century more than 400 systems of therapeutic interventions have been documented worldwide, ranging from mindfulness to soap opera therapy. Professional helpers today clearly have a wide variety of theories from which to choose.

Reflective Question

What comes to your mind when you think of theoretical techniques to helping? Which techniques would you be most comfortable with—for example, talking, acting, or emoting? How often do you think therapeutic techniques should be used? How long do you think an ideal counseling/helping process should last?

Although theory development has not stopped, Okun (1990) states that the present emphasis, at least in helping circles, is on connecting counseling theories instead of creating them. This focus rests on the fundamental assumption that "no one theoretical viewpoint can provide all of the answers for the clients we see today" (p. xvi).

Another current trend is helping practitioners adapt techniques and interventions from different theoretical approaches into their work without actually accepting the premises of some theoretical points of view. This flexibility can be seen in the widespread use of **microskills**—atheoretical helping methods, such as active listening, reflection of feeling and content, immediacy, confrontation, and summarization—that promote relationship formation and exploration of a problem or concern. The microskills approach, which is useful in many cases, does not rely on a comprehensive approach of addressing personal difficulties, but assumes that some therapeutic skills transcend theory. Nonetheless, as therapists consider intrapersonal, interpersonal, and external factors when working with clients, theories generate counseling techniques and blend all these dimensions in unique, inclusive, and effective ways.

THEORIES AND ECLECTICISM

Most professional helpers, including those involved in counseling, identify themselves as **eclectic**—that is, combining theories or techniques from a wide variety of therapeutic approaches (Sharf, 2016). These practitioners use various theories and techniques to match their clients' needs, with "an average of 4.4 theories making up their therapeutic work with clients" (Cheston, 2000, p. 254). As needs change, clinicians may depart from one theory and adopt another—a phenomenon called **style shift counseling**.

Counselors make changes related to their clients' developmental levels (Ivey et al., 2018). To be effective, practitioners must consider how far their clients have progressed in their development, as described by theorists like Jean Piaget, and what their needs are, as outlined by Abraham Maslow. For example, according to Piaget's theory, clients who are not developmentally aware of their environments may need a therapeutic approach that focuses on "emotions, the body, and experience in the here and now," whereas clients at a more advanced level of development may respond best to a "consulting-formal operations" approach, in which the emphasis is on thinking about actions (Ivey & Goncalves, 1988, p. 410). Likewise, according to Maslow, clients who are lacking basic physical needs should have these addressed before trying to meet their higher needs such as self-esteem. Clinicians must start with where their clients are and help them develop in a holistic manner (see Figure 1.2).

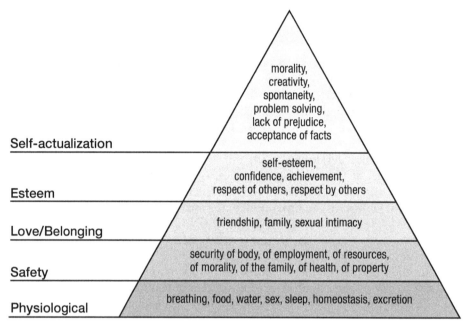

Figure 1.2 Abraham Maslow's hierarchy of needs

Even though eclecticism can draw on various theories, techniques, and practices to meet clients' needs, this approach does have its drawbacks. For instance, an eclectic approach can be hazardous if helpers are not thoroughly familiar with all aspects of the theories involved. In such situations, helping specialists may become technicians who do not understand why certain approaches work best with specific clients at certain times and in certain ways (Cheston, 2000). In such cases, an eclectic orientation often does more harm than good.

To combat this problem, McBride and Martin (1990) advocate a hierarchy of eclectic practices and discuss the importance of having a sound theoretical base as a guide. They describe the first or lowest level of eclecticism as **syncretism**—a sloppy, unsystematic process of putting unrelated clinical concepts together. It is encouraged when students are urged to formulate their own theories without first having experienced how tested models work. The second level of eclecticism is traditional. It incorporates "an orderly combination of compatible features from diverse sources [into a] harmonious whole" (English & English, 1956, p. 168). Theories are examined in greater depth and breadth than in syncretism, but no mastery is expected.

The third level of eclecticism is described as theoretical or as **theoretical integrationism** (Lazarus & Beutler, 1993; Simon, 1989). This type of eclecticism requires that helpers master at least two theories before attempting any combinations. This approach assumes a degree of equality between theories, which may not be accurate, and the existence of criteria "to determine what portions or pieces of each theory to preserve or expunge" (Lazarus & Beutler, 1993, p. 382).

A fourth level of eclecticism is called **technical eclecticism** and is exemplified in the work of Arnold Lazarus (2000, 2009) and the BASIC ID acronym (behavior, affect, sensation, imagination, cognition, interpersonal, and drugs and biology). In this approach, procedures from different theories are selected and used in treatment

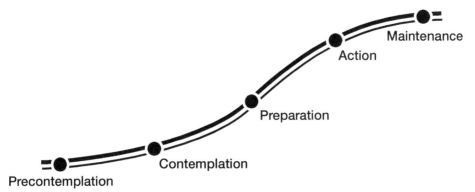

Figure 1.3 Transtheoretical levels of change from precontemplation to maintenance

"without necessarily subscribing to the theories that spawned them" (Lazarus & Beutler, 1993, p. 384). The idea is that techniques, not theories, are used in treating individuals. Therefore, after properly assessing clients, practitioners can use behavioral methods (such as assertiveness training) with interpersonal techniques (such as confronting persons about the meaning they find in relationships) or other combinations. This approach is in line with what Cavanagh and Levitov (2002) propose as a healthy way to conduct helping. It requires clinicians in all helping specialties to have:

- A sound knowledge and understanding of the theories used.
- A basic integrative philosophy of human behavior that brings disparate parts of differing theories into a meaningful collage.
- A flexible means of fitting the approach to the client.

The critical variables in being a healthy eclectic helper are a mastery of theory and an acute sensitivity to knowing which approach to use when, where, and how (Harman, 1977).

A final type of eclectic approach is the **transtheoretical model (TTM) of change** (Prochaska & DiClemente, 1992; Prochaska & Norcross, 2018). This model is developmentally based and has been empirically derived over time. It is "an alternative to technical eclectic approaches that tend to be inclusive to the point that various components are 'poorly' held together" (Petrocelli, 2002, p. 23). The model proposes five stages of change—precontemplation, contemplation, preparation, action, and maintenance. Not everyone is ready to change when help is available. Some are not aware they need to change and are precontemplative. Others are contemplative of making a change but are not prepared to act. They need to get ready. Once action is taken, it needs to be maintained if it is going to make a difference. As an entity and progressive model, the transtheoretical levels of change look like Figure 1.3.

Reflective Question

Think of when you have made a change in your life. When and how did you realize you needed to change? What behaviors just listed did you experience?

"Counseling from a TTM perspective allows for a more macroscopic approach (involving a broad and comprehensive theoretical framework) and personal adaptation (involving an increase in critical, logical, accurate, and scientific-like thinking) rather than simple personal adjustment" (Petrocelli, 2002, p. 25). Its main drawbacks are its comprehensiveness and complexity and the fact that TTM has been tested only among limited groups, such as addicted populations.

THEORIES AND APPLICATION: THE CASE OF LINDA

The major theories discussed in subsequent chapters have significant differences in their approaches to psychological helping: counseling. To highlight those differences and show the ways in which therapists would operate from each of the theoretical perspectives, each theory is applied to a common case—that of a young woman named Linda. She is the person seeking help and in therapeutic terms is called a **client**. Comparing different theories at work with the same person should reveal those theories in action and permit an informed decision about their use, either singly or in combination.

Linda is a recently divorced, 32-year-old Caucasian woman seeking help because of relationship problems. Linda was married for 7 years but recently ended her marriage with her Arab American husband, Amir, because she no longer found him exciting and thought he was verbally abusive—he often criticized her looks, weight, and dress. During her marriage, Linda had an abortion because of Amir's insistence and the fact that she did not feel ready to be a responsible parent. However, she states that her former husband's insistence on remaining childless was the primary reason for the abortion. That event took place about 2 years ago, and Linda still has mixed emotions about it. When discussing it, she is both sad and angry.

Linda grew up in a lower-class neighborhood in a mid-sized Western city. Her father, Ralph, was a construction worker with a seventh grade education. He drank heavily on weekends but otherwise seemed to have a good work ethic and a positive attitude toward his work. Ralph had definite conservative opinions about politics, religion, and the place of women in society, and he never hesitated to voice his views, sometimes quite loudly. Linda kept her distance from him. Linda's mother, Marian, did not work outside the home. Instead, she took care of Linda and her three siblings: Ted, 2 years older than Linda; Patricia, 3 years younger; and Claudia, 13 months younger. A high school graduate, Marian took in sewing to earn extra income for the family. She was a rather quiet and introverted woman, and although Linda felt close to her in many ways, she never really identified with her mother. In fact, Linda reports that she is not emotionally close to her family at all.

As a teenager, Linda was mildly rebellious. She occasionally skipped school and church services and engaged once in petty theft at a local department store. She dated older boys, most of whom were friends of her brother. Linda was flirtatious but never really acted out sexually. She states that her brother was her protector; she was grateful for his presence in her adolescent life. Otherwise, she would have probably gotten into trouble. She might even have gotten married before finishing high school.

All of Linda's siblings graduated from high school but, like their parents, married young and got jobs either in a trade or in retail. Linda made good enough grades to have been accepted into a regular 4-year college. However, she did not feel confident enough to apply because it would have gone against family norms and she would have been seen as "uppity." She states that her father openly discouraged her further education. As a compromise, Linda enrolled in a local community college, where she completed a course in business administration. Since graduation, Linda has drifted from job to job as an administrative assistant or a secretary, never challenged in any of her jobs. She admits to having a temper and says that she is fed up with the treatment she receives from her bosses, who have all been men and sexist. She also gets tired of the routine work, especially the filing, that she must do.

Linda likes to read romance novels, watch the home-and-garden television channel, and go to action movies featuring car chase scenes. All these activities make her feel better; they take her away from her mundane existence. Since her divorce, she has felt aimless, anxious, and depressed. She has not found a peer group of singles or divorcees to associate with, and most of her former friends and acquaintances have either married or moved away. Both of her younger sisters are still in town, as are her parents, but Linda receives no support from them. In fact, she finds them boring. They do not "stretch their minds." Still, she sees them only once a week, for Sunday lunch, and leaves as soon as possible after the meal.

Linda reveals that she has had suicide ideations about ending her life by stepping out in front of a truck. However, she swears she would never do such a thing. She has recently contemplated finding a new job or going to a nearby college to earn a 4-year degree. She has recently given 2 weeks' notice to her employer. She does not want life to pass her by, but she is beginning to think it is doing just that. Her voice sounds almost desperate as she asks for help and direction.

SUMMING UP

Current ways of working with people who have concerns or problems are based on theories that have been researched and tested for effectiveness with client populations. Such was not always the case. The first theories for the treatment of people in mental pain were degrading, based on superstition, and potentially deadly. Clients were thought to be possessed by evil spirits that had to be driven out. This viewpoint eventually gave way to more humane approaches, and theories of treatment, initially slow to evolve, exploded in number during the last half of the 20th century.

Today, the creation and development of theories have slowed; movement is toward the combination of approaches and eclecticism. Most counselors use multiple theories, and some focus more on techniques than theories. Nonetheless, the value of theories remains. They provide the foundation for the most effective counseling approaches.

CHAPTER 1 RECAP: COUNSELING THEORIES

What Is a Theory?

A theory may be thought of as a group of related laws or relationships used to provide explanations for an action. Theory explains human thought and behavior, including what causes people to change. In practice, a theory creates the goals of therapy and specifies how to pursue them.

Characteristics of Thorough Theories
- Clear, easily understood, and communicable.
- Comprehensive. A good theory encompasses explanations for a wide variety of phenomena in human development.
- Explicit and heuristic. Theory generates research because of its design, inviting others to explore its uses.
- Specific in relating means to desired outcomes. A well-crafted theory includes a way of achieving a desired product.
- Useful to its intended practitioners.

The Pragmatic Value of Theories
Theories are the *why* behind the *how* of helping.

Six practical functions of theories:

- Theories help practitioners find unity and relatedness within their diversity of experience.
- Theories compel helpers to examine relationships they would otherwise overlook.
- Theories give practitioners operational guidelines by which to work and help them evaluate their development as specialists.
- Theories assist helpers in focusing on relevant data.
- Theories enable practitioners to assist clients in making effective behavior modifications when appropriate.
- Theories assist helpers in evaluating old and constructing new approaches to the processes they are using.

Evolution of Theories
Antiquated theories came first, for example, trephining.
    In the Middle Ages emphasis was placed on ridding persons of evil spirits and included practices such as exorcism, burning, and chaining.

Modern Theories
Emphasis is placed on humane treatment and talk therapies.

Importance is placed on connecting theories instead of creating them.
The assumption is held that some therapeutic skills (microskills) transcend
    theory.

Theories and Eclecticism
Most modern practitioner helpers identify themselves as eclectic: combining theories or techniques from a wide variety of therapeutic approaches.
    As needs change, practitioners may depart from one theory and adopt another—a phenomenon called style shifting.
    Helpers make changes related to their clients' developmental levels.
    Hierarchy of eclectic practices:

- Lowest level (syncretism)—a disordered, unsystematic process of putting unrelated clinical concepts together.

- Second level (traditional)—an orderly combination of compatible features from diverse sources into a harmonious whole, but no mastery is expected.
- Third level (theoretical integrationism)—requires that helpers master at least two theories before attempting any combinations; assumes a degree of equality between theories.
- Fourth level (technical eclecticism)—exemplified in the BASIC ID acronym of Arnold Lazarus (behavior, affect, sensation, imagination, cognition, interpersonal, and drugs and biology). The idea is that techniques, not theories, are used in treating clients. Technical eclecticism is a flexible means of fitting the approach to the client.
- Fifth level (transtheoretical model) (TTM)—developmentally based and empirically derived over time. Stages of change in this model—precontemplation, contemplation, preparation, action, and maintenance. Not everyone is ready to change when help is available. Varied behaviors are associated with this model.

KEY TERMS

bedlam 6
client 10
humane theory 6
microskills 7
style shift counseling 7
syncretism 8
talk therapies 6

technical eclecticism 8
theoretical integrationism 8
theory 2
transtheoretical model (TTM) of
  change 9
trephining 5

LEARNING MORE

The website http://changingminds.org/explanations/theories/a_alphabetic.htm gives an alphabetical list of theories on which persuasion techniques are based. In looking at the website think of how many theories there are for explaining other aspects of human behavior.

CLASSROOM ACTIVITIES

1. How does the transtheoretical model of change help you understand why some individuals make changes in their lives while others do not? Think of historical or literary people who have made dramatic changes in their lives, such as Scrooge in Charles Dickens's *A Christmas Carol*, and talk to a classmate about the behaviors that changed in these individuals.
2. Microskills are prevalent in counseling. What does that tell you about the common qualities counselors share?
3. What are your thoughts about theories and their usefulness now that you have read this chapter? How has your thinking changed?

2

Psychoanalysis and Psychodynamic Therapies

■ ■ ■

All our baggage is behind us
as we rumble down the tracks
past the people and the places
that are changing.
At each station we entrust
those events now in our minds
will come to have new meaning
as we talk past fleeting scenery.

"Baggage" © S. T. Gladding

CHAPTER OVERVIEW

From reading this chapter you will learn about

■ Freud's central ideas about levels of consciousness and the interaction of the id, ego, and superego in the formation of personality.
■ Psychosexual and psychosocial stages of development.
■ Major defense mechanisms and major techniques used in psychodynamic theory.

As you read consider

■ How much you think your behaviors are impacted by your unconscious.
■ How often you have used defense mechanisms and which ones have been most prevalent for you.
■ How familiar you are with psychodynamic techniques such as free association, and how comfortable you would feel receiving therapy originating from this theory.

Psychoanalysis and psychodynamic theories are important both historically and currently. Psychoanalysis was the first theory to gain public recognition and acceptance, especially in Europe and the Americas. Sigmund Freud created psychoanalysis and from his ideas other psychodynamic theories sprang—for example, those of Anna Freud, Erik Erikson, Harry Stack Sullivan, Melanie Klein, Karen Horney, and Heinz Kohut.

In addition, many prominent therapists who did not become psychoanalysts were directly influenced by Freud's concepts, either through interaction with Freud or through instruction about his ideas—for example, Alfred Adler, Carl Jung, Albert Ellis, Rollo May, and Fritz Perls. Other theorists—including Carl Rogers, B. F. Skinner, and Otto Rank—developed theories in direct opposition to Freud's principles. Thus, Sigmund Freud and concepts of psychoanalysis permeate counseling literature in direct and indirect ways. To be uninformed about psychoanalysis and psychodynamic theories is to be undereducated as a helping specialist.

MAJOR THEORIST: SIGMUND FREUD

The life of Sigmund Freud (1856–1939) has been the focus of many books, such as Irving Stone's *Passions of the Mind*. His official biographer, Ernest Jones, wrote a definitive three-volume work (1953, 1955, 1957) on Freud's life and the development of his ideas.

Sigmund Freud was born in Freiburg, Austria, the first son of Jacob Freud's second marriage. His mother, Amalia, gave him special privileges because she had higher hopes for her Sigmund than for the five daughters and two sons born later. Consequentially, Freud grew up feeling special since his mother's attention centered on him. In 1860, Freud's father moved the family to Vienna, where Freud spent most of the remainder of his life.

Although he was an excellent student, Freud was limited in his occupational choices because of finances and the discrimination in Europe at the time against Jews' entering certain lines of work. Thus, Freud enrolled at the University of Vienna in 1873 with the idea of pursuing medicine since this was a career open to Jews. He received his medical degree in 1881, having mastered research methods as well as the normal coursework. He married Martha Bernays in 1886 and fathered six children, the youngest of whom, Anna, became famous in her own right as a child psychoanalyst.

Freud supported his family through his private practice in neurology, working primarily with individuals with hysteria. Initially, he used hypnosis as his main form of treatment, a technique he had mastered in France under the tutelage of neurologist Jean Charcot. Though Freud was not a good hypnotist, he soon discovered that this deficit was beneficial. Indeed, much of his success depended on the relationship he developed during the treatment process rather than on the hypnosis. This revelation led Freud to explore how he might use his clinical relationship with a client in combination with the client's concentration to bring about change (Freud, 1925/1959).

During medical school, Freud had been impressed with Joseph Breuer's **cathartic method** of treating people with hysteria. This method was coined "the talking cure" by one of Freud's most famous patients, Anna O., who also had sessions with Breuer. In his sessions, Breuer had his patients relive painful experiences and work through emotional events suppressed for years. Breuer's method also used hypnosis. However, Freud modified the approach by dropping the hypnosis and sitting behind his patients as they lay on couches. From this position, he would press his hand on their foreheads whenever they began to block out memories, assuring them they could remember long-forgotten important events and thoughts. Freud called this method **free association** and used it to explore the unconscious minds of his patients. The material uncovered in the process became the stuff of interpretation and analysis, and thus psychoanalysis was born. Freud's work with others, as well as years of self-analysis, gave him new insight into the nature of persons, and he began to stress the importance of the unconscious in understanding personality.

Many of Freud's colleagues, and later the public, were outraged by his emphasis on the importance of sexuality and aggression in the etiology of personality. Nevertheless, his ideas attracted a number of followers, and in 1902, he formally organized in his home the Wednesday Psychological Society, which met to discuss personality theory. This group, which at times included Carl Jung and Alfred Adler, became known in 1908 as the Viennese Psychoanalytic Society. It acquired international prominence when Freud and some of his followers accepted an invitation in 1908 to lecture at Clark University in the United States. Even though Freud suffered a number of personal and professional setbacks, his theory of psychoanalysis continued to develop. Practitioner journals and international congresses devoted to the theory, as well as Freud's prolific and heuristic writings, assured the historical prominence of psychoanalysis. Freud died in 1939 in London, a refugee from the Nazi occupation of Austria.

Freud's theory of psychoanalysis evolved throughout his lifetime. Many of its main tenets were set down in his books *The Interpretation of Dreams* (1900/1955), *New Introductory Lectures on Psychoanalysis* (1923/1933), and *The Ego and the Id* (1923/1947). The Freudian view of human nature is dynamic—that is, Freud believed in the transformation and exchange of energy within the personality (Hall, 1954). Much of what he described, however, is metaphorical because most of the hypotheses he proposed could not be proven scientifically at the time (Olson & Hergenhahn, 2011). Nevertheless, Freud hoped his theory would eventually be empirically verified, and he developed techniques for working with his patients based on that hope.

VIEW OF HUMAN NATURE/PERSONALITY

The psychodynamic view of human nature and personality, especially Freud's theory of psychoanalysis, is layered and complex. It is focused on levels of consciousness, the formation of personality, psychosexual development, and defense mechanisms.

Levels of Consciousness

For Freud human nature can be explained in terms of a **conscious mind**, a **preconscious mind**, and an **unconscious mind**. The conscious mind is attuned to events in the present, to an awareness of the outside world. The preconscious mind is an area between the conscious and unconscious minds and contains aspects of both. Within the preconscious mind are hidden memories or forgotten experiences that can be remembered with the proper cues. For example, after a long separation a person may recall another person's name if enough reminders are generated. Finally, beneath the preconscious mind is the unconscious mind, the most powerful and least understood part of the personality. The instinctual, repressed, and powerful forces of the personality exist in the unconscious mind.

Formation of Personality

Freud hypothesized that the personality is formed from the interaction of three developing parts—the **id**, the **ego**, and the **superego**—imbedded in the various conscious states. The id and the superego are confined to the unconscious, whereas the ego operates primarily in the conscious but also in the preconscious and the unconscious (see Figure 2.1).

The id comprises the inherited givens of the personality and is present from birth. It is amoral, impulsive, and irrational and works according to the **pleasure principle**—that is, it pursues what it wants because it cannot tolerate tension. The id operates

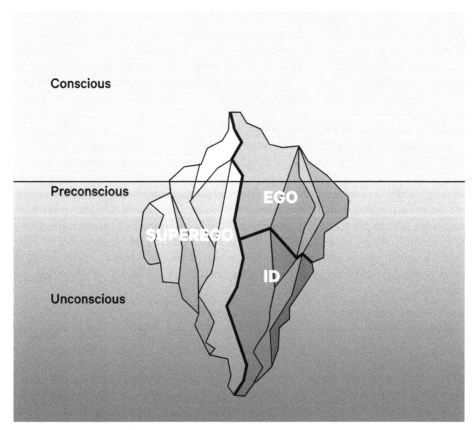

Figure 2.1 Freud's view of human personality

Shiri Esh'har for Zebra on Wheels

through drives, instincts, and images (such as dreaming, hallucinating, and fanta-sizing), a thought process known as the **primary process**. Although primary process thinking may bring temporary relief, it is ultimately unsatisfying. Consequently, the id discharges energy to the ego, which is another way of obtaining what it wants.

If empowered and left on its own, the id would probably destroy a person, or at least cause trouble by acting on its primitive, aggressive, and sexual drives. Those who let their ids guide their actions lack insight into the consequences of what they are doing. The id contains basic life energy, collectively known as **eros**, and basic death instincts, known as **thanatos**. At first, Freud associated eros with sexuality, but he later modified this idea, describing all life-preserving instincts as eros and the psychic energy that accompanies them as **libido**. The idea that each person has some sort of death wish was the result of Freud's observation of the destructiveness of World War I and his belief that humans, composed of inorganic matter, ultimately have a desire to return to this state of being. The premise of thanatos was never fully developed, but Freud saw it in acts of aggression, as well as in foolishly dangerous behaviors such as taking unnecessary risks.

The ego, the second system to develop, moderates the wishes and desires of the id and the superego in order to keep the person from being too self-indulgent or too morally restrained. It keeps the id from getting out of control and often is called "the executive of the mind." When the ego is fully developed, it functions to keep the desires of the id and the superego in check while helping the person interact realistically with the outside world. The ego works according to the **reality principle**, with reality being what exists (Hall et al., 1998). The ego devises ways to achieve appropriate goals, obtain energy for activities from the id, and keep the person in harmony with the environment. The ego's way of thinking is known as the **secondary process**, which is rationally thinking through situations. A strong ego is essential to healthy functioning.

The superego, in contrast to the id, is the moral branch of the mind, operating according to what is ideal. The superego arises from the moral teachings of a child's parents and functions according to the **moral principle**. Through a mechanism known as the **ego ideal**, it strives for perfection and rewards actions that follow parental and societal dictates. For example, children who have been taught that neatness is a virtue feel good when they keep a neat room. On the other hand, those who act against what they have been taught are punished through the part of the superego called the **conscience**, which induces guilt. The superego locks a person into rigid moral patterns if given free reign. Because its goal is perfection, the superego sometimes forces people into restrained action or no action when they face a dilemma.

Reflective Question

Reflect on your life when you engaged in foolish or admirable behaviors. What messages did you give yourself that influenced your actions? How does this information affect your acceptance of Freud's idea of personality and consciousness?

Psychosexual and Psychosocial Stages of Development

In addition to levels of consciousness and his concept of personality, psychoanalysis is built on what Freud referred to as **psychosexual developmental stages**. Each of four main stages focuses on a zone of pleasure dominant at a particular time. In the first stage, the **oral stage**, the mouth is the chief pleasure zone. Children under the age of 1 are in this stage and obtain basic gratification from sucking and biting. In the second stage, the **anal stage**, children between the ages of 1 and 2 delight in either withholding or eliminating feces. This stage involves the first significant conflict between a child's internal instincts and external demands, such as toilet training.

In the third stage, the **phallic stage**, children from 3 to 5 attempt to resolve their sexual identities. The chief zones of pleasure are the sex organs, and children of both genders must work through their sexual desires in a conflict of feelings known as the Oedipus complex. Freud thought that the conflict was clearer and more completely resolved in boys than in girls. Initially, both boys and girls are attracted to the mother because she is the source of great pleasure. Both genders see the father as a rival for the mother's love and attention. However, feelings about the mother change as boys and girls discover their own sexual identities.

For a boy there is a desire to possess his mother sexually. Yet there is a fear that if he makes his wishes known, his father, who is bigger and stronger, will become angry and castrate him. A boy assumes his penis is the source of conflict between his father and himself and girls, because they lack a penis, have been castrated.

Although the boy may feel hostile toward his father, he represses his desire for his mother and comes to identify with his father, thereby gaining vicarious satisfaction through father-mother interactions.

The Oedipus complex for a girl, sometimes called the Electra complex, is less clearly resolved. A young girl comes to notice she does not have a penis and boys do. Freud says she blames her mother for the lack of this valued organ and envies her father for possessing one (i.e., penis envy). Thus she has both negative and positive feelings toward each parent and is sexually ambivalent at the end of this stage. She takes some consolation from learning she has the ability to have babies because boys cannot. Therefore, she identifies with her mother and, according to Freud, hopes to receive later gratification by having children, especially boys.

The wishes of young boys and girls are not manifested directly during the phallic stage. Rather they are disguised in dreams, fantasy, and play. Nevertheless, the wishes are real. If not resolved, they will lead to future intra- and interpersonal difficulties. Freud thought the basic ingredients of the adult personality had formed by the end of the phallic stage.

After the phallic stage, between the ages of 6 and 12, comes a period known as **latency**, at which time there is little manifest interest in sexuality. Instead, energy is focused on peer activities and personal mastery of cognitive learning and physical skills. Around puberty occurs the last of the psychosexual phases, the **genital stage**. If all has gone well previously, each gender takes more interest in the other and normal heterosexual patterns of interaction appear. If there were unresolved difficulties in any of the first three stages, collectively known as the **pregenital stages**, the person may have difficulty adjusting to the adult responsibilities that begin in the genital stage. Freud believed two difficulties could arise in the pregenital stages—excessive frustration or overindulgence—causing a person to become **fixated**, or arrested, at that level of development and overly dependent on the use of defense mechanisms. For example, if someone becomes fixated at the oral stage, they may become oral dependent (a persistent need for oral stimulation like smoking and drinking) or oral aggressive (manifested in a biting or sarcastic personality).

Reflective Question

How do you think Freud's ideas about psychosexual stages of development match up with what society knows about sexuality today?

Freud's psychosexual stages of development are the aspects of his theory that have been modified most by others who have stayed in this tradition. Psychoanalysts Melanie Klein, Ronald Fairbairn, and Donald Winnicott proposed a much less sexually based view of childhood development. Their psychodynamic approach is known as **object relations theory**. An **object** is anything that satisfies a need, whether it is a person or a thing. The term "object" is used interchangeably with the term "other" to refer to an important person to whom the child and later the adult becomes attached. Infants perceive others as not-me objects for gratifying basic and instinctive needs, rather than as individuals with separate identities.

Object relations theory proposes that children introject what they perceive from others as good and both reject and project what they perceive as bad. In this way, children form an identity with others through interactions, both real and imagined.

The challenge for children "is to learn to negotiate with this outside world without trading away satisfaction of such fundamental needs as love, security, and esteem for individual autonomy and a sense of self" (Bankart, 1997, p. 179). Mature individuals are both independent and attached to others, able to integrate all aspects of themselves and avoid **splitting**, a defense mechanism that keeps incompatible feelings separate from oneself.

Erik Erikson (1963) went even further than the object relations theorists in modifying Freud's psychosexual theory of development. For Erikson development extends over the life span, and **psychosocial development** is most important. Thus Erikson's theory extends Freud's development emphasis from birth to death and focuses on the achievement of specific life-enhancing tasks. Like a number of other modifiers of Freud's theory, Erikson emphasizes the central role of the ego in life tasks rather than the interplay between the id, the ego, and the superego. Because of this emphasis, he and theorists like him are sometimes known as ego psychodynamic theorists. Erikson's stages of development and the accompanying ages and tasks are presented in Table 2.1. They encompass eight distinct stages. The first five deal with individual development through age 18. The last three focus on interpersonal relationships, productivity, and integrity/integration.

Defense Mechanisms

Defense mechanisms are the last crucial part of Freud's theory as it relates to human nature and personality. As a group, **defense mechanisms** protect a person from being overwhelmed by anxiety through adapting to situations or distorting or denying events. Such mechanisms are normal and operate on an unconscious level. Anna Freud (1936) and other ego psychodynamic theorists elaborated on Freud's original ideas. Among the main defense mechanisms are the following:

- **Repression.** Repression is the most basic defense mechanism, the one on which others are built. Using this mechanism, the ego involuntarily excludes from consciousness any unwanted or painful thoughts, feelings, memories, or impulses. The ego must use energy to keep excluded areas from consciousness,

Table 2.1   Erikson's Stages of Psychosocial Development

Stage	Age	Tasks
Trust vs. mistrust	Birth to 1	Emphasis on satisfying basic physical and emotional needs
Autonomy vs. shame/doubt	2 to 3	Emphasis on exploration and developing self-reliance
Initiative vs. guilt	4 to 5	Emphasis on achieving a sense of competence and initiative
Industry vs. inferiority	6 to 11	Emphasis on setting and attaining personal goals
Identity vs. role confusion	12 to 18	Emphasis on testing limits, achieving a self-identity
Intimacy vs. isolation	19 to 35	Emphasis on achieving intimate interpersonal relationships
Generativity vs. stagnation	36 to 65	Emphasis on helping next generation, being productive
Integrity vs. despair	66 +	Emphasis on integration of life activities, feeling worthwhile

but sometimes the repressed thoughts slip out in dreams or verbal expressions. Repression is considered the cornerstone or foundation stone of psychoanalysis (Nye, 2000).

- **Projection.** Persons using projection attribute an unwanted emotion or characteristic to someone else in an effort to deny that the emotion or characteristic is part of themselves. For example, a woman may say her boss is angry at her instead of saying she is angry at her boss.
- **Reaction formation.** With this mechanism, anxiety-producing thoughts, feelings, or impulses are repressed and their opposites are expressed. For example, a host at a party may shower a disliked guest with attention. A reaction formation is often detected by the intensity with which the opposite emotion is expressed.
- **Displacement.** Displacement channels energy away from one object to an alternative—that is, to a safe target. For instance, a person who has had a hard day at the office may come home and yell at the dog.
- **Sublimation.** A positive form of displacement is known as sublimation. It occurs when a drive that cannot be expressed directly is channeled into constructive activities. For example, those unable to express themselves sexually may take care of children. Freud thought sublimation was a major means of building civilization.
- **Regression.** In regression, a person returns to an earlier stage of development. For example, after suffering a trauma during early adolescence, a child may begin to wet the bed. Virtually all people regress if placed under enough pressure or stress.
- **Rationalization.** Rationalization allows a person to find reasonable explanations for unreasonable or unacceptable behaviors, to make them sound logical and acceptable. An individual might say, "I did it because everyone else was doing it," or "I really didn't think it was going to be worth the time I'd have to spend, so I didn't do it."
- **Denial.** A person in denial does not consciously acknowledge an unpleasant or traumatic event or situation. Denial protects people from having to face painful experiences. For instance, a couple may deny they are having marital problems even though both are aware the relationship is deteriorating. Denial may initially help a person cope with certain situations, such as war, but if perpetuated, it ultimately becomes destructive and can result in acute or post-traumatic stress disorders.
- **Identification.** In identification a person incorporates the qualities of another, thereby removing any fear that person might have of the other and giving him or her new behavioral skills. For example, a child might identify with a feared parent. Identification, like sublimation, differs from other defense mechanisms in that it can help a person realistically solve problems.

Reflective Question

How can a knowledge of defense mechanisms give counselors insight into the needs of clients?

Freud's view of human nature stresses conflict between conscious and unconscious forces (Luborksy et al., 2011; Sollod et al., 2009). A battle is going on inside every person between these forces, and therapists and counselors emphasize making the unconscious conscious in order to live more fully. This theory is also deterministic. It holds that a person's adult personality is formed by resolving the gender-specific stages of childhood. If a person has a traumatic childhood and fails to resolve a psychosexual stage, that person will need to work through this unresolved stage later in life.

ROLE OF THE COUNSELOR

Practitioners of psychodynamic theories, especially psychoanalysis, play the role of experts. They encourage their clients to talk about whatever comes to mind, especially childhood experiences. To create an atmosphere in which clients feel free to express difficult thoughts, psychodynamic theorists may have clients lie down on a couch while the clinician remains out of view, usually seated behind the client's head (see Figure 2.2).

The analyst's role is to let clients gain insight by reliving and working through unresolved past experiences that come into focus during therapy sessions. To help clients deal realistically with unconscious material therapists encourage them to project onto the therapist emotions associated with others in the clients' lives, a process known as **transference**. Unlike some other approaches, psychoanalysis encourages clinicians to interpret for their clients.

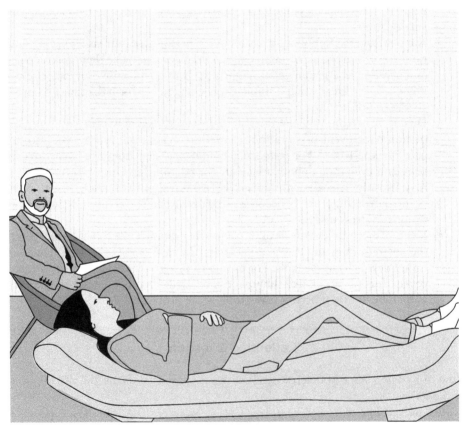

Figure 2.2 Client-analyst position during therapy
Shiri Esh'har for Zebra on Wheels

Overall, psychodynamic therapists employ both active and passive techniques. Psychological assessment instruments are sometimes employed, especially perceptual tests such as the Rorschach Ink Blots (Exner & Erdberg, 2005). Psychoanalytic and psychodynamic practitioners usually use diagnostic labels to classify clients and from those labels develop treatment plans. As a group, they rely on the latest edition of the American Psychiatric Association's *Diagnostic and Statistical Manual* (*DSM*), the standard reference for diagnoses.

GOALS

The goals of psychoanalysis and psychodynamic approaches vary according to the clients being treated. However, clinicians in these traditions focus mainly on personal adjustment, usually inducing a reorganization of internal forces within the persons they see. In most cases, a primary goal is to help clients become more aware of the unconscious aspects of their personalities, including repressed memories and wishes too painful or threatening to have been dealt with initially. Repression does not stop thoughts from having influence; it just makes identifying them more difficult. Psychoanalytic and psychodynamic approaches strive to help clients gain insight into themselves.

A second major goal, often tied to the first and most prevalent in object relations theory and self-psychology, is to help clients work through developmental stages not previously resolved. If accomplished, clients become unstuck and are able to live more productively. However, working through unresolved developmental stages may require a major reconstruction of the personality. Consequently, classical psychoanalysis, as practiced by Freud (drive psychology), is often a long, intense, and expensive process (Nye, 2000).

A final goal of psychoanalytic and psychodynamic approaches is helping clients cope with the demands of the society in which they live. According to these theories, unhappy people are not in tune with themselves or society. Thus psychoanalytic and psychodynamic approaches stress environmental adjustment, especially in the areas of work and intimacy. The focus is on strengthening the ego so that perceptions and plans become more realistic.

PROCESS AND TECHNIQUES

Although short-term psychodynamic approaches are prevalent, traditional psychodynamic therapy, especially psychoanalysis, are time consuming. Clients are usually seen a minimum of three times a week for several months or even years. Psychodynamic techniques are most often applied within a specific setting, such as a therapist's office or the interview room of a hospital. Among the most prominent techniques are free association, dream analysis, analysis of transference, analysis of resistance, and interpretation. Although each technique is examined separately here, in practice they are integrated into the process of therapy whether it is short or long term.

Free Association. Repressed material in the unconscious is always seeking release. On a daily basis this material may be expressed in the form of sexual or aggressive jokes or through **Freudian slips**, errors of speech such as "I loathe you" instead of "I love you." In psychoanalysis and psychodynamic therapies, clients are encouraged to relax and freely recall early childhood memories or emotional experiences. During free association, clients abandon the normal way of censoring thoughts by consciously repressing them and instead say whatever comes to mind, even if the thoughts seem silly, irrational, suggestive, or painful. In this way the id is requested to speak and the ego remains silent (Freud, 1936). Unconscious material thus enters the conscious mind, and there clinicians interpret it.

At times clients resist free association by blocking their thoughts, denying their importance, or both. Often such resistance is concerned with significant earlier unresolved relationships. Nonetheless, therapists attempt to help clients work through their resistance, assuring them that even seemingly trivial thoughts or feelings are important. Many times, such assurance is enough to overcome the resistance.

Dream Analysis. Clients report dreams to their therapists on a regular basis. Freud believed dreams are "the royal road to the unconscious," an attempt to fulfill a childhood wish or express unacknowledged sexual desires. He insisted on getting at the nature of dreams by breaking them down into parts and treating them in as much detail as possible.

In **dream analysis**, clients are encouraged to dream and remember dreams, even though not everything in a dream is considered important. Clinicians are especially sensitive to two aspects—the **manifest content** (obvious meaning) and the **latent content** (hidden but true meaning) (Jones, 1979)—and help interpret both. Some dream symbols are obvious, such as hostility expressed as death or an accident (Nye, 2000). Other symbols are vague and difficult to interpret. Freud's method of dream analysis is considered the first scientific approach to the study of dreams.

Analysis of Transference. Transference denotes a client's response to a clinician as if the clinician were some significant figure in the client's past, usually a parent figure. As mentioned before, clinicians encourage transference and interpret the positive or negative feelings expressed. The release of feelings is therapeutic, providing an emotional catharsis, but the real value lies in clients' increased self-knowledge, which comes through therapists' analysis of the transference. Clients who experience transference and learn from it are freed to move on to another developmental stage (Singer, 1970). It should be stressed that "working through" transference is a continual process that consists of repetition, elaboration, and amplification (Luborksy et al., 2011). Understanding and insight grow with each analysis of the transference experience.

Analysis of Resistance. Sometimes clients make initial progress while undergoing psychoanalysis or psychodynamic treatment and then slow down or stop. Their **resistance** to the therapeutic process may take many forms, such as missing or being late for appointments, not paying fees, persisting in transference, blocking thoughts during free association, or refusing to recall dreams or early memories. When resistance occurs in any form, clinicians must deal with it immediately. Analysis of resistance can help clients gain insight into it as well as other behaviors. However, if resistance is not dealt with, the therapeutic process will probably come to a halt.

Interpretation. Interpretation is part of the other techniques already examined and complementary to them. Through interpretation therapists help clients understand the meaning of past and present personal events. The technique also encompasses explanations and analysis of clients' thoughts, feelings, and actions. However, counseling practitioners must carefully time the use of interpretation. If it comes too soon in a relationship, it can drive a client away. On the other hand, if it is not employed at all or is used infrequently, a client may fail to develop insight. Only when clients are ready can interpretation make a significant impact on their growth and development.

Reflective Question

A number of Freudian techniques are frequently brought up in public discussions. Which ones have you heard most often? How useful and effective do you think these techniques are?

DIVERSITY AND MULTICULTURAL ISSUES

Sigmund Freud and his psychodynamic theory were influenced by the times in which they emerged: the late Victorian era and the beginning of the 20th century in Vienna, Austria. The period was one of repressed sexuality, rigidity conformity, and authoritarianism. Consequently, many of the concepts and ideas in psychodynamic approaches are not considered as relevant in the 21st century as they were in the 20th. In addition, because Freud worked with upper-class Viennese women, many of whom suffered from hysteria, the application of the concepts created do not seem appropriate to clients who come seeking help for a wide variety of other problems. Thus, some clinicians today dismiss psychoanalysis and psychodynamic theory as irrelevant (Zalaquett et al., 2019).

However, a good deal of psychodynamic theory has transcended cultural barriers and has much to contribute. A specific aspect of the psychodynamic approach relevant for today is its emphasis on **intraindividual diversity** (i.e., diverse components of being that exist within the individual) (Hansen, 2010). These components have to do with the unconscious, specifically a person's unconscious. The psychodynamic approach focuses on promoting insight, which although not universally valued, is of value in many cultures, especially in the West.

In addition to this inside focus, psychoanalysis and psychodynamic ways of working are also diverse in where they are practiced (Fulmer, 2018). Outside the United States, psychodynamic theories are practiced in Spain, South Africa, Brazil, and Argentina (Allodi, 2012; Knight, 2013; Volnovich, 2017). In addition, the work of Anna Freud and Erik Erikson in studying the development of children and child-rearing practices with an emphasis on the ego has helped make psychodynamic practices more palatable and useful than originally set forth. Furthermore, concepts ranging from transference to defense mechanisms seem to have relevance for people in different parts of society throughout the world even if they do not subscribe to psychoanalytic or psychodynamic tenets.

Gender-sensitive issues in psychodynamic theory are also being reconsidered from a diversity point of view. Freud's concept of the Electra complex and penis envy caused many women to avoid anything to do with psychodynamics and its offshoots because of what they considered a bias in the theory, which saw women as inferior to men. Now a variety of disciplines and theoretical orientations combine feminism with psychodynamics and postmodern theories to celebrate diversity in gender and sexual experience (Glassgold & Iasenza, 2004). Freud's views on the inferiority of women and the superiority of men have largely been discredited and are not advocated by most who practice this theory. In addition to sex, there is evidence in favor of utilizing psychodynamic interventions with older adults (Choudhury et al., 2020).

Reflective Question

How do you think intraindividual diversity complements cultural diversity?

EVALUATION OF THE THEORY

Strengths and Contributions

As developed by Freud and modified by others, psychoanalysis and psychodynamic theory has several unique emphases. First, the psychodynamic approach emphasizes the importance of sexuality and the unconscious in human behavior. Before this theory, sexuality (especially childhood sexuality) was denied, and little attention was paid to unconscious forces. Now many theories acknowledge both the importance of the person as a sexual being and the power of the unconscious mind.

Another positive aspect of psychoanalytic and psychodynamic theories is they lend themselves to empirical studies; they are heuristic. Since the early 1900s Freud's proposals have generated a tremendous amount of research. Much of the research supporting the theory has been reported in the form of case histories and reactions in journals such as the *American Psychoanalytic Association Journal*, *International Journal of Psychoanalysis*, and *Psychoanalytic Review*. A good deal of the research attacking Freud's theory has been reported as empirical studies in other reputable journals. Psychoanalysis and psychodynamic theories challenge researchers to develop sophisticated methods of inquiry.

A third contribution of psychodynamic theories is they provide a theoretical base of support for a number of diagnostic instruments. Some psychological tests, such as the Thematic Apperception Test and the Rorschach Ink Blots, are rooted in psychodynamic theories. Many other tests therapists use are outgrowths of these theories or reactions to them.

Another strength of psychodynamic approaches is their focus on the complexity of life and human nature. Counselors can gain a greater appreciation of human development and various associated problems connected with development by understanding psychodynamic theories (Sollod et al., 2009).

A fifth strength of psychodynamic theories is they have become more diverse through the years. The United States has more than 10,000 classical psychoanalysts and many clinicians who engage in a modified form of psychodynamic theories. Two of these modified forms of psychoanalysis are **ego psychology** (which focuses on the ego's normal and pathological development) and object relations theory (which postulates that relationships, beginning with the mother-infant dyad, are primary, and that intrapsychic, interpersonal, and group experiences lay the foundation for the development of individual identity. This theory is the basis for attachment theory.). Psychodynamics continues to evolve and recently has emphasized adaptive processes, social relations, and brief forms of treatment.

Another contribution of psychodynamic theories is they appear to be effective for those who suffer from a wide variety of disorders. These include hysteria, narcissism, obsessive-compulsive reactions, character disorders, anxiety, phobias, and sexual difficulties (Luborksy et al., 2011).

A final strength of psychoanalysis and psychodynamic theories is they stress the importance of developmental growth stages. This emphasis on growth is important for practitioners since much of the focus in the counseling profession is on development. A significant amount of investigation since Freud's time, especially the work of Erikson (1963) and Levinson et al. (1978), has stressed developmental aspects of people. Such knowledge of human development is invaluable to practitioners.

Limitations and Criticisms

Despite the unique emphases of psychoanalysis and psychodynamic theories, most clinicians do not use this approach. The reasons are numerous. First, classical psychoanalysis and some psychodynamic theories are time consuming and expensive. A person undergoing psychoanalysis is usually seen three to five times a week for a period of years (Bankart, 1997; Nye, 2000). Although psychodynamic-oriented psychotherapy, an alternative to psychoanalysis, is a briefer form of treatment, it still takes considerable time.

Another drawback is that psychoanalysis and psychodynamic theories do not seem to lend themselves as well as other theories to working with older people as much as with younger adults. The reason is they take longer than many other forms of counseling. Life span and practical issues play a part in how useful this approach can be with individuals nearing or in the latter stages of their lives. However, psychodynamic theories are beginning to change and working with older adults is occurring more often.

A third limitation of psychoanalysis and psychodynamic theories is practitioners of these approaches tend to be rather restricted professionally and geographically. Most nonmedical mental health practitioners are members of the American Academy of Psychoanalysis and the National Psychological Association for Psychoanalysis, organizations that are less prestigious than the American Psychoanalytic Association to which most medical professionals who use this theory belong. Geographically, most psychodynamic practitioners work in large cities. This approach is rarely used outside of these big metropolitan areas.

A fourth limitation of psychoanalysis in particular is many of its concepts are not easily communicated or understood. For instance, the id, the ego, and the superego are metaphors that represent thoughts and behaviors as do many other terms that at times may be complicated.

Another criticism of the psychodynamic approaches, especially associated with Freud, is they are deterministic. For example, Freud attributed certain limitations in women to their gender. This controversial aspect of his theory has subsided because of the influence of ego psychology and women scholars' interpretation of Freud, yet the appropriateness of psychoanalysis for women continues to be questioned.

A sixth and final limiting aspect of the psychodynamic approaches is that much of them, especially psychoanalysis, do not lend themselves to the needs of most individuals. The psychodynamic model has become associated with people who have major adjustment difficulties or who want or need to explore the unconscious. However, most individuals who seek counseling have less disruptive developmental or situational problems.

TREATING LINDA WITH PSYCHODYNAMIC THERAPIES

Conceptualization

As a psychodynamic practitioner, you notice several problems in Linda's life. She states she never felt close to her mother and is not close to her father either. You therefore hypothesize she has never really resolved the phallic/Electra stage of childhood.

If that is true, then it is little wonder she has not been able to sustain a marriage and she continues to have trouble with her bosses at work. Linda's psychosexual development is a major theme you identify immediately.

You also note, not surprisingly, that Linda is dependent on a number of defense mechanisms, one of which is repression of her hostile thoughts about the way she has been and is being treated in life. Instead of dealing with these thoughts and feelings constructively and in a straightforward manner, Linda uses escape literature, movies, and television to help her feel better. Overall, Linda has a stronger-than-average death wish and a weak ego. She has not found satisfaction in either love or work, and she is most likely diagnosable under one of the *DSM* categories dealing with depression or personality disorders.

Treatment Process

As a counselor steeped in psychodynamic approaches, you are the expert who directs the course of treatment. You are particularly interested in Linda's past and early childhood memories. You hope Linda can gain insight into her situation by reliving past experiences and thereby resolving them. To help Linda, you employ a number of procedures to bring out repressed and unconscious material. For example, you encourage Linda to engage in free association and dream analysis. Your goal is to enable her to adjust to society and to be intimate with others as she chooses.

You begin your work with Linda in one of two ways. If you wish to help her using the classical psychoanalysis method you see Linda four times a week for 1 hour at a time, stressing to her that treatment is likely to take years. To be unobtrusive and yet facilitate Linda's therapy, you have her lie down on a couch while you sit behind her head and encourage her verbalization about events in her life. In addition to free association and dream analysis, you try other standardized psychoanalytic techniques, including analysis of transference, analysis of resistance, and interpretation. If you use a more modified psychodynamic model with Linda, your focus with her is on strengthening her ego and relationship skills. You see her weekly and the main agenda in your sessions is on consciously assisting Linda in becoming more skilled in her interpersonal relationships by becoming more competent as a person.

In either of these procedures conscious and unconscious material Linda has repressed comes into greater awareness. Often the process is a struggle, and Linda is surprised at what she says. For example, she blurts out that she loathed (instead of loved) her father. The interpretation of the latent content of her dreams astonishes her too. In addition, she works through her transference of feelings related to her father and her former husband.

Through the procedures found in the psychodynamic process, Linda gains insight into her defense mechanisms and comes to understand why she has been depressed and has become obsessed with escape materials. When she ends treatment, she has made considerable progress, manifest in a less passive and more productive role within her family, especially with her mother. She has also begun to date and is feeling optimistic her next relationship will be healthy.

SUMMING UP

Many clinicians consider psychoanalysis and psychodynamic theories the grandparent of most modern theories of helping. Although Freud's ideas were and still are controversial to some, his thoughts about human nature and the helping process are comprehensive. They have been elaborated on and refined by his daughter Anna Freud. She enlarged his explanation of defense mechanisms and childhood problems. Many of Freud's followers, such as Melanie Klein and Heinz Kohut, have concentrated on interpersonal relationships. In addition, life span theorists, such as Erik Erikson, have focused on life cycle development and have emphasized psychosocial rather than psychosexual aspects of life. Helping professionals still widely practice psychodynamic approaches in some areas, mainly large metropolitan areas.

Overall, psychoanalysis and psychodynamic approaches stress biological causality, psychosexual development, the dynamics of the mind, and defense mechanisms. These approaches make use of psychological diagnoses. However, many counselors do not use psychodynamic treatments because they are costly, time consuming, and are usually not ones in which they are educated. In addition, these approaches are not applicable for the client populations most counselors serve, and they lack empirical evidence of their effectiveness.

CHAPTER 2 RECAP: PSYCHOANALYSIS AND PSYCHODYNAMIC THEORIES

Major Theorists
Sigmund Freud, Anna Freud, Melanie Klein, Karen Horney
Heinz Kohut, Erik Erikson, Donald Winnicott, Harry Stack Sullivan

View of Human Nature/Personality
Personality development occurs during early childhood.
Psychosexual stages of development are crucial.
Emphasis is on the unconscious and its impact.
Ego defense mechanisms are protective but can be detrimental.
Biological and deterministic aspects of behavior are prevalent in the original
    theory.

Role of the Counselor
Functions as experts in relationship with clients
Encourages transference from clients
Focuses on the unconscious, except in briefer models that emphasize the
    conscious
Explores defense mechanisms and how they are used
Uses interpretation

Goals
Make the unconscious conscious
Work through unresolved developmental stages
Help client learn to cope and adjust
Reconstruct client's personality

Process and Techniques
Several sessions per week except in briefer models of theory
Free association
Analysis of transference
Exploration of dreams
Interpretation of conscious and unconscious material
Attention to resistance
Encouragement of client insight

Diversity and Multicultural Issues
Practiced worldwide
Inappropriate for some cultures because of emphasis or techniques
Emphasis in approach on intraindividual diversity (i.e., diverse components
   of being that exist within the individual)
A variety of disciplines and theoretical orientations combine feminism with
   psychodynamic and postmodern theories to celebrate diversity in gender
   and sexual experience

Strengths and Contributions
First modern theory to emphasize sexuality and the unconscious
Supports diagnostic instruments and diagnoses
Is multidimensional
Continues to evolve
Focuses on developmental stages—psychosexual and psychosocial

Limitations and Criticisms
Classic psychoanalysis is time consuming and expensive.
Use of theory is limited geographically.
Focus is on pathology.
Deterministic
Inefficient for less disturbed individuals

KEY TERMS

anal stage 18
analysis of resistance 24
analysis of transference 24
cathartic method 15
conscience 18
conscious mind 16
defense mechanisms 20
denial 21
displacement 21
dream analysis 24
ego 16
ego ideal 18

ego psychology 26
eros 17
fixated 19
free association 15
Freudian slips 23
genital stage 19
id 16
identification 21
interpretation 24
intraindividual diversity 25
latency 19
latent content 24

LEARNING MORE

A number of periodicals are devoted to the theory, research, and practice of psychoanalysis. Among the best are the following:

American Journal of Psychoanalysis
Bulletin of the Menninger Clinic
Contemporary Psychoanalysis
International Journal of Psychoanalysis
Journal of American Psychoanalytic Association
Journal of Clinical Psychoanalysis
Modern Psychoanalysis and Psychotherapy
Psychoanalytic Inquiry
Psychoanalytic Psychology
Psychoanalytic Quarterly
Psychoanalytic Review

In addition to journals, there are several training institutes where clinicians can learn psychodynamic and psychoanalytic processes and skills. Associations to contact about training include:

American Psychoanalytic Association
309 East 49th Street
New York, NY 10017–1601
212-752-0450; www.apsa.org

National Psychological Association for Psychoanalysis
40 West 13th Street
New York, NY 10011–7891
212-924-7440; www.npap.org

Sigmund Freud Museum, Vienna home page
http://www.freud-museum.at/cms/index.php/en_home.html

CLASSROOM ACTIVITIES

1. Think of defense mechanisms you have used. Share your examples with a classmate and then with the class.
2. What specific aspects of psychodynamic theories do you think need further research? Why? Write down your responses and share them with the class.
3. In a group of three to five, discuss the appeal of psychodynamic theories and determine why your group believes they are attractive or unattractive for mental health practitioners.

3
Adlerian Therapy

■ ■ ■

Compared to others
you're physically small
so your heart must be big
and your senses strong,
Amid such a contrast
people may see
the gifts you bring to humanity
and know anew quality in life
is not measured in inches.

"A Note to Tim on Life" © S. T. Gladding

CHAPTER OVERVIEW

From reading this chapter you will learn about

- Adler's views on lifestyles and his emphasis on social interests as a primary motivator of people.
- Five basic mistakes associated with personal beliefs (i.e., fictions).
- Four different phases of treatment that are part of the Adlerian therapeutic process: establishing a relationship, performing analysis and assessment, promoting insight, and reorienting.

As you read consider

- How you view motivation and human development.
- People you have known who seem to have an inferiority or superiority complex.
- When you have seen others act "as if" they were the person they wished to be.

Adlerian counseling is an internationally popular form of helping. It is based on the commonsense thinking of Alfred Adler, a contemporary of Sigmund Freud who proposed his ideas in the early days of psychotherapy. Adler had a keen interest in people and their motivations for behavior. He noted the inherent social interest of individuals and based his ideas around this concept. From the Adlerian point of view, the **essence of normality** is feeling concern for others (Corsini, 1988; Sweeney, 2019). Such an emphasis is manifested in activities that center on social development, cooperation, and education.

In addition to his emphasis on social interests, Adler focused his theory on the influence of early memories on a person's life. The impact of one's family of origin was another focus of Adler's, especially the ordinal position of children in the family. Adler based his therapeutic approach on such concepts as lifestyle, beliefs (which he referred to as **fictions**), psychological environment, and the importance of striving for completeness and wholeness.

MAJOR THEORIST: ALFRED ADLER

Alfred Adler (1870–1937) was born in Penzig, Austria, a suburb of Vienna. He was the second of six children in a middle-class Jewish family. Adler shared a close relationship with his mother until his younger brother was born. Then, feeling abandoned, he sought the support of his father. Adler was also close to his older brother, Sigmund.

Adler was a sickly child and was injured often. He was run over in the street, suffered from rickets, and almost died of pneumonia at age 5. At age 3 he had witnessed the death of a younger brother. It is little wonder that he was later attracted to the profession of medicine.

To make up for his physical limitations, Adler spent a great deal of his childhood outside playing with other children and went out of his way to cultivate their friendship. Initially, he was not a good student. In fact, he did so poorly in mathematics at the secondary level that his teacher suggested his father take him out of school and apprentice him to a shoemaker. Adler reportedly overheard the conversation and studied to overcome this deficiency. Eventually, he became skilled in math.

In 1895 Adler received a degree in medicine from the University of Vienna. In his first practice he worked as an ophthalmologist, but his interests turned to neurology and finally to psychiatry. As a practicing psychiatrist, Adler was invited in 1902 to join Freud's Vienna Psychoanalytic Society, where he quickly gained prominence. Adler always thought of himself as a colleague rather than a disciple of Freud and disagreed early on with much of Freud's theoretical approach, especially his emphasis on biology and sexuality. Adler developed a theoretical orientation that was less deterministic and more practical and hopeful. Unlike Freud, Adler stressed the importance of subjective feelings rather than biological drives as the primary motivating force of life (Datler & Gstach, 2001).

Because of his differences with Freud, Adler resigned as president of the Vienna Psychoanalytic Society in 1910 and gave up his co-editorship of the *Journal of Psychoanalysis*, a periodical he had cofounded with Freud. Adler then established the rival Society of Individual Psychology.

During World War I Adler served as a physician in the Austrian army. After the war, in 1922, he was instrumental in setting up child guidance clinics in Vienna schools and eventually in other parts of Europe. All the while Adler worked to refine his theory and spoke widely in Europe and the United States. Adler fled Hitler's rise to power and in 1932 was appointed to a position in medical psychology at the Long Island College of Medicine. He died of a heart attack in 1937 while on a lecture tour in Aberdeen, Scotland. He was survived by his wife, two daughters, and a son.

Although Adler was a popular speaker and the author of more than 300 published papers and books, he has not generally received credit for many of the concepts he formulated. Such terms as "inferiority complex," "social interest," "empathy," and "lifestyle" originated with Adler and were quickly absorbed by other scholars and the public. His theory waned in popularity during the 1940s and 1950s and was revitalized during the 1960s and 1970s. It has been widely used since. Three excellent introductions to Adlerian theory are *The Practice and Theory of Individual*

Psychology (Adler, 1969), *Theories of Psychotherapy Series, Adlerian Psychotherapy* (Carlson & Englar-Carlson, 2017), and *Adlerian Counseling* (Sweeney, 2019).

VIEW OF HUMAN NATURE/PERSONALITY

Adler thought people are primarily motivated by social interests, such as having an interest in others and wanting to contribute to society (Wedding & Corsini, 2019). Thus **social interest** is "not only an interest in others but an interest in the interests of others" (Ansbacher, 1977, p. 57).

In addition, Adler's theory holds that conscious aspects of behavior, rather than the unconscious, are central to the development of personality. A major Adlerian tenet is that individuals strive to become successful—that is, the best they can be. Therefore, their behavior is goal directed and purposeful. Underlying this paramount belief is Adler's conviction that each person strives for growth and has a need for wholeness. Adler gave his theory the name Individual Psychology to emphasize the holistic perspective, with the term "Individual" deriving from the Latin *individuum*, meaning "indivisible" (Maniacci & Sackett-Maniacci, 2019).

The tendency of people to try to fulfill their own unique potential is a process Adler called **striving for perfection** or completeness (Adler, 1964). Another tendency for each person is to feel initially inferior to others. If not overcome, this feeling leads to an **inferiority complex** and can become the basis for defining one's personality. A person who overcompensates for feelings of inferiority develops a **superiority complex** (Ansbacher & Ansbacher, 1964), which Adler described as another **neurotic fiction** that is unproductive.

Reflective Question

How do you think a knowledge of Adler's view of human nature—that is, people have social interests and strive to be the best they can be—can help you as a counselor practitioner?

Adler believed that people are as much influenced by future (**teleological**) **goals** as by past causes. His theory places considerable emphasis on birth order (Eckstein & Kaufman, 2012). He thought those who share ordinal birth positions (e.g., firstborns) may have more in common with one another than with their siblings (Dreikurs, 1950). Adlerian literature on the family emphasizes **five ordinal positions: firstborns, secondborns, middle children, youngest children,** and **only children** (Dreikurs, 1967; Dreikurs & Soltz, 1964; Sweeney, 2019).

Firstborns. Firstborns are initially the "reigning monarchs" of a family because they receive undivided attention from parents. They are socialized to conform, achieve, behave, and please. They take responsibility when parents are absent and often act as parent substitutes in large families. All firstborns experience the loss of their unique position in the family when a second child is born. The experience of being "dethroned" may cause them to become resentful or it may help them better understand the significance of power and authority.

Secondborns. The position of secondborn is an enviable one, according to Adler. However, it does have drawbacks. Secondborns never have to worry about issues of power and authority because they are born into a family atmosphere in which they will never be dethroned. Usually, these individuals are more outgoing, carefree, and creative. They are less concerned with rules than firstborns. They frequently pursue roles not taken by firstborns and are likely to be just the opposite of their older siblings.

Middle children. Children born in the middle positions of a family often feel squeezed in and treated unfairly. They do not develop the close, personal types of alliances that an oldest or a youngest child may form, but because of their position, middle children learn a great deal about family politics and the art of negotiation. These skills can prove useful in manipulating events to get what they want and choosing areas where they can be successful.

Youngest children. Youngest children in the family have difficulties and opportunities that are different from those of their older siblings. Youngest children receive a great deal of attention from others, who are likely to cater to their needs. These children may become charmers but may also have difficulty breaking out of the role of baby or family pet. They face the danger of becoming spoiled but at the same time may make great strides in achievement because of role models older siblings provide.

Only children. Any child born 7 or more years apart from siblings is psychologically an only child. These children, as a group, are never dethroned and are at an advantage, like oldest children, in receiving a great deal of attention. They may mature early and become high achievers. They may also develop rich imaginations because of the amount of time they spend alone. Major disadvantages are that only children may become pampered and selfish and may not be well socialized.

Reflective Question

How do you think your ordinal position within your family of origin has influenced you? What influence do you think ordinal position has had on your siblings or other relatives?

In addition to birth order, the family environment is important to a person's development, particularly in the first 5 years of life. Adlerian theory stresses that by age 5 each person creates a lifestyle, or **style of life**, which is a person's characteristic way of relating to others, viewing the world, behaving, and pursuing long-term goals. This lifestyle is gained primarily through interacting with other family members. A **negative family atmosphere** might be authoritarian, rejecting, suppressive, materialistic, overprotective, or pitying (Dreikurs & Soltz, 1964), whereas a **positive family atmosphere** might be democratic, accepting, open, and social. Nevertheless, perception of the family atmosphere, rather than any events themselves, is crucial to the development of a lifestyle (Adler, 1964).

Individuals are also guided by their fictions—that is, their subjective evaluations of themselves and their environments. **Five basic mistakes** are caused by fictions (Maniacci & Sackett-Maniacci, 2019):

- **Overgeneralizing**—viewing everything as the same—for example, believing that all African Americans think similarly.
- **False or impossible goals of security**—trying to please everyone—for example, being aggressive or passive to please certain individuals.

Table 3.1   Adler's Five Healthy Lifestyle Tasks Each Requiring Courage

1. Social Interest (i.e., contributing to others and society, interdependence)
2. Work
3. Sex
4. Spirituality
5. Coping with Ourselves

- **Misperceptions of life and life's demands**—believing that one never gets any breaks.
- **Minimization or denial of one's worth**—thinking that one will never amount to anything.
- **Faulty values**—believing in the necessity of being first no matter what needs to be done to achieve that goal.

In contrast, a **healthy style of life** focuses on three main areas—society (i.e., social tasks), work, and sexuality. Adlerian theory places strong emphasis on contributing to society. It also holds that work is essential for human survival and that we must learn to be interdependent. Furthermore, individuals must define their sexuality in regard to self and others, in a spirit of cooperation rather than competition. Adler mentions two other challenges of life, although he does not fully develop them—spirituality and coping with self (Dreikurs & Mosak, 1966). Adlerian theory emphasizes that every life task requires **courage**, a willingness to take risks without knowing what the consequences may be (see Table 3.1).

ROLE OF THE COUNSELOR

Adlerian counselors function primarily as diagnosticians, teachers, and models in the egalitarian relationships they establish with their clients. Adlerian clinicians try to assess why clients are oriented to a certain way of thinking and behaving. They are active in making an assessment by gathering information on the family constellation and clients' earliest memories. They then share interpretations, impressions, opinions, and feelings with their clients and concentrate on promoting the therapeutic relationship. Those with whom they work are encouraged to examine and change a faulty lifestyle by developing social interests (Adler, 1927, 1931). Adlerian practitioners frequently share hunches or guesses with clients and are often directive when assigning clients homework—for example, suggesting that they act as if they were the persons they want to be.

Adlerians employ a variety of techniques, some of which are borrowed from other approaches. Adler was not specific in detailing how those who help others should operate when using his theory. As a rule, Adlerian specialists make little use of assessment tools, such as psychological tests, but usually employ life-history questionnaires to gather data. They avoid the types of diagnoses found in formal assessment texts, such as the *Diagnostic and Statistical Manual of Mental Disorders*, but use their own language (e.g., "discouraged") to describe the dynamics they encounter in clients.

Reflective Question

How might the use of homework as advocated by Adler help counselors assist clients in reaching their goals? What are the drawbacks to assigning homework?

GOALS

The goals of Adlerian practitioners revolve around helping individuals develop healthy, holistic lifestyles. This focus may mean educating or reeducating clients about such lifestyles, as well as helping them overcome feelings of inferiority.

One of the major goals of Adlerian specialists is to encourage clients to cultivate and increase social interest (Adler, 1931). According to Adler, social interest is an innate potentiality "that must be consciously developed or trained" (Watts, 1996a, p. 169). A faulty style of life is self-centered and based on mistaken goals and incorrect assumptions associated with feelings of inferiority. Therefore, it is important that clients change self-defeating thoughts and behaviors. These thoughts might stem from a physical or mental defect, pampering by parents, or neglect. Regardless, Adlerian practitioners try to help clients increase their self-understanding and encourage clients to see equality among all people (see Table 3.2).

To correct faulty thoughts and stop inappropriate forms of behavior, practitioners must assume the roles of teachers and interpreters of events. In short, Adlerians deal with the whole person, and clients must ultimately decide whether to pursue social or self-interests (Kern & Watts, 1993).

Table 3.2 Five Goals of Adlerian Therapy

1. Increase social interest
2. Make a lifestyle change
3. Change self-defeating thoughts and behaviors
4. Increase self-understanding
5. Encourage clients to see equality among all people

PROCESS AND TECHNIQUES

Adlerian techniques are practiced in conjunction with the four different phases of treatment that are part of the Adlerian therapeutic process (Nystul, 2019). These phases are identified as: establishing a relationship, performing analysis and assessment, promoting insight, and reorienting (Dreikurs, 1967; Kottman & Warlick, 1990; Maniacci & Sackett-Maniacci, 2019).

1. **Establishing a Relationship**

   Establishing a relationship is crucial if the goals of Adlerians are to be achieved. Certain techniques enhance this process. Counselors who practice Adlerian theory try to develop a warm, supportive, empathic, friendly, and egalitarian relationship with clients.

   They are encouraging and try to win the respect of those with whom they work. Adlerian helping is seen as a collaborative effort (Adler, 1956), with encouragement and hope a part of the process. Clinicians actively listen and respond in reflective and probing ways (James & Gilliland, 2003), trying to help their clients define specific goals and discover what prevents the achievement of these goals. Adlerians may focus on clients' strengths but may confront at times, pointing out clients' inconsistencies. The primary objectives are to maintain a flexible interaction process that stresses clients' responsibilities and abilities (Dinkmeyer & Sperry, 2000).

2. **Performing Analysis and Assessment**

   After a relationship has been established, Adlerian counselors concentrate on analyzing their clients' lifestyles, examining family constellations, early memories, dreams, priorities, and ways of responding. As previously noted, the family constellation and the atmosphere in which children develop influence both self-perception and perceptions of others. Clients are encouraged to recall early memories, especially events before the age of 10. Adler (1931) contended that people remember childhood events that are consistent with their present view of self, others, and the world in general. Adlerian counselors look both for themes and for specific details within these early recollections (Slavik, 1991; Statton & Wilborn, 1991; Watkins, 1985). Figures from the past are treated as prototypes rather than specific individuals; they may represent clients' attitudes toward power, weakness, men, women, or almost anything else. Recent and past dreams are also a part of lifestyle analysis. Adlerian theory holds that dreams are a possible rehearsal for future courses of action, making recurrent dreams especially important.

   A look at client priorities is helpful in understanding style of life and ways of responding. Unless challenged, a client may persist in one predominant lifestyle filled with basic mistakes (Maniacci & Sackett-Maniacci, 2019). These faulty or irrational views of life, or fictions, have already been elaborated on. In this second phase of counseling, lifestyle priorities and ways of responding are challenged.

3. **Promoting Insight**

   Counselors next try to help clients develop insight, especially by asking open-ended questions and offering interpretations. **Open-ended questions** invite a thoughtful response of more than a few words. They allow clients to explore patterns in their lives that may have gone unnoticed. **Interpretation,** from an Adlerian perspective, often takes the form of intuitive guesses, sometimes based on counselors' general knowledge of ordinal positions and family constellations. However, true to the egalitarian spirit of the process, clients are never forced to accept a practitioner's point of view. **Empathy,** the ability to feel what it is like to be the client, is especially important in this process.

4. **Reorienting**

   To accomplish behavioral change and put insight into action, counselors use the following specific techniques.

   <u>Confrontation</u>: In this process counselors challenge clients to consider their own private logic. When clients examine their logic, they often realize they can change it as well as their behavior.

   <u>Asking the question</u>: In this procedure counselors ask, "What would be different if you were well?" Clients are often asked this question during the initial interview, but it is appropriate at any time.

   <u>Encouragement</u>: Encouragement implies faith in a person (Dinkmeyer & Losoncy, 1996; Dreikurs & Soltz, 1964). Counselors encourage their clients by stating their belief that behavior change is possible. Encouragement is the key to making productive lifestyle choices.

   <u>Acting "as if"</u>: Clients are instructed to act as if they are the persons they want to be—for instance, the ideal persons they see in their dreams (Gold, 1979). Adler originally got this idea from Hans Vaihinger (1911), who wrote that people create the worlds they live in by making assumptions about the world.

Spitting in the client's soup: In this technique, counselors point out certain behaviors to clients, thereby ruining the payoff for the behaviors. For example, a mother who always shows up her daughter in order to feel superior may continue to do so after the behavior has been pointed out, but will no longer reap the reward of feeling superior.

Catching oneself: Clients learn to become aware of self-destructive behaviors or thoughts. At first, counselors may help in the process, but eventually clients take over this responsibility.

Task setting: Clients initially set short-range, attainable goals and eventually work up to long-term, realistic objectives.

Push button: Clients are encouraged to realize that they have choices about the stimuli to which they pay attention. They are taught to create the feelings they want by concentrating on their thoughts. The technique is like pushing a button because clients can choose to remember negative or positive experiences (Maniacci & Sackett-Maniacci, 2019).

In the process of using these techniques, counselors must avoid the "tar baby"—that is, "the perceptions on life that the client carries into counseling and attempts to fit into the counselor. Anger, discouragement, seductiveness, martyrdom, and a host of other traps are set for the unwary counselor as the client resists change" (James & Gilliland, 2003, p. 121).

Reflective Question

The four-step process of Adlerian counseling seems straightforward. What parts of the process do you think are most difficult? Why?

DIVERSITY AND MULTICULTURAL ISSUES

Because of its emphasis on social interest, Adlerian counseling is well suited for use with diverse and multicultural populations (Sharf, 2016). For example, many minority cultures in the United States—such as Native Americans, Asian Americans, African Americans, and Latinx—value social interaction, social groups, and social justice (Ergüner-Tekinalp et al., 2018). The Adlerian approach is helpful in working with these populations in a number of ways (Chavez et al., 2018; Lemberger-Truelove, 2018; Yee, 2018). Adlerians emphasize that healthy people need to extend their worldview beyond themselves and their families, regardless of their heritage and group identity. This process often requires learning about and understanding different cultural groups. In the process individuals learn much about themselves. They also may come to realize that certain Adlerian concepts need to be modified within a cultural context.

The Adlerian approach is sensitive to equality issues between the genders (Ansbacher & Ansbacher, 1978; Sweeney, 2019). Adler believed that both men and women want to be superior—that is, perfect (their best) and never inferior. He referred to this attitude in women as the **masculine protest**, since men in his era held superior roles to those of women. Because Adler's concern for women's rights and equality is still a part of Adlerian theory and practice, both women and men find Adlerian counseling appropriate.

Reflective Question

Why do you think Adler's emphasis on equality of the genders makes this theory attractive to men as well as women and society as a whole?

EVALUATION OF THE THEORY

Strengths and Contributions

Adlerian therapy has a number of unique emphases that make it an important theory. The Adlerian approach fosters an egalitarian atmosphere through positive counseling techniques. Rapport and commitment are enhanced, thereby increasing the chances for change. Adlerian counselors offer encouragement and support and approach their clients with an educational orientation and an optimistic outlook on life.

Adlerian therapy is also versatile over the life span. "Adlerian theorists have developed counseling models for working with children, adolescents, parents, entire families, teacher groups, and other segments of society" (Purkey & Schmidt, 1987, p. 115). **Play therapy** for children ages 4 to 9 seems especially effective, allowing children to communicate through the language of play and then talk about their feelings (Kottman & Meany-Walen, 2016; Kottman & Warlick, 1990). An approach that emphasizes verbal and behavioral consequences is recommended for adolescents, particularly those dealing with the faulty goals typical of this age group (Kelly & Sweeney, 1979; Sweeney, 2019). Parents may benefit from Adlerian theory through **educational support groups** that help them understand their children better and plan effective intervention strategies (Dinkmeyer, 1982a, 1982b; Dinkmeyer et al., 1997; Dinkmeyer et al., 1998). The Adlerian approach has been successfully applied to complex family interactions too (Lowe, 1982; Walsh & McGraw, 1996).

In addition, the Adlerian approach is useful in the treatment of a variety of disorders, including those listed in the *Diagnostic and Statistical Manual*—for example, conduct disorders, antisocial disorders, anxiety disorders of childhood and adolescence, some affective disorders, and personality disorders (Seligman & Reichenberg, 2014).

Another valued aspect is the Adlerian contribution to other helping theories and to the public's knowledge and understanding of human interactions. Adlerian concepts such as freedom, phenomenology, interpretation of events, life scripts, growth, and personal responsibility are found in existential therapy, Gestalt therapy, rational emotive behavior therapy, person-centered therapy, and reality/choice counseling and therapy. Adlerian terms such as "inferiority complex" have also become part of the public's vocabulary.

A final strength of Adlerian therapy is that it can be employed selectively in different cultural contexts, especially those that are collectivist (Brown, 1997). The reason is the theory's emphasis on working for the common good, social interest, and acting collaboratively. For instance, the concept of encouragement is appropriately emphasized in working with Hispanic and Asian American groups, which have traditionally emphasized collaboration.

Limitations and Criticisms

The Adlerian approach, like any theory, has limitations and weaknesses. First, the therapy lacks a firm, supportive research base (Watts, 2018). Although neuroscience supports the principles of social embeddedness, purposefulness of behavior, and holism in Adlerian theory (Miller & Taylor, 2016), relatively few empirical studies clearly outline the effectiveness of Adlerian counseling. More investigations are needed if the theory is to develop systematically. Journals devoted to the Adlerian viewpoint, such as the *Journal of Individual Psychology*, may rectify this situation, but scholars still need to conduct much research if the Adlerian approach is to gain respectability as an evidence-based treatment.

In addition, the Adlerian approach is vague regarding some of its terms and concepts. Corey (2017) notes that Adler emphasized practice and teaching rather than theoretical definitions and organization. Although a number of prominent educators—such as Dreikurs, Mosak, Dinkmeyer, and Sweeney—have attempted to clarify the Adlerian approach, some of its ideas remain unclear. Adler was especially nebulous about how to work with clients.

A third factor that may be considered a drawback is that this therapy may be too optimistic about human nature. Indeed, Adler had a more positive view of people than originators of many other theories. However, Adler, who called his theory "individual psychology" and stressed social cooperation and interests, was clear that many clients had to put forth a lot of effort to achieve meaningful change. Some critics overlook this factor or contend Adler did not stress it enough and thus consider his view neglectful of other life dimensions, such as the power and place of the unconscious.

Yet a fourth possible limitation of the Adlerian approach centers on some of its basic principles. For instance, a concept like democratic family structure may not fit well with clients whose cultural contexts stress a lineal social relationship, such as that of traditional Arab Americans (Brown, 1997). If all basic principles of Adlerian counseling cannot be followed, then the impact of the theory may be lessened.

Finally, the Adlerian approach relies heavily on verbal erudition, logic, and insight and may be limited in its applicability to clients who are not intellectually bright (James & Gilliland, 2003). This limitation applies to many theories and is not singularly targeted to Adlerian work.

TREATING LINDA WITH ADLERIAN THERAPY

Conceptualization

From an Adlerian viewpoint, Linda is discouraged; she has tried to succeed, but has failed. Yet she is goal directed and wants more in her life than escape mechanisms. Linda is also seeking to connect socially. Her family life and her former husband were both less than ideal. In addition, Linda has an inferiority complex that has kept her from reaching her potential vocationally and interpersonally. As the secondborn child in her family and the first girl, Linda is in an enviable position. However, her negative perception of her family and its authoritarian, suppressing, and rejecting attitude has handicapped her.

Linda has bought into a couple of fictions that hinder her too. She has overgeneralized, believing that she will never get a break. And she has minimized her worth as a person, hence her thoughts about suicide. Linda's style of life—especially as it relates to work, society, and sexuality—has been unhealthy and needs to be rectified.

Treatment Process

As an Adlerian practitioner, you recognize first that Linda is discouraged. To promote a positive relationship with Linda, you are warm, supportive, empathic, encouraging, and collaborative in working with her. You actively listen and give her feedback. In addition, you ask Linda about early childhood memories. These memories center around staying clean, being neat and proper, and doing what she was told. They are not pleasant recollections, and you share your impressions of what it must have been like as you continue to develop your relationship with Linda. You note that Linda has developed a faulty lifestyle that has made her overly dependent on the opinions of others. Therefore, in the therapeutic session you take the role of an interpreter and teacher.

As your work progresses, you as well as Linda begin to concentrate on her strengths. You ask her what her dreams are and how she would like to respond to situations around her. To give Linda practice in being the person she wishes to be, you invite her to act as if she were that person. In addition, you ask Linda open-ended questions and allow her to explore her life more closely, especially regarding how she wants it to be.

As your time with Linda moves toward a conclusion, you help Linda reorient to a new life by confronting her and challenging her private logic, which tells her that she is not capable of being more than she is now. You also ask her the question about how her life would look if she were well. You encourage her to live a more productive lifestyle and to catch herself when she begins to have destructive or negative thoughts. You urge Linda to set short-term goals too, such as taking a course at a nearby college, hoping that the achievement of these short-term goals will lead to long-term goals. Overall, you help Linda strive toward her own perfection or completeness and resist getting trapped into her former unproductive lifestyle.

SUMMING UP

Alfred Adler, a contemporary of Sigmund Freud, developed a theory of individual psychology based on the premise that people have a specific concern and need for social interest. The theory has been clarified and expanded since his death, especially by Rudolph Dreikurs, Don Dinkmeyer, and Thomas Sweeney. They have made the approach more understandable and popular, particularly in North America. Adlerian theory is a socially-based, interpersonal, and subjective (i.e., phenomenological) approach to counseling. It emphasizes the future, holism, collaboration, and choice and focuses on the importance of childhood (i.e., working through real or perceived unresolved situations) and behavioral goals. Ordinal family positions, lifestyle, and the importance of socialization and encouragement are a few Adlerian concepts that have made strong contributions to the helping professions.

The Adlerian approach stresses definable techniques and is widely practiced in educational and institutional settings. Its popularity can be attributed to its hopefulness and its useful application in multiple settings, such as in groups and families. Even though more research needs to be conducted on its practice, this approach remains a popular way of working with people of all stages and backgrounds.

CHAPTER 3 RECAP: ADLERIAN THERAPY

Major Theorists
Alfred Adler, Rudolph Dreikurs, Terry Kottman, Jon Carlson
Don Dinkmeyer, Thomas Sweeney, Richard Watts

View of Human Nature/Personality
Emphasis on social interest
Focus on birth order
Personality expressed in lifestyle
Future goals influential

Role of the Counselor
Establishes egalitarian relationship
Models, teaches, and assesses
Shares hunches, directs, encourages

Goals
Cultivate client's social interests
Help client make a lifestyle change
Correct client's self-defeating thoughts and behaviors
Develop client's insight
Promote equality among all people

Process and Techniques
Four-stage process: establishing a relationship, performing analysis and
    assessment, promoting insight, and reorienting
Multiple techniques: empathy, confrontation, acting as if, asking the ques-
    tion, spitting in the client's soup, support, catching oneself, encourage-
    ment, task setting, push button (emphasizing choices), stressing client
    strengths and awareness, examining memories and dreams, interpreting,
    challenging

Diversity and Multicultural Issues
Emphasizes social interest
Is appropriate for most cultural groups, requires modification for some
Is sensitive to gender equality and equality in general
Sees both men and women as wanting to be superior

Strengths and Contributions
Supportive egalitarian relationship
Versatile approach
Useful therapy for specific disorders
Contribution of ideas and vocabulary to the helping professions

Limitations and Criticisms

Weak evidence-based research on effectiveness of approach
Some vagueness of concepts and terms
Narrow emphasis, does not consider some complex phenomena

KEY TERMS

acting "as if"   39
catching oneself   40
courage   37
educational support groups   41
empathy   39
encouragement   39
essence of normality   33
five basic mistakes caused by
   fictions   36
false or impossible goals of
   security   36
faulty values   37
minimization (denial of one's
   worth)   37
misperceptions of life and life's
   demands   37
overgeneralizing   36
five goals of Adlerian therapy   38
five ordinal positions   35
firstborns   35
secondborns   35

middle children   36
youngest children   36
only children   36
healthy style of life (Adler)   37
inferiority complex   35
interpretation   39
masculine protest   40
negative family atmosphere   36
neurotic fiction   35
open-ended questions   39
play therapy   41
positive family atmosphere   36
push button   40
social interest   35
spitting in the client's soup   40
striving for perfection   35
style of life (lifestyle)   36
superiority complex   35
task setting   40
teleological goals   35

LEARNING MORE

Many periodicals feature articles on the theory, research, and practice of Adlerians. A journal specifically devoted to Adlerian therapy is the *Journal of Individual Psychology.*

Adlerian theory is practiced worldwide; its emphasis on social living makes it a popular approach in helping. For more information on Adlerian organizations and institutes, contact

North American Society of Adlerian Psychology
65 East Wacker Place, Suite 1710
Chicago, IL 60601–7298
312-629-8801 http://www.alfredadler.org/

CLASSROOM ACTIVITIES

1. With a classmate, discuss how an Adlerian approach might be used in the following settings: a mental hospital, a public secondary school, a rehabilitation center, and a community agency.

2. As a class, divide into five groups according to Adler's description of the five ordinal positions in a family: firstborns, secondborns, middle children, youngest children, and only children. Appoint a scribe in each group to take notes. Then discuss with other group members your perceptions of being a child in that position. Have each scribe report back to the class as a whole.

3. Divide into groups of three with each member taking the role of a counselor, a client, or an observer. Try to implement some of the specific ways (such as examining lifestyle beliefs) an Adlerian would work with clients who have the following problems: depression, anxiety, poor self-identity, and phobias. After each role-play, discuss what you observed and learned.

4
Existential Therapy

■ ■ ■

He struggles with life
as he rides the subways
beneath the boroughs of New York City
Afraid he may have lost the dreams
he nurtured in the open fields
outside of Omaha.
He looks for new horizons
amid a sea of brownstones.

"The Dream" © S. T. Gladding

CHAPTER OVERVIEW

From reading this chapter you will learn about

■ Beliefs existentialists share.
■ The focus existentialists have on ultimate human concerns (death, freedom, isolation, and meaninglessness).
■ Techniques of existentialist counselors.

As you read consider

■ Your beliefs about the meaning of life and what you find meaningful.
■ Your thoughts and feelings about ultimate human concerns (death, freedom, isolation, and meaningfulness).
■ How focused you are on living in the present and forming relationships with others.

Existentialism is a philosophy that addresses what it means to be human, including thoughts, feelings, and anxieties (Haddock & Diambra, 2018). The basis for existentialism comes from a number of sources but may well be attributed to 19th-century theologian and philosopher Soren Kierkegaard. He was one of the first to develop a philosophy focused on the pursuit of becoming an individual, "formulating truth as a guidepost, and emphasizing the necessity of commitment. His approach was named 'existentialism' by German and French theorists Martin Heidegger and Jean Paul Sartre. The approach was later formulated into a therapeutic process by Swiss psychiatrist Ludwig Binswanger" (Austin, 1999, p. 53). It has been applied to the helping professions since the mid-1940s by drawing from writers such as Martin Buber, Paul Tillich, Steve Biko, and Frederick Nietzche.

The essence of existentialism as a therapeutic approach is represented in the writings of several prominent American theorists—including Sidney Jourard, Abraham Maslow, Irvin Yalom, Rollo May, Clemmont Vontress, James Bugental, and Clark Moustakas—even though its philosophical roots are European. Other notable contributors to existentialism include Fyodor Dostoyevski, Albert Camus, Edmund Husserl, Friedrich Nietzsche, Martin Buber, and Viktor Frankl. In recent years, the most prominent practitioners of existential psychotherapy in the United States and Europe have been Rollo May, Viktor Frankl, Irvin Yalom, and Clemmont Vontress. May and Frankl are probably the best known of these theorists.

As a group, existentialists differ widely in their emphases. For example, Dostoyevski stressed the importance of consciousness, Kierkegaard concentrated on human anxiety and dread, and Buber (1970) focused on the treatment of persons in "it" or "thou" relationships—that is, treating others as inanimate objects or as unique individuals. However, despite their diversity, existentialists hold some beliefs in common:

- The importance of anxiety, values, freedom, and responsibility in human life.
- An emphasis on finding meaning in one's actions.
- The belief people form their lives by their choices.

MAJOR THEORISTS: ROLLO MAY AND VIKTOR FRANKL

Rollo May (1909–1994) was born in Ada, Ohio. Like Alfred Adler, May was the second of six children, but unlike Adler, May was the oldest son in his family. The relationship between May's parents was discordant, leading May to describe his boyhood home life as unhappy. Consequently, he became a loner and a rebel during his adolescence (Rabinowitz et al., 1989).

In 1930, May graduated with a degree in English from Oberlin College and accepted a position teaching English at Anatolia College in Greece. During two of his summer vacations there, he traveled to Vienna and enrolled in seminars conducted by Alfred Adler, which sparked his interest in psychodynamic theory and in therapy. However, during his years in Greece, he was extremely lonely and began working incessantly, which resulted in a breakdown. As he reflected years later, "I had learned enough psychology at college to know that these symptoms meant that something was wrong with my whole way of life. I had to find some new goals and purposes for my living and to relinquish my moralistic, somewhat rigid way of existence" (May, 1985, p. 8).

In 1933, May returned to the United States to enter Union Theological Seminary, where he was strongly influenced by Paul Tillich, an existential theologian. After a brief career as a Congregationalist minister, May decided to pursue a degree in clinical psychology at Columbia University, but tuberculosis interrupted his studies. He struggled with the illness for almost 2 years, during which time he was strongly impressed with the writings of Danish existentialist Soren Kierkegaard. After his recovery, May completed his doctorate at Columbia in 1949 and joined the faculty of the William Allanson White Institute in New York City.

May's most influential book, *The Meaning of Anxiety*, was published a year later. May believed that anxiety could work for the good as well as the detriment of people. He lectured on this subject at some of the most distinguished universities in the United States, including Yale and Harvard, while continuing to practice psychotherapy and serve "as an adjunct faculty member at the New School of Social Research and New York University" (Rabinowitz et al., 1989, p. 437). May was a cofounder of the Association for Humanistic Psychology in the 1960s and later wrote two other well-known books, *Love and Will* (1969) and *The Courage to Create* (1975). In the 1980s, he retired to the San Francisco area, where he concentrated on writing about the meaning of myths for modern society and continued to promote a humanistic approach to psychology until his death at the age of 85.

Viktor Frankl (1905–1997) was born in Vienna, Austria. He received a medical degree in 1930 and a PhD in 1949 from the University of Vienna. Frankl established the Youth Advisement Centers in Vienna and directed them from 1928 to 1938. He also held several hospital appointments in the city between 1930 and 1942.

Although Frankl was a contemporary of Freud and Adler and interacted with both, he became interested in existentialism in the 1930s while reading philosophers such as Heidegger, Scheler, and Legan. He began formulating his ideas about an existential approach to counseling, using the term "**logotherapy**" as early as 1938. The Greek word *logo* implies a search for meaning.

During World War II Frankl was imprisoned from 1942 to 1945 in Nazi concentration camps at Auschwitz and Dachau, where his parents, a brother, and his wife died. The impact of the concentration camps crystallized his thoughts about the meaning of life and suffering, and it was partly his determination to share those beliefs that kept him alive.

In 1947 Frankl joined the faculty of the University of Vienna and later became associated with the United States International University in San Diego, lecturing at many prestigious universities throughout the world. He wrote extensively also; his best-known books are *Man's Search for Meaning* (1985), which has been translated into 24 languages, and *The Will to Meaning* (1969b). "According to Frankl, the will to meaning is the central drive of human existence" (Dollarhide, 1997, p. 181), but meaning is attained as a by-product of discovery rather than through direct pursuit.

Frankl is sometimes referred to as the founder of the third school of Viennese psychotherapy (i.e., logotherapy), with Freud's psychoanalytic theory first and Adler's individual psychology second. At the age of 92, Frankl died of heart failure in Vienna.

VIEW OF HUMAN NATURE/PERSONALITY

As a group, existentialists believe that people form their lives by the choices they make. Even the worst situations, such as the Nazi death camps, provide an opportunity to make important life-and-death decisions, such as whether to struggle to stay alive (Frankl, 1969b). Existentialists focus on this freedom of choice and the action that goes with it, viewing people as the authors of their lives. Existentialists contend that people are responsible for any choices they make and that some choices are healthier and more meaningful than others. For example, individuals who prize creativity, service to others, friendship, and self-growth within a community or family environment may, as Abraham Maslow describes, have **peak experiences**, in which they feel truly integrated and connected with the universe in a very emotional way (Hoffman, 1990). Such persons are characterized as having "a holistic perspective of the world, [having] a natural tendency toward synergy [cooperative action], [being] intrapsychic, interpersonal, intercultural and international, [being] more consciously and deliberately metamotivated" (Chandler et al., 1992, p. 168).

Reflective Question

What healthy choices have you made in your life? How have they helped shape the person you are today?

On the other hand, individuals who are self-indulgent may feel a sense of normlessness and valuelessness. They may experience what Frankl (1959) calls an **existential vacuum**, a sense that life has lost all meaning. If this attitude is carried to an extreme, these individuals would develop a disorder Frankl calls **noogenic neurosis**, characterized by a feeling that one has nothing to live for (Das, 1998).

According to Frankl (1962), the "meaning of life always changes but it never ceases to be" (p. 113). **Meaning** goes beyond self-actualization and exists at three levels: (a) **ultimate meaning** (e.g., an order to the universe), (b) **meaning of the moment**, and (c) **common, day-to-day meaning** (Das, 1998). Frankl believes we can discover life's meaning in three ways:

- **By doing a deed**—that is, by achieving or accomplishing something.
- **By experiencing a value** such as a work of nature, culture, or love.
- **By suffering**—that is, by finding a proper attitude toward unalterable fate.

Existentialists believe that **psychopathology** is a failure to make meaningful choices and maximize one's potential (McIllroy, 1979). Choices may be avoided and potentials unrealized because of the anxiety involved in action. Anxiety is often associated with paralysis, but May (1977) argues normal anxiety can be healthy and motivational and can help people change. Clients may leave existential counseling more anxious than they began, but in such cases, they are consciously aware of their anxiety and can therefore channel it toward constructive use (May, 1967). Thus, existentialism, unlike other theories, focuses on the meaning of anxiety in human life, emphasizing the inner person and the ways in which authentic individuals search for value in life. By being aware of feelings and the finite nature of human existence, people come to make healthy, life-enhancing choices.

ROLE OF THE COUNSELOR

Existentialists do not adopt any uniform roles. Indeed, the existential approach to counseling is unique in its diversity. Nor is there agreement among existentialists about how systematically to formulate their ideas into a uniform way of helping others. Part of the reason for this variety among practitioners is that existentialists believe every client is distinctive, regardless of similar concerns, heritages, or backgrounds. Therefore, existentialists are sensitive to the discrete aspects of their clients' characteristics, "such as voice, posture, facial expression, even dress and apparently accidental movements of the body" (May, 1939, p. 101). Existentialists concentrate on being authentic with their clients and entering deep and personal relationships with them.

In the therapeutic process, it is not unusual for helpers to share personal experiences with their clients to deepen the relationship and help clients realize a shared humanness and struggle. Buhler and Allen (1972) suggest that existentialists focus on person-to-person relationships that emphasize mutuality, wholeness, and growth.

Existentialists who practice from Frankl's perspective are Socratic in engaging their clients in dialogue (Das, 1998). However, all existentialists serve as a model of how to achieve individual potential and make decisions. They concentrate on helping clients experience subjective feelings, gain clearer self-understanding, and move toward a new way of being in the world. The focus is on living productively in the present, not recovering a personal past. They also focus on ultimate human concerns (death, freedom, isolation, and meaninglessness) (Yalom & Josselson, 2011).

Existentialists do not use psychological tests, nor do they make diagnoses in accordance with the latest *Diagnostic and Statistical Manual* (*DSM*). Both procedures would be antithetical to the thrust of the approach, which stresses the uniqueness of each client. It is interesting to note, however, that some psychological instruments, such as the Purpose of Life Test, are based on existential premises and that the *DSM* deals with anxiety on several levels. In addition, existentialists do assess how meaningfully and purposefully individuals they are working with see life.

Reflective Question

How do you think focusing on ultimate human concerns, such as death, freedom, isolation, and meaninglessness, can be helpful to clients in formulating and carrying out their goals individually or in a group?

GOALS

The goals of existential helping include assisting clients to realize the importance of meaning, responsibility, awareness, freedom, and potential. Existentialists hope that during the course of the helping relationship, clients will take more responsibility for their lives: "The aim of therapy is that the patient experience his existence as real" (May et al., 1958, p. 85). If all works well, clients are freed from being observers of events and become shapers of meaningful personal activity.

Clients become more responsible through the relationships they build with their existential helper because in relationships they develop a greater awareness of personal freedom. Thus, a major goal is for clients to shift from an outward to an inward frame of reference, no longer depending on the judgment of others but evaluating their own activities first. Further goals include

- Making clients sensitive to their existence.
- Calling attention to clients' unique traits and characteristics.
- Helping clients improve their encounters with others.
- Assisting clients in establishing a will to meaning.
- Encouraging clients to decide about both present and future directions in life (Cunningham & Peters, 1973; Das, 1998; May, 1975; Reeves, 1977).

Reflective Question

What unique traits and characteristics do you have? How do you use them? How might you use them more?

PROCESS AND TECHNIQUES

Because the existential approach is not a clearly defined process for most of its practitioners, specific techniques are rarely used repeatedly. In fact, the existential approach claims fewer techniques than almost any other major model of helping. "Approaching human beings merely in terms of techniques necessarily implies manipulating them," and manipulation is opposed to what existentialists espouse (Frankl, 1967, p. 139).

This apparent weakness is paradoxically a strength because it allows existentialists to concentrate on building deep and meaningful relationships with their clients, thereby helping them become more aware of themselves and others. It also allows these practitioners to borrow ideas from other areas and to use a wide range of skills in a highly personal manner. Thus they are free to use techniques as widely diverse as desensitization and free association or to disassociate themselves from these practices entirely (Corey, 2017).

Clients usually benefit from existentialists who can address their needs in a multidimensional and highly customized way. For example, depressed persons tend to adopt emotion-focused strategies for dealing with their pain, whereas nondepressed individuals use multiple and vying strategies (Stevens et al., 1987). Thus, assessing whether a person is depressed gives an existentialist an idea of what approach to use. Existentialists can offer a variety of approaches—some that may be cognitive or even behavioral, as well as some that may be emotionally oriented—to help depressed individuals and assist them in seeing options. Of uppermost importance is the existential view that working with clients is open and inquiring. As such, they accept the truth unique to each individual (Kemp, 1976).

In addition, developing some vision of the true, the good, and the beautiful is essential from an existential perspective. Such a vision gives meaning to individuals' personal lives and humanizes society as well (Partenheimer, 1990). However, sometimes the process of finding personal truth requires a willingness to work through ambiguity, which is a central concept in existentialism. In such cases existentialists have a most effective and powerful tool to aid in exploration—their relationships with clients. Ideally, existentialists transcend their own needs and focus on their clients during this phase of therapy (Wallace, 1986), remaining open and self-revealing in an attempt to help their clients become more in touch with personal feelings and experiences. The emphasis is on authenticity, honesty, and spontaneity.

Existentialists also make use of confrontation; clients are confronted with the idea that everyone is responsible for his or her life. For this purpose, existentialists borrow some techniques from other models, such as imagery exercises, awareness exercises, and goal-setting activities. For example, existentialists may lead clients through a typical day in their lives 5 years in the future. Through this process, clients can see more clearly meaning in life by recognizing the choices they are making now that will shape their futures.

DIVERSITY AND MULTICULTURAL ISSUES

Because existentialists concentrate on human conditions that are universal in most lifestyles and circumstances, this approach to helping is probably as diverse and multicultural as any. A leading proponent of the existentialist approach in the United States for many years was Clemmont Vontress, an African American who proposed existential theory as a base for multicultural counseling (Moodley & Walcott, 2010;

Vontress, 1979; Vontress et al., 1999). In addition, Viktor Frankl's form of existentialism, logotherapy, is highly adaptable to multicultural concerns (Zalaquett et al., 2019). As Hoffman et al. (2016) point out, meaning must be seen in a multicultural context, and clinicians need to be aware of the complexities of meaning and culture to effectively work with diverse clientele.

Gender issues are deemphasized in the existential approach. Both men and women have feelings of meaninglessness, isolation, and anxiety with which they must deal. Even though ways of addressing these feelings and other conditions in life may vary with the genders, a common emphasis remains within existentialism on working with men and women in unique ways that help them transcend common human difficulties such as disabilities or socioeconomic circumstance.

Likewise, the settings where existential counseling is practiced vary. They range from prisons (Murphy, 2018) to counseling centers (Du Plock, 2019). Existentialism is found worldwide and has been influenced by Taoism and Buddhism (Bradford, 2017) as well as by Western European thinkers such as Buber and Heidegger.

Reflective Question

Both Adlerian and existential approaches to counseling deemphasize gender issues. Do you think this approach devalues the uniqueness and concerns of men and women? Why or why not?

EVALUATION OF THE THEORY

Strengths and Contributions

A strength of existentialism is its emphasis on the uniqueness of each individual. It is a very humanistic way of working with others (Yalom, 1980). It also stresses continued human growth and development, including the unending possibility for individuals to create meaning for a renewed life offering hope (Zyromski et al., 2018). The life of Viktor Frankl is a good illustration of this strength. Furthermore, existential therapy recognizes that anxiety is not necessarily a negative condition. Anxiety is a part of human life and can motivate some individuals to make healthy and productive decisions, realizing time is limited and they cannot put off making choices forever.

Another contribution of existentialism is its effectiveness in culturally diverse situations (Moodley & Walcott, 2010). Because of its global view of human existence, existentialism allows clinicians to focus on the person of the client in an I-thou manner without regard to ethnic, social, or sexual background (Epp, 1998; Jackson, 1987; Miars, 2002). In addition, an existential approach gives practitioners access to a tremendous amount of philosophy and literature that is both informative and enlightening about human nature. This philosophical base has the potential to support a systematic counseling theory.

Existential theory also helps connect individuals to universal problems faced by humankind, difficulties such as the search for peace, the absence of caring, or finding employment (Baldwin, 1989; Schultze & Miller, 2004). In the latter situation, the existential themes of death, freedom/responsibility, aloneness, and meaninglessness may serve as a process-oriented framework that the existential counselor uses to support a person in entering or reconnecting with a turbulent and unpredictable job marketplace (Maglio et al., 2005).

Finally, an existential approach is valuable to helping relationships because it can be combined with other perspectives and methods, such as those based on learning principles and behaviorism, to treat extremely difficult problems—for example, addiction. In these cases, a major focus is on the existential value of facing "life problems and feelings through honest expression" (Wilbur et al., 1990, p. 157). Overall, existentialism has a wide appeal because the theory behind it focuses on a person's reason for being in life (Marino, 2019).

Limitations and Criticisms

Despite its strengths and contributions, the existential approach has been criticized for a lack of a coherent framework of practice or a fully developed model of counseling (Correia et al., 2017). Practitioners who stress developmental stages of growth are particularly vehement in this criticism. Research is being undertaken to address this deficit, but it remains problematic.

A related limitation is that existential counseling is difficult to implement beyond an individual level because of its subjective nature. Existentialism lacks the type of methodology and validation processes prevalent in most other therapeutic approaches and the uniformity and systematic outline that beginning helpers readily understand.

Another shortcoming of the existential approach, according to some critics, is that existentialists as a group do not diagnose or test their clients. Critics claim that due to the failure to evaluate and diagnose, therapists may miss opportunities to assess their clients more thoroughly and subsequently gear their practices more specifically to clients' needs.

Finally, critics charge that existential theory and therapy are closer to existential philosophy than to other counseling theories and therapies. This distinction and separation limit the usefulness of existentialism according to this argument.

Reflective Question

How useful do you think you could be to people in need if you were an existentialist? What makes you think so?

TREATING LINDA WITH EXISTENTIAL THERAPY

Conceptualization

From an existential perspective, Linda seems to be living a meaningless life, just drifting. She has contemplated suicide and has had anxiety about her ability to succeed at work and in relationships. Thus her life is characterized by a feeling that she has nothing to live for. Although Linda has made a number of bad choices, you, as an existentialist, believe she is capable of making healthy choices and maximizing her potential.

Treatment Process

As an existentialist, you focus on Linda's uniqueness and distinctiveness. You attempt to be authentic with her and to enter a deep relationship. You self-disclose and share with Linda some of your own struggles as she reveals hers. You try to serve as a role model for her and help her focus on living a productive life in the present.

Your hope in working with Linda is that she will take more responsibility for her life. You want her to shift from an outer to an inner frame of reference, from which she can evaluate situations first. You want her to be more sensitive to herself. To help her envision the good and the beautiful, you borrow several techniques from guided imagery and use them with her. You also confront Linda with the fact that she alone is responsible for her life. Because Linda likes to read, you assign her books on the lives of Viktor Frankl and Rollo May as well as the existential writings of Irvin Yalom, including some of his popular fiction such as *Love's Executioner* and *Momma and the Meaning of Life*. When she returns for her appointments, you discuss the books with her and talk about how each of these individuals has had to overcome obstacles to find meaning in life.

Linda leaves counseling with a new sense of herself and others. She begins to engage in social activities within the community and to explore opportunities for personal and professional growth. She maintains a relationship with you even after treatment has officially ended.

SUMMING UP

Existentialism is both a philosophy and a philosophical approach to counseling. It has European roots, yet it has been adopted and adapted by a number of prominent American clinicians. The approach is centered on the premise that human beings have universal feelings and experience universal conditions such as anxiety, loneliness, death, and the search for meaning in existence. Leading existentialists of the 20th century include Rollo May and Viktor Frankl. Notable therapists and educators today include Irvin Yalom and Clemmont Vontress.

There is no uniform existentialist approach, although one form of existentialism, Frankl's logotherapy, is more systematic than others and scholars are attempting to bring existentialists together in more unified ways (Van Dueren & Adams, 2016). Nonetheless, the focus in all forms of existentialism is on the relationship between the helper and client, and on that relationship a dialogue about issues relevant to the client is built. In the process, existentialists confront and share personal experiences. Most borrow techniques from other approaches and concentrate on working with clients in the moment, using whatever techniques further insight and the movement within clients to address their concerns.

In recent years some have argued existential psychotherapy is a positive psychology because it focuses on both possibilities and limitations and recognizes human potential without succumbing to an unrealistic optimism (Bretherton & Orner, 2003). Existential counseling remains an effective approach for working in diverse and gender-sensitive venues.

CHAPTER 4 RECAP: EXISTENTIAL THERAPY

Major Theorists
Rollo May, Irvin Yalom, Mick Cooper
Viktor Frankl, Clemmont Vontress, James F. T. Bugental

View of Human Nature/Personality
Belief in human freedom and choice of lifestyle
Focus on meaning of anxiety, meaning of life, relevance of individual
   experience

Role of the Counselor
Emphasize authenticity
Understand clients as unique individuals
Stress personal relationship, modeling, sharing experiences

Goals
Help clients realize responsibility, awareness, freedom, potential
Shift clients from outward to inward frame of reference

Process and Techniques
Use of counseling relationship that is open, inquiring, accepting
Variety of borrowed and diverse techniques

Diversity and Multicultural Issues
Recognizes and respects culture and uniqueness
Transcends gender differences
Focuses on meaningfulness for all individuals

Strengths and Contributions
Emphasizes human interests and concerns
Recognizes uniqueness of individuals
Focuses on anxiety and meaning as motivators
Uses a wide range of philosophy and literature
Stresses continuous growth
Is strongly multicultural and gender sensitive
Connects individuals to universal problems

Limitations and Criticisms
Is not as fully developed as some other theories
Lacks centralized training facilities, varies from country to country
Is more subjective than most theories
Lacks uniformity and uniform teachable processes
Does not use standardized diagnostic labels from the DSM nor does it utilize
   testing
Is closer to philosophy than to most other counseling therapies

KEY TERMS

by doing a deed   50
by experiencing a value   50
by suffering   50

discovering life's meaning   50
existential vacuum   50
existentialism   47

logotherapy   49
meaning   50
noogenic neurosis   50

peak experience   49
psychopathology   50

LEARNING MORE

A number of periodicals on existential theory may be helpful in exploring this approach to counseling.

Humanistic Psychology
Journal of Humanistic Counseling
Journal of Humanistic Psychology
Journal of Phenomenological Psychology
Journal for the Society of Existential Analysis
Review of Existential Psychology and Psychiatry

In addition to journals, several training institutes and practitioner associations allow clinicians to learn more about existentialism in therapeutic settings. Two of the best are listed next.

Society for Existential Analysis
BM Existential
London, England WC1N 3XX
07000 473337
http://www.existentialanalysis.org.uk/

Existential Humanistic Institute
1368 Lincoln Ave., Suite 214
San Rafael, CA 9490
415–689-1475
http://ehinstitute.org

CLASSROOM ACTIVITIES

1. Rollo May believed that the best helpers are those who have been psychologically wounded—that is, who have suffered and been healed. What do you think are the advantages of having experienced suffering and situations similar to those you help? What do you think are the disadvantages?
2. Tell how you think an existentialist might work with the following types of clients: an alcoholic, a school-phobic child, a spouse abuser, and an unemployed person. Discuss your thoughts with a classmate. Do you think the techniques existentialists use would be different or the same in these situations? Why or why not?
3. What experiences have been most meaningful in your life—for example, graduation, love relationships, birth of children? How do you think existentialists might use such significant and momentous life experiences in their work?

5

Person-Centered Therapy

■ ■ ■

Unless I am true to myself
and genuine with you
our words are worthless
our relationship hollow.

"Relating" © S. T. Gladding

CHAPTER OVERVIEW

From reading this chapter you will learn about

■ The development of person-centered therapy and its phenomenological perspective.
■ The necessary and sufficient (core) conditions of counseling according to Carl Rogers: empathy, positive regard/acceptance, and congruence/genuineness.
■ The difference between the ideal self and the real self.

As you read, consider

■ When you have been accepted conditionally and unconditionally and how such acceptance felt.
■ How you view other people.
■ How you would recognize if someone were a fully functioning person.

Carl Rogers created person-centered counseling in the early 1940s. It was considered a radical approach when it began because it differed greatly from the primary theories in use. At that time, the predominant theories of counseling were counselor centered (e.g., E. G. Williamson), symptom focused (e.g., behaviorism), or personality change oriented (e.g., psychoanalysis). Rogers altered the counseling landscape with his initial emphasis on being nondirective and letting clients take the lead in directing change.

Rogers's approach to helping was revolutionary. He emphasized caring, empathy, understanding, and acceptance in ways never tried before. He trusted his clients would grow if the right conditions were established. His journey as a clinician, his development as a person, and the growth of his theory were achieved despite resistance and, at times, adversity. The validity of the person-centered approach to counseling may seem obvious in the 21st century, but its therapeutic process and procedures were considered anything but routine when it emerged.

MAJOR THEORIST: CARL ROGERS

Carl Rogers (1902–1987), the individual most identified with person-centered counseling, was born in Oak Park, Illinois, a suburb of Chicago. He was the fourth of six children. As fundamentalist Christians, his parents discouraged Rogers from forming friendships outside the family because of the bad influence others might have on him. Due to this parental message, Rogers (1980) describes his childhood as solitary, with "no close friend and only superficial personal contact" (p. 29). When he was 12, his family moved to a farm outside Chicago, where he developed a strong interest in science and reading. Among his early scientific experiments was one investigating a species of moth.

As a teenager Rogers read everything he could, including encyclopedias and dictionaries. However, his academic interests and abilities did not help him socially, and Rogers (1967a) describes himself as generally inept in interpersonal relations during his high school years. A major turning point occurred when Rogers enrolled at the University of Wisconsin in 1919 to study agriculture. There he became involved with a YMCA group and began to develop friendships. He also started dating and began to trust others. A life-changing event for him was a 6-month trip in 1922 as 1 of 10 American students attending the World Student Christian Federation conference in Peking, China. The trip exposed him to people of other cultures, religions, and ways of thinking (Kirschenbaum, 2007).

After his return, Rogers broke away from the domination of his parents and changed his major to history, intending to become a minister. After graduation in 1924, he enrolled in New York's Union Theological Seminary but became discouraged 2 years later about the prospect of entering the ministry. He transferred to Teachers College, Columbia University, "a hotbed of radical behavioristic thinking in the 1920s" (Bankart, 1997, p. 293). There he studied clinical and educational psychology, receiving an MA degree in 1928 and a PhD in 1931. As a graduate student, Rogers studied briefly with Alfred Adler, who was a visiting instructor at the Institute for Child Guidance in New York City, where Rogers was an intern (Watts, 1996a).

After completing his studies, Rogers took a position with a child guidance agency in Rochester, New York. His 12-year tenure there was productive and significantly influenced his later theory of counseling. He found that the psychoanalytic approach, which was dominant in this work setting, was time consuming and often ineffective. However, clients with whom Rogers formed an open and permissive relationship seemed to improve. During this time Rogers was reinforced in his clinical beliefs by the works of Otto Rank and his followers (Raskin et al., 2019).

Rogers left Rochester in 1940 to accept a professorship at Ohio State University. Two years later, he published his ideas on counseling in his first book on theory, *Counseling and Psychotherapy* (1942). He refined and revised those ideas during extensive research in the 1950s and 1960s at the University of Chicago and the University of Wisconsin. At Wisconsin Rogers first examined the effectiveness of his approach in a hospital setting with persons diagnosed as schizophrenic. In 1964, he became a resident fellow at the Western Behavioral Sciences Institute, and in 1968, he helped establish the Center for the Study of Persons in La Jolla, California.

A prolific writer, Rogers published more than 200 articles and 15 books (Heppner et al., 1990). Among his most noteworthy books are *Counseling and Psychotherapy* (1942), which laid the foundation for person-centered counseling; *Client-Centered Therapy* (1951), which thrust him and his theory into national prominence; and

On Becoming a Person (1961), which "solidified his reputation in his chosen profession" (Whiteley, 1987, p. 8) and with the public at large.

Rogers wrote five books after the age of 65, including *Freedom to Learn* (1969), *Carl Rogers on Encounter Groups* (1970), and *A Way of Being* (1980). He considered his theory to be constantly evolving, becoming relevant in groups, marriages, families, and international relations, especially the peace movement of the 1980s (Goodyear, 1987; Rogers, 1987). He died unexpectedly at the age of 85 on February 4, 1987, from complications following hip surgery.

VIEW OF HUMAN NATURE/PERSONALITY

Implicit in person-centered counseling is the view that people are essentially good (Rogers, 1961). Humans are characteristically "positive, forward-moving, constructive, realistic, and trustworthy" (Rogers, 1957, p. 99). From infancy on, each person is aware, inner-directed, and moving toward self-actualization.

- Whatever an infant perceives is that infant's reality. An infant's perception is an internal process of which no one else can be aware.
- All infants are born with a self-actualizing tendency satisfied through goal-directed behavior.
- An infant's interaction with the environment is an organized whole, and everything an infant does is interrelated.
- The experiences of an infant may be seen as positive or negative according to whether they enhance the actualization tendency.
- Infants maintain experiences that are actualizing and avoid those that are not. (Rogers, 1959)

According to Rogers, self-actualization is the most common and motivating drive of existence; it encompasses actions that influence the total person. "The organism has one basic tendency and striving, to actualize, maintain, and enhance the experiencing organism" (Rogers, 1951, p. 487). Person-centered theorists believe that each person can find a personal meaning and purpose in life. As such, the approach is anti-deterministic.

Rogers views the individual from a **phenomenological perspective**: what is important is a person's perception of reality rather than an event itself (Rogers, 1955). This view is similar to Adler's, as is the concept of self. However, for Rogers the concept is so central to his theory that his ideas are often referred to as **self-theory**. The self is an outgrowth of what people experience, and an awareness of self helps individuals differentiate themselves from others (Nye, 2000).

For a healthy self to emerge, people need **positive regard**—love, warmth, care, respect, and acceptance. However, in childhood, as well as in later life, individuals often receive conditional regard from parents and others. **Conditional acceptance** teaches persons to feel valued only when they conform to others' wishes. Those persons may thus have to deny or distort a perception when others on whom they depend for approval see a situation differently. Individuals caught in such a dilemma become aware of incongruities between their self-perceptions and their experiences. If they conform, they open a gap between the **ideal self** (what they are striving to become) and the **real self** (what they are). The further the ideal self is from the real self, the more alienated and maladjusted persons become.

Reflective Question

How do you picture your ideal self? How are you striving to achieve it?

ROLE OF THE COUNSELOR

Person-centered counselors take on a holistic role in their work. They set up and promote a climate in which clients are free and encouraged to explore all aspects of their lives (Rogers, 1951, 1980). This atmosphere focuses on the counselor-client relationship, which Rogers describes as having a special **I-Thou personal quality** (Buber, 1970). Person-centered counselors are aware of the verbal and nonverbal language of their clients, and they reflect what they hear or observe (Braaten, 1986). Neither clients nor counselors know what direction sessions will take or what goals will emerge in the process. Yet counselors trust clients to develop the agenda with counselors working as **facilitators** rather than as directors. In the person-centered approach counselors are process experts and expert learners. Patience is essential (Miller, 1996).

Person-centered counselors make limited use of psychological tests. Testing is usually done only at the request of clients and only after clients have had an opportunity to be reflective about their past decisions. If testing does take place, counselors focus on the meaning of the test for clients rather than on test scores. One innovative test Rogers used initially in evaluating clients was the **Q Sort Technique** (Olson & Hergenhahn, 2011). In this evaluative method, the client is given 100 cards, each of which contains a self-descriptive sentence such as "I am intelligent" or "I despise myself." Next, the client is asked to place the cards in nine piles, from most-like-me to least-like-me. Then the client sorts the cards again according to how he or she would like to be. The final step of the process is correlating the degree of similarity between the sorting before, during, and after counseling.

The use of diagnosis, at least on a formal level, is eschewed in person-centered counseling because diagnosis is philosophically incompatible with the objectives of the approach. Diagnosis categorizes people, implying that each person is not unique. It also puts the counselor in charge because, once a diagnosis is made, a treatment plan follows. Thus, person-centered counselors do not usually use the *Diagnostic and Statistical Manual for Mental Disorders*. However, clinicians who are person-centered are aware of the degree to which individuals they work with are functioning and at least on an informal level assess their growth and development over time.

Reflective Question

Do you think displaying unconditional positive regard is enough to establish rapport with a client? If not, what else might be needed?

GOALS

The goals of person-centered counseling are geared to clients as people, not to their problems. Rogers (1977) emphasizes that people need to be assisted in learning how to cope with situations so that they become fully functioning persons with no need to apply defense mechanisms to everyday experiences. Such individuals are increasingly willing to change and grow; they are more open to experience, more trusting of self-perception, and more engaged in self-exploration and evaluation (Rogers, 1961). Fully functioning persons develop a greater acceptance of themselves and others and become better decision makers.

Ultimately, person-centered counseling helps clients identify, use, and integrate their own resources and potential (Boy & Pine, 1982; Miller, 1996). Rogers (1961) holds that clients should become

- More realistic in their self-perceptions.
- More confident and self-directing.
- More positively valued by themselves.
- Less likely to repress aspects of their experiences.
- More mature, socialized, and adaptive in their behavior.
- Less upset by stress and quicker to recover from it.
- More like a healthy integrated well-functioning person in their personality structures (p. 375).

Thus, a major goal of person-centered counseling is harmony "between the client's real self-concept and his or her perceived self-concept" (Benjamin & Looby, 1998, p. 92).

Reflective Question

How likely do you think it is that a person can achieve and maintain the qualities of a fully functioning person? Why?

PROCESS AND TECHNIQUES

Person-centered processes and techniques have evolved over the years. Hart (1970) identifies **three periods of evolution**, each distinctively different in its emphasis.

- **Nondirective period** (1940–1950). During this period, person-centered counselors emphasized relationship with clients by creating a permissive atmosphere of nonintervention. Their main techniques were acceptance and clarification.
- **Reflective period** (1950–1957). This 7-year span was characterized by an emphasis on nonthreatening relationships. Techniques included responding to clients' feelings and reflecting underlying affect back to clients. During this period, Rogers changed his terminology from nondirective to client-centered to deemphasize techniques and focus on the therapeutic relationship.
- **Experiential period** (1957–1980). This period began when Rogers (1957) issued his statement on the necessary and sufficient or core conditions of counseling: empathy, positive regard or acceptance, and congruence or genuineness

(Gelso & Carter, 1985; Watts, 1996a). **Empathy** is the ability to feel with clients and convey this understanding back to them. It is an attempt to think with rather than for or about them (Brammer et al., 1993). Empathy is more than an amorphous concept. Carkhuff (1987) has developed a 5-point scale to measure verbal responses from those that are high to those that are low in empathy. The essence of these responses is in Table 5.1.

Rogers (1975) notes, "The research keeps piling up and it points strongly to the conclusion that a high degree of empathy in a relationship is possibly the most potent and certainly one of the most potent factors in bringing about change and learning" (p. 3). Positive regard, also known as acceptance, is a deep and genuine caring for clients as persons—that is, prizing people just for being (Rogers, 1961, 1980). **Congruence** is the condition of being transparent in the therapeutic relationship by giving up roles and facades (Rogers, 1980). This period helped make person-centered counseling more active and well defined.

Since 1980 person-centered counselors have tried a number of other procedures for working with clients, such as limited self-disclosure of counselors' feelings, thoughts, and values. However, because clients grow by experiencing themselves and others in relationships (Cormier et al., 2017), Rogers (1967b) holds that "significant positive personality change" cannot occur except in relationships (p. 73). He lists six necessary and sufficient conditions for a counseling relationship:

- Two persons are in psychological contact.
- The first person, the client, is in a state of incongruence and is vulnerable or anxious.
- The second person, the counselor, is congruent or integrated in the relationship.
- The counselor experiences unconditional positive regard for the client.
- The counselor experiences an empathic understanding of the client's internal frame of reference and attempts to communicate his or her experience to the client.
- There is at least a minimal degree of communication to the client of the counselor's understanding and unconditional positive regard.

According to Rogers (1959), these six conditions exist on a continuum and, except for the first condition, are not on an all-or-nothing basis.

Table 5.1   Cakhuff's Levels of Empathy

1. **Low** to no level of empathy response—responder communicates little or no awareness of other person's feelings, changes the subject, or gives advice
2. **Moderately low** level of empathy response—responder is inaccurate in identifying feelings or inappropriately qualifies them—for example, "somewhat," "kind of"
3. **Interchangeable or reciprocal** level of empathy—responder shows understanding that is essentially interchangeable with the client's, accurately reflects the client's story and surface feelings or state of being
4. **Moderately high** level of empathy response—responder is aware of underlying aspects of other person's feelings and helps them get in touch with somewhat deeper feelings
5. **High** level of empathy response—responder gets at emotional nuances of message using voice and intensity of expressions attuned to the client's surface and underlying feelings and meanings

Methods that promote the counselor-client relationship include, but are not limited to, the following:

- Active and passive listening.
- Accurate reflection of thoughts and feelings.
- Clarification.
- Summarization.
- Confrontation.
- General or open-ended leads.

All these techniques have been incorporated into other helping approaches and systematic human-relations training courses.

Overall, the person-centered approach places minimal emphasis on formal techniques and maximal focus on creating a therapeutic relationship (Purswell, 2019). A classic example of this emphasis can be seen in Rogers's (1965) interview with a client named Gloria, in which he focuses on her acceptance of herself and their relationship rather than on Gloria's problem. As with any vibrant theory, person-centered counseling continues to evolve and develop based on research and practice (Luke, 2018).

Reflective Question

When have you been totally accepted by someone? How did it feel? How did you respond?

DIVERSITY AND MULTICULTURAL ISSUES

Person-centered counseling did not initially receive positive reviews regarding its appropriateness in multicultural contexts, although it had been used in a number of countries to promote cross-cultural communication and understanding and is even referred to as multicultural. Rogers himself conducted many such workshops in countries as diverse as Japan, Mexico, China, Northern Ireland, and the former Soviet Union. That work continues, and as Spangenberg (2003) points out, the person-centered approach provides an excellent cross-cultural approach in South Africa, where there is a relationship between person-centered counseling and traditional African healing practices. Furthermore, Wiryosutomo et al. (2019) point out that research in the 21st century conducted in countries such as Brazil, Malaysia, Iran, and the United States has provided empirical evidence that supports person-centered counseling as an effective treatment for culturally diverse populations.

As a theory, person-centered theory has some similarities to Eastern philosophies and psychologies in which there is an openness to the development of people, and the self is seen as a process rather than a fixed being (Sharf, 2016). There is a deep appreciation in the person-centered approach of the many ways clients can benefit from therapy (Cooper & Mcleod, 2011). Recent multicultural research studies in both the United States and countries worldwide suggest that person-centered therapy is an effective and acceptable treatment for clients from collectivist-oriented cultures of origin as well as those that are more individualistic (Quinn, 2013).

Gender issues receive a mixed report. On one hand, Rogers appears to be effective with Gloria, a young, divorced woman in the film demonstrating his approach. A number of other incidents are documented in which person-centered therapy conducted by Rogers seems to be successful with both women and men, in groups and other settings. Gender-related concerns arise primarily because Rogers did not address them in his lifetime and some question whether people of one gender can truly empathize with and relate to others of another gender or whether those without disabilities can empathetically relate to individuals who have them. Decisive data are still out.

EVALUATION OF THE THEORY

Strengths and Contributions

Person-centered therapy revolutionized the counseling profession by demystifying the helping process. Rogers provided actual transcripts of counseling sessions (Goodyear, 1987) and "turned the field of counseling upside down" (Rogers, 1974, p. 115). Furthermore, he made the person-centered approach applicable to a wide range of human problems, including institutional changes, labor-management relationships, leadership development, career decision making, and international diplomacy. He summed up his view of the approach in this way: "I am no longer talking about psychotherapy, but about a point of view, a philosophy, an approach to life, a way of being, which fits any situation in which growth, of a person, a group, or a community is part of the goal" (Rogers, 1980, p. ix).

Besides transforming the therapeutic community, the person-centered approach has contributed to the profession by generating a great deal of research (Kirschenbaum, 2004, 2007). Initially, it set the standard for doing research on counseling variables, especially those that Rogers (1957) deemed necessary and sufficient to bring about therapeutic change. In addition, Rogers was the first clinician to make audiotape recordings of counseling sessions and insisted that the person-centered approach be compared only to theories that were empirically verified (Rogers, 1986). "Above all, Rogers was the quintessential scientist practitioner. He continually put his formulations to the test of research. In fact, no model of therapy is more extensively researched than his own" (Goodyear, 1987, p. 523).

A third contribution of person-centered counseling is its focus on open relationships. More than most, Rogers's theory emphasizes the importance of an accepting counselor-client relationship. Specific dimensions of that relationship have been examined for their impact on the total helping process (Carkhuff, 1969a, 1969b).

Another strength of the person-centered approach is its effectiveness. It helps improve psychological adjustment, learning, and frustration tolerance and helps decrease defensiveness (Grummon, 1972). In addition, person-centered counseling is appropriate in treating mild to moderate anxiety states, depression, self-esteem issues, adjustment disorders, relationship concerns, and conditions not attributable to mental disorders, such as uncomplicated bereavement or interpersonal relations (Neukrug, 2017a; Seligman & Reichenberg, 2014).

A fifth strength of person-centered counseling is that the basics of the approach take a relatively short time to learn, although a lifetime to master. With its emphasis on relationship and listening skills, the person-centered approach has become a foundation for training many practitioners to work in varied settings (Glauser & Bozarth, 2001).

Yet another beneficial aspect of person-centered therapy is its positive view of human nature (Heppner et al., 1990; Kirschenbaum, 2004), which is different from the more pessimistic and deterministic views some theories hold. One of the strongest reasons people change is the belief that they can change, and person-centered helpers are strong believers in the change process.

Finally, the person-centered approach has generated a number of relatively new therapeutic ways of conducting counseling that claim to be either person centered or based on Rogers's theory. These treatment methods include child-centered play therapy, person-centered expressive therapy, mindfulness, focusing-oriented psychotherapy, and process-experiential/emotion-focused therapy (Kirschenbaum, 2012). In addition, Rogers's daughter, Natalie, claims the person-centered approach of her father as the theoretical underpinnings of her person-centered expressive arts therapy (Rogers et al., 2012).

Limitations and Criticisms

One initial drawback to person-centered therapy is that it provides few instructions for counselors on how to establish relationships with clients and bring about change. The work of Carkhuff (1969a, 1969b) and Gazda (1973) have helped rectify this deficiency; however, person-centered theory is still sometimes viewed as an approach without clearly defined terms or techniques (Nye, 2000).

Another limitation of the person-centered approach is that it depends on bright, insightful, hard-working clients for best results. Thus this theory of helping has limited applicability and is seldom employed with the severely handicapped or with young children (Henderson & Thompson, 2016).

A third criticism of being person-centered is that practitioners of this theory ignore diagnosis, the unconscious, and innately generated sexual and aggressive drives. Many critics think the theory is overly optimistic. Even though Rogers compiled a great deal of data supporting his point of view, much of that research has been attacked as simplistic and based on self-reports (Olson & Hergenhahn, 2011).

A fourth limitation of person-centered counseling is that it is directed by clients and may thus deal only with surface issues. Believing that only deep change is lasting, critics charge that clinicians who are person-centered do not challenge their clients to explore those deeper areas. Because the person-centered approach is relatively brief in nature and is not directed by an expert practitioner, critics claim that it cannot have a permanent impact on clients.

Reflective Question

What changes have you made that were not directed by others? Do you think Rogers is right in stating human beings are self-directed? Why?

TREATING LINDA WITH PERSON-CENTERED THERAPY

Conceptualization

From a person-centered perspective, what is important is that Linda has been accepted conditionally throughout her life. She has been valued as a daughter and a wife only when she has performed these roles as others have defined them. Linda's relationship with her ex-husband lasted only as long as she conformed to his wishes that she look and act in a certain way. Now she is searching to be accepted for herself unconditionally, and so far, she has not found people that value her just for herself. She does not get close to her family members because they too judge her.

As Linda looks at life, she sees a rather hostile environment. Men are mean or sexist. Families do not offer support or comfort. Thus it is little wonder that she has retreated to books, television, and movies as ways to escape and feel safe. On the other hand, Linda knows that she is more capable than she has been allowed to be.

Treatment Process

As a person-centered therapist, you immediately set up a therapeutic environment in which Linda is accepted and encouraged. You use yourself and the relationship you establish with Linda to help her see herself. You actively listen and reflect back to her what you hear her saying. You empathize, clarify, confront, and show her unconditional positive regard. You convey to her that you trust her to make observations, insights, and decisions. You are genuine in your statements and try to create an atmosphere in which Linda can be herself. In the process, she begins to feel like a person capable of finding her own direction in life.

As Linda begins to disclose, she initially ventilates anger toward her father, her former husband, and individuals in her work environments. You self-disclose and reveal that you would be angry too if you had been through her experiences. After a while, Linda shifts away from her anger and begins to concentrate on who she can be and how she can be. Her thoughts and feelings move into the present, and she recognizes that she has a quick mind and can go back to school or find a higher-level job. She also realizes that not all men are like her father or her ex-husband and that she might be able to be in a relationship in which she is valued for herself.

With these ideas in mind, Linda begins to make plans that will expand her environment and her opportunities, such as taking a yoga class at the Y and joining a reading club at the library. After a few more sessions, Linda reveals that she is ready to trust herself to make other plans and arrangements. Thus she leaves therapy with an optimistic sense of hope and a new perspective on herself.

SUMMING UP

The person-centered approach to counseling created a great deal of excitement and controversy when Carl Rogers introduced it to the therapeutic community in 1942. It emphasized that clients could and would make important and needed changes in their lives if a proper relationship was set up and someone listened to them. The emphasis on being nondirective was just the opposite of prominent theories of the time that put therapists in charge of change. Yet this approach has prevailed because of research supporting its underlying tenets.

Even though the person-centered approach has undergone a number of changes since its introduction, it still places priority on creating a therapeutic relationship and fostering the conditions necessary for change to take place. It continues to be one of the most popular theories of helping and has been used both domestically and internationally in a number of venues, ranging from group work to peace talks.

CHAPTER 5 RECAP: PERSON-CENTERED THERAPY

Major Theorists
Carl Rogers

View of Human Nature/Personality
Emphasis on the good and the positive
Phenomenological view of self
Self-direction and orientation toward growth

Role of the Counselor
Stresses holism and I-Thou relationship
Facilitates
Focuses on client uniqueness
Conveys empathy, acceptance, genuineness

Goals
Promote self-exploration and openness
Emphasize self-direction and realistic orientation
Encourage acceptance of self and others
Focus on here and now

Process and Techniques
Includes six necessary and sufficient conditions for change
Involves varied techniques: acceptance, clarification, reflection, empathy, congruence
Uses active listening, self-disclosure, summarization, and unconditional positive regard

Diversity and Multicultural Issues
Used in numerous countries
Like some Eastern philosophies and African healing practices
Inappropriate in some cultures
Successful with men and women
Questionable in closing gender gap through empathy

Strengths and Contributions
Credited with revolutionizing the world of therapy and helping it evolve
Applicable to varied problems and concerns
Effective with specific disorders
Short-term
Useful in training paraprofessional helpers

Positive in its view of people
Has generated a number of new approaches to counseling

Limitations and Criticisms
Lacks concrete direction in relationship formation
Depends on articulate and insightful clients
Ignores the unconscious and innate drives
May not resolve in-depth problems

KEY TERMS

conditional acceptance   60
congruence   63
empathy   63
facilitator   61
ideal self   60
I-Thou personal quality   61
Levels of Empathy (Carkhuff)   63
phenomenological perspective   60

positive regard   60
Q Sort Technique   61
real self   60
self-theory   60
Three periods of evolution for
   person-centered processes and
   techniques   62

LEARNING MORE

A limited number of periodicals are devoted to the theory, research, and practice of person-centered therapy. The best is probably *The Person-Centered Journal*, published by the Association for the Development of the Person-Centered Approach.

In addition, the *Journal of Counseling and Development*, *Counselor Education and Supervision*, and other major counseling journals carry articles and research periodically on person-centered counseling.

Several training institutes offer clinicians a chance to learn more about person-centered counseling. Two of the best known are:

Center for Studies of the Person
1150 Silverado, Suite #112
La Jolla, CA 92037
www.centerfortheperson.org

Association for the Development of the Person-Centered Approach
http://www.adpca.org/

CLASSROOM ACTIVITIES

1. How do you think a person-centered counselor would handle reluctant clients, such as an adolescent who is mandated to seek help or a person on probation who must receive court-ordered counseling? Discuss your ideas in pairs and then share them with the class.

2. In *A Way of Being* (1980), Carl Rogers traces his professional and personal development. Think of your own life and the events and people who have shaped who you are. What influence have they had on your philosophy of life? Your worldview? Make a timeline charting out these events and people. What did you learn in the process?

3. Compare the person-centered approach with Adlerian counseling. How are the two similar? How do they differ? Without considering money or time, which do you think most clients would prefer and why?

6
Gestalt Therapy

■ ■ ■

They wait stiff and still in the summer sun
for the boys who loved them to return,
But those boys,
having grown to an age where swing sets
are part of their history
have new interests
As they sit on front porch steps
trading stories and waiting for the cool of evening
when the girls they knew,
now young women,
will walk by, sometimes stop,
and send their hearts into orbit.

"Time and Motion" © S. T. Gladding

CHAPTER OVERVIEW

From reading this chapter you will learn about

■ The importance of and difference between figure and ground and **top dog** (thinking what you should do) versus **bottom dog** (doing what you want to do).
■ The emphasis in Gestalt therapy on the "now" of human experience.
■ The five layers of neurosis that interfere with being authentically in touch with oneself.

As you read, consider

■ What unfinished business, if any, you may have.
■ How comfortable you are with the Gestalt emphasis on "doing."
■ What you think about major techniques in Gestalt therapy and how emotionally comfortable you would be in doing them.

Gestalt therapy is an experiential and humanistic approach to change associated with Gestalt psychology, a school of thought that stresses the perception of completeness and wholeness. In fact, the translation of the term *gestalt* means "whole figure." Gestalt therapy arose as a reaction to the reductionist emphasis in other schools of counseling and psychotherapy, such as psychoanalysis and behaviorism, which tried to break down the personality or client behaviors into explainable parts. In contrast, Gestalt theory emphasizes how people function in their totality—a major emphasis of counseling (Levine, 2012).

Gestalt therapy was popularized in the 1960s by Fritz Perls, who focused on helping individuals become more aware of the many aspects of their personhood. Laura Perls, Fritz's wife, and Paul Goodman, a colleague, helped Perls write, enlarge, and refine his original ideas (Masquelie, 2006). Later theorists, particularly Joen Fagan and Irma Lee Shepherd (1970), developed the model still further. However, since Fritz Perls is the best known of the Gestalt theorists, he is highlighted here.

MAJOR THEORIST: FRITZ PERLS

Frederick Salomon Perls (1893–1970) was born into a middle-class Jewish family in Berlin. He had a younger and an older sister. Even though his parents fought bitterly and Perls disliked his older sister, he remembered his childhood as happy. Initially, he loved to read and was a top student in his grade school. However, in secondary school Perls encountered difficulty because of a conservative learning environment and his own rebellious spirit. He had trouble obeying authorities and failed the seventh grade twice. Nevertheless, he completed his secondary education once placed in a more permissive environment and was later awarded a medical degree from Frederich Wilhelm University in 1920. World War I interrupted his schooling, and he served as a medic in the German army.

Perls trained as a psychoanalyst in both Vienna and Berlin. Wilhelm Reich and Karen Horney participated in Perls's analysis as part of his training. Subsequently he took a position in Frankfurt at the Institute for Brain Injured Soldiers. There Perls became associated with Kurt Goldstein, from whom he learned to view humans as complete or holistic entities rather than as individuals made of separate parts.

In 1933 Perls fled Nazi Germany, first to Holland and then to Johannesburg, South Africa, where he and his wife, Laura Posner Perls, built a strong psychoanalytic practice, as they had previously done in Germany. In 1936, Perls sailed his private yacht 4,000 miles from South Africa to Germany to attend an international psychoanalytic congress in Czechoslovakia. There he arranged an audience with Freud, which left Perls feeling humiliated because of Freud's comments to him. Having been frequently demeaned by his father, Perls dedicated himself to proving Freud and psychoanalysis wrong as a revenge for the incident.

Perls immigrated to the United States in 1946. Although his ideas were not readily accepted, he gained prominence through the publication of *Gestalt Therapy* (1951), which he coauthored with Ralph Hefferline and Goodman. Perls also established the Institute for Gestalt Therapy in New York City in 1952 and offered lectures and workshops around North America. In 1960, he moved to the Esalen Institute in Big Sur, California.

Perls was an actor at heart and loved to parade his ideas before the public at Esalen. Laura Perls, long separated from Fritz, continued to support her husband until his death in British Columbia at the Gestalt kibbutz, a commune he had founded (Bankart, 1997). Perls recounted many of the more personal moments of his life in his autobiographical book, *In and Out of the Garbage Pail*, published posthumously in 1972.

Reflective Question

How do you think Perls's rejection by his father and Freud may have affected the development of his theory?

VIEW OF HUMAN NATURE/PERSONALITY

Gestalt therapists believe that human beings work for wholeness and completeness in their lives. Each person has a self-actualizing tendency that emerges through the beginning of self-awareness and personal interaction with the environment. Self-actualization is centered in the present; it "is the process of being what one is and not a process of striving to become" (Kempler, 1973, p. 262). The Gestalt view of human nature places trust in the inner wisdom of people, much as person-centered counseling does. People seek to live in an integrative and productive way, striving to coordinate the various parts of their personhood into a healthy, unified whole. From a Gestalt perspective, persons are more than a sum of their parts.

The Gestalt view is anti-deterministic: each person can change and become responsible (Hatcher & Himelsteint, 1997). Thus individuals are actors in the events around them, not just reactors to actions. Overall, the Gestalt point of view is existential, experiential, and phenomenological: the now is what really matters. People discover different aspects of themselves through experience rather than talk, and individuals' own assessments and interpretations of their lives at any given moment are what matter most.

According to Gestalt therapy, many troubled persons have an overdependence on intellectual experience (Simkin, 1975). Such an emphasis diminishes the importance of emotions and the senses, limiting people's abilities to respond to various situations. Another frequent problem is the inability to identify and resolve **unfinished business**—that is, earlier thoughts, feelings, and reactions that still affect personal functioning and interfere with living life in the present. The most common unfinished business is the failure to forgive parents for their mistakes. Gestaltists do not attribute either of these difficulties to any unconscious force within persons but rather to a lack of awareness, "the ability of the client to be in full mental and sensory" contact and to be "experiencing the now" (James & Gilliland, 2003, p. 142).

Every person operates on some conscious level, ranging from very aware to very unaware. Healthy individuals are those who are most aware. Such people realize that body signs, such as headaches or stomach pains, may indicate a need to change behaviors. They are also conscious of personal limitations. For instance, in conflicts with others, they may be able to resolve the situation or they may have to dismiss it. Healthy people avoid complicating such situations, refusing to embellish them with fantasy. Instead, they focus sharply on one need (**the figure**) at a time while relegating other needs to the background (**the ground**). A pictorial example of the figure and ground dichotomy can be seen in the Rubin face-vase drawing (Figure 6.1). Which pattern is the figure and which one is the ground is dependent on a person's perceptions. Regardless, when a figure need is met or the Gestalt is closed or completed, the figure is relegated to the background and a new need comes into focus and becomes the figure (Henderson & Thompson, 2016).

Figure 6.1 Rubin face-vase drawing of figure-ground phenomenon
Shiri Esh'har for Zebra on Wheels

Reflective Question

How do you think Gestalt therapy is like person-centered and Adlerian therapy? What makes it distinct?

In the Gestalt worldview, functioning requires that persons recognize internal needs and learn how to manipulate those needs and the environment (Perls, 1976). However, persons experience difficulties in several ways.

- They may lose contact with the environment and the resources in it.
- People may become overinvolved with the environment and thus grow out of touch with themselves.
- Individuals may fail to put aside unfinished business.
- They may become fragmented or scattered in many directions.
- Persons may experience conflict between the **top dog** (what they think they should do) and the **underdog** (what they want to do).
- People may have difficulty handling the dichotomies of life, such as love/hate, masculinity/femininity, and pleasure/pain (Assagioli, 1965).

Neurotic individuals try to attend to too many needs at one time and therefore do not take care of any one need fully. They also depend on others for care instead of caring for themselves, as they are capable of doing.

ROLE OF THE COUNSELOR

The role of the Gestalt clinician is to create an atmosphere that encourages clients to explore what they need to grow. Practitioners provide such a climate by being intensely and personally involved with clients, by being honest, and being nonjudgmental (Miller, 2008). They must be exciting, energetic, and fully human as well (Polster & Polster, 1973). Involvement occurs in the now, which is a continuing process (Perls, 1969) in which practitioners help clients redirect energy in positive and adaptive ways (Zinker, 1978). The now also entails helping clients recognize patterns in their lives (Fagan, 1970).

Gestalt therapists follow several rules in helping clients become more aware of the now (Levitsky & Perls, 1970):

- The **principle of now**—always using the present tense.
- An **"I-and-thou relationship"**—always addressing someone directly instead of
- talking about him or her.
- The **use of I**—substituting the word "I" for "it," especially when talking about one's body.
- The **use of an awareness continuum**—focusing on how and what rather than why.
- The **conversion of questions**—asking clients to convert questions into statements.

Gestaltists do not use standardized assessment instruments such as psychological tests. Furthermore, they do not diagnose their clients according to the *Diagnostic and Statistical Manual of Mental Disorders*. However, they do assess individuals with whom they work on their willingness to engage in activities that help them act and become more mature.

GOALS

The goals of Gestalt therapy are well defined. They include an emphasis on the here and now and a recognition of the immediacy of experience (Bankart, 1997). The importance of these first two goals can be seen in the fact that the term "contact" is used to refer to the sensory and motor immediacy that can be experienced when the environment is met directly (Perls et al., 1951). Further goals include a focus on both nonverbal and verbal expression and on the concept that life involves making choices (Fagan & Shepherd, 1970).

The Gestalt approach concentrates on helping clients become integrated by resolving the past, completing the process of growing up mentally and becoming mature (Perls, 1969). It emphasizes the coalescence of the emotional, cognitive, and behavioral aspects of a person. A primary focus is the acceptance of polarities within the person (Gelso & Carter, 1985).

As a group, Gestalt therapists stress action, pushing their clients to experience feelings and behaviors. They also emphasize the meaning of the word "now." Perls (1970) developed a formula that expresses the word's essence: "Now = experience = awareness = reality. The past is no more and the future not yet. Only the now exists" (p. 14).

To be mature in the now, a person must often shed neurotic tendencies. Perls (1970) identifies **five layers of neurosis** that interfere with being authentically in touch with oneself.

- The **phony layer** consists of pretending to be something one is not, often involving game playing and fantasy enactment. When persons become more aware of the games they are playing, they can be more honest, open, and in touch with unpleasantness and pain.
- The **phobic layer** is an attempt to avoid recognizing aspects of oneself an individual would prefer to deny. People at this layer of awareness are afraid that they will be rejected if they acknowledge who they are and present that to others.
- The **impasse layer** has no sense of direction. Individuals wonder how they are going to make it in the environment and are adrift in a sea of helplessness and dread.
- The **implosive and explosive layers** are often grouped together; people at these layers frequently feel vulnerable to feelings. As they peel back the layers of defensiveness built up over the years (the implosive layer), they may explode in intense feelings of joy, sorrow, or pain (the explosive layer). When persons reach this point, they can become authentic with themselves and others.

Reflective Question

The Gestalt approach emphasizes action and resolution of the past while living in the present. What actions do you think people can take that will help them resolve matters in their lives? What is an advantage of doing as opposed to thinking?

PROCESS AND TECHNIQUES

Some of the most innovative counseling techniques ever developed are found in Gestalt therapy (Harman, 1997). These techniques take two forms—exercises and experiments. **Exercises** are ready-made techniques, such as the enactment of fantasies, role-playing, and psychodrama (Covin, 1977). They are employed to evoke a certain response from clients, such as anger or exploration. **Experiments**, on the other hand, are activities that grow out of the interaction between counselors and clients. They are not planned, and what is learned is often a surprise to both participants. Even though many of the techniques of Gestalt therapy do take the form of unplanned experiments (Zinker, 1978), the concentration here is on exercise-oriented techniques.

One common exercise is **dream work**. Perls describes dreams as messages that represent a person's place at a certain time (Bernard, 1986). It is the royal road to integration (Perls, 1969). Unlike psychoanalysts, however, Gestalt counselors do not interpret; instead, clients present dreams and are then directed to experience what it is like to be in each part of the dream—a type of **dramatized free association**—in which individuals become all parts of the dream. In this way, clients get more in touch with the multiple aspects of themselves. People with repetitive dreams are encouraged to realize that unfinished business is being brought to their awareness and that they need to take care of the message being delivered.

Another effective method is the **empty chair technique** (see Figure 6.2). In this procedure clients focus on an empty chair and talk to the various parts of their personality, such as the part that is dominant and the part that is passive. Clients may use the chair as a representative of the self or may use different chairs to represent different parts of themselves. In this dialogue both rational and irrational parts of the client come into focus, and the client becomes able to deal with the inner dichotomies. Overall, the empty chair technique is a **three-stage model: opposition, merging, and integration.** It is an emotionally charged exercise and works well with many clients, such as those who may be in a pre-divorce situation (Mackay, 2002). However, this technique is not recommended for the severely emotionally disturbed (Bernard, 1986).

One of the most powerful Gestalt exercises is confrontation. In **confrontation,** counselors point out to clients incongruent behaviors and feelings, such as smiling when nervous. Confrontation involves asking clients what and how questions. Why questions are avoided because they lead to intellectualization. Therapists may purposely frustrate their clients to help them move beyond present states of denial (Harman, 1975), hoping clients will make valuable interpretations when confronted.

Figure 6.2 The empty chair
Shiri Esh'har for Zebra on Wheels

Techniques that center on working in the here and now help clients break out of old habits and become more in touch with themselves.

Other powerful Gestalt exercises that are oriented to individuals are often used in groups (Harman, 1997).

- **Making the rounds.** Counselors use this exercise to get clients to say something they usually do not verbalize. It is particularly effective in a group to become aware of feelings and work through unfinished business. For instance, a client may say, "I am prone to depression." The client is then instructed to repeat this sentence to each person in the group, becoming more mindful in the process. The exercise is flexible and may include nonverbal as well as positive feelings.
- **I take responsibility.** In this exercise clients make statements about perceptions and close each statement with the phrase "and I take responsibility for it." The exercise helps clients integrate and own their perceptions and behaviors.
- **Exaggeration.** Clients accentuate their own unwitting movements or gestures, such as using their hands when trying to talk about something difficult they have never shared before. In the process they make the inner meaning of these behaviors more apparent.
- **May I feed you a sentence?** Aware of implicit attitudes or messages in what a client is saying, the counselor asks whether the client will repeat a certain sentence that makes the client's thoughts explicit, such as "I am afraid to tell you what I really think because you might reject me." If the counselor is correct about the underlying message, the client will gain insight as the sentence is repeated.

Reflective Question

Which of the exercises just described appeals the most to you? Ask yourself what it is about the exercise that you think would be most effective in bringing about change in someone.

DIVERSITY AND MULTICULTURAL ISSUES

Gestalt therapy is widely used throughout the world—for example, in a survey of European psychotherapy training, Gestalt therapy was one of only four modalities practiced in the majority of the 32 countries polled (Zerbetto & Tantam, 2001). One reason for this popularity may be that Gestalt therapy is described by many of its practitioners as highly sensitive and adaptable to culturally diverse clients. The reason is the openness and inclusiveness found in its philosophy, theory, and methodology (Reck, 2009). Gestalt experiments can be used to help individuals deal with and perceive their own culture and its influence on them more fully (Sharf, 2016). For example, Gestalt experiments may help clients recognize polarities between cultures in which they live, such as a minority culture within a majority culture.

However, because Gestalt therapy is very individualistic, it contrasts sharply with cultures that are more oriented to group values and traditions. Thus, for Gestalt therapy to be practiced effectively and ethically in such communities, it needs to focus more attention on the importance of human interconnectedness (Ivey et al., 2012). Hence, Gestalt therapy must continue to evolve (Frew, 2016), which it appears to be doing.

On another positive note, Gestalt therapy is probably as open to sensitive gender issues as any other counseling modality. At its conception and during its formative years, women such as Laura Perls, Joen Fagan, and Irma Lee Shepherd influenced the approach strongly.

Reflective Question

How can helping individuals perceive and deal with their own culture contribute to their self-development?

EVALUATION OF THE THEORY

Strengths and Contributions

A strength of Gestalt therapy is its emphasis on helping people incorporate and accept all aspects of their lives. An individual cannot be understood outside the context of the whole person, who is choosing to act on the environment in the present (Levine, 2012; Passons, 1975).

The Gestalt approach also helps clients focus on resolving areas of unfinished business so that their lives can be more integrated and they can live productively.

A third contribution of Gestalt therapy is that it places primary emphasis on doing rather than talking. Activity helps individuals experience what the process of change is about and thus make more rapid progress. In addition, the change is likely to be enduring (Melnick, 2003).

Furthermore, the Gestalt approach is flexible and is not limited to a few techniques (Mann, 2010; Yontef et al., 2019). Any activity that helps clients become more integrative can be employed in Gestalt therapy. Such activities are readily available in the *Gestalt Journal*, which disseminates research, theory, and innovative techniques of the approach.

A final strength of Gestalt therapy is its versatility. It is appropriate for certain affective disorders, anxiety states, somatoform disorders, adjustment disorders, occupational problems, and interpersonal problems (Glinnwater, 2000), as well as for addiction and couple communication.

Limitations and Criticisms

Gestalt therapy lacks a strong theoretical base. In fact, some critics view Gestalt counseling as all experience and technique—that is, too gimmicky (Corey, 2017). They maintain that it is antitheoretical and often cite a line from Fritz Perls: "Lose your mind and come to your senses."

A second limitation of Gestalt therapy is that it deals strictly with the now and how of experience (Perls, 1969). Thus it does not allow for passive insight and internal change, which some clients are more likely to use.

A third criticism of Gestalt therapy is that it eschews diagnosis and testing in formal ways, such as using the *Diagnostic and Statistical Manual of Mental Disorders* or standardized tests. However, Gestalt clinicians do assess. For example, they screen individuals for emotional stability before exposing them to their intense methods of promoting therapeutic change.

Finally, Gestalt therapy is too concerned with individual development and a self-centered approach to helping; it focuses primarily on feelings and personal discovery. Although many other counseling theories are also centered on individual development, some consider Gestalt therapy extreme. An example of its self-centeredness is seen in the Gestalt prayer, which centers on being yourself, not living up to anyone's expectations, and letting relationships happen (Perls, 1969).

TREATING LINDA WITH GESTALT THERAPY

Conceptualization

From the perspective of Gestalt therapy, Linda is having relationship problems, but her difficulties are as much internal as they are external. Linda is not aware of how fragmented she is as a person and how much unfinished business she has in regard to her family of origin and her former husband. Although Linda did some mild acting out as a teenager, she was mostly submissive, as her father insisted. Instead of breaking away from family constraints by going to college or moving away, she denied herself that opportunity and earned a 2-year degree locally in an area in which she was not interested. As a result, Linda has hopped from one glorified secretarial position to another because of boredom. Externally she blames the situation on her bosses, but internally she blames herself.

In addition to her resentment about the past, Linda is angry about her present situation. She is lonely and does not have a support system. Consequently, she reads fantasy novels and watches exciting movies and instructional television programs. All of this activity is an attempt to escape rather than to construct a productive life.

Treatment Process

As a Gestalt therapist, you establish rapport with Linda and then begin to challenge her about what she is aware of and what she is doing now. At first, Linda may want to guide you back into the past and discuss what has been, but you insist on staying in the present, even if it involves dealing with unfinished business. You direct Linda to act as opposed to react. You are also adamant that she use "I messages" to promote responsibility and that she focus on how rather than why questions. You notice that Linda sometimes smiles when she talks about being abused by her husband or put down by her father. To get her to be more aware, you call her on this action, saying that she is playing games and being phony. Linda becomes angry with you in the process but continues in therapy.

In order to help Linda become more congruent and real, you ask her to engage in some anger exercises with you. In one of these, she shows you, by hitting a pillow with her hand, how angry certain events, people, or situations make her. As Linda completes this exercise, she starts growling spontaneously each time she hits the pillow. You then move her into a chair and have her talk as the more active person she is now to the inactive, passive side of herself. She switches chairs as she switches from active to passive. This empty chair technique helps her integrate an aspect of her life. As homework, you ask her to keep a diary of her dreams and to bring it with her each time so that she can reenact and understand the messages that her unconscious is sending her.

As Linda continues to be active in therapy, she begins to gain insight into what she is doing and feels more empowered. She realizes she cannot dwell on what has been but can live in the now. She decides to complete a 4-year degree, join a women's support group, and participate in several community clubs that engage in interesting activities such as biking and cooking. She lets her family know what she is doing and talks with them about how she is changing. She resists their attempts to pull her back and continues to develop greater self-awareness as she begins to accomplish new tasks.

SUMMING UP

Gestalt therapy has been a force in the field of counseling and therapy since the 1950s. It was initially associated primarily with Fritz Perls, but since Perls's death in 1970, a number of other proponents—including Dave Mann, Gary Yontef, Talia Bar-Yoseph Levine, Philip Brownell, and Phil and Charlotte Sills—have been its main developers as well as its strong advocates.

As a therapeutic modality Gestalt therapy is action oriented. It stresses acting in the present—that is, the now. Changes in thoughts and feelings follow changes in behaviors. Gestalt therapy uses both structured exercises and spontaneous experiments. Exercises are planned, whereas experiments grow out of client-counselor relationships. Both may lead clients to greater awareness of themselves and others, which is a primary goal.

Although the Gestalt approach helps individuals and groups act differently, it has been criticized for not having a stronger theoretical base and for dealing too much with the here and now, eschewing formal diagnosis and standardized tests, while being too self-centered—that is, focused on the individual. Nevertheless, Gestalt therapy is quite flexible and holistic, helps clients resolve unfinished business, and is flexible and appropriate for certain affective disorders.

CHAPTER 6 RECAP: GESTALT THERAPY

Major Theorists
Fritz Perls, Laura Perls, Dave Mann, Gary Yontef, Talia Bar-Yoseph Levine, Philip Brownell, Violet Oaklander, Jim Simkin, Phil and Charlotte Sills

View of Human Nature/Personality
Emphasizes wholeness and completeness
Focuses on the inner wisdom of individuals
Is phenomenological and anti-deterministic
Stresses human change through action

Role of the Counselor
Must be authentic, exciting, energetic
Emphasizes the here and now
Helps clients resolve unfinished business
Assists clients in using I messages

Goals

Focus on the here and now
Attend to both nonverbal and verbal expression
Recognize that life presents choices
Help clients become more integrated and mature
Bring together emotion, cognition, and behavior
Help clients accept internal polarities and shed neurotic tendencies

Process and Techniques

Exercises, or planned interactions—for example, dream work, empty chair, confrontation
Experiments or spontaneous interactions
Group exercises—for example, making the rounds, taking responsibility, exaggerating, repeating a sentence

Diversity and Multicultural Issues

Used worldwide
Inappropriate for some cultures
Open to sensitive gender issues

Strengths and Contributions

Incorporates all parts of life
Resolves the past so individuals can live more effectively in the present
Stresses doing and acting
Helps in the treatment of certain affective disorders
Is flexible in using exercises and experiments

Limitations and Criticisms

Lacks a strong theoretical base
May become gimmicky
Does not allow for passive learning
Eschews standardized testing and formal diagnosis
Is too self-centered

KEY TERMS

LEARNING MORE

A number of periodicals devoted to Gestalt therapy and theory might prove helpful in exploring this approach to counseling.

Gestalt Journal
Gestalt Review
International Gestalt Journal

In addition to journals, several training institutes and practitioner associations offer clinicians an opportunity to learn more about Gestalt therapy.

The Association for the Advancement of Gestalt Therapy http://www.aagt.org/

The Gestalt Therapy Page http://www.gestalt.org/

Gestalt Theory: Society for Gestalt Theory and Its Applications http://gestalttheory.net/

CLASSROOM ACTIVITIES

1. Approximately 50 Gestalt institutes exist in the United States. With the help of your instructor or a librarian, locate as many of them as you can and find out what types of training programs they offer. If possible, interview a professional who practices Gestalt and ask how he or she compares the Gestalt approach to other ways of counseling.
2. Make a list of questions people might direct to others such as "Why are you smiling?" Then convert the questions into statements such as "I see you are smiling." Note the differences in your group between questions and statements. Share your impressions with your classmates.
3. In a group of five discuss and then role-play how a clinician and a client might devise an experiment to depict anger. How easy or difficult did you find this experiment? What advantages do you think an experiment like this has over a more formalized exercise? What are the disadvantages?

7

Choice Theory/Reality Therapy

■ ■ ■

When I leave the office with a headache
I know I have done your work
and you are without a plan.
When I go home with a heartache
it is because I have seen you fail
to capture your dreams.
Give me heartaches any day
for embedded in them
is the pain that often leads to change.

"Headaches and Heartaches" © S. T. Gladding

CHAPTER OVERVIEW

From reading this chapter you will learn about

■ The physical and psychological growth forces within individuals.
■ Identity and suitable/healthy behavior.
■ The WDEP system and other ways of helping and bringing about change.

As you read, consider

■ How you meet your psychological growth needs (belonging, power, freedom, fun).
■ How you form a successful identity.
■ How difficult and elegant reality therapy is—for example, not accepting excuses and the continuous making of plans if previous plans have not worked.

William Glasser formulated **choice theory**, originally referred to as reality therapy, in the early 1960s. It began as a major theoretical approach in 1965 with the publication of Glasser's book *Reality Therapy*. This approach emphasizes the choices people can make to change their lives and focuses on two general concepts: the environment necessary for counseling and the procedures leading to change (Wubbolding, 1998, 2011, 2017). It is usually essential to establish a safe environment before change can occur.

Reality therapy is a flexible, friendly, and firm approach to working with clients. It is also action oriented. Overall, it emphasizes the fulfillment of psychological needs, the resolution of personal difficulties, and the prevention of future problems.

MAJOR THEORIST: WILLIAM GLASSER

William Glasser (1925–2013) was born in Cleveland, Ohio, the third and youngest child in a close-knit family. He describes his childhood as happy and uneventful but like his theory, he does not emphasize the past. In school, he played in the band and developed a strong interest in sports. After graduating at the age of 19 from the Case Institute of Technology with a degree in chemical engineering, he began graduate work in clinical psychology. He finished work for a master's degree in 1948, but his doctoral dissertation was rejected. He then entered medical school at Western Reserve University, graduating with a medical degree in 1953.

Glasser moved to California with his wife, Naomi Judith Silver, for a psychiatric residency at UCLA, which he completed in 1957. Although he hoped to establish a private psychiatric practice, he found that referrals were slow in coming because of his open resistance to traditional psychoanalytic treatment. Therefore, he took a position as head psychiatrist at the Ventura School for Girls, a state-operated facility for juvenile delinquents (Roy, 2014).

At Ventura in the 1960s, Glasser began to formalize his approach to counseling. One of Glasser's faculty supervisors during his residency, G. L. Harrington, had supported his doubts about the effectiveness of classical psychoanalysis. Harrington helped Glasser develop some of the basic tenets of reality therapy and even assisted Glasser in verifying these primary concepts. Glasser's first book, *Mental Health or Mental Illness?* (1961), contained many of the ideas later more formally expressed in *Reality Therapy: A New Approach to Psychiatry* (1965). Glasser developed reality therapy because he thought "conventional psychiatry wastes too much time arguing over how many diagnoses can dance at the end of a case history" (1965, p. 49). He wanted an approach that was practical and more easily understood by both clinicians and the public. By using the basic principles of reality therapy, he cut recidivism at the Ventura School to only 20%.

Shortly after the publication of *Reality Therapy*, Glasser founded the Institute of Reality Therapy in Canoga Park, California, where he did some of his most creative work. He applied reality therapy to school settings in *Schools without Failure* (1969) and to areas of identity in *The Identity Society* (1972). In *Positive Addiction* (1976), he asserted that individuals could become stronger instead of weaker from so-called addictive habits. For example, both jogging and meditation may improve physical and mental health.

In 1981, Glasser linked his original ideas with **control theory**, which argues that all behavior is generated internally. Thus the only thing that people obtain from the outside world is information (Glasser, 1988). Two of Glasser's books, *Stations of the Mind* (1981) and *Control Theory: A New Explanation of How We Control Our Lives* (1984), reflect this theoretical stance and emphasize how the brain influences inner perceptions. However, Glasser abandoned control theory as a part of his approach in 1996 and incorporated choice theory in its place, asserting that people choose to be the way they are. This tenet is reflected in Glasser's writings since the late 1990s (Wubbolding, 2015). It is also found in the writings of Robert Wubbolding, a major practitioner and proponent of reality/choice theory (Klingler & Gray, 2015).

Glasser died at his home in Los Angeles on August 23, 2013, in the company of his wife, Carleen, and others. The cause of death was respiratory failure stemming from pneumonia.

VIEW OF HUMAN NATURE/PERSONALITY

Reality therapy does not include a comprehensive explanation of human development. Instead, it offers practitioners a focused view of some important aspects of human life and human nature. One major tenet of reality therapy is its focus on consciousness: human beings operate on a conscious level and are not driven by unconscious forces or instincts (Glasser, 1988, 2005).

A second belief about human nature is that a health/growth force exists within everyone (Glasser & Wubbolding, 1995; Wubbolding & Brickell, 2017). This force is manifested on two levels—the physical and the psychological. Physically, there is the need to obtain and use life-sustaining essentials such as food, water, and shelter. According to Glasser, human behavior was once controlled by the physical need for survival. He associates behaviors such as breathing, digesting, and sweating with **physical** or **old brain needs** because the body automatically controls them. In modern times, most important behavior is associated with **psychological** or **new brain needs**. The four **primary psychological needs** include the following:

- **Belonging**—the need for friends, family, and love.
- **Power**—the need for self-esteem, recognition, and competition.
- **Freedom**—the need to make choices and decisions.
- **Fun**—the need for play, laughter, learning, and recreation. (see Figure 7.1)

Reflective Question

What do you do for fun? Think of at least three things.

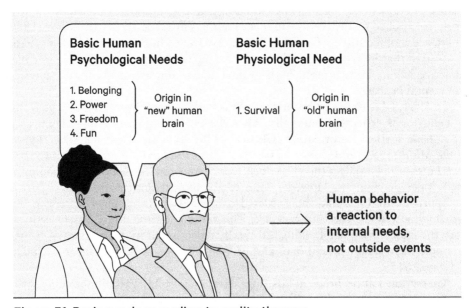

Figure 7.1 Basic needs according to reality therapy
Shiri Esh'har for Zebra on Wheels

Associated with these psychological needs is the need for **identity**—that is, a psychologically healthy sense of self. Identity needs are met when others accept a person. Especially important in this process is the experience of love and worth. When these needs are met, people achieve a **success identity**. Those whose needs are not met establish a **failure identity**, a maladjusted personality characterized by a lack of confidence and a tendency to give up easily. Because "almost everyone is personally engaged in a search for acceptance as a person rather than as a performer of a task," personal identity precedes performance (Glasser, 1972, p. 10).

Glasser thinks there are two critical periods in children's lives related to identity. First, between the ages of 2 and 5, children learn early socialization skills—such as how to relate to their parents, siblings, and friends—and they begin to deal with frustrations and disappointments. During this period children especially need the love, acceptance, guidance, and involvement of their parents. If that is not forthcoming, a child may begin to establish a failure identity. Second, between the ages of 5 and 10, children are involved with school, where they gain knowledge and self-concept. Many children establish a failure identity during this period because of socialization difficulties or learning problems (Glasser, 1969).

Reality therapy proposes that human learning is a lifelong process based on choice. If individuals do not learn something early in life, such as how to relate to others, they can choose to learn it later. In the process, they may change their identity and the way they behave (Glasser & Wubbolding, 1995).

A final tenet of reality therapy is a new psychology of personal freedom called choice theory (Glasser, 1998, 2000). The idea is that people have mental images of their needs and behave accordingly; individuals are thus ultimately self-determining (Glasser, 1984; Wubbolding, 1994). Individuals may choose to be miserable or mentally disturbed; they may also choose to behave in positive ways and give up trying to control others. People who are mentally healthy are in noncontrolling relationships with significant others, such as a parent, a child, a spouse, or an employee/employer. They choose to "care, listen, support, negotiate, encourage, love, befriend, trust, accept, welcome, and esteem" rather than "coerce, force, compel, punish, reward, manipulate, boss, motivate, criticize, blame, complain, nag, badger, rank, rate, and withdraw" (Glasser, 1998, p. 21).

Reflective Question

Do you think performance could ever precede personal identity? Why or why not? If so, what might that mean for someone achieving a success identity?

ROLE OF THE COUNSELOR

Practitioners who use reality therapy serve primarily as teachers and models, accepting their clients in a warm, involved way and creating an environment in which choice and change can take place. They immediately seek to build relationships with clients by developing trust through friendliness, firmness, and fairness (Wubbolding, 1998, 2000, 2017). They also use "ing" verbs, such as "angering" or "bullying," to describe clients' thoughts and actions. Thus there is an emphasis on choice, on what clients choose to do—internal control and personal responsibility (Wubbolding,

2015). Counselor-client interactions focus on behaviors that clients would like to change and ways to go about achieving these desires. Positive, constructive actions are emphasized (Glasser, 1988, 2005), with special attention paid to metaphors and themes that clients verbalize.

Those who use reality therapy make little attempt to test, diagnose, interpret, or otherwise analyze clients' actions, except to ask questions such as "What are you doing now?" "Is it working?" and "What are the consequences?" Reality therapists do not concentrate on early childhood experiences, clients' insights, aspects of the unconscious, mental illness, blame, or stimulus-response perceptions of interaction. They emphasize the aspects of clients' lives that can be controlled and give little consideration to the latest editions of diagnostic manuals.

GOALS

The primary goal of reality therapy is to help clients become psychologically strong and rational and realize that they have choices in how they treat themselves and others. If this goal is reached, individuals become autonomous and responsible (Wallace, 1986; Wubbolding, 1988, 1991). **Responsible behavior** allows individuals to take charge of their actions and attain their goals; it also keeps them from interfering with others or getting into trouble. In addition, it leads to the formation of a success identity, which enables clients to live more productive and harmonious lives. Glasser (1981) contends that to help people "we must help them gain strength to do worthwhile things with their lives and at the same time become warmly involved with the people they need" (p. 48). Reality therapy strives to prevent problems from occurring.

A second goal is to help clients clarify what they want in life. It is vital for individuals to be aware of their life goals if they are to act responsibly. In assessing goals, reality therapists help their clients examine personal assets as well as environmental supports and hindrances. It is then the responsibility of clients to choose behaviors that fulfill personal needs. Glasser (1976) lists six criteria with which to judge whether a person is choosing suitable and healthy behavior.

- The behavior is **noncompetitive**.
- The behavior is **easily completed without a great deal of mental effort**.
- The behavior **can be done by oneself**.
- The behavior **has value for the person**.
- The client believes that **improvements in lifestyle** will result from the behavior.
- The client **can practice the behavior without being self-critical**.

Another goal of reality therapy is to help clients formulate a realistic and viable plan to achieve personal needs and wishes. Poor mental health is sometimes the result of not knowing how to achieve what has been planned. Glasser advocates that plans be as specific and concrete as possible. Once a plan is formulated, alternative behaviors, decisions, and outcomes are examined; often a contract is written. The focus is on helping individuals become more responsible and realize that no single plan is absolute. According to Wubbolding (2007), a **viable plan** has eight features and can be represented by the acronym SAM I2 C3:

- **Simple**—clear, understandable.
- **Attainable**—the client can accomplish it.

- **Measurable**—can be tangibly recorded what was done, when.
- **Immediate**—can be started on right away.
- **Involves** the clinician in some appropriate way such as giving feedback.
- **Controlled by the client**—not under the control of someone else.
- **Committed to be kept by the client** realizing change is important.
- **Consistent** in that the client will keep at it and repeated needed changes.

An additional goal of reality therapy is to have counselors establish meaningful relationships with their clients (Glasser, 1980, 1981). Such relationships are based on understanding, acceptance, empathy, and faith in a client's ability to change. Counselors help their clients establish boundaries for behaviors but do not give up on their clients if they are unable to complete a behavior. Often, to facilitate effective relationships, those who work from a reality therapy basis risk disclosing personal information to clients.

Another goal of reality therapy is to focus on behavior and the present. Glasser (1988) believes that behavior—that is, thought and action—is interrelated with feeling and physiology. A change in behavior also brings about other positive changes. Glasser emphasizes now activities because clients, who have no control over the past, can control them.

Finally, reality therapy aims to eliminate both fear of punishment and excuses from clients' lives. Clients often use the excuse that they cannot formulate and carry out a plan because they fear being punished by either their counselors or outside people if they fail. Reality therapy helps clients formulate new plans if old ones do not work. The emphasis is on planning, revision, and eventual success regardless of setbacks. The entire procedure empowers clients and enables them to be more productive.

Reflective Question

What "now activities" are you engaged in? How are you enjoying them? How productive are they for you?

PROCESS AND TECHNIQUES

Reality therapy relies on action-oriented techniques that help clients realize they have choices in how they respond to events and people and that other people do not control them any more than they control other people (Glasser, 1998; Onedera & Greenwalt, 2007). Reality therapy eschews external control psychology and what Glasser (2000) calls its seven deadly habits (i.e., "criticizing, blaming, complaining, nagging, threatening, punishing, and bribing") (p. 79). Some of the more effective and active techniques are teaching, employing humor, confronting, role-playing, giving feedback, formulating specific plans, and making contracts.

Reality therapy relies heavily on teaching as a primary technique. Glasser (1965) states that "the specialized learning situation ... is made up of three separate but interwoven procedures" (p. 21). First, there is involvement between counselors and clients in which clients begin to face reality and see that a behavior is unrealistic.

Second, therapists reject the unrealistic behavior of their clients without rejecting the clients as persons. Finally, counselors teach clients better ways to fulfill needs within the confines of reality. One strategy counselors use is positiveness, in which they talk about, focus on, and reinforce positive and constructive planning and behaving (James & Gilliland, 2003).

In reality therapy, **humor** is the ability to see the absurdity within a situation and view matters from a different and amusing perspective. It is an appropriate technique if used sparingly. Most clients do not instinctively see difficult situations as funny, yet if counselors offer a well-timed remark, clients may come to see some silliness in their behavior. The ability to laugh at oneself promotes the ability to change because the situation can be seen in a new and often insightful way. Humor should never be used as a sarcastic put-down because use in this way usually leads to a deterioration of the therapeutic relationship and adversely affects the process of change.

In **confrontation**, counselors challenge clients about certain behaviors as a way of helping clients accept responsibility for their actions. This procedure does not differ much from the confrontation used in other approaches. **Role-playing** in reality therapy is also similar to that employed in other counseling approaches. However, its purpose in reality therapy is to help clients bring the past or future into the present and assess how life will be different when they start behaving differently. Role-plays are almost always followed by counselor feedback. After specific plans are formulated for improving their lives, clients develop contracts to carry out these plans in a timely and systematic way.

Reality therapy uses the **WDEP system** as a way of helping counselors and clients make progress. In this system, the **W** stands for **wants**; at the beginning of the counseling process, counselors find out what clients want and what they have been doing to get it (Wubbolding, 1988, 1991, 2000). Counselors, in turn, share their wants for and perceptions of clients' situations. The **D** in WDEP involves clients' exploration of the **direction** of their lives. The effective and ineffective self-talk clients use is discussed. Strategically incorporated in these two steps are establishing a relationship and focusing on present behavior.

The **E** in the WDEP process stands for **evaluation**, which is the **cornerstone of reality therapy**. In this procedure, clients evaluate their personal behaviors and determine how responsible they are. Behaviors that do not contribute to meeting client needs often alienate clients from themselves and significant others. If clients recognize a behavior as unproductive, they may be motivated to change. However, if there is no recognition, the therapeutic process may break down. It is crucial, therefore, that clients, not counselors, do the evaluation.

The final letter, **P**, of the WDEP system stands for **plan**, which clients make to change behaviors. The plan stresses actions clients will take, not behaviors they will eliminate. The best plans are simple, attainable, measurable, immediate, and consistent (Wubbolding, 1998, 2000). They are also controlled by clients and are often supported by written contracts in which responsible alternatives are spelled out.

Clients are then requested to make a commitment to the action plans. Therapists make clear that no excuses will be accepted for failing to carry out plans of action; neither will there be blame or punishment. Responsibility is thus placed entirely on clients. If they fail to accomplish their plans, Glasser thinks they should suffer the natural or reasonable consequences of that failure (Evans, 1982).

According to Glasser (1965, 1980), reality therapists should not give up on their clients even if they fail to accomplish their goals. Instead, counselors should stubbornly and tenaciously encourage their clients to make new plans or revise old ones. Most clients, who are used to being put down or abandoned when goals are not achieved, find in Glasser's approach an opportunity to alter that cycle of failure.

Reflective Question

Do you think counselors should give up on some clients? Why? When have you been tenacious and made new plans instead of giving up?

DIVERSITY AND MULTICULTURAL ISSUES

Reality therapy respects cultural differences. Clients "decide on the changes they wish to make that are consistent with their own cultural values" (Sharf, 2016, p. 445). Thus, reality therapy focuses on the responsibility of clients to themselves, others, and society. This emphasis puts it in accord with Native American Indian and Asian and Asian American value systems (Ivey et al., 2012). Reality therapy has been used and found effective with a wide range of people from varied cultures such as those of Korea, Singapore, Canada, Japan, and Australia. It has also been found effective with students of color and those with various clinical issues (Haskins & Appling, 2017). In addition, it has also been found effective with the deaf and those suffering from arthritis and depression (Wubbolding, 2013). However, despite these strengths reality therapy is said not to take into account "environmental forces such as discrimination and racism that affect people from different cultures" (Sharf, 2016, p. 445).

Concerning gender issues, reality therapy emphasizes the empowerment of clients to make choices regardless of gender. This approach may be especially good for men who are achievement oriented because it concentrates on specific plans and behaviors without broaching the area of feelings and emotions, which many men eschew. However, this therapy may be limited in what it can do for women because it does not advocate for social change or address societal ills such as sexism.

EVALUATION OF THE THEORY

Strengths and Contributions

First, reality therapy is versatile (Mason & Duba, 2009). It can be applied to many different disorders and populations; it is especially appropriate in treating conduct disorders, substance-abuse disorders, impulse-control disorders, personality disorders, and antisocial behavior. It can also be employed in individual counseling with children, adolescents, adults, and the aged as well as in group, marriage, and family counseling. This approach has such flexibility that it is helpful in almost any setting that emphasizes mental health and adjustment, such as hospitals, mental health clinics, schools, prisons, rehabilitation centers, and crisis centers (Glasser, 1986, 2000; Seligman & Reichenberg, 2014).

A second advantage of reality therapy is its concreteness. Both counselors and clients can assess how much progress is being made and in what areas, especially if a goal-specific contract is drawn up. When clients are doing well in modifying one behavior but not another, increased attention can be given to the underdeveloped area.

Another advantage of reality therapy is that it promotes responsibility and freedom within individuals without blaming, criticizing, or attempting to restructure entire personalities. To act in a responsible manner is "to fulfill one's needs and to do so in a way that does not deprive others of the ability to fulfill their needs" (Glasser, 1965, p. 13). Many individuals need help in becoming responsible, and reality therapy provides this assistance.

Reality therapy also addresses the resolution of conflict. Glasser (1984) believes that conflict occurs on two levels, true and false. On the true level, conflict develops over interpersonal disagreements about change. In such cases, no single solution exists, and people should expend their energy in other, nonconflicted areas. In false conflict, however, such as losing weight, change is possible if persons are willing to give the effort. Responsible behavior in such situations can bring resolutions.

An additional strength of reality therapy is its stress on the present; current behavior is most amenable to clients' control. Reality therapists are not interested in the past.

Furthermore, reality therapy emphasizes short-term treatment. It is usually limited to relatively few sessions that focus on present behaviors. Clients work with conscious and verifiable objectives that can be achieved quickly. This approach is especially valuable in a time-limited, managed care environment.

One other strength of reality therapy is that it has national training centers and advocates. The Institute for Reality Therapy in Los Angeles and the Center for Reality Therapy in Cincinnati promote a uniform educational experience among practitioners employing this theory. The centers also publish professional literature. The strongest advocate for the theory is Robert Wubbolding, who continues publishing in this area and who has furthered the theory through his writings on it. He has been especially creative in his use of metaphors people may use to understand reality therapy and their lives—for example, Metaphor 34: "M34: A car has four wheels. All four wheels move at the same time. Likewise, total behavior has four parts—acting, thinking, feeling, and physiology. All four parts happen at the same time. When you experience a feeling, what else is happening at the same time?" (Rapport, 2019, p. 34).

Finally, reality therapy has contributed to counseling by successfully challenging the medical model of client treatment. The rationale and positive emphasis of this approach are refreshing alternatives to pathology-centered models.

Limitations and Criticisms

By emphasizing so strongly the here and now of behavior, reality therapy tends to ignore other concepts, such as the unconscious and personal history. However, people may sometimes be informed by the unconscious—for example, in dreams—or they may need to relive and resolve past traumas. Reality therapy makes little allowance for these situations.

A second limitation of reality therapy is its belief that all forms of mental illness are attempts to deal with external events (Glasser, 1984). Mental illness does not just happen, Glasser contends; persons choose mental illness to help control their world. Thus Glasser ignores biology as a factor in mental illness, a stance some critics consider naive and irresponsible.

Reality therapy is also criticized for being too simple because it has few theoretical constructs. Even though it is becoming more sophisticated by virtue of its link to choice theory, reality therapy does not deal with the full complexity of human life, preferring to ignore most developmental stages. Its critics state that the theory behind the therapy lacks comprehensiveness.

Another limitation is that reality therapy is susceptible to becoming overly moralistic, a potential difficulty rather than a certain disadvantage. Glasser (1972) asserts that reality therapy was never intended to function in this way. Therapists who practice reality therapy are not to judge clients' behaviors; clients judge their own behaviors. The role of therapists is to support their clients in a personal exploration of values. Nonetheless, overzealous practitioners may impose their values on clients.

Yet another limitation of reality therapy is its dependence on establishing a good counselor-client relationship. Without sufficient involvement, counselors may settle for general client goals, force a plan, or proceed too quickly to commitment (Wubbolding, 1975).

A related limitation of reality therapy is its dependence on verbal interaction and two-way communication. Consequently, it may falter in helping clients who, for any reason, cannot adequately express their needs, options, and plans (James & Gilliland, 2003).

Finally, reality therapy keeps changing its focus and emphasis, despite an initial denial of that charge by Glasser (1976). Acceptance is now emphasized more than it previously was. Furthermore, the integration of control theory and then its replacement by choice theory as the bedrock of the approach necessarily altered the theory's earlier focus. Thus far, there has been no attempt to document these changes and to note which emphases are most essential to the practice, leaving reality therapy less well understood and utilized than it might otherwise be.

Reflective Question

What arguments could you make that all mental illness is chosen? Give examples. What are the arguments (besides biological) against the idea that mental illness is chosen? Give examples.

TREATING LINDA WITH CHOICE THEORY/REALITY THERAPY

Conceptualization

From the perspective of reality therapy, Linda is avoiding making choices. She has let others decide for her, such as whether to have a baby. She mainly has excuses as to why her life has been relatively unproductive. In addition, Linda has not taken care of her psychological needs for belonging, power, freedom, and fun. By neglecting these needs, Linda has taken on a failure identity.

However, Linda can choose to be different. She can choose to be in noncontrolling relationships with her family and friends. Furthermore, she can choose to take other constructive action and stop failing and depressing herself. If she makes these choices, Linda can become more autonomous, responsible, and successful. She can also clarify what she wants in life and find internal and external support for realistic pursuit of her goals. If she does, her mental health will improve, and she will be able to live in the present in a productive way.

Treatment Process

As a reality therapist, you are active in Linda's treatment process. You base your work on a good, strong, and trusting client-counselor relationship. You try to teach Linda how she can reject unrealistic behaviors without rejecting herself or being rejected by you. In addition, you reinforce her positive and constructive plans and behaviors.

You use humor with Linda as she gains insight into herself and sees the folly of her ways. However, you are mostly serious and confront Linda with the fact that she is responsible for her actions, especially now in the present. You role-play with her how she can act responsibly.

After you confront, you use the WDEP acronym to help Linda articulate her wants and the direction she wishes to travel. You help her evaluate behaviors that will contribute to her growth, and then you support her in formulating a plan for moving on. As a part of this process, you draw up a contract with Linda to help her see how she is carrying out her ambitions. Even though Linda has been discriminated against in the past and treated in sexist ways, you do not dwell on what has been or what might recur. Instead, you encourage and support her as she begins anew.

When Linda fails to carry out some part of her plan, such as returning to college, you do not blame or punish her. Instead, you help her formulate another plan. For Linda the ultimate achievement is to become more responsible and free and to accomplish that within a relatively brief period.

SUMMING UP

Reality therapy is an ever-evolving system of counseling that began with William Glasser in the 1960s. It focuses on present situations that clients wish to change. Counselors work to establish collaborative relationships with clients and use those relationships to help clients develop plans involving concrete and goal-oriented choices. Excuses and blame are not a part of the process, and counselors do not give up on their clients.

Counselors use a number of techniques to help clients reach their goals. Besides strong relationships and persistence, counselors also teach, use humor, confront, and role-play with clients. Wubbolding's WDEP system—wants, direction, evaluation, plan—is sometimes used as a guide to help counselors evaluate what they need to do to help their clients be successful. If all goes well, clients become more focused and skilled in reaching realistic and productive goals.

CHAPTER 7 RECAP: REALITY THERAPY

Major Theorists
William Glasser
Robert Wubbolding

View of Human Nature/Personality
A health/growth force in all individuals
Problems arise from failure to take responsibility for behavior
Lifelong learning
A need for love, worth, success, and control

Role of the Counselor
Teacher and model
Collaborative relationship with client
Active, direct, practical, didactic style

Goals
Become psychologically strong and rational
Take responsibility
Formulate a realistic plan focused on behavior
Accept no punishment; offer no excuses
Develop new plans when needed

Process and Techniques
Help clients see choices
Use action-oriented techniques: teaching, employing humor, confronting, role-playing, giving feedback, formulating specific plans, making contracts
Use Wubbolding's WDEP system

Diversity and Multicultural Issues
Respects cultural differences
Does not address environmental forces
Emphasizes the empowerment of clients
Does not deal with societal ills such as sexism, racism, etc.

Strengths and Contributions
Is versatile, concrete, short-term
Promotes responsibility and freedom
Addresses conflict resolution
Stresses the present
Has national and international training centers
Challenges medical model of client treatment

Limitations and Criticisms
Ignores some human concepts (e.g., the unconscious and personal history)
Glasser believes mental illness has no biological aspects.
Has few theoretical constructs
Does not deal with the full complexity of human life
Susceptible to becoming overly moralistic
Depends on good counselor-client relationship
Keeps changing focus

KEY TERMS

attainable 88
belonging 86
can be done by oneself 88
can practice the behavior without
   being self-critical 88
choice theory 84
committed to be kept by client 89
confrontation 90
consistent 89
control theory 85
controlled by the client 89
easily completed without a great
   deal of mental effort 88
evaluation - cornerstone of reality
   therapy 90
failure identity 87
freedom 86
fun 86
has value for the person 88
humor 90

identity 87
immediate (start right away) 89
improvements in lifestyle 88
involves clinician in appropriate
   way 89
measurable 89
noncompetitive 88
physical or old brain needs 86
power 86
primary psychological or new brain
   needs 86
responsible behavior 88
role-playing 90
simple 88
six criteria for healthy behavior 88
success identity 87
viable plan 88
WDEP – wants, direction, evaluation,
   plan 94

LEARNING MORE

Articles on the theory, research, and practice of reality therapy are found in a number of counseling and therapy publications. Probably the best journal devoted exclusively to reality therapy is published by the William Glasser Institute—*International Journal of Choice Theory and Reality Therapy.*

That institute also maintains an international resource library, both at its headquarters in California and at Northeastern University in Boston.

For more information on reality therapy organizations and institutes, contact the following:

William Glasser Institute
22024 Lassen Street, Suite #118
Chatsworth, California 91311-3600
818-700-8000 or 800-899-0688 http://www.wglasser.com/

Center for Reality Therapy
5490 Windridge Court
Cincinnati, OH 45243
513-561-1911 http://www.realitytherapywub.com/

CLASSROOM ACTIVITIES

1. Discuss with another classmate how you meet each of the four primary psychological needs in your life—belonging, power, freedom, and fun.

2. Write down what you think of choice theory and the idea that we choose how we are and how we behave. How do you see choice theory working in your life? What do you think are the weaknesses in choice theory?

3. Explore the websites mentioned in this text for training in reality therapy. How do they compare? What do you see as the strengths and limitations of each center?

8

Behavioral Therapies

■ ■ ■

She was lonely so she cut herself
to get her friends' attention,
He was scared so he hit someone
and now he has detention,
Neither one knew what to do
so they did their best,
The trouble is now they wear labels:
"Different from the rest!"

"Different" © S. T. Gladding

CHAPTER OVERVIEW

From reading this chapter you will learn about

■ The common and diverse factors within behaviorism as a therapeutic approach.
■ The three main approaches to behaviorism: stimulus-response model, applied behavior analysis, and social-cognitive theory.
■ The multiple techniques available to behavioral counselors.

As you read, consider

■ When you have reinforced others for their behaviors, how, and on what schedule.
■ How you have used punishment and aversive techniques with others.
■ How comfortable you are in using behavioral techniques to influence behaviors in others.

Behavioral theories and the origins of behavioral therapy date back to the beginning of the 20th century. They focus on how to reinforce, extinguish, or modify a broad range of behaviors. Over the years, these approaches have become quite popular because people who seek counseling often have difficulties due to behavioral deficits, excessive behaviors, or a repertoire of inappropriate behaviors.

The term "behavioral" encompasses a wide range of ideas, practices, and theories. In its infancy (1900s–1930s), behaviorism was concerned almost entirely with external observations and was promoted as a scientific approach to the study of human life. The first major advocate for behaviorism was John B. Watson (1913, 1925), who, building off the classical conditioning research of Ivan Pavlov, used his work with a child named Little Albert to demonstrate that human emotions are amenable to conditioning (Watson & Raynor, 1920). After World War I, behaviorist ideas were explored by researchers such as Mary Cover Jones (1924), who demonstrated how a process known as **counterconditioning** can be employed to help people overcome phobic reactions.

In the 1940s and 1950s behaviorism achieved even more prominence. In this period, behavioral therapists were seen as scientific practitioners who based their work on research, such as that by Edward Thorndike on learning theory. Prominent scientist-practitioners included B. F. Skinner (1953) and his work in operant conditioning, Joseph Wolpe (1958) and his study of respondent conditioning, Hans Eysenck (1960) and his treatment of abnormal behavior, and Albert Bandura (Bandura & Walters, 1963) and his study of the effects of vicarious learning. During the 1950s, the term **"behavior therapy"** was introduced to describe diverse behavioral approaches to resolving client problems.

John Krumboltz (1966) is credited as being one of the major personalities to popularize behaviorism in counseling. He drew upon Bandura's earlier work and revolutionized the counseling profession of his time with behavioral concepts such as observational learning (Hosford, 1980). Krumboltz's ideas, as well as behaviorism in general, gained widespread acceptance in the 1970s. By the late 1980s behavioral approaches to therapy had generally split into three main theories: the stimulus-response model, applied behavior analysis, and social-cognitive theory.

This chapter examines the dominant behavioral counseling approaches, except cognitive behaviorism, which is covered in the next chapter. As advocates of a school of thought, behaviorists "stress instrumental rationality, control over emotions, enhanced human liberty, efficiency in ways of achieving self-defined goals, and opposition to irrational authority or arbitrary privilege" (Christopher, 1996, pp. 19–20).

MAJOR THEORIST: B. F. SKINNER

B. F. (Burrhus Frederick) Skinner (1904–1990) was born in Susquehanna, Pennsylvania. He was the older of two sons, but his younger brother died at the age of 16. Skinner's home environment was warm, comfortable, and stable, imbued with the virtues of small-town, middle-class America at the turn of the century (Skinner, 1976). His parents did not use corporal punishment.

Skinner's father, a wealthy attorney, wanted his son to become an attorney also, but Skinner showed skills in other areas, such as an early facility with mechanical devices. The young Skinner made roller skate scooters, blowguns, model airplanes, and a flotation system to separate green from ripe elderberries (Skinner, 1967). These inventions were precursors of later devices such as the infant air crib and the Skinner Box. Skinner was also interested in animal behavior and was highly impressed by a troupe of performing pigeons at a county fair. He later used pigeons to demonstrate aspects of his theory, teaching them to do a variety of tasks. In addition, Skinner enjoyed music and played the saxophone in a jazz band.

As a young adult, Skinner wanted to be a writer. He majored in English literature at Hamilton College, where he earned Phi Beta Kappa honors and graduated in 1926. Back home he set about the task of writing, having been encouraged in his efforts by Robert Frost. After a year, he moved to New York's Greenwich Village to live among writers and benefit from a stimulating environment. There he discovered the works of Ivan Pavlov and John B. Watson, as well as those of Bertrand Russell and Francis Bacon. Soon he gave up his writing ambitions to become a psychologist, although he had never taken a psychology course in college. He was accepted for graduate study at Harvard, where he received a master's degree in 1930 and a PhD in 1931. After another 5 years of postdoctoral training, he joined the faculty of the University of Minnesota in 1936, the same year in which he married Yvonne Blue.

Other major works followed Skinner's first book, *The Behavior of Organisms* (1938), and he rapidly developed a national reputation. He left Minnesota for the University of Indiana in 1945, where he chaired the department of psychology until he returned to Harvard in 1948. At Indiana, he wrote an influential futuristic novel, *Walden Two* (1948), which describes a utopian society functioning without punishment and following the principles of learning. The writing process itself was a remarkable experience for Skinner, filled with much emotion (Elms, 1981).

At Harvard, Skinner continued to be prolific. His best book on theory, *Science and Human Behavior* (1953), was published while he was there; it describes how learning principles can be applied to all areas of society. *Beyond Freedom and Dignity* (1971), also influential, outlined the steps necessary for civilization to survive and flourish. In the early 1980s, Skinner wrote about how behavioral principles could be applied to problems of the aged (Skinner & Vaughan, 1983).

Overall, Skinner can be classified as a **behavioral determinist** because of his emphasis on learning as the primary determinant of human actions. He died at the age of 86, a much admired and respected pioneer in the helping professions (Fowler, 1990).

VIEW OF HUMAN NATURE/PERSONALITY

Despite the great diversity of thought among behaviorists, certain characteristics are basic to their overall view of human nature and the development of personality. Commonalities that behaviorists share include:

- Behaviorists assume that all **behavior is learned,** whether it is adaptive or maladaptive.
- Behaviorists believe that **learning can be effective in changing maladaptive behavior or acquiring new behavior.**
- Behaviorists **reject the idea that the human personality is composed of traits** (Antony et al., 2020; Rimm & Cunningham, 1985).

Reflective Question

Reading is a learned behavior. Think of how you were taught to read. What behaviors were involved for you and your teacher?

As mentioned earlier, the three main approaches in contemporary behavioral therapy are the **stimulus-response model, applied behavior analysis,** and **social-cognitive theory.** These ways of learning are used by all organisms, although only human learning is addressed here.

The Stimulus-Response Model

The stimulus-response (S-R) model is basically **classical conditioning**, sometimes called **respondent learning**. In this model, the person need not be an active participant to learn because learning occurs through the association of two stimuli, also known as the conditioning of involuntary responses.

The best-known example of S-R learning is Pavlov's famous experiments with his laboratory dogs. Pavlov found that when a dog's food was paired with the sound of a bell, the dog would associate the bell with food and would begin to salivate in response to the bell before the food was served. The bell, initially a neutral stimulus, became a conditioned or learned stimulus (CS) because of its association with an unconditioned or natural stimulus (UCS)—that is, the food. Salivating at the sound of the bell became a conditioned or learned response (CR), as opposed to the unconditioned response (UCR) of naturally salivating when presented with food. S-R learning in this case is represented in the following sequence (Holden, 1993b):

> CS does not initially elicit CR
> UCS elicits UCR
> CS + UCS elicit UCR
> CS + UCS presented simultaneously or
> CS followed immediately by UCS CS + UCS repeated several times
> CS elicits CR

In a similar way, many human emotions, such as phobias, arise because of paired associations. For example, a person may have an accident after eating a certain food. The association of the food with the accident, even though the two are unrelated, may result in that person's eventual fear or avoidance of the food. (I, as your author, had that experience when I had an appendectomy shortly after eating licorice. Now I do not eat licorice). Clients often associate feelings with certain events and vice versa. The sound of music, the smell of certain odors, the sight of certain colors, and the touch of a stranger are experiences to which individuals may react emotionally because of S-R learning. Once learned, these associations can be unlearned and replaced in a process known as **counterconditioning**.

Reflective Question

What associations do you have with stimuli in your environment? Which are pleasant? Which are not?

Applied Behavior Analysis

Applied behavior analysis (ABA) is a direct extension of Skinner's (1953) radical behaviorism (Wilson, 2011), and is based on operant conditioning. According to that theory, learning occurs only when a person is involved as an active participant with the environment. **Operant conditioning**—along with its successor, ABA—focuses primarily on how individuals operate in the environment. In general, the idea is that a person learns to discriminate between behaviors that bring rewards and those that do not and is then likely to increase behavior that is rewarded and decrease behavior that is either punished or not reinforced. Applied behavior analysis makes use of reinforcement, punishment, extinction, stimulus control, and other procedures derived from laboratory research (Wilson, 2011).

Skinner's (1953) basic premise is the foundation on which applied behavior analysis is built. It states that when a certain behavior is followed closely by a **reinforcer,** or reward, chances increase that the behavior will recur in similar or identical circumstances. Individuals do not shape their environments as much as they are shaped by them through rewards and punishments. In other words, the consequences of a behavior determine whether that behavior will be learned or repeated. This idea can be thought of as the **ABC model (antecedent-behavior-consequence).**

Social-Cognitive Theory

In **social-cognitive learning,** people acquire new knowledge and behavior by observing other people and events without engaging in the behavior themselves and without any direct consequences to themselves. Synonyms for social-cognitive theory include observational learning, imitation, social modeling, and vicarious learning.

The social-cognitive approach depends on the theory that behavior is based on three separate but interacting regulatory systems (Bandura, 1986). They are (a) external stimulus events, (b) external reinforcement, and (c) cognitive mediational processes. In social-cognitive learning "the behavior of an individual or a group, the model, acts as a stimulus for similar thoughts, attitudes, or behavior on the part of another individual who observes" (Perry & Furukawa, 1980, p. 131). Driving a car, using the correct fork at a dinner party, giving oneself positive messages, and reacting appropriately to a new client are often learned in this way. Learning through social-cognitive processes emphasizes the self-regulation of behavior and deemphasizes external reinforcers. Thus learning may be independent of reinforcement (Olson & Hergenhahn, 2011). The advantages of social-cognitive learning are many, but chief among them is saving time, energy, and effort in acquiring new skills. In addition, social-cognitive theory is easily administered and is directed toward positive behavioral change. It is visually appealing and is of little or no risk to clients.

Bandura (1969) finds that models closest to the observer's age, gender, race, and attitude have the greatest impact. Live models, symbolic models (i.e., those on films and videos), and multiple models (i.e., groups of people) are equally effective in producing desired behavior change. In addition, covert models are quite effective, whereby a client imagines a model performing a socially desired activity (Cautela, 1976).

Reflective Question

Think of how you behave in certain situations, such as at parties or when attending an athletic or artistic event. Where did you learn to act as you do? Is some of your behavior a result of copying behaviors you once saw?

ROLE OF THE COUNSELOR

Behaviorists concentrate on behavioral processes—that is, processes closely associated with overt behavior. Counselors who take a behavioral approach help clients learn new, appropriate ways of acting or modify or eliminate excessive actions;

adaptive behaviors replace those that are maladaptive. Generally, behaviorally based counselors are active in sessions and serve as learning specialists so that clients can learn, unlearn, or relearn specific ways of behaving. In this process, counselors function as consultants, teachers, advisers, reinforcers, and facilitators (James & Gilliland, 2003). They may also instruct or supervise support people in a client's environment who are assisting in the change process. An effective behaviorist operates from a broad perspective, involving the client in every phase of the counseling. Counselors who are oriented toward social-cognitive learning serve as models for emulation, whereas those who lean toward S-R or applied approaches are more direct and prescriptive in offering assistance.

Counselors using a behavioral approach differ widely in their use of psychological tests and diagnoses. Most employ some form of client assessment device, but often these instruments measure behavior and action. Rarely do counselors use paper-and-pencil personality tests. For diagnosis, counselors describe clients according to the behaviors they display, many of which are listed in the *Diagnostic and Statistical Manual of Mental Disorders*.

GOALS

Behaviorists focus on changing, modifying, or eliminating behaviors; they set up well-defined therapy goals with their clients. Behavioral counselors want to help clients achieve definable personal and professional objectives. The focus is on helping clients acquire healthy, constructive ways of acting. Just eliminating a behavior is not enough; unproductive actions must be replaced with productive responses.

In reaching mutually agreed-upon goals, counselors and clients follow four specific steps (Blackham & Silberman, 1979):

- **Define the problem.** If a problem is to be solved, it must be stated concretely. Therefore, clients are asked to specify when, where, how, and with whom the problem arises. Counselors may benefit from observing the problem behavior.
- **Take a developmental history.** It is useful for both clients and counselors to know whether the presenting problem is organically based and how clients have handled past circumstances.
- **Establish specific goals.** Behavioral therapists help clients break goals down into small, achievable units. Counselors also set up learning experiences for clients to develop any needed skills (Krumboltz & Thoresen, 1976). For example, if a woman wishes to complete college, she must first select and then pass courses during a school term. She may also need to learn new study habits and new ways of interrelating with others, such as roommates.
- **Determine the best methods for change.** Usually several behavioral methods can help clients reach desired goals. If one method does not work, it can be modified, or a new one can be generated and tried. Continual assessment of the effectiveness of methods is critical.

In general, behavioral counselors specialize in helping clients learn how to set up and achieve specific goals and the subgoals that go with them. Counselors are concrete, objective, and collaborative in their work to help clients define and reach the goals they are seeking.

PROCESS AND TECHNIQUES

Behavioral therapy is a process; it takes time and dedication. Accentuating, eliminating, adding, or modifying behaviors requires a collaborative effort between therapist and client. Behaviorists concentrate on the here and now as opposed to the then and there of behavior. Therefore, they focus on presenting symptoms and concerns and ways in which they can be immediately treated.

Behavioral counselors have at their disposal some of the best-researched and most effective counseling techniques available. They stress the importance of obtaining empirical evidence and scientific support for any techniques they use. A sample of behavioral procedures is discussed here, although behaviorally oriented publications offer many additional techniques.

General Behavioral Techniques

General behavioral techniques are applicable to all behavioral theories, although a given technique may be more applicable to a particular approach at a given time or in a specific circumstance.

Use of Reinforcers. Reinforcers are those events that, when they follow a behavior, increase the probability of the behavior recurring. A **positive reinforcer** is valued and considered pleasurable by the person affected. Certain events and objects frequently serve in this capacity, such as social recognition, money, and food. A **negative reinforcer** is an aversive stimulus, the removal of which is contingent upon performance of a desired action; that removal is reinforcing for the person involved. For example, when a mother nags her son until he washes the dishes, the nagging could be viewed as a negative reinforcer, especially if the son values peace. In behavioral counseling, positive reinforcers are used more frequently than negative ones.

A reinforcer may also be either primary or secondary. A **primary reinforcer** is one that is valued intrinsically, such as food. A **secondary reinforcer**—for example, money or a token—acquires its value by being associated with a primary reinforcer. Clients know best which activities or items are most reinforcing for them.

Schedules of Reinforcement. When a behavior is initially being learned, it should be reinforced every time it occurs—that is, by **continuous reinforcement**. After a behavior is established, however, it should be reinforced less frequently— that is, by an **intermittent reinforcement schedule**. Schedules of reinforcement operate according to either ratio (the number of responses between reinforcers) or interval (the length of time between reinforcers). Both ratio and interval schedules are either fixed or variable. A **fixed-ratio schedule** delivers reinforcement based on the number of responses made—for instance, being paid for the number of items produced. A **fixed-interval schedule** occurs on a regular time schedule, such as a salary payment every two weeks. A **variable-ratio schedule** offers reinforcement irregularly, as a slot machine does, but averages out to a given figure. The irregular reinforcement is one reason people addicted to gambling continue to play slot machines. They hope they will be playing when the machine finally pays off. A **variable-interval schedule** follows an irregular time schedule so that reinforcement takes place unpredictably—for example, the boss might congratulate an employee twice in one day and then not again for a month. A counselor who knows what type of schedule a client prefers can set up reinforcers accordingly.

Shaping. **Shaping** occurs when a behavior is learned gradually in steps through successive approximation. When clients are learning new skills, counselors may help break behavior down into manageable units. Clients may practice a behavior or may imagine doing more of a task than they had previously done (i.e., focused imagery). Before undertaking shaping, however, counselors and clients need to be aware of the specific response sequence they wish to establish—that is, what follows what and how, a process known as **chaining**. When carefully planned, such a procedure usually leads to new or improved behaviors.

Generalization. **Generalization** involves the display of behaviors in environments other than those in which the behaviors were originally learned. Generalizing behaviors and transferring them to another setting requires a number of procedures, including the assignment of behavioral homework, training significant others to reinforce appropriate behaviors, and consulting with clients about particular problems in making behavioral switches (Rose, 1993).

Maintenance. **Maintenance** is consistent performance of desired actions without depending on anyone else for support. Maintenance emphasizes increasing a client's self-control and self-management. When clients learn to modify their own behaviors, **self-monitoring** occurs in two related processes: **self-observation** and **self-recording** (Goldiamond, 1976). Self-observation requires that clients notice particular behaviors they exhibit; self-recording focuses on keeping track of these behaviors. Self-monitoring interferes with learned habits by having clients count the occurrences of specific behaviors, which are normally done without thought. Such self-monitoring increases client awareness of targeted behaviors and the ways in which they occur. In weight control, for example, individuals monitor their calorie intake and their reactions to eating certain foods.

Reflective Question

Many specialized behaviors, such as swinging a golf club or playing a musical instrument, are learned gradually and involve shaping, generalization, and maintenance. What skills have you learned in this way?

Extinction. **Extinction** is the elimination of a behavior by withdrawal of its reinforcement. Few individuals continue doing something that is not rewarding. For example, when clients are no longer reinforced for talking about the past, they stop bringing it up. Talking about that subject has disappeared and is said to be extinct.

Punishment. **Punishment** is the presentation of an aversive stimulus in order to suppress or eliminate a behavior. A counselor might punish a client with a critical statement such as "I don't want to hear you talk like that." Usually, however, behavior therapists do not use punishment in their treatment of clients. Holden (1993a) identifies the differences in behavioral consequences, which are summarized in Table 8.1.

Specific Behavioral Techniques
Specific behavioral techniques are refined behavioral methods that combine general techniques in precise ways. They are found in different behavioral approaches but are used only after rapport and trust have been established between counselors and clients.

Table 8.1   The Effect of Behavioral Consequences on Behavior

Use of Pleasurable Stimulus	Use of Aversive Stimulus	Effect
Positive Reinforcement (response followed quickly by pleasurable stimulus)	Negative Reinforcement (response followed quickly by termination of aversive stimulus or response precludes aversive stimulus)	Increased rate or strength of response
Extinction (response no longer followed by pleasurable stimulus)	Punishment (response followed quickly by aversive stimulus)	Decreased rate or strength of response

Behavioral Rehearsal. **Behavioral rehearsal** consists of practicing a desired behavior until it is performed in the way a client wishes (Lazarus, 1985). The process involves gradually shaping a behavior and getting corrective feedback. It is frequently used after clients have viewed a model enacting the desired behavior. In such cases, especially with complex behavior, clients who wish to acquire the behavior will practice in a counselor's presence what they have observed. Clients then receive feedback and suggestions and make modifications accordingly. Clients also receive homework designed to help them practice the new behavior outside the counselor's office. Practice in real-life conditions often leads to success and generalization; if not, modifications can be made during the next counseling session (Kipper, 1986). Behavioral rehearsal is sometimes called **role-playing** because clients are practicing new roles. Improvisational role-playing of new behavior is an effective mechanism for change (Zimbardo & Leippe, 1991).

Environmental Planning. In **environmental planning** a client sets up part of the environment to promote or limit certain behaviors (Krasner & Ullmann, 1973). For example, if a client associates painful memories with a certain place, a daily schedule might be designed to avoid that setting. Similarly, to control a situation and therefore promote desirable interaction, a client might arrange a room or chairs in a certain way.

Reflective Question

What are the advantages and disadvantages of using behavioral rehearsal over environmental planning and vice versa?

Systematic desensitization. **Systematic desensitization** is designed to help clients overcome anxiety in particular situations. Clients are asked first to describe a situation that causes anxiety and then to rank this situation and related events on a hierarchical scale, from aspects that cause no concern (0) to those that are most troublesome (100) (see Table 8.2). The higher up the scale an event or situation is the more anxious clients are about it. To help clients avoid anxiety and face situations, counselors teach them to relax physically or mentally. Then the hierarchy is reviewed, starting with low-anxiety items. When clients' anxieties begin to mount, they are

Table 8.2   Anxiety Hierarchy

Amount of Anxiety	Event
90	Talking to a girl I like
80	Talking to my algebra teacher
70	Talking to my father
60	Talking to a new kid at school
50	Talking to an older adult
40	Talking to my minister
30	Going to a fast food restaurant
20	Going to sleep
10	Watching television

helped to relax again. The underlying idea is that people cannot feel anxious and relaxed at the same time, a phenomenon called **reciprocal inhibition** (Wolpe, 1958).

Assertiveness training. The major tenet of **assertiveness training** is that people should be free to express thoughts and feelings appropriately without feeling undue anxiety (Alberti & Emmons, 2017). The technique consists of counterconditioning anxiety and reinforcing assertiveness. Clients are taught that everyone has the right, not the obligation, of self-expression. Clients then learn the differences among aggressive, passive, and assertive actions. Clients tell their counselors at the beginning of the counseling relationship what their objectives are, such as being able to speak out at public meetings. Counselors then give their clients feedback, both positive and negative, about present behaviors. The next steps involve modeling the desired behaviors and having clients role-play them. Counselors reinforce these behaviors and help shape their clients' actions. Finally, clients receive homework to be completed between sessions (Bellack & Hersen, 1998). Assertive behaviors should be shaped gradually to keep clients encouraged and on track. The objective is for individuals to feel good about their ability to express themselves in a nonaggressive or manipulative way.

Contingency Contracts. **Contingency contracts** spell out behaviors to be performed, changed, or discontinued, the rewards associated with the achievement of these goals, and the conditions under which rewards are to be received. Most often contracts are used with children rather than adults, who may find them offensive (see Figure 8.1). The contracts are frequently written out as quasi-formal documents as in Figure 8.1.

Implosion and Flooding. **Implosive therapy** involves desensitizing clients to a situation by having them imagine an anxiety-producing situation that may have dire consequences, without having been taught to relax first (as in systematic desensitization). This technique should not be used by beginning counselors or with clients who have heart conditions. In **flooding**, which is less traumatic, the imagined anxiety-producing scene does not have dire consequences. Instead, clients are overwhelmed with images of anxiety-producing stimuli.

Aversive Techniques. Although most behaviorists recommend that positive techniques be employed first, sometimes it is necessary to use aversive techniques, such as punishment. Such techniques, which vary in their severity, are useful when one behavior must be eliminated before another can be taught.

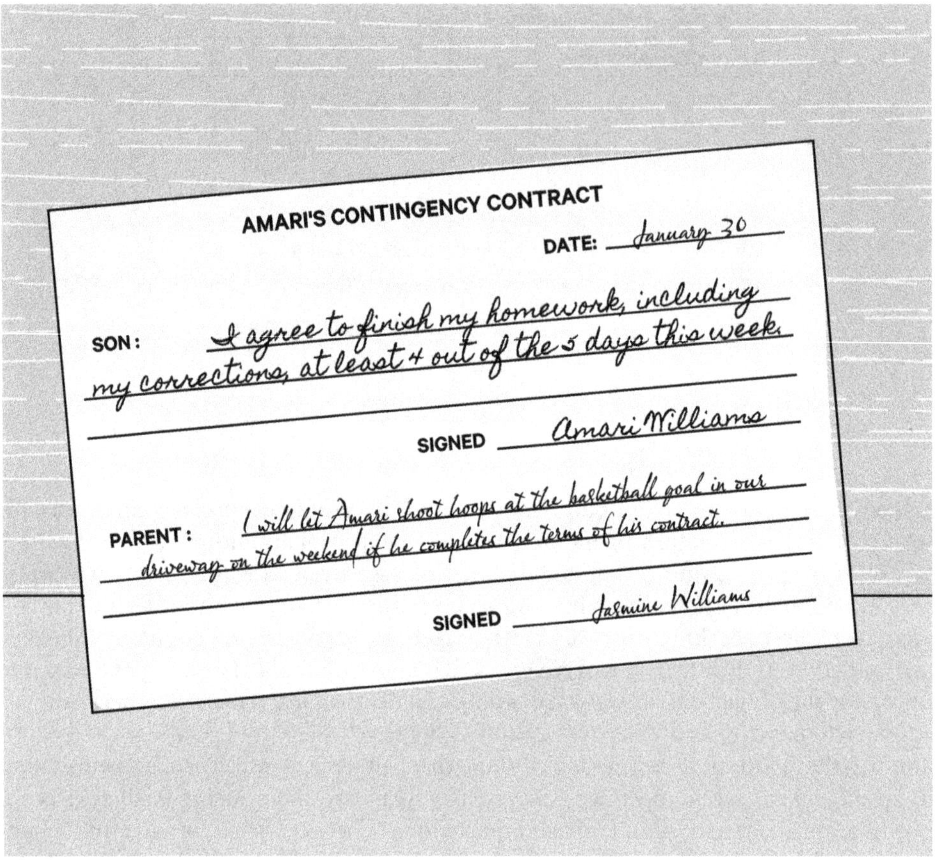

AMARI'S CONTINGENCY CONTRACT

DATE: _January 30_

SON: _I agree to finish my homework, including my corrections, at least 4 out of the 5 days this week._

SIGNED _Amari Williams_

PARENT: _I will let Amari shoot hoops at the basketball goal in our driveway on the weekend if he completes the terms of his contract._

SIGNED _Jasmine Williams_

Figure 8.1 Contingency contract
Shiri Esh'har for Zebra on Wheels

Among the most powerful aversive techniques are time-out, overcorrection, and covert sensitization. **Time-out** separates clients, usually children, from the opportunity to receive positive reinforcement. It is a mild aversive technique that requires careful monitoring and is most effective when employed for short periods of time, such as 5 minutes. One example is separating a child from classmates when he or she misbehaves. **Overcorrection** is a technique in which clients first restore the environment to its natural state and then make it better. For example, children who throw food in the lunchroom might be required to clean up their mess and then wax the floor. **Covert sensitization** eliminates undesirable behavior by associating it with unpleasantness. It is used in treating clients who have problems with smoking, obesity, substance abuse, and sexual deviation.

In the long run, aversive stimuli are usually not effective by themselves.

- Their negative emotional effects soon dissipate.
- They may interfere with the learning of desired behaviors.
- They may encourage escape, which, when successful, becomes a positive reinforcement.

Furthermore, ethical and legal concerns are associated with all aversive techniques. Before administering them, counselors should obtain written permission for their use, especially if minors are involved, and be sure that they are adequately trained and supervised.

DIVERSITY AND MULTICULTURAL ISSUES

Like most approaches, behavioral therapy has strengths and weaknesses when it comes to working with clients from cultures and backgrounds that differ from that of the counselor. A behavioral approach may help clients be more specific about what they want to do within their subcultures and larger cultural groups, such as depression or sleep (Knight & Johnson, 2014). Thus clients in a behavioral orientation may define more precisely the behaviors that are troubling for them and may then be better able to address these behaviors, especially if they learn new ways of responding. The drawback to such work, however, is that counselors must become attuned to culture-specific behaviors and ways to address them appropriately.

Concerning matters of gender, behavior therapy terms and techniques are free of reference to gender. In addition, the behavioral approach allows clients to acquire new skills that may enhance their status across gender lines. Observational learning may be especially powerful in helping clients make changes related to nontraditional gender-role behavior, such as that involved in careers (Bussey & Bandura, 1999).

EVALUATION OF THE THEORY

Strengths and Contributions

Behavioral therapy works well with clients who are predominantly goal and action oriented with a need for achievement and results. It is a good approach for clients who are interested in changing either a discrete response or a limited number of behaviors.

A second strength of behavioral therapy is that it deals directly with symptoms; it is objective in defining and addressing problems. It demystifies the process of counseling and makes it possible for clients and outside evaluators to assess levels of change in a measurable way. Moreover, by working directly with symptoms, counselors are often able to assist clients immediately. Because behavioral approaches focus on the here and now, clients do not have to examine the past to obtain help in the present, thus saving time and money.

Another positive aspect of behavioral counseling is its appropriateness in working with certain disorders—for example, attention deficit disorders, conduct disorders, eating disorders, substance abuse disorders, psychosexual dysfunction, impulse control disorders, and phobic disorders. Behavioral approaches are also useful in addressing difficulties associated with anxiety, stress, assertiveness, parenting, and social interaction (Hackney & Bernard, 2017; Seligman & Reichenberg, 2014).

In addition, behavioral therapy offers numerous techniques for counselors to use. Behavioral techniques, which more than doubled from 1969 to 1976, continue to increase. Moreover, therapists can employ these techniques in numerous settings, including institutions such as mental hospitals or sheltered workshops. Many behaviorally oriented counseling journals are also available, such as the *Journal of Applied Behavior Analysis*.

Another strength of behavioral therapy is that it is based on learning theory, which is a well-formulated way of documenting how new behaviors are acquired (Krumboltz & Thoresen, 1976; Thoresen, 1969). Furthermore, learning theory continues to evolve and generate pragmatic applications for treatment in a wide variety of areas (Rescorla, 1988).

The Association for the Advancement of Behavior Therapy (AABT), which publishes ethical guidelines for its members, also buttresses behavioral therapy. The AABT promotes the practice of and education about behavioral counseling methods while protecting the public from unscrupulous practitioners.

In addition, behaviorism is supported by exceptionally good research on how techniques and processes affect the process of counseling. Thus novice counselors can follow many research designs. A common denominator among all behavioral approaches is a commitment to objectivity and evaluation.

Limitations and Criticisms

Behavioral therapy does not deal with the total person, just with explicit behaviors. Critics contend that many behaviorists, such as B. F. Skinner, have taken the person out of personality and replaced it with an emphasis on laws that govern actions in specific environments. This emphasis may be too simplistic in explaining complex human interaction (Olson & Hergenhahn, 2011).

A second criticism is that behaviorism is sometimes applied mechanically. Goldstein (1973) notes that "the most common error of neophyte behavior therapists is to start employing techniques too quickly" (p. 221). Even though most behaviorists are careful to establish rapport with their clients and make counseling a collaborative effort, those who do not initially stress the counselor-client relationship have hurt the approach's image.

A third limitation of the behavioral approach is that it is often best demonstrated under controlled conditions that are difficult to replicate in normal counseling situations. Implicit in this criticism is an uneasiness that much of behavioral theory has been formulated using other animal forms, such as rats and pigeons. Many counselors wonder whether a behavioral approach can work with human clients who operate in less than ideal environments.

Another weakness of behaviorism is that techniques may be ahead of theory (Thoresen & Coates, 1980). Behavioral counselors have generated a proliferation of new methods, yet the theory that should underlie these methods has not kept pace.

Yet another criticism is that behaviorism ignores clients' histories and unconscious forces. Although it may work quite well with someone who clearly has a behavioral concern, those who wish to resolve past issues or deal with insight from the unconscious may not be helped.

A related concern is that behaviorism does not consider developmental stages. Skinner (1974) notes that a child's world does develop, but he and many other behaviorists think that developmental stages do little to explain overt behavior.

Finally, critics charge behaviorists program clients for minimum or tolerable levels of behavior, reinforce conformity, stifle creativity, and ignore client needs for self-fulfillment, self-actualization, and feelings of self-worth (James & Gilliland, 2003).

TREATING LINDA WITH BEHAVIORAL THERAPY

Conceptualization

From a behaviorist point of view, Linda has been reinforced for being passive, dependent, depressed, and submissive. She has been punished when assertive. Thus the behaviors Linda has learned have prevented her from utilizing many of her talents and have resulted in her now being isolated and relying on things she can manipulate, such as the pages of books and the remote control of the television.

Linda has lacked models of strong and competent women in her life. Her mother was rather withdrawn, her sisters have achieved little, and Linda has never had a woman supervisor. Overall, Linda lacks the behaviors that would help make her successful as a person and a professional.

Treatment Process

As a behavioral therapist, you want to help Linda learn new, appropriate ways of acting, replacing maladaptive behaviors with adaptive ones. Therefore, you function as a consultant, teacher, adviser, reinforcer, and facilitator. Initially, you work with Linda to identify behaviors she wants to acquire and those she wants to eliminate. For instance, Linda reveals that she would like to be more assertive instead of passively accepting the dictates of others and then getting angry about it. Linda also wants to explore how to make the most of her talents and possibly gain new job skills.

You set up specific and mutually agreed-upon goals by concretely defining the problem (i.e., a lack of adequate social and vocational skills), taking a developmental history, establishing specific goals, and determining the best method for change. In Linda's case, you believe that an assertiveness training course offered by a community agency would be helpful, as would an assessment of her vocational interests and skills. As an active learning specialist, you set up both experiences.

During therapy sessions, you discover reinforcers for Linda and begin to help her shape and generalize the assertive behavior she wants by role-playing different scenarios with her. You also set up a self-observation and self-monitoring schedule for Linda to use outside counseling sessions so that she becomes ever more aware of her behavior. In addition, you encourage Linda to reinforce herself when she realizes that she is speaking up for herself or when she takes positive steps to acquire additional vocational skills.

As therapy continues, Linda becomes more independent and joins a number of community organizations in which she has an interest. She finds out how best to use the business skills she already has and takes some additional courses at a nearby college. Without being aggressive or passive, she lets her family know how she wants to relate to them and even plans some of the regular Sunday outings so that they are fun for her and educational for her family. Overall, behavioral therapy helps Linda become a more accomplished person.

SUMMING UP

Behavior therapy is a diverse way of working with clients to help them improve their personal and interpersonal skills. Through behavioral therapy, individuals learn how to manage excessive behaviors, extinguish unwanted behaviors, and learn new behaviors. The three primary approaches to behavioral change are the stimulus-response model, applied behavior analysis, and social-cognitive theory. Behaviorists employ many general techniques with their clients, including reinforcement, shaping, generalization, extinction, and problem-solving rehearsals. They also use specialized and refined techniques such as environmental planning, systematic desensitization, assertiveness training, contracts, implosion, flooding, time-out, and overcorrection.

A real strength of behavioral therapy is its solid learning theory base; excellent research supports the behavioral approaches. In addition, behavioral therapy is extolled for dealing directly with symptoms and behaviors, working in the present, being relatively brief, demystifying the counseling process, having a plethora of available techniques, and being buttressed by a professional association of practitioners and researchers in the field—the Association for the Advancement of Behavior Therapy. On the other hand, behaviorism is limited by conducting some of its research with animals, ignoring clients' histories and the unconscious, dismissing developmental stages as unimportant, and reinforcing conformity.

CHAPTER 8 RECAP: BEHAVIORAL THERAPY

Major Theorists
John B. Watson, Mary Cover, Jones B. F. Skinner, Ivan Pavlov
Joseph Wolpe, Albert Bandura, John Krumboltz, Edward Thorndike

View of Human Nature/Personality
All behavior is learned.
There are no human personality traits.
Clients earn through respondent learning, operant conditioning, and social modeling.

Role of the Counselor
Teacher, director, expert
Active participant in counseling sessions
Aids in clarifying goals and modifying behaviors

Goals
Extinguish or adjust behavior
Learn productive responses
Establish and achieve behavioral goals

Process and Techniques
Reinforcement: positive/negative, primary/secondary, continuous/intermittent
Shaping and extinction: ABC Model (antecedent-behavior-consequence)
Environmental planning and systematic desensitization
Implosion and flooding
Time-out and overcorrection

Diversity and Multicultural Issues

May be applied to clients in every culture
Requires sensitivity to cultural context
Cuts across gender lines

Limitations and Criticisms

Does not focus on the whole person
May be applied too mechanically
Cannot always replicate lab conditions in the field
Ignores history and the unconscious
Does not consider developmental stages

KEY TERMS

ABC Model (antecedent-behavior-consequence) 102
applied behavior analysis 100
assertiveness training 107
aversive techniques 107
behavior therapy 99
behavioral rehearsal 106
chaining 105
contingency contracts 107
continuous 104
counterconditioning 99
covert sensitization 108
environmental planning 106
extinction 105
fixed-ratio schedule 104
flooding 107
generalization 105
implosive therapy 107
intermittent 104
maintenance 105
negative 104
overcorrection 108

positive 104
primary 104
punishment 105
reciprocal inhibition 106
reinforcers 102
role-playing 106
secondary 104
self-monitoring 105
self-observing 105
self-recording 105
shaping 105
social-cognitive learning, aka modeling 102
social-cognitive theory 100
stimulus-response model – classical conditioning, aka response learning 101
systematic desensitization 106
time-out 108
variable-interval schedule 104
variable-ratio schedule 104

LEARNING MORE

A number of periodicals devoted to behavioral therapy may prove helpful in exploring this approach.

Advances in Behaviour Research and Therapy
Behavior Analysis
Behavior Modification

Behavior Therapist
Behavior Therapy, Cognitive and Behavioral Practice
Behavioral Assessment
Journal of Applied Behavior Analysis
Journal of Behavior Therapy and Experimental Psychiatry
Progress in Behavior Modification

In addition to journals, several training institutes and professional associations offer clinicians a chance to learn more about behavior therapy and its uses in therapeutic settings.

Association for Behavioral and Cognitive Therapies
http://www.abct.org/Home/
Behavior Online: The Mental Health and Behavioral Science Meeting Place
    www.behavior.net

CLASSROOM ACTIVITIES

1. Discuss your own positive and negative reinforcers in life with another classmate. How has punishment affected your life, especially concerning learning?
2. As a class discuss how and what you have learned in life by way of each of the three behavioral models: stimulus-response conditioning, applied behavior analysis, and social-cognitive learning.
3. Find examples of behaviors that have either been generalized or extinguished in society. As a class, discuss these behaviors and the impact their generalization or extinction has had.

9

Cognitive and Cognitive-Behavioral Therapies

■ ■ ■

Miss Alice sits in her chair all day
rocking back and forth pretending it's a sleigh
She doesn't talk for that would give it away
within her mind she hears voices.

"Delusions" © S. T. Gladding

CHAPTER OVERVIEW

From reading this chapter you will learn about

■ The importance of self-talk and the negative impact cognitive distortions have.
■ Three categories of thought: cold, warm, and hot cognitions.
■ A basic four-step procedure cognitive counselors use to bring about change and prevalent cognitive techniques.

As you read, consider

■ When you have heard others give positive or negative self-statements.
■ When you have encountered others who have used cognitive distortions.
■ The impact of cold, warm, and hot cognitions in the lives of those you know and how effective you might be in using prevalent cognitive techniques with others.

Cognitions are thoughts, beliefs, and internal images people have about events in their lives. **Cognitive counseling theories—cognitive therapy (CT) and cognitive-behavioral therapy (CBT)**—focus on mental processes and their influence on mental health. A common premise of all cognitive approaches is: how people think largely determines how they feel and behave (Beck & Weishaar, 2019). As Burns (1980) points out, "Every bad feeling you have is the result of your distorted negative thinking" (p. 28). Therefore, most cognitive theorists agree with the biblical verse from Proverbs 23:7—"As people think, so shall they be"—and with Shakespeare's Hamlet, who said, "There's nothing either good or bad but thinking makes it so." In short, cognitive theorists and clinicians believe that if individuals change their ways of thinking, their feelings and behaviors will be modified.

Cognitive approaches to counseling are relatively new. They came into prominence in the 1970s and were known as the second wave of behavioral therapy after the first wave based on classical and operant conditioning. This second wave of behavioral therapies included cognitions in the form of using behavioral tasks to modify faulty perceptions, irrational beliefs, and interpretations of important life events. Among the best-known cognitive theories in the second wave have been Aaron Beck and Judith Beck's cognitive-behavioral therapy and David Burns's new mood therapy. Cognitive-behavioral therapeutic approaches in the third wave of cognitive-behavioral theory and therapy have been acceptance and commitment therapy (ACT) and relational cultural theory (RCT), which are not covered here.

Researchers and practitioners such as Donald Meichenbaum (1977, 1985) and Neil Jacobson have been among the most prominent cognitive behaviorists. Their work emphasizes mental processes in human behavior and views thoughts as a type of behavior. The essence of the cognitive-behavioral approach is the blending of behavioral and cognitive strategies to help people make needed changes in their lives. Cognitive behaviorists thus form a bridge between counselors who are exclusively focused on either cognitive or behavioral changes.

MAJOR THEORISTS: AARON BECK AND DONALD MEICHENBAUM

A prolific writer of more than 400 articles and 15 books, Aaron T. Beck (1921–) is a Philadelphia psychiatrist originally trained as a psychoanalyst. He developed a cognitive approach to mental disorders in the late 1950s and early 1960s, emphasizing the importance of cognitive thinking, especially dysfunctional thoughts, which are unproductive, unrealistic, and may produce depression (Beck & Beck, 2021; Weinrach, 1988).

Beck served for many years as the director of the Center for Cognitive Therapy at the University of Pennsylvania's Department of Psychiatry. There he refined his theory and rigorously tested it (see Beck, 1991; Newman & Beck, 2009). In the process, he found that cognitive therapy is effective as a short-term treatment for a number of problems and disorders, especially depression and general anxiety (Beck & Alford, 2009; Clark & Beck, 2012). In these maladies there are "interpretations and expectations that lead to the painful effects of sadness and anxiety, to avoidance and inhibition" (Weinrach, 1988, p. 161). Cognitive counselors trained in Beck's methodology try to help clients become more realistic in their interpretation of events by generalizing less in the case of depression or projecting less in the case of anxiety. This approach uses a Socratic method that is problem oriented, educational, brief, and collaborative. In short, Beck's approach emphasizes that affect and behavior are determined by the ways in which people mentally structure their worlds, especially their thinking.

Donald Meichenbaum (1940–) is one of the founders of cognitive-behavioral therapy (CBT). He was born and raised in New York City, where he observed many people talking to themselves. He concluded that helping people talk to themselves differently and constructively might be an excellent goal for therapy and might bring about behavioral changes (Meichenbaum, 1995, 1997).

Meichenbaum is the author of numerous articles, chapters, and books, some of which are now considered classics in the field of therapy, such as *Cognitive-Behavioral Modification: An Integrated Approach* (1977) and *Stress Inoculation Training* (1985). He is noted especially for his work on treating individuals with anger and aggressive behavior and adults with posttraumatic stress disorder. In a survey reported in the *American Psychologist*, North American clinicians voted Meichenbaum 1 of the 10 most influential psychotherapists of the 20th century.

He has served on the editorial boards of numerous journals and has lectured and consulted worldwide. Prior to retirement Meichenbaum was a professor of psychology at the University of Waterloo in Waterloo, Canada, where he also had a private practice as a clinical psychologist.

VIEW OF HUMAN NATURE/PERSONALITY

A concern of cognitive and cognitive-behavioral therapies is the impact of thinking on personality. These counseling approaches usually are employed with individuals who are not visibly impaired but who suffer from dysfunctional automatic thoughts specific to an event. These thoughts are known as schemata, which are general rules about oneself or the world associated with an event, such as how a person should think or behave (Beck, 2021; Holden, 1993b). These individuals often engage in **self-statements** that affect their behaviors in much the same way as statements made by another person. For instance, a guest slighted at a party may automatically think, "That person is a jerk!" The schema that follows may be "I'm offended" or "I'm hurt."

For Beck and for cognitive therapists in general, a counselor should be attuned to a number of **cognitive distortions**. These include at least nine ways of mentally assessing a situation (Arnkoff & Glass, 1992; DeRubeis et al., 2019).

- **All-or-nothing thinking** (also known as **dichotomous thinking**) occurs when people think they must do something a certain way or else they are failures. For example, in giving a speech, if all-or-nothing thinkers do not say every word written, they believe they will be seen as incompetent.
- In **selective abstraction**, individuals pick out an idea or fact to support their negative thinking. For instance, if a person who usually makes straight As in school suddenly makes a B, that person might use the B to conclude, "I'm not really very smart."
- **Overgeneralization** makes a rule based on a few incidences or events. For example, someone may think that all white people are insensitive because of encounters with some white people who were rude and uncaring.
- **Magnification** and **minimization** are two sides of the same thought process. In magnification a cognitive distortion occurs when an imperfection is exaggerated beyond reality. For instance, a high school student could fail a test and conclude, "I will never be able to get into a good college." In minimization a person downplays good points or notable achievements. The student who is an accomplished artist may not apply to appropriate colleges, thinking, "I am not up to the quality of these colleges."
- **Personalization** occurs when an event unrelated to a person is distorted and made to appear related. For example, a woman may begin to think that the elevators in her office complex are slow even though she uses them only at peak times.
- **Labeling** and **mislabeling** are common cognitive distortions that arise when people characterize themselves in certain ways. For instance, a man who goes to a batting cage to hit balls and misses most of them during his first visit may label or mislabel himself as a poor hitter, instead of a person needing more practice.
- **Catastrophizing** is similar in both Beck's and Ellis's theories. It involves mentally distorting an event so that one becomes fearful of it. For example, if a shy but accomplished young man is attracted to an outgoing, sophisticated, and

good-looking young woman, he may say to himself, "She is far superior to me in every way. I cannot ever talk to her, let alone ask her out for a date." He precludes any possible relationship and becomes completely discombobulated any time he is near her.

- **Mind reading** refers to the tendency of some people to guess what others are thinking about them. An older adult may believe that others who see him think, "There is an incompetent old fool who is good for nothing." Therefore he fails to interact with people in his environment and becomes a recluse.
- **Negative predictions** are beliefs that something bad is going to happen. They may have little basis in fact, but they influence a person's actions just the same. For instance, a person may believe "I will get sick if I eat chicken, because I once got sick after a meal that included chicken." Thus the prediction keeps that person from eating chicken, which would have no negative impact.

Reflective Question

When have you seen people display any of the distorted cognitions just described? All-or-nothing thinking, overgeneralization, and negative predictions seem to be especially prevalent in society.

ROLE OF THE COUNSELOR

The role of cognitively oriented counselors is to collaborate with clients (Beck, 1976), sharing the responsibility to select goals and bring about change. In this relationship, counselors function as educators and as experts on cognitions, behaviors, and emotions. Clients collaborate by participating in assignments. Initially, cognitively oriented counselors do not try to disprove beliefs but let clients examine the functionality of their beliefs. Beck's model is exploratory in working with clients and Socratic in letting them assess what is correct and incorrect in their belief systems (Holden, 1993a). Cognitive therapy is ever evolving so that as new data come in, the counselor-client team can make new strategies.

Overall, cognitively based helping requires empirical testing on the part of clients to understand how functional or dysfunctional their beliefs are. Counselors, especially cognitive-behavioral counselors, may use diagnoses, such as those in the *Diagnostic and Statistical Manual*, in working with clients. However, diagnoses are employed only as a way of working with clients to overcome a disorder, such as posttraumatic stress.

GOALS

Both cognitive and cognitive-behavioral approaches to helping employ specific learning experiences to teach clients ways to monitor their negative or automatic thoughts (Beck & Beck, 2021). Clients are taught to recognize the relationship between these thoughts and their emotions and behaviors. In addition, counselors with this orientation help clients compile evidence for and against their distorted automatic thoughts. Ideally, clients are freed to alter their distorted beliefs and to substitute reality-based interpretations for unrealistic thoughts.

In order to help clinicians achieve these goals, profiles and treatment plans have been developed, especially by Beck, for disorders such as depression (Beck et al., 1987), suicide, anxiety (Dattilio, 2010), anger, and worry (Gillihan, 2018). However, goals are constantly reexamined and modified to fit clients; cognitive approaches are tailored to individual situations.

PROCESS AND TECHNIQUES

Cognitive and cognitive-behavioral therapy are specific and goal directed (Sharf, 2016), emphasizing the modification of thoughts to bring about therapeutic change. One way to organize thoughts is in three categories: cold, warm, and hot cognitions. A **cold cognition** is descriptive and nonevaluative, such as "I lost my job." A **warm cognition** emphasizes preferences and nonpreferences, such as "I lost my job and I really don't want to have to start looking for another one." **Hot cognitions** "are heavily laden emotional-demand statements" (James & Gilliland, 2003, p. 238) that may reveal varied distortions, such as overgeneralizing, catastrophizing, magnification, and all-or-nothing thinking—for example, "I must get a job just like the one I lost." Hot cognitions usually lead to dysfunctional behaviors because they are filled with both demands and distortions.

A cognitive approach to change must first establish a relationship between client and counselor and then implement cognitive strategies in a basic four-step procedure (Burns, 1989; Schuyler, 2003). These four steps and the premises behind them are at the heart of change.

The first step is to use standardized guidelines for understanding in a concrete manner the events in clients' lives—that is, what is happening in their environments. The second step is to set up a way of recording or reflecting clients' thoughts about these events to understand their cognitions in a clear, precise way. Often thoughts are written down so that they can be seen in as concrete a manner as possible.

In the third step, counselors and clients work to find a means to identify and challenge distorted thoughts. For instance, if a client believes that no one likes her, an empirical test might be set up whereby she records all positive as well as negative interactions. The final step is to implement new ways of thinking that are realistic and productive. Thus the client might change her thinking from "Nobody likes me" to "Some people like me and some do not." This process frees her to act more positively with specific individuals and with people in general.

Cognitive Techniques

The following are among the most prevalent cognitive techniques in use.

- **Specifying automatic thoughts.** As mentioned earlier, automatic thoughts are cognitions that occur without effort. They are usually distorted and lead to unhealthy emotional responses. Therefore, a major focus of cognitive therapy is to identify—that is, specify—and then correct such thoughts.
- **Homework.** As with other types of therapy, much change that occurs in cognitive therapy happens outside actual counseling sessions. Clients may practice giving themselves different thoughts at home, on the job, or in particular settings. Such practice makes it easier for clients to achieve the desired changes in their thinking.
- **Cognitive interventions.** A number of processes occur under the heading of cognitive interventions. All of them focus on bringing cognitive distortions

into greater awareness—for example, challenging absolutes and all-or-nothing thinking, reattribution, labeling of distortions.

- **Cognitive rehearsals.** Because practice makes perfect, it is important for clients to consistently rehearse healthy thoughts. They may do so covertly or overtly, privately through mental rehearsal, or publicly, as in a gathering of friends. Cognitive rehearsals ensure that clients will say to themselves and others the right words in the right way—at least most of the time.
- **Scriptotherapy.** In the process of writing, which is scriptotherapy, individuals improve their thoughts by expressing them concretely. Pennebaker and Smyth (2016), among others, has noted both mental and physical changes in clients who write about stressful situations in their lives.

Reflective Question

How helpful do you find it to write your thoughts down? Look at what you write and how you write about success and disappointment in your life.

Cognitive-Behavioral Techniques

Some of the most exciting new techniques in counseling have been originated by cognitive-behaviorists (Craighead et al., 1994; Mahoney, 1995). Cognitive-behavioral techniques are "usually active, time-limited, and fairly structured. They are designed to enlist the client" and others in "a collaborative process" (Meichenbaum, 1986, p. 347). Although "there is no single definition of cognitive-behavioral theory ... the individual theories are tied together by common assumptions, techniques, and research strategies" (Powers & Kalodner, 2016, p. 227). CBT approaches maintain a diversity of views about the role cognitions play in behavior change, but all agree that cognitions play a part in such change.

CBT procedures emphasize the present, the environment, and learning. Common to cognitive-behavioral intervention is "a directive style; structured, goal-directed, and time-limited treatment; use of homework assignments and skill practice; and a focus on problem-solving ability" (Powers & Kalodner, 2016, p. 227). Dozens of interventions can be included under the cognitive-behavioral banner—for example, "cognitive restructuring, problem-solving, relaxation training, behavioral and imaginal rehearsal, self-monitoring, self-reinforcement, and efforts at environmental change" (Meichenbaum, 1985, p. 21). Following are some of the interventions most common to cognitive-behavioral approaches to counseling.

- **Self-instructional training.** One of the best methods for changing clients' cognitions and behaviors is a process known as self-instructional training (Meichenbaum, 1977). In this procedure counselors first perform a task or engage in appropriate behaviors while verbalizing aloud through self-talk the reasons behind what they are doing. Clients then do the same task or behavior and give themselves instructions aloud. Next, clients engage in the behaviors while whispering self-instructions. Finally, they perform the behaviors while silently repeating the reasons behind what they are doing. These covert messages thus become the basis for the clients' behaviors, and in the future, they may

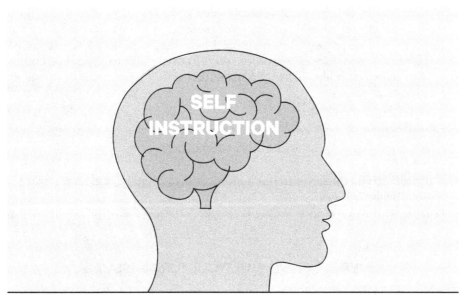

Figure 9.1 Self instruction
Shiri Esh'har for Zebra on Wheels

communicate with themselves in this manner. As a strategy, self-instructional training is especially powerful and popular in working with impulsive, defiant, or attention-deficit children and adolescents (see Figure 9.1) (Barkley, 1987, 1991; Kendall, 2007).

- **Stress-inoculation training.** Stress inoculation is a preventive technique, like medical inoculation, in which individuals are taught coping skills to handle stressful events. First, clients are helped to understand the nature of stress and coping. Second, clients learn specific coping skills and are reinforced for using the ones they already possess. The final phase emphasizes practice: clients use coping skills in clinical settings and real situations. Overall, stress inoculation involves focusing on what lies ahead, grouping stressful events into manageable doses, thinking of ways to handle small stressful events, and practicing coping skills (Meichenbaum, 1985, 1986). The major drawback to this procedure is that its initial results sometimes do not generalize into permanent behavior changes (Arnkoff & Glass, 1992). Therefore, follow-up and booster sessions are often necessary.
- **Thought stopping.** Thought stopping helps clients who ruminate about the past or who have irrational thoughts to stop such self-defeating behavior and live more productively. Counselors initially ask their clients to think in a self-defeating manner and then, in the midst of such thoughts, suddenly yell, "Stop!" The shout interrupts the thought process and makes it impossible to continue. The thought-stopping process comprises several components (Cormier et al., 2017); it teaches clients to progress from outer to inner control of negative thought patterns. It also helps clients replace self-defeating thoughts with assertive, positive, or neutral ones.
- **Cognitive restructuring.** Among the most effective cognitive-behavioral techniques is cognitive restructuring, which includes stress inoculation and thought

stopping. In cognitive restructuring clients are taught to identify, evaluate, and change self-defeating or irrational thoughts that negatively influence their behavior. This process is accomplished by getting them to vocalize their self-talk and then change it, when necessary, from negative to neutral or positive. This technique is like Ellis's (1962) and Beck's (1976) proposals for modifying thought processes.

Reflective Question

How difficult do you think it is to teach individuals to cognitively change or restructure their thoughts? Why?

DIVERSITY AND MULTICULTURAL ISSUES

Cognitive therapy and CBT approaches are applicable to diverse populations because they let clients take the lead in assessing whether their thoughts and beliefs are appropriate to their cultures. A number of studies have shown the positive use of cognitive and cognitive-behavioral counseling approaches with a variety of populations including African American and Latino men as well as with Malaysians and Chinese (Pantalone et al., 2010; Sharf, 2016; Shea & Leong, 2013; Wilson & Cottone, 2013).

Cognitive therapy and CBT approaches may also be appropriate for both men and women in dealing with gender-specific concerns as well as concerns in general (Sokol & Fox, 2019). LGBTQIA clients may also benefit from this approach (Hall et al., 2019). By examining their beliefs, men and women may better understand the cognitive distortions that hinder their overall functioning. The only major drawback in this regard is that some clients may become dependent on their counselors to structure sessions and help them examine their beliefs, thus failing to become empowered.

Reflective Question

French philosopher Rene Descartes founded his views on human nature on thinking. How can thinking make a person or group a counselor works with more functional and aware of the diversity of others around them?

EVALUATION OF THE THEORIES

Strengths and Contributions

Cognitive therapy and CBT are both focused on teaching clients how to identify and monitor their thoughts and behaviors and to change or modify them. For instance, Clark and Beck (2012) have published an anxiety and worry workbook that provides readers with practical strategies for identifying their anxiety triggers and challenging the thoughts and beliefs that lead to distress. In addition, cognitive and cognitive-behavioral therapists have published workbooks for clients and instructional guides for clinicians in numerous private and public settings including schools (Creed et al., 2011). Overall, both approaches are proactive, providing training to clients that helps them prepare for and then successfully deal with a variety of specific and general problems.

Another contribution of these counseling theories is that they demystify the process and techniques associated with choice and change. Clients realize that to become someone different and act in a more functional manner, they have to think, behave, and feel in ways that are different from those of the past.

Cognitive therapy and CBT are also generally empowering for clients. When they learn new ways to think and behave, they are free to generalize their learning to new situations and end their treatment. For example, CBT has been found to be an excellent treatment for all types of eating disorders with those receiving help generalizing their behaviors to not only eat a variety of foods but also to eat out in public at restaurants (Fursland et al., 2012).

Furthermore, cognitive therapy and CBT are applicable to a wide range of client disorders, such as depression, guilt, phobias, distress, and pain. Because they work with children, adolescents, adults, and the aging, they are beneficial for a large group of clients. Cognitive therapy and CBT have published a plethora of research documenting the effectiveness of these approaches (Clark & Beck, 2010; Dobson & Dozois, 2019) and comparing cognitive-behavioral therapy with other brief therapeutic approaches such as short-term psychoanalytic psychotherapy (STPP) (Bhar & Beck, 2009).

A fifth strength of cognitive and CBT approaches is they have set up training centers like the Academy of Cognitive Therapy (Dodson et al., 2005) to identify and credential mental health professionals who demonstrate competence in cognitive therapy. By setting up training centers, cognitive counseling has ensured its future, thus strengthening its place as a major player in professional therapeutic circles.

Finally, behaviorism is the foundation for two postmodern theories:

- **Dialectical behavior therapy** (DBT)—a behaviorally based treatment to teach people how to live in the moment, develop healthy ways to cope with stress, regulate their emotions, and improve their relationships with others; it is often used in treating mood disorders, suicidal ideation, and negative behavioral patterns such as self-harm and substance abuse.
- **Acceptance and commitment therapy** (ACT)—a psychological intervention that uses acceptance and mindfulness strategies, together with commitment and behavior change strategies, to increase psychological flexibility—that is, being in the moment.

Limitations and Criticisms

Clients cannot be psychotic or disabled by present problems if they are to succeed with cognitive or cognitive-behavioral approaches. Both cognitive and CBT methods depend on clients being able to think clearly.

Another drawback is that clients must be motivated and willing to complete systematic homework assignments. Change comes about as a result of practice. Clients must be willing to work on their own as well as with their therapists.

In addition, clients must possess a repertoire of behavioral skills and responses or be able to learn such behaviors. Clients who cannot or will not apply what they know or learn are not good candidates for these approaches.

Finally, cognitive therapy and CBT do not explore to any great extent the past influences in clients' lives, including the unconscious or underlying conflicts. Even though surface thoughts and behaviors may be of greatest concern and may be most susceptible to change, previous difficulties and the history behind them may be pertinent as well.

Reflective Question

Homework is helpful in learning. If you have ever had to memorize something you know repetition over time helps, and that often means doing homework. When have you engaged in homework to master a behavioral or a cognitive-behavioral skill? Describe the experience.

TREATING LINDA WITH COGNITIVE AND COGNITIVE-BEHAVIORAL THERAPY

Conceptualization

From a cognitive and cognitive-behavioral perspective, Linda is having difficulty with her life because of her thinking. She is using demoralizing or depressing self-statements. In many ways she is repeating in her own mind what her father, her former husband, and even some of her bosses have said to her—for example, "You are no good unless you obey us" or "Women are inferior and will never amount to anything." These thoughts have become automatic and have prevented Linda from doing anything constructive with her life. In fact, these thoughts have led her to contemplate suicide. Thus Linda has labeled herself a failure and has acted accordingly. She has sabotaged her own life by not venturing out or speaking out. Indeed, she has engaged in catastrophizing and negative predictions to the point that these mental distortions now control her life.

Treatment Process

As a cognitive or cognitive-behavioral therapist you work in collaboration with Linda to select goals and to bring about change. You encourage Linda to examine her beliefs functionally, using a Socratic method to determine which beliefs are correct and which are incorrect. For instance, in mulling over the idea that women are inferior and will never amount to anything, Linda quickly dismisses such a notion as she thinks of famous historical and contemporary women who have been high achievers.

As you engage Linda in this way, you are also helping her see the link between thoughts and feelings; if she gives herself negative messages, she is going to depress herself. You urge Linda to keep a written record of her thoughts so that she can see what messages she is sending herself.

In addition to helping Linda decipher and challenge the automatic negative thoughts that are most pervasive in her life, you help her cognitively rehearse healthy thoughts. You use the CBT technique of self-instructional training, in which you perform a task or engage in appropriate behavior while verbalizing aloud the reasons behind what you are doing—for example, behaving civilly to someone you dislike. Linda then does the same task or behavior, at first giving herself instructions aloud and then performing the action while whispering self-instructions. Finally, she does the task silently.

You also teach Linda stress inoculation as a preventive technique. In this procedure you teach her a set of coping skills to help her handle stressful events like interacting with sexist men and her father. In addition, you instruct Linda on how to thought stop so that she does not persist in her negative thinking. By the end of therapy, Linda is engaged in healthy thinking, and her actions reflect a woman who is much more self-confident and realistic about who she is and what she can do.

SUMMING UP

Cognitive therapy and CBT approaches to treatment are some of the most creative and effective in counseling. They are based on the belief that cognitions are directly related to behaviors and in the case of CBT that beliefs are behaviors. As a rule, cognitive and cognitive-behavioral therapies are straightforward and successful with a wide variety of clients; the results can be seen in a timely and concrete way. In addition, the number of sessions involved is usually minimal, and the outcomes are usually long lasting.

Although Beck's approach to cognitive therapy provides a common ground for linking psychodynamic and behavior therapies (Beck & Weishaar, 2019), cognitive therapy and CBT are distinct in their emphasis. They focus on the present as opposed to the past, and they target specific behaviors instead of general ways of acting. Furthermore, they continue to evolve in their techniques and processes. A common misconception of these approaches is that they neglect emotions; however, they do deal with the affective by attending to the cognitive and cognitive-behavioral aspects of life first.

Overall, Beck's cognitive approach and Meichenbaum's cognitive-behavioral therapy are among the most used and useful theories in practice today. They will most likely continue to gain in popularity because of their pragmatic nature and their applicability to the concerns of many clients. Their suitability for people of both genders, all ages and stages of life, and multiple cultures adds to the prestige and practicality of these counseling approaches.

CHAPTER 9 RECAP: COGNITIVE THERAPY AND COGNITIVE-BEHAVIORAL THERAPY

Major Theorists
Aaron Beck, Judith Beck, Donald Meichenbaum, Neil Jacobson
Arnold Lazarus, Michael J. Mahoney, Marvin Goldfried

View of Human Nature/Personality
Problems caused by dysfunctional automatic thoughts and schemata
Examples of dysfunctional cognitions: all-or-nothing thinking, selective
    abstractions, overgeneralization, magnification and minimization, person-
    alization, labeling and mislabeling, catastrophizing

Role of the Counselor
Function as experts and educators on cognitions, behaviors, emotions
Allow clients to examine their beliefs
Collaborate in helping clients formulate new cognitive strategies

Goals
Monitor negative/automatic thoughts
Recognize relationship between thoughts, emotions, behaviors
Individualize approaches

Process and Techniques
Establish client-counselor relationship
Understand events, record thoughts, challenge distortions, implement new ways of thinking
Utilize varied techniques: specifying automatic thoughts, homework, cognitive interventions, cognitive rehearsals, scriptotherapy, self-instruction training, stress inoculation, thought stopping, and cognitive restructuring

Diversity and Multicultural Issues
Applicable to multiple populations
Appropriate for gender concerns
Hindered by potential dependence

Strengths and Contributions
Teaches clients to identify and modify thoughts and behaviors
Approaches therapy proactively
Demystifies the process of choice and change
Empowers clients
Applies to a wide range of clients and disorders
Strong research base especially for depression and anxiety
Focused on symptom removal in the present
Supported by many behavioral procedures
Based on learning theory and well researched
Effective for certain disorders
Increasing in sophistication and effectiveness
Can be combined with other theoretical positions
Foundation for Dialectical Behavior Theory & Acceptance & Commitment Therapy

Limitations and Criticisms
Requires at least average intelligence for maximum effectiveness
Excludes many psychotic or mentally disabled clients
Necessitates systematic homework
Favors clients with behavioral skills and learning ability
Does not explore past influences or the unconscious

KEY TERMS

LEARNING MORE

A number of periodicals are devoted to the theory, research, and practice of cognitive and cognitive-behavioral therapy.

Behavioural and Cognitive Psychotherapy
Cognitive & Behavioral Practice
Cognitive Therapy and Research
Journal of Cognitive Psychotherapy: An International Quarterly

In addition, several training institutes enable clinicians to learn cognitive and cognitive-behavioral processes and skills.

Beck Institute for Cognitive Therapy and Research
GSB Building
City Line and Belmont Avenues, Suite 700
Bala Cynwyd, PA: 19004-1610 http://www.beckinstitute.org

American Institute for Cognitive Therapy
136 East 57th Street, Suite 1101
New York, NY 10022 www.CognitiveTherapyNYC.com

National Association of Cognitive-Behavioral Therapy http://www.nacbt.org

CLASSROOM ACTIVITIES

1. Think about the following situations and try to assess how distorted or realistic your thoughts are about each: a wedding, a funeral, the birth of a baby, a graduation, moving. How do your thoughts impact your feelings and behaviors?
2. Cognitive therapy and CBT have grown in their influence because of a strong research base. Find a journal article on either approach and critique it. Present to the class the findings of the article and your evaluation of how the research was conducted.
3. How are the cognitive therapy and cognitive-behavioral counseling approaches similar? How do they differ? What do you think the future of each is likely to be, either separately or combined? Why?

10

Rational Emotive Behavior Therapy (REBT)

■ ■ ■

He measured his words out carefully
like a fine chef contemplating cups of confection
for he wanted to be as perfect in his speech
as he was for the cakes.
But as he spoke, he mumbled
his sentence structure crumbled
as he awkwardly asked for a raise
in a room that felt much too hot.
Imperfection won the day
but with a smile he walked away
knowing, like Albert Ellis, he had done his best
and his mind deserved a rest
before he practiced and tried again.

"Imperfection" © S. T. Gladding

CHAPTER OVERVIEW

From reading this chapter you will learn about

- The effects of rational and irrational beliefs.
- The ABCs of rational emotive behavior therapy.
- The primary emphases of REBT.

As you read, consider

- When you have seen others have irrational thoughts and how they have impacted decision making.
- How you might think of a situation from a positive, negative, neutral, and mixed perspective.
- How REBT compares to cognitive therapy, which was covered in the previous chapter.

Rational emotive behavior therapy (REBT) originally was known as rational therapy (RT). Albert Ellis changed its name to rational-emotive therapy (RET) in 1961 and then changed its name again in 1993 to rational emotive behavior therapy to better reflect what the theory actually did—focus on behaviors as well as cognitions (Backx, 2011).

Although the name change came in 1993, the various forms of REBT had been evolving for decades (Dryden, 1994). While it initially was more similar to the cognitive therapy of Aaron Beck than to any other counseling approach, REBT evolved. That is why it is treated on its own here.

MAJOR THEORIST: ALBERT ELLIS

Albert Ellis (1913–2007), the founder of rational emotive behavior therapy (REBT), was once described by Weinrach (1980) as "abrasive, impatient, and lacking in some of the basic social graces that my mother spent hours indoctrinating me with" but also as "brilliant, sensitive, perceptive, humorous, and stimulating" (p. 152). That Ellis fit both descriptions is partially the result of his life experience.

Albert Ellis was born into a Jewish family in Pittsburgh, Pennsylvania; his parents eventually had a daughter and another son. In his early childhood, Ellis's family moved to New York City, where Albert spent most of the rest of his life. Ellis described his father in positive and neutral terms, although the elder Ellis was often absent from home. From his father Ellis thought he acquired his intelligence, drive, and persistence (Newhorn, 1978). His mother was quite independent for her time, often idiosyncratic in her behavior as well as happy and nonsmothering. Ellis described her way of parenting as benign neglect (Dryden, 1989).

At the age of 5, Ellis almost died from tonsillitis and later suffered from acute nephritis and diabetes (Dryden, 1989; Morris & Kanitz, 1975). He thought most members of his family were crazy and by the age of 7, he was largely on his own (Weinrach, 1980). Ellis's parents divorced when he was 12 years old, which caused him to give up plans to be a Hebrew teacher. As a result, he became a self-described probabilistic atheist—someone who does not believe God exists but would accept empirical evidence to the contrary.

Ellis's dream as an adolescent was to become a writer. He planned to make enough money to retire early in life and then devote his time to writing. In 1934, he graduated in business from the City College of New York and worked in the business world until the mid-1940s. When not working, he wrote fiction, but his literary efforts proved unsuccessful, and he decided to study psychology. From Columbia University, Ellis received a master's degree in 1943 and a PhD in clinical psychology in 1947.

Ellis wanted to become a psychoanalytic clinical psychologist, a wish that was frustrated at first because institutions that specialized in such training admitted only medical professionals. He finally succeeded in obtaining his own analysis from the Karen Horney group and practiced classic psychoanalysis in the early 1950s. Dissatisfied with that approach, Ellis formulated and began practicing his own theory in 1955 (Backx, 2011; Hickey & Doyle, 2018).

Rational emotive behavior therapy was primarily a cognitive theory in the beginning. Its main tenets were first published in Ellis's *Reason and Emotion in Psychotherapy* (1962). REBT has since broadened its base considerably and now includes behavioral and emotional concepts.

Ellis established a nonprofit institute to promote REBT—the Albert Ellis Institute. A prolific writer, he produced more than 500 articles, 50 books, and numerous films and tapes (Ellis, 2019). Up until his death Ellis's weekly schedule included as many as 80 clients for individual sessions and up to eight group sessions. Annually, he gave about 200 workshops and talks. Despite such a workload, Ellis did not consider himself a compulsive professional because he did not have to work or prove himself (Weinrach, 1980). He relaxed by reading, listening to music, and socializing.

Ellis was married twice and stated that he learned something about himself and the nature of women from both marriages. Starting in 1964, he had a solid love/companionship relationship with Janet Wolfe, who helped him build the Albert Ellis Institute. Besides being a devout practitioner of his own theory, Ellis was recognized in professional circles in many ways, including being named Humanist of the Year by the American Humanist Association. Although he was flamboyant in a humorous and startling manner, Ellis was affectionate and warm too (Dryden, 1989). Indeed, he was a man of contrasts who saw ways of combining ideas that, on the surface, might appear to clash, such as religion and REBT (Powell, 1976).

VIEW OF HUMAN NATURE/PERSONALITY

REBT assumes that people are both "inherently rational and irrational, sensible and crazy" (Weinrach, 1980, p. 154). According to Ellis (1995), this duality in people is biologically inherent and is perpetuated unless a new way of thinking is learned (Dryden, 1994). **Irrational thinking**, or as Ellis defines it, **irrational Beliefs (iBs)**, may include the invention of upsetting and disturbing thoughts regarding self, others, and life. Examples of such beliefs are: "I'm a product of my past. I cannot change anything. I've always been this way" and "It's easier to avoid than to face this problem; hopefully, it will just go away." These fallacies and others like them have been used in formulating various tests, which have been correlated "with various kinds of emotional disturbance" (Ellis, 1984, p. 266). Ellis organizes irrational beliefs under three main headings:

- "I absolutely must perform important tasks well and be approved by significant others, or else I am an inadequate, pretty worthless person!" Result: severe feelings of anxiety, depression, and demoralization, often leading to severe inhibition.
- "Other people, especially my friends and relatives, truly must treat me kindly and fairly, or else they are rotten, damnable people!" Result: severe feelings of anger, rage, fury, often leading to fights, child abuse, assault, rape, murder, and genocide.
- "The condition under which I live absolutely must be comfortable, unhassled, and enjoyable, or else it's awful, I can't stand it, and my life is hardly worth living!" Result: severe feelings of low frustration tolerance, often leading to compulsion, addiction, avoidance, inhibition, and public reaction. (Ellis, 1996b, p. 77)

Although Ellis did not deal with the developmental stages of individuals, he thought that children are more vulnerable to outside influences and irrational thinking than adults are. He believed that human beings are by nature gullible, highly suggestible, and easily disturbed. Overall, people have within themselves the means to control their thoughts, feelings, and actions, but they must first realize what they are telling themselves (i.e., **self-talk**) to gain command of their lives (Ellis, 1962). This matter is one of personal, conscious awareness; the unconscious mind is not involved.

Ellis believed that it is a mistake for people to evaluate or rate themselves beyond the general idea that everyone is a fallible human being. He especially discouraged the use of any form of the verb "to be" (e.g., is, was, am, has been, being) to describe a person. He reasoned that human problems do not come from the id, as Freud envisioned, or from the what if, but rather from the is; the verb "to be" makes it difficult to separate people from their actions. Therefore, Ellis advocated that individuals speak and think of their behavior as separate from their personhood—for example, "I act badly" rather than "I am bad" (Ellis & Harper, 1975). Avoiding the verb "to be" fosters a more rational thought process and gives a person the freedom to change, to focus on altering specific behaviors instead of overhauling personality.

Reflective Question

What do you think of Ellis's idea about calling yourself a fallible human being and not using the verb "to be" to describe yourself? What are the strengths to such an approach? What are the drawbacks?

ROLE OF THE COUNSELOR

In the REBT approach counselors are active, direct, provocative, and confrontational (Backx, 2011). They are instructors who teach and correct clients' cognitions. Countering a deeply ingrained belief requires more than logic; it requires consistent attention and repetition (Krumboltz, 1992). Therefore, REBT therapists listen carefully for illogical or faulty statements from their clients and challenge them. In the process, they show concern and care for their clients by "attending to their behavior, by frequently asking questions for clarification, by recalling personal details about the client and his or her problems, by the use of gentle humor, and by active attempts to help the client solve difficult issues" (Vernon, 1996, p. 122).

Ellis (1980) and Walen et al. (1992) have identified several characteristics desirable for REBT counselors. They should be bright, knowledgeable, empathetic, respectful, genuine, concrete, persistent, scientific, interested in helping others, and involved in using REBT themselves. They should also adopt the humanistic core REBT philosophies of unconditional self-acceptance, unconditional other-acceptance, and unconditional life-acceptance (Ellis & Ellis, 2019). A counselor's main assessment instrument is the evaluation of a client's thinking. Some formal tests may be employed to measure rational and irrational thinking, but the evaluation process is primarily accomplished in counselor-client sessions. As a rule, REBT practitioners do not rely heavily on the diagnostic categories in the *DSM*.

Reflective Question

Why is it important that REBT counselors use the theory in their daily life if they are going to practice it?

GOALS

The primary goals of REBT focus on helping people realize that they can live more rational and productive lives. In general, rational emotive behavior therapy constitutes "an attempt to correct mistakes in a client's reasoning as a way of eliminating undesirable emotions" (Cohen, 1987, p. 37).

REBT is heavily influenced by stoic philosophy, and Ellis was fond of quoting a first-century stoic, Epictetus: "Men feel disturbed not by things, but by the views which they take of them." Thus individuals often disturb themselves by changing wishes and desires into demands. Ellis points out that when people use words such as "must," "ought to," "have to," and "need," they make demands of wishes and think irrationally. For individuals who think that wishes must or should occur, a wish unfulfilled results in a catastrophe. REBT helps clients stop catastrophizing and making such demands. Clients in REBT may express some negative feelings, but a major goal is to help them avoid a more emotional response than is warranted by the event.

Another goal of REBT is to help people change self-defeating habits of thought or behavior. One way this goal is accomplished is through the ABCs of REBT: A signifies an activating experience, B represents how the person thinks about the experience, and C is the emotional reaction to B (see Figure 10.1).

Many clients believe that an experience directly causes feelings—a concept called **cognitive bypass**. Left out of this conceptualization is the thought process that leads to the development of emotions. For example, a person may lose a job or an opportunity and then assert that the experience caused depression. REBT helps people recognize their emotional anatomy—that is, how feelings are attached to thoughts.

Thoughts about experiences may be characterized in four ways: positive, negative, neutral, or mixed. A positive thought leads to positive feelings. For example, if a host at a party reminds a man that he has had too much to drink, the man may think about the host's care and concern on his behalf and have positive emotions. On the other hand, the man may think that the host is criticizing him and has no right to do so, resulting in negative feelings about that same experience. If the latter thought process occurs, the man becomes angry. With a neutral thought, the man might simply note the host's actions and move on to another thought, having no emotional reaction. Mixed thoughts occur when a person has both negative and positive thoughts at once—for example, "I'm glad something was said, but I dislike the way it was said." The resulting feeling is ambivalence.

REBT encourages clients to be more tolerant of themselves and others, for everyone is a fallible human being. People are encouraged through REBT to achieve personal goals, rather than dwell on mistakes or miscues. Such goals are accomplished when individuals learn to think rationally, to change self-defeating behavior, and to unconditionally accept themselves.

A	B	C
Events	Thoughts	Feelings

	1. Positive
	2. Negative
	3. Neutral
	4. Mixed

Figure 10.1 The ABC model of human interaction

Reflective Question

Keep a chart for a couple of days on how often you use "must," "should," and "ought." See if you can avoid using these words and what a difference it makes.

PROCESS AND TECHNIQUES

The two primary emphases of REBT are teaching and disputing. Before any changes can be made, clients must learn the basic ideas of REBT and understand how thoughts are linked to emotions and behaviors. Consequently, REBT is highly didactic and very directive. In the first few sessions, counselors teach their clients the anatomy of an emotion—that is, feelings are a result of thoughts, not events, and self-talk influences emotions. This process, generally known as **rational emotive education** (REE), has had a high success rate with children, adolescents, and adults with a wide variety of problems and from a wide range of backgrounds (Wilde, 1996).

It is also critical in the REBT process that clients be able to dispute irrational thoughts. Disputing thoughts and beliefs takes one of three forms—cognitive, imaginal, or behavioral—and is most effective when all three forms are used (Walen et al., 1992). **Cognitive disputation** involves the use of direct questions, logical reasoning, and persuasion. Direct questions challenge clients to prove that their responses are logical. Sometimes these inquiries use the word "why," which is seldom employed in other counseling approaches because it puts many people on the defensive and closes off exploration. However, why questions help REBT clinicians cut through defenses and educate clients to new ways of thinking, feeling, and behaving. For example, counselors might ask, "Why must you?" or "Why must that be so?" These inquiries help clients learn to distinguish between rational and irrational thoughts and appreciate the superiority of rational thoughts.

Another form of cognitive disputation involves the use of **syllogisms**, "a deductive form of reasoning consisting of two premises and a conclusion" (Cohen, 1987, p. 37). Syllogisms help clients and counselors more thoroughly understand inductive and deductive fallacies that underlie emotions. For example, in irrational can't-stand-it-ism the process might go as follows (Cohen, 1987, p. 39):

> Major premise: "Nobody can stand to be lied to."
> Minor premise: "I was lied to."
> Conclusion: "I can't stand it."
> Certainly being lied to is not pleasant, but it is often a part of life, and concluding "I can't stand it" is silly, false, and illogical.

Imaginal disputation depends on a client's ability to imagine and employs a technique known as **rational emotive imagery** (REI) (Maultsby, 1984). REI may be used in one of two ways. First, a client may be asked to imagine a situation in which she is likely to become upset and to examine her self-talk during that imagined situation. Then she is asked to envision the same situation but to be more moderate in her self-talk this time. Second, a counselor may ask a client to imagine a situation in which he feels or behaves in a different way from that of a real occurrence. The client is then instructed to examine the self-talk he used in this imagined situation. REI takes practice.

The **emotional control card (ECC)** is a device that helps clients reinforce and expand the practice of REI (Sklare, Taylor, & Hyland, 1985). Wallet-sized ECCs list four emotionally debilitating categories—anger, self-criticism, anxiety, and depression (Ellis, 1986). Under each category is a list of inappropriate or self-destructive feelings and a parallel list of appropriate or non-defeating feelings. In potentially troubling situations, clients can refer to the cards and change the quality of their feelings about the situations. At their next counseling sessions, clients can discuss the use of the cards in cognitively restructuring their thoughts from irrational to rational.

Behavioral disputation involves behaving in a way that is the opposite of the client's usual way of acting. Sometimes behavioral disputation takes the form of **bibliotherapy**, in which clients read a self-help book such as those distributed by the Albert Ellis Institute. At other times, behavioral disputation includes **role-playing** and completing a **homework** assignment in which clients do activities they previously considered impossible. In both cases, clients bring their completed assignments to their scheduled counseling sessions and evaluate them with their counselors.

If disputation of **irrational beliefs (iBs)** is successful, a new and effective philosophy will emerge. This philosophy will include a new cognitive Effect (cE), which is a restatement of original rational Beliefs (rBs). For example, "It is not awful, merely inconvenient, that I was rejected by a particular person."

Ellis has devised a number of homework assignments, such as **shame attack exercises,** to help clients learn to behave differently. These exercises usually include an activity that is harmless but dreaded, such as introducing oneself to a stranger or asking for a glass of water in a restaurant without ordering anything else. By participating in such exercises, clients learn the ABCs of REBT on a personal level and come to realize more fully that the world does not stop if a mistake is made or if a want remains unfulfilled (Ellis & Ellis, 2019). Clients also learn that others are fallible human beings and need not be perfect. Finally, clients learn that goals can be achieved without "awfulizing" or "terriblizing" personal situations.

In addition, Ellis frequently used puns and other humorous devices to help his clients see how irrational thinking develops and how silly the consequences of such thinking are. He cautioned clients not to "should on themselves" (a demand using the word "should," e.g., the world should be perfect), not to "awfulize" (characterizing an event as "awful," not just inconvenient), and advises people to avoid "musterbation" (an illogical mandate that a situation must be a certain way). Ellis even composed a number of songs to remind himself and others to think rationally.

Other REBT counselors, such as Richard Watts (1996b), have also written rational emotive behavior therapy songs to common tunes—"I've Been Working on the Railroad," "Jimmy Cracked Corn," "Twinkle, Twinkle, Little Star," and "O Susannah." These songs address cognitively distorted thoughts in a humorous and therapeutic way.

Reflective Question

Pick a familiar tune and write lyrics that are humorous and rational, such as the one that follows, to the melody of "I've Been Working on the Railroad."

"I've been working on my thinking all the live long day.
I've been working and not drinking and I believe that it's okay.

Can't you see me speaking rationally to everyone I meet
Don't you know I'm acting calmly and my mind is now upbeat!"

How do you think singing this song or another like it might be helpful to you or someone with whom you work? What are the drawbacks to such songs?

Two other powerful REBT techniques are **confrontation** and **encouragement**. As previously noted, REBT counselors explicitly encourage their clients to abandon thought processes that are not working. Sometimes counselors challenge or confront clients who claim to be thinking rationally but who are not. At other times, counselors encourage clients to continue working from an REBT base even when they are discouraged. Confrontation need not be done in the style of Ellis—that is, vigorously confronting and attacking a client's beliefs (Johnson, 1980). Instead, counselors can be empathetic and insistent at the same time.

DIVERSITY AND MULTICULTURAL ISSUES

Almost from its beginning, REBT has been concerned with its effectiveness as a treatment with multicultural and diverse populations (Dryden & Bernard, 2019). In the 1970s, Ellis (1977) provided research data on the effectiveness of REBT with different types of clients in specific settings across the life span. His research has since been verified in numerous settings (e.g., Deen et al., 2017; Johnson, 2013). In addition, REBT counselors are generally sensitive to their clients' cultures and adjust their actions to respect those they are helping (Sharf, 2016). James and Gilliland (2003) summarized REBT effectiveness with minority culture clients and revealed that it was usually positive.

REBT is also attuned to the needs and specific concerns of women (O'Kelly & Gilson, 2019). Because REBT practitioners realize that women may be stereotyped according to their gender and gender roles, REBT counselors give female clients a voice as to what they will work on (e.g., assertiveness, career, life change, stress) and how (e.g., in a group or individually).

Reflective Question

Is thinking enough to become aware of diversity or do other factors, such as behavior, have to be a part of the process?

EVALUATION OF THE THEORY

Strengths and Contributions

One of the major strengths of REBT is that it is clear, easily learned, and effective. Most clients have few problems in understanding the principles or terminology of REBT. Furthermore, REBT is effective with many different types of individuals, including adolescents, and can be used as a preventive approach to mental health in educational settings (Banks, 2011). Moreover, Seligman and Reichenberg (2014) note REBT is appropriate for the treatment of affective disorders, anxiety disorders, and adjustment disorders.

A second strength of REBT is that it can easily be combined with other behavioral techniques to help clients experience more fully what they are learning (Ellis, 2002). REBT is like cognitive-behavioral counseling in that it borrows and integrates other techniques that are compatible with its theoretical foundation.

Another asset of REBT is that it is relatively short term, usually lasting 10 to 50 sessions. Thereafter, clients can continue to use the approach on a self-help basis. Thus the economy and efficiency of REBT is impressive (Ellis, 1996b; Ellis & Ellis, 2011).

Moreover, REBT has generated a great deal of literature and research for clients and counselors. Few other theories have developed as much bibliotherapy material; Ellis was a prolific writer and researcher, as are many other REBT practitioners today. Each year the Albert Ellis Institute produces a catalog filled with an array of books, booklets, audiotapes, and videotapes on rational emotive behavior therapy. In addition, Ellis's institute is constantly engaged in empirical studies on the use of REBT with a wide variety of clients.

A final strength of REBT is that it has continued to evolve over the years as its processes and techniques have been refined. An example of this evolution is found in the difference between inelegant and elegant REBT (Dryden, 2010). **Inelegant REBT**, which developed first, focuses on the activating event and the distortions that clients usually have about such events (Ellis, 1977, 1995). It does not give clients any coping strategies for dealing with situations in which perception matches reality. Instead, clients are encouraged to assure themselves that they will do better in the future or that they are good persons. **Elegant REBT**, on the other hand, concentrates on the beliefs of clients and focuses on their taking responsibility for their own feelings. In the process, clients realize that success in everything is not essential and that catastrophe does not result from every unfulfilled want.

Limitations and Criticisms

One drawback to REBT is that it cannot be used effectively with individuals who have mental problems or cognitive limitations, such as those with schizophrenia and those with severe thought disorders. Nor is it productive with people who are severely mentally impaired. Intellectually bright individuals benefit most from this approach.

Another limitation of REBT is that it may be too closely associated with its founder, Albert Ellis. Many individuals have difficulty separating the theory from Ellis's eccentricities. Although Johnson (1980) urges counselors to adapt the theory and its techniques to their own personalities and individual styles of counseling, some therapists still eschew the approach because of its connection with Ellis.

REBT also has limited usefulness if its practitioners do not combine its cognitive base with more behavioral and emotive techniques. Ellis says that REBT has always been a diverse approach, and he advocates its use in various settings. Indeed, the theory is now much broader than it was originally, but some counselors still concentrate on the cognitive side of REBT, thus limiting its effectiveness.

Furthermore, REBT's direct and confrontive approach to clients may be a limitation for some individuals. There is the potential for counselors to be overzealous and pushy, with the result that clients may resist change more strongly than might otherwise be the case and/or drop out of treatment.

Yet another drawback to REBT is its lack of a strong research base. The theory makes sense intuitively, but it has not been well researched as some other theories. For example, research on the effectiveness of REBT pales when compared to Beck's cognitive therapy, which is similar in its emphasis on the therapeutic importance of changing client thinking.

Finally, REBT's emphasis on changing thinking may not be the simplest way of helping clients change their behaviors or emotions. Gestalt theorists would challenge REBT and charge that emotions should be experienced before interventions are made.

TREATING LINDA WITH RATIONAL EMOTIVE BEHAVIOR THERAPY

Conceptualization

From the perspective of rational emotive behavior therapy (REBT), Linda is demonstrating her inherently rational and irrational sides through her thoughts, feelings, and behaviors. This duality is to be expected, but Linda is unduly upsetting herself with her irrational beliefs that life is not worth living and that she is worthless. Linda's negative self-talk is dangerous to her well-being, as is her assessment of herself as inadequate.

Treatment Process

As an REBT therapist, you work actively to teach Linda the ABCs of REBT. You show her that events do not cause feelings but thoughts do, and she has a choice as to how she is going to think—with positive, negative, neutral, or mixed thoughts. Right now, she is engaged almost exclusively in negative thinking. As a user of REBT yourself, you show genuine concern for Linda and build rapport with her by asking questions and using gentle humor. You even give her a personal example of how REBT has helped you.

You talk with Linda about how the use of words such as "must," "should," "ought," "have to," and "need" make demands of wishes and lead to irrational thinking. You also work with her on not responding more emotionally to an event than is warranted. You then teach Linda how to dispute thoughts—cognitively, imaginably, and behaviorally. She decides that she will dispute cognitively, and when things do not go her way, she will ask herself why questions—for example, "Why must things go my way?" By engaging herself in this way, she empowers herself.

To help Linda even more, you give her some of the bibliotherapy writings from REBT practitioners. You also encourage her to monitor her thoughts regularly and to challenge irrational ones. Treatment ends when Linda is more rational in her thinking and playful in her outlook. Through REBT, she can see that the world will not end if her family does not become more functional or her workplace friendlier. On the other hand, she has become more aware that she can take control of her thoughts and the emotions and behaviors that go with them. She uses this knowledge to explore new vocational possibilities, new clubs and community activities in which she has an interest, and new and appropriate relationships with men.

SUMMING UP

Rational emotive behavior therapy is a popular approach in the helping professions. It makes use of affective, behavioral, and cognitive methods to bring about change. A primary focus of this approach is teaching clients to realize that feelings are derived from thoughts, not events.

REBT stresses role-play and homework assignments as well as recognition of thoughts. Disputations are employed to counteract faulty, irrational thinking and help clients take control of their lives. REBT is both a psychoeducational and a psychotherapeutic means of promoting change in clients.

CHAPTER 10 RECAP: RATIONAL EMOTIVE BEHAVIOR THERAPY

Major Theorist
Albert Ellis

View of Human Nature/Personality
People are inherently rational and irrational.
Thoughts, not events, cause disturbances.
People trouble themselves by using the verb "to be."

Role of the Counselor
Teaches, confronts, corrects
Concentrates on clients' self-talk
Challenges irrational thinking
Encourages tolerance and acceptance of self and others

Goals
Live more rational and productive lives
Stop making demands of self and others
Recognize irrational thinking and its consequences
Change self-defeating habits
Become more tolerant of self and others
Have unconditional self-acceptance

Process and Techniques
Teaching the anatomy of an emotion
Disputing thoughts and beliefs: cognitive, imaginal, and behavioral points of
    view
Using homework assignments

Diversity and Multicultural Issues
Sensitive and adaptive to client cultures
Sensitive to women's needs and concerns

Strengths and Contributions
Is direct, clear, effective, and easily learned
Combines well with other theories
Is short-term
Has a centralized training center
Continues to evolve

Limitations and Criticisms
Not applicable to all clients
Associated with unconventional theorist Albert Ellis
Still primarily cognitive
Direct and confrontive
Limited research on REBT's effectiveness

KEY TERMS

behavioral disputation   134
bibliotherapy   134
cognitive bypass   132
cognitive disputation   133
confrontation   135
elegant REBT   136
emotional control card (ECC)   134
encouragement   135
homework   134
inelegant REBT   136

irrational thinking, aka irrational
  beliefs (iBs)   130
rational emotive education
  (REE)   133
rational emotive imagery (REI)   133
role-playing   134
self-talk   130
shame attack exercises   134
syllogism   133

LEARNING MORE

A number of journals publish articles on the theory, research, and practice of REBT. However, the best journal devoted solely to REBT is the *Journal of Rational Emotive and Cognitive Behavior Therapy.*

Further training in the clinical practice of REBT is available:

Albert Ellis Institute
145 East 32nd Street, 9th floor
New York, NY 10016; https://albertellis.org/
(212) 535-0822

Rational-Emotive-Behavior Therapy Sites
https://positivepsychology.com/rational-emotive-behavior-therapy-rebt/
https://www.psycom.net/rebt/
https://www.healthline.com/health/rational-emotive-behavior-therapy

CLASSROOM ACTIVITIES

1. Compare an article or a book written by Albert Ellis in the 1970s and the 2000s. What differences in emphasis, if any, do you notice? Share your findings and impressions with classmates.
2. Using the ABC criteria, examine prominent thoughts you have about a person or an event. How were your thoughts modified using this method?
3. With a classmate make up a humorous rational song set to a familiar and popular tune. Perform your song before the class. What is your underlying message? How do you think your song might help you be more rational in the future?

11

Transactional Analysis

■ ■ ■

He acted like a child running wild
talking trash with a bottle in his hand
and liquor on his breath.
She was smart, played the part of a grown-up,
calming him down, while giving him coffee.
In the middle of what was chaos
quiet reigned again.

"Chaos and Calm" © S. T. Gladding

CHAPTER OVERVIEW

From reading this chapter you will learn about

■ The three major ego states in transactional analysis: parent, adult, and child.
■ The four major methods of understanding and predicting human behavior: structural analysis, transactional analysis, game analysis, and script analysis.
■ The three levels on which transactions may occur: complementary, crossed, or ulterior.

As you read, consider

■ How similar and distinct transactional analysis is from classic psychoanalysis.
■ How useful the language of transactional analysis is.
■ When you or others you know have been involved in playing games.

Some clinicians classify transactional analysis (TA) as an almost purely cognitive theory with a linkage to psychoanalysis. Others consider it a versatile and comprehensive system of psychotherapy (Widdowson, 2010). TA was formulated by Eric Berne in the early 1960s and rose to prominence after the publication of two best-selling books: Berne's *Games People Play* (1964) and Thomas Harris's *I'm OK, You're OK* (1967). Although Berne was fearful that the popularity of these books would undermine the seriousness of his work, they simply made the theory more attractive and familiar to the public.

Since the 1970s, TA has not been as popular in the United States as it has been in some other countries. One explanation is that the theory has not continued to evolve much, and research supporting it has been sparse. In addition, TA has suffered from the rise of cognitive therapy and REBT, both of which have had stronger proponents and a plethora of research supporting their use. Nevertheless, a number of practitioners still use TA in counseling, coaching, management, organizational development, and learning, and it is therefore important to understand (Cornell et al., 2018).

MAJOR THEORIST: ERIC BERNE

Eric Berne (1910–1970) was born in Montreal, Canada, where his father was a doctor and his mother was a writer and an editor. Berne was 5 years older than his only sibling, a sister. He was close to his father, who died at the age of 38, when Eric was only 9 years old. Berne followed in his father's footsteps, earning a medical degree from McGill University in 1935. He then completed a psychiatric residency at Yale, set up a private practice in Connecticut and New York, became a US citizen, and married. During World War II, he served as an army psychiatrist in Utah, where he started practicing group therapy.

After the war Berne settled in Carmel, California, where he separated from his wife and completed his first book, *The Mind in Action* (1947), which was a critical survey of psychiatry and psychoanalysis. In California, he resumed the psychoanalytic training he had started before the war, part of which was his own analysis, supervised by Erik Erikson. Erikson insisted that Berne not remarry until after the analysis was finished, and Berne complied. He remarried in 1949 and fathered two children, as he had in his first marriage. He built a study in his house away from the noise of the children and, in 1950, began a demanding schedule that included consultations and practice in Carmel, San Francisco, and Monterey. His only breaks occurred on Friday nights, when he played poker at his house.

In 1956, Berne was turned down for membership in the Psychoanalytic Institute, a rejection that proved to be a turning point in his life. He reacted by disassociating himself from psychoanalysis and devoting his time to the development of transactional analysis, which has a psychoanalytic aspect.

Dusay (1977) describes the formulation of TA in four phases. In the first (1955–1962) Berne developed the concept of **ego states**. His ideas were influenced by his clients' descriptions of behaving like a parent, an adult, or a child—the three ego states (as represented in the following diagram below with the parent ego state on top and the child ego state on the bottom).

(P) Parent
(A) Adult
(C) Child

In the second phase (1962–1966), Berne concentrated on transactions and games. The International Transactional Analysis Association was created in 1964, and Berne published the popular *Games People Play*. In the third phase (1966–1970), he emphasized the reasons some individuals choose to play certain games in life. In the fourth phase (from 1970 on), he and his followers emphasized action and energy distribution.

Berne was involved in the first three phases of TA development. After a second divorce in 1964, he spent a great deal of time writing; at one point, he was working on the manuscripts of six books and editing the *Transactional Analysis Bulletin*. He also gave numerous lectures and seminars. Berne's third marriage was short-lived; he died of a heart attack at the age of 60.

VIEW OF HUMAN NATURE/PERSONALITY

Transactional analysis is an optimistic theory: it assumes that people can change despite any unfortunate events of the past. According to Barrow (2007), TA is a kind of positive psychology because of its emphasis on optimism among other things. Regardless, besides stressing optimism TA is also anti-deterministic, proposing that people have choices in their lives and that what was once decided can be redecided. As James and Jongeward (1971) emphasize, "Transactional analysis is a rational approach to understanding behavior and is based on the assumption that all individuals can learn to trust themselves, think for themselves, make their own decisions, and express their feelings" (p. 12).

TA focuses on four major methods of understanding and predicting human behavior:

- **Structural analysis**—understanding what is happening within the individual.
- **Transactional analysis**—describing what happens between two or more people.
- **Game analysis**—understanding transactions that lead to bad feelings.
- **Script analysis**—understanding an individual's life plan.

Structural Analysis

In structural analysis each person is considered to have three functional ego states—child, parent, and adult. Berne (1964) defined an ego state as "a consistent pattern of feeling and experience directly related to a corresponding consistent pattern of behavior" (p. 364). He noted that the findings of Wilder Penfield (1952) and Penfield and Jasper (1954) supported this definition. Penfield, a neurosurgeon, found that an electrode applied to different parts of the brain evokes memories and feelings long forgotten by the person. The implication is that the brain functions like a tape recorder to preserve complete experiences in a sequential form recognizable as ego states.

The **child ego state**, the first to develop, is that part of the personality characterized by childlike behaviors and feelings. Childlike behavior might be described as inquisitive, affectionate, selfish, mean, playful, whiny, and manipulative. The child ego state consists of two subdivisions—the natural or free child and the adaptive child (Figure 11.1). The **natural child** is the part of the person that is spontaneous,

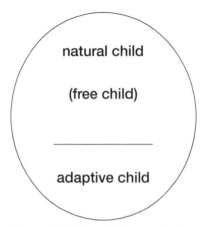

Figure 11.1 The child ego state

impulsive, feeling oriented, and often self-centered and pleasure loving. The natural child is also intuitive, creative, and responsive to nonverbal messages. The **adaptive child** is the compliant part of the personality that conforms to the wishes and demands of parental figures. These adaptations of natural impulses occur in response to traumas, natural life experiences, and training.

The **parent ego state** incorporates the attitudes and behaviors of parental figures— that is, the dos, shoulds, and oughts. Outwardly, these messages are expressed through critical or nurturing behavior. Parental messages are present throughout a person's life; any response to a thoughtful question that occurs within 10 seconds usually comes from the parent ego state. This ego state also consists of two subdivisions (Figure 11.2). The **nurturing parent** is the part that comforts, praises, and aids others. The **critical parent** is the part that finds fault, displays prejudices, disapproves, and prevents others from feeling good about themselves. These two parts are revealed in nonverbal behaviors such as pointing a finger at someone and in verbal statements such as "That's too bad, but don't worry."

The **adult ego state** is not subdivided or related to a person's age. It is the objective, thinking, data-gathering part of a person. The adult ego state tests reality, much as the ego does in Freud's system. The adult is rational and organized, functioning in some ways like a computer by processing data without feelings and expressing itself through phrases such as "I understand" and "I'm going to."

Sometimes the different ego states operate simultaneously. For example, a woman may observe an attractive man and go through the following self-dialogue: "He is really good looking and well spoken [adult], but he's probably stuck up [critical parent], although I've heard he's very sensitive [nurturing parent]. I wonder how I could attract him and get him to notice me [natural child]. Oops! I'd better stop looking and get back to work, or my boss will get mad at me [adaptive child]."

A major focus of transactional analysis is determining which ego state(s) a person is using. Although TA does not favor one ego state over another, the theory stresses the importance of being able to balance responses when necessary and appropriate. Those who constantly exhibit just one ego state do not function as well as those who are more flexible.

One way of assessing which ego state(s) a person employs most is by using an **egogram** (Dusay & Dusay, 1989). An egogram remains fixed unless an individual

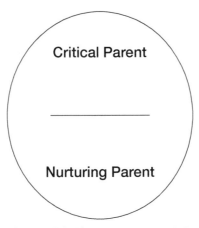

Figure 11.2 The parent ego state

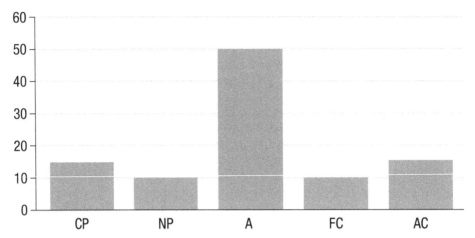

Figure 11.3 An egogram (of a person's interaction with others on a typical day) represented by percentages. CP—Critical Parent, NP—Nurturing Parent, A—Adult, FC—Free Child, AC—Adaptive Child

invests energy in changing response patterns. The egogram of a person who responds primarily from the adult ego state is shown in Figure 11.3.

Reflective Question

Make an egogram of your speech in different situations such as asking for a favor, ordering a meal, and recapping your day to a friend. What do you notice about the TA ego states you tend to use in these situations?

Transactional Analysis

The second way of understanding and predicting human behavior involves ego state transactions. In contrast to the intrapersonal focus of structural analysis, transactional analysis is interpersonal. Transactions may occur on one of three levels: complementary, crossed, or ulterior. In a complementary transaction both persons are operating either from the same ego state (e.g., child to child, adult to adult) or from complementary ego states (e.g., parent to child, adult to parent). In such cases, responses are predictable and appropriate.

An adult-to-adult transaction might look like this:

(P)   (P)

(A) What time is it? ⟶ (A)

⟵ It is 7 o'clock.

(C)   (C)

A child-to-child transaction would involve more playfulness:

(P)   (P)

(A)   (A)

(C) Let's go play with Billy. ⟶ (C)

⟵ Yeah! We could have lots of fun with him!

A parent-to-parent transaction, however, would be more nurturing or critical:

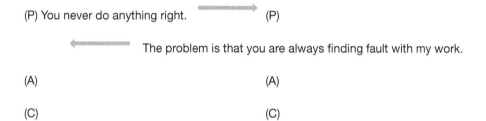

(P) You never do anything right. ⟶ (P)

⟵ The problem is that you are always finding fault with my work.

(A)   (A)

(C)   (C)

In a crossed transaction, an inappropriate ego state is activated, producing an unexpected response. Crossed transactions hurt, prompting individuals to withdraw from each other or switch topics. In a crossed transaction, one person might be operating from a child ego state and hoping for a complementary parent ego state response but might receive instead a comment from the other person's adult ego state:

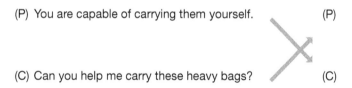

(P) You are capable of carrying them yourself. (P)

(C) Can you help me carry these heavy bags? (C)

An **ulterior transaction** is one in which two ego states operate simultaneously and one message disguises the other. Ulterior transactions appear to be complementary and socially acceptable even though they are not. For example, at the end of a date one person might say to the other, "Do you want to come in and listen to a little music?" On the surface this question might seem to be coming from an adult ego state, but in reality it is masking a child ego state: "Want to come in and have some fun together?"

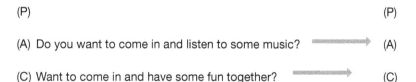

(P)   (P)

(A) Do you want to come in and listen to some music? ⟶ (A)

(C) Want to come in and have some fun together? ⟶ (C)

Game Analysis

Games are ulterior motivated transactions that appear complementary on the surface but end in bad feelings. Games confirm and reinforce script decisions (Tyrangiel, 2011). People play games to structure time, achieve recognition, make others predictable, and prevent intimacy. Because intimacy involves risks, games keep people safe from exposing their thoughts and feelings. There are first-degree, second-degree, and third-degree games, and all have predictable ends. Berne (1964) offers examples of each degree.

First-degree games are played in social circles with anyone who is willing to participate. They generally lead to mild upsets. An example of a first-degree game is Seducto, which can be exciting and fun initially. In this game, a male and a female enjoy an evening flirting with each other until one turns the other down and both leave feeling slightly uncomfortable.

A **second-degree game** occurs when the players go after bigger stakes, usually in more intimate circles, and end up with bad feelings. An example of a second-degree game is Uproar, in which two persons get angrier and angrier until one or both get very upset about being called a name or put down.

A **third-degree game** usually involves injury; the players end up in jail, the hospital, or the morgue. An example of this game is Cops and Robbers, in which people dare those in authority to catch them and yet leave clues about where they can be cornered. With each increasing degree, there is greater danger of permanent damage. Very few games have a positive or neutral outcome (Berne, 1964).

Individuals who play games operate from one of three positions: victim, persecutor, or rescuer (Karpman, 1968, 2014). To keep games going, people often assume new roles. For example, in the game Why Don't You/Yes, But, one person plays the rescuer, responding to a complaint from the victim by saying, "Why don't you … ?" The victim answers, "Yes, but … " When this game becomes tiresome, the rescuer may switch off to a persecuting role and respond sarcastically to the victim's complaint: "Ain't it awful!" Figure 11.4 represents the three positions people assume

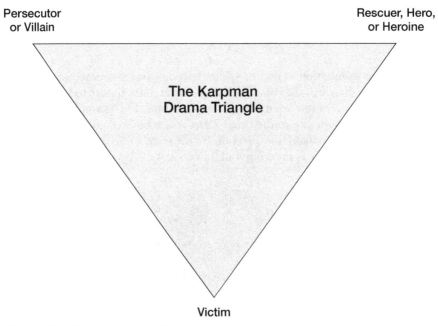

Figure 11.4 Karpman triangle

during game interactions. The list of possible games is almost endless, and it is easy for individuals to get hooked into playing them. In the end, however, game players avoid meaningful and healthy human interactions.

Reflective Question

What games have you observed in your life? Are some games more prevalent than others in certain situations? Describe their dynamics and give them a name.

Script Analysis

Berne contends that everyone makes a **life script** or **life plan** by the age of 5. These scripts, which determine how individuals interact with others, are based on interpretations of external events. Positive messages given to children function as permissions and do not limit them in any way. Negative messages or injunctions are more powerful and may become the basis for destructive scripts. Many parental injunctions begin with don't: "Don't question." "Don't contradict." "Don't play with them." Unless people make conscious attempts to overcome such injunctions, they may experience negative consequences.

Most life scripts revolve around giving and receiving **strokes** (i.e., verbal or physical recognition). Berne points out that negative strokes or punishments are better than no strokes at all—that is, being ignored. Strokes result in the accumulation of either good or bad feelings, known as **stamps**. When individuals collect enough stamps, they cash them in on certain behaviors. For example, a teenager may collect enough bad feelings from frequent failing grades to justify quitting school or enough good feelings from studying hard to justify attending a party. Healthy people give and receive positive strokes most often.

The following negative scripts are common:

- **Never scripts:** Individuals never get to do what they want (e.g., "Marriage is bad; never get married").
- **Until scripts:** Individuals must wait until a certain time to do something they want to do (e.g., "You cannot play until you have all your work done").
- **Always scripts:** Individuals tell themselves that they must continue doing what they have been doing (e.g., "You should always continue a job once you've started it").
- **After scripts:** Individuals expect difficulty after a certain event (e.g., "After age 40 life goes downhill").
- **Open-ended scripts:** Individuals do not know what they are supposed to do after a given time (e.g., "Be active while you're young").

There are also **miniscripts** that focus on minute-by-minute occurrences. Some of the most common miniscripts are "Be perfect," "Be strong," "Hurry up," "Try harder," and "Please someone." These five messages, called **drivers**, allow people to escape their life scripts, but the escape is only temporary.

You are OK with me

	I'm not OK You're OK One down position Feeling helpless "get away from"	I'm OK You're OK Healthy position Feeling happy "get on with"	
I'm not OK with me	I'm not OK You're not OK Hopeless position Feeling hopeless "get nowhere with"	I'm OK You're not OK One-up position Feeling angry "get rid of"	I'm OK with me

You are not OK with me

Figure 11.5 OK positions in transactional analysis

The ideal life script in TA terms is informed by the position **I'm OK, You're OK** (i.e., a get-on-with position) (Harris, 1967). But people may operate from three other positions: **I'm OK, You're not OK** (i.e., a get rid of position); **I'm not OK, You're OK** (i.e., a get away from position); and **I'm not OK, You're not OK** (i.e., a get nowhere position). Figure 11.5 shows these positions.

Everyone operates from each of these four positions at various times, but well-functioning individuals learn to recognize unhealthy positions and modify their thoughts and behaviors accordingly. Berne holds that life scripts can be rewritten if people become more conscious of what they are thinking and make concerted efforts to change.

Reflective Question

What miniscripts are you likely to give yourself when encouraged? When discouraged? When in doubt? When happy? When mad?

ROLE OF THE COUNSELOR

TA treatment assigns counselors the initial role of teacher. They must explain to their clients the language and the concepts of TA, a new way of thinking about self. Thereafter, counselors contract with clients for specific changes and help them achieve them. Counselors also help their clients obtain the tools or skills necessary for change and empower them through various techniques.

TA counselors do not rely heavily on formal psychological tests, although they do assess client functioning. However, assessment is usually done through an egogram or another less formal method. The purpose is to determine how clients are spending time and from which ego states they are operating. Diagnosis based on *DSM* categories is not stressed and is only done if necessary.

GOALS

The primary goals of TA focus on transforming clients from frogs into princes and princesses. It is not enough that clients learn to adjust, as in psychoanalysis. Instead, the emphasis is on attaining health and autonomy. Counselors help their clients identify and restore distorted or damaged ego states, develop the capacity to use all ego states, use the adult ego state with its reasoning powers, alter inappropriate life scripts, and adopt a position of "I'm OK, you're OK" (Berne, 1966).

In becoming autonomous, clients exhibit more awareness, intimacy, and spontaneity, become free of games, and eliminate self-defeating scripts. They become more in touch with their past but at the same time are freed from previous negative influences. One of Berne's most important contributions was to depathologize mental health issues by helping people see that the psychological symptoms they developed were the best options they had in childhood to try to take care of themselves (Steward & Joines, 2011, 2012). A major emphasis of TA is on learning about the self in order to decide what changes to make and whom one wishes to become (Goulding & Goulding, 1997).

PROCESS AND TECHNIQUES

TA has initiated a number of techniques for helping clients reach their goals. Most TA counselors begin with analysis—structural, transactional, game, and/or script—as described earlier. Other techniques include the following:

- **Treatment contract**—emphasizes agreed-upon responsibilities for both counselors and clients (Dusay & Dusay, 1989); reveals when counseling goals have been reached
- **Interrogation**—involves speaking to a client's adult ego state until an adult response is given; can be confrontational; can be ineffective, supplying only historical material
- **Specification**—identifies the ego state that initiated a transaction; takes place on an adult-to-adult level
- **Confrontation**—involves pointing out inconsistencies in client behavior or speech
- **Explanation**—teaches the client about some aspect of TA; occurs on an adult-to-adult ego state level
- **Illustration**—enlightens the client or elaborates on a point; may speak to both the child and the adult ego states
- **Confirmation**—points out recurrence of previously modified behavior; can be effective only when the client has a firmly established adult ego state
- **Interpretation**—explains to the child ego state of the client the reasons for the client's behavior; can be effective only when the client has a functioning adult ego state
- **Crystallization**—involves an adult-to-adult transaction in which the client becomes aware that game playing may be given up; frees the client; completes the TA process

Almost all the techniques in TA involve some combination of questioning, confrontation, and dialogue. The following questions are among those most frequently asked by TA counselors:

> What are the nicest and worst things your parents ever said to you? What is your earliest memory?
> What is the family story about your birth? What is your favorite fairy tale, story, or song? How would you describe your mother and father?
> How long do you expect to live?

To be most effective, TA counselors must always carefully assess the ego strengths of individual clients. Clients are usually capable of making new decisions about life once they discover different aspects of themselves.

TA was divided into three main schools of treatment in the 1970s: the **classical San Francisco** school (with an emphasis on explanation, diagrams, contracts, and behavioral change), the **cathexis** school (which emphasized confrontation and reparenting), and the **redecision** school (which emphasized the child's compliance with injunctions and the power to make new decisions) (Barnes, 1977). Today there are more than a dozen TA schools. Each represents a particular theoretical slant—for example, psychodynamic transactional analysis, constructivist transactional analysis, relational transactional analysis, and body-centered transactional analysis (Erskine, 2009). All these schools use contracts as their primary method of intervention and have autonomy as the final goal of treatment.

Reflective Question

Since almost all techniques in TA involve some combination of questioning, confrontation, and dialogue, think about which of these three ways of communicating is easiest for you and which is hardest. How could you make your weakest area stronger?

DIVERSITY AND MULTICULTURAL ISSUES

Transactional analysis appears as an appropriate theory to use in many cultures. Indeed, there are TA associations in 65 countries from Argentina to the Ukraine. TA has an appeal in countries with diverse populations, largely because the contract basis acts as a safeguard against therapists' imposing their values on clients. In addition, the cognitive nature of TA and the instructive methods it uses are appealing to some cultural groups within the United States, such as African Americans, Latinx, and Asian Americans (Henderson & Thompson, 2016).

Likewise, TA seems to be an appropriate theory for work on gender-sensitive issues. The emphasis on empowerment and contracts strengthens the position of women in TA therapy. Furthermore, the exploration of life scripts and family messages may help both men and women explore their roles and decide whether they wish to make any changes in what they do and how they do it (Campos, 2018).

EVALUATION OF THE THEORY

Strengths and Contributions

Transactional analysis uses terms that are easily understood and clearly defined. Consequently, it can be used in settings with varied populations—for example, with students who want to overcome math anxiety (Eisenberg, 1992). Another strength of TA is that it is easily and effectively combined with other more action-oriented counseling theories. The use of TA and Gestalt therapy together has been especially powerful (James & Jongeward, 1971).

One other positive aspect of TA is that it puts the responsibility for change on clients. Individuals can choose to change or remain the same, but it is their decision, not their therapists'. In addition, TA is goal directed. The contractual nature of the counseling process makes it possible for both counselors and clients to know when treatment should be terminated (James & Gilliland, 2003).

A final benefit of TA is a worldwide association that sponsors certification, conferences, and publications related to the theory. The International Transactional Analysis Association (ITAA) is active in training and certifying its members and in publishing a scholarly journal, the *Transactional Analysis Journal*.

Limitations and Criticism

TA has been criticized for its cognitive orientation; to understand is only the beginning of change. Although TA promotes understanding, it is limited in its effectiveness unless it is used with another, more action-oriented theory.

The TA approach is criticized too for its simplicity, structure, and popularity. TA is so widely known that some people use the terminology but do not practice the theory. These individuals intellectualize their problems but take few actions to modify them. Moreover, TA terms such as "I'm OK, You're OK" have become so popular that they sometimes lose their punch.

A further criticism is that TA does not emphasize the authenticity of the counselor. Counselors and clients are seen as equals, and little attention is paid to the person of the counselor in the process.

A more serious criticism of TA is that the research behind it is relatively weak (Widdowson, 2018). Methodological improvements are needed to study populations receiving TA treatment. In addition, some clinicians charge that the approach has not developed much since Berne's death in 1970. Although distinct emphases and schools of TA have emerged, few new ideas have been conceptualized. In addition, there are no prominent new theorists or disciples of TA on the national or international scene. Unless there is renewal within the theory and those who practice it, TA will lose prominence as a counseling modality.

TREATING LINDA WITH TRANSACTIONAL ANALYSIS

Conceptualization

From a transactional analysis (TA) perspective, Linda has made some decisions that have not been productive. Many of these decisions have been made out of her adaptive child ego state, the compliant part of the personality that conforms to the wishes and demands of parental figures. She has conformed to the wishes and demands of her father, her former husband, and her bosses at work. She has not found any of this acquiescent behavior satisfactory; in fact, it has been just the opposite, and hence her involvement with escape literature and movies. Linda has an overdeveloped child ego state and an underdeveloped adult ego state.

In addition, Linda does not operate on a complementary level in her interpersonal relationships. Instead, her responses are crossed, as when unequals speak. Most of the time these transactions leave Linda dissatisfied and discouraged. She feels that others talk down to her, and she is frustrated. Consequently, Linda plays games, most of which have left her with bad feelings, except for her most recent third-degree game involving suicide, which could have left her in the morgue. Linda feels like a victim in the games she plays and in life.

You also note that Linda has injunctions in her life, such as "Don't be too competent." Therefore, Linda's life is limited in how much she can achieve. Because Linda has received mainly negative strokes in her life, she has followed negative scripts that have allowed her to distance herself from her family, divorce her husband, and find fault with her work. Her miniscript has been to please others. She is definitely in the "I'm-not-OK" position, as are most of those with whom she associates.

Treatment Process

As the TA therapist, you are first a teacher. You explain to Linda the language and concepts of TA and the ways in which she can use these tools to think about herself. You want Linda to achieve a healthy lifestyle, to develop a strong adult ego state, and to adopt a position of "I'm OK, you're OK." You want Linda to become autonomous and exhibit more awareness, intimacy, and spontaneity, become free of games, and eliminate self-defeating scripts. Therefore, you draw up a treatment contract with Linda with mutually agreed-upon goals and responsibilities.

When necessary, you confront Linda about inconsistencies in her behavior, explaining, illustrating, confirming, and interpreting as appropriate. Almost all of the TA techniques you use involve some combination of questions, confrontation, and dialogue. The techniques are aimed at helping Linda gain insight into not only what she is doing now but also how she can transform herself in time. To help in this pursuit, you use some Gestalt techniques that add action and emotion to the thought process. In the end, Linda is able to experience what it is like to be talking to others from an adult ego state and to be successful instead of frustrated and angry.

SUMMING UP

Eric Berne formulated transactional analysis in the 1960s. It parallels psychoanalysis with its emphasis on ego states, yet it has a number of other assumptions and practices that differ from those of psychoanalytic theory. For instance, TA holds that people can change if they gain insight into their thinking process; thinking influences feeling and behavior. The unconscious is not important. The TA approach also stresses that therapy is a learning process and that counselors operate in the role of instructors. TA theory emphasizes the importance of clients' homework outside formal therapeutic sessions and requires clients to learn new vocabularies. TA can be used in a number of settings and with a variety of client problems.

Although TA has strengths, it likewise has limitations. TA is so cognitively based and has so few techniques that TA counselors often must combine their theory with other approaches, such as Gestalt, to make it more active and stronger. In addition, the TA research database is not strong. Many clinicians think that TA has stagnated in its development and that its popular appeal weakens its impact on clients and its status in the world of therapy.

Reflective Question

How effective do you think TA can be by itself since it focuses mainly on cognitively teaching clients awareness of ego states and ways of communicating?

CHAPTER 11 RECAP: TRANSACTIONAL ANALYSIS

Major Theorist
Eric Berne, Thomas Harris, Vann Joines

View of Human Nature/Personality
Optimistic view of change
Three interacting ego states—child, parent, adult
Importance of intrapersonal integration
Analysis of transactions, games, and scripts

Role of the Counselor
Teaches
Contracts with clients for change
Instructs in the language of TA

Goals
Transformation of clients
Client health and autonomy
Increased awareness, freedom from games, being OK

Process and Techniques
Emphasis on teaching and learning
Treatment contract
Interrogation, specification, confrontation
Explanation, illustration, confirmation, interpretation, crystallization

Diversity and Multicultural Issues
Theory is international
Appeals to diverse populations because of contract basis
Strengthens women through empowerment and contracts
Helps men and women explore life scripts and family messages

Strength and Contributions
Uses easily understood and clearly defined terms
Can be combined easily and effectively with other theories
Makes clients responsible for change
Is goal directed
Has a worldwide association

Limitations and Criticisms
Cognitive orientation
Simplicity, structure, and popularity
Lack of emphasis on authenticity of the counselor
Relatively weak research base
Little development since 1970s

KEY TERMS

adaptive child 143

adult ego state 143

after scripts 147

always scripts 147

child ego state 142

confirmation 149

confrontation 149

critical parent 143

crystallization 149

drivers 147

ego states – parent, adult, child 140

egogram 143

explanation 149

first-degree games 146

four major methods of understanding and predicting human
behavior 142

game analysis 142

games 146

illustration 149

I'm OK, You're OK 148

I'm OK, You're not OK 148

I'm not OK, You're OK 148

I'm not OK, You're not OK 148

interpretation 149

interrogation 149

life script (life plan) positions 147

miniscripts 147

natural (free) child 142

negative scripts 147

never scripts 147

nurturing parent 143

open-ended scripts 147

parent ego states 143

script analysis 142

second-degree games 146

specification 149

stamps 147

strokes 147

structural analysis 142

techniques in transactional
analysis 149

third-degree games 146

transactional analysis 142

transactional analysis - three main
schools of TA – San Francisco,
cathexis, redecision 150

treatment contracts 149

ulterior transaction 145

until scripts 147

LEARNING MORE

A number of periodicals include articles on the theory, research, and practice of transactional analysis. However, one is devoted exclusively to TA—the *Transactional Analysis Journal.*

For more information on transactional analysis organizations and institutes, contact

International Transactional Analysis Association
2843 Hopyard Road, Suite 155
Pleasanton, CA 94588 USA
http://itaaworld.org/

CLASSROOM ACTIVITIES

1. In groups of three, role-play how you think a TA counselor would act in helping an individual with the following concerns: procrastination, interpersonal conflict, stress, adjustment to a new living situation, and grief. Each student should take one role: client, counselor, or observer. After the role-playing, the observer should give feedback to the counselor; the counselor and the client should explain how they experienced the process. Then switch roles until everyone has had a chance to play each role.

2. Keep a list of the number and types of games you think TA analysis would classify you playing in a week, such as "Just made it to class on time" or "Oops, I forgot." Try to notice any patterns that emerge. Share your findings with classmates in an open class discussion.

3. What support does recent professional literature offer on the effectiveness of transactional analysis? Conduct a search of the literature for articles written in the past 3 years.

12
Feminist Therapy

■ ■ ■

Her eyes are trained
on the people she meets
especially when she's on the streets.
For it is how they see her
that matters as much
as who she really is.

"Glances" © S. T. Gladding

CHAPTER OVERVIEW

From reading this chapter you will learn about

- The major foci of feminist therapists.
- The similarities and differences of feminist theory and therapy compared with other therapeutic approaches.
- The techniques feminist therapists use to bring about change in clients.

As you read, consider

- How you would be treated by a counselor who uses feminist therapy.
- The advantages and disadvantages of advocating for clients.
- If therapeutic approaches can be or should be politically neutral.

Feminist therapy is a growing approach in counseling. Feminist views of counseling sprang from the emergence of the women's movement in the late 1960s and 1970s (Pitts & Kawahara, 2017) and the development of **feminist theory** which begins "with the experience of women and uses women's values and beliefs as the assumptive framework" (Nwachuku & Ivey, 1991, p. 106).

Initially, the **feminist movement** was seen as a challenge to patriarchal power. However, as feminism has grown and gone through a number of stages, its focus has centered more on the development of females as human beings with common and unique qualities (Brown, 2018; Maass, 2021). One of the most powerful writers in the formation of feminist theory was Jean Baker Miller. In her classic book, *Toward a New Psychology of Women* (1987), she focused on how sexual stereotypes restrict the psychological development of women.

The infusion of feminist theory into counseling was gradual at first. It started to escalate after the publication of Carol Gilligan's *In a Different Voice* (1982) as the distinctions between and commonalities of women and men were more clearly defined.

This approach encourages women and men to become aware of socialization patterns and personal options in altering traditional gender roles. When women face societal discrimination and subordination because of their gender, feminist theory and therapy offers them a nonsexist, active way of addressing social ills and creating a positive sense of self (Ballou et al., 2008; Miller, 1986; Okun, 1990). Furthermore, this approach encourages women to become involved not only in personal but also in social change activities that stress equality as a way of life (Enns & Hackett, 1993).

Overall, the major goals of feminist theory and therapy besides equality are change, balancing independence and interdependence, empowerment, self-nurturance, and valuing diversity (Herlihy & Park, 2016; Schwarz, 2017). The feminist approach emphasizes analyzing the meaning of power and privilege in each person's life and its placement of that life into the larger social and political context as a strategy for understanding oppression, joy, and good functionality (Brown, 2018).

MAJOR THEORIST: HARRIETT LERNER

Feminist therapy can claim a number of individuals as its founders; the translation of feminist theories into therapy has seen a number of proponents. Rachel Hare-Mustin, Ellyn Kaschak, E. Kit Childs, Paula Caplan, Reiko Homma-True, Laura S. Brown, Annette Brodsky, Harriett Lerner, Lenore Walker, Nancy Chodorow, Oliva Espín, Carol Travis, Phyllis Chesler, Miriam Greenspan, Jean Baker Miller, Hannah Lerman, Jeanne Marecek, Mary Gergen, and Carol Enns all stand out as persons who have been outstanding in this process (Pitts & Kawahara, 2018), as does Mikki Kendall. Because of the diversity in their backgrounds and emphases, no one of these outstanding women is the prototype for a feminist therapist. However, the life of Harriett Lerner is featured here.

Harriett Lerner (1944–) was born and raised in Brooklyn, New York. She was the younger of two daughters. Her parents were first-generation Americans, and her grandparents on both sides were Russian Jewish immigrants. Although her parents were high school graduates, they held ambitions for their daughters far beyond their educational levels. Lerner decided at a young age to be a clinical psychologist. Part of the reason was being put in therapy with her sister around the age of 3 by her mother, who thought it would be a good learning experience.

Lerner received her PhD from the City University of New York and moved in 1972 with her psychologist husband, Steve, to join the Menninger Clinic in Topeka, Kansas, for postdoctoral training. Feminism had not arrived in Topeka and Lerner had a difficult time as the only feminist voice at Menninger. After difficulties explaining feminist views to male colleagues and problems publishing feminist opinions of psychoanalytic theory in the *Menninger Bulletin*, Lerner found support from two prominent women, Teresa Bernardez and Jean Baker Miller. They reached out to Lerner from afar and invited her to present and correspond with them. Bernardez was a major influence in Lerner's 1985 book *The Dance of Anger* while Miller urged Lerner to write more simply rather than academically, which Lerner did with considerable success.

Lerner sees truth telling and authenticity as the heart of feminism and therapy. Pretending and denying who women are, which was dominant before the women's movement, is the opposite. Rather than calling herself a "feminist therapist," Lerner self-identifies as a feminist and a therapist (Lerner, 2017). She sees her work as a therapist and a writer through the lens of feminist theory. She longs for a world where the dignity and integrity of all women and all human beings are honored and respected. She notes identifying as a feminist is important for there "is no 'post-feminist' era and no resting place in the struggle to create a just and safe world for women ... As therapists and mental health professionals, we can't afford silence." (Lerner, 2017, p. 402).

VIEW OF HUMAN NATURE/PERSONALITY

Feminist theory and the therapy that has sprung from it are not monolithic; diverse views about human nature exist among feminist counselors. Various feminist theories have been described as liberal, cultural, radical, or socialist with each having its unique emphasis. Yet the different points of view share some beliefs in common about people and the nature of problems within society.

Feminist counselors believe that women have been constrained and oppressed in society (Ballou et al., 2008). Their strengths have been devalued, and they have been socialized to take care of others and deny their own needs. Thus, many problems that women experience are the result of sociopolitical and cultural forces. In addition, feminist counselors believe that clients know what is best for their lives—for example, women should determine their sexual and procreative lives.

Another assumption underlying the feminist approach is that societal relationships and institutions, as well as gender relationships, are primarily based on noncooperative values. If society and its individuals are to be more mentally healthy, values must change and society must become more nurturing, cooperative, and relational. Individual change will best occur through social change (Okun & Kantrowitz, 2015).

Reflective Question

How does feminist theory promote the dignity, worth, and uniqueness of individuals, especially women?

ROLE OF THE COUNSELOR

Counselors who work from a feminist perspective play a number of roles in the treatment of their clients. As educators, they demystify counseling and inform clients about how the therapeutic process works. Furthermore, feminist therapists assume an egalitarian and collaborative role and often use self-disclosure to reduce the power differentiation between client and counselor.

Counselors also attempt to make the client active in the therapeutic process by focusing on the inner power a client has that may have been previously unrecognized or discounted, thus enhancing self-esteem. Through open dialogue a feminist therapist helps the client make goals and follow through on them, often using contracts to make therapy more overt and concrete.

In addition, feminist counselors challenge the traditional ways of assessing psychological health. They do not usually make diagnoses using the *Diagnostic and Statistical Manual of Mental Disorders* but rather include clients in the assessment and treatment process. Somewhat like Adlerian therapists, feminists have their own descriptive terms to define the concerns and problems clients bring. They tend to reframe and relabel disorders that are especially prevalent in women—for example, depression, eating disorders, and posttraumatic stress—as ways of coping or responding to unfair societal norms and standards. There is also a focus on relationships and recognizing the differences between dependence, independence, and interdependence.

Reflective Question

How might you reframe or relabel depression? How about anxiety? What are the challenges of trying to reframe or relabel a disorder? How could it be harmful as well as helpful?

GOALS

Counselors with a feminist therapy focus have a number of goals and objectives. While some are individual, a number are societal (Erford et al., 2020). These emphases are quite different from most other theories, especially the goals that target social change. The goals can be summarized in the following way.

Individual goals are:

- To develop client awareness of the gender-role socialization process and internalized gender-role messages and replace them with functional beliefs.
- To foster personal empowerment and the development of a wide range of freely chosen behaviors.
- To enable clients to balance independence and interdependence.
- To assist clients in becoming more self-nurturing.
- To develop and exercise freely chosen behaviors.
- To develop the skills needed to bring about social change.
- To enhance self-esteem.

Societal goals are:

- To value diversity in all its forms, especially regarding gender, culture, and lifestyle (Enns, 2004)
- To help clients acquire skills to bring about change in the environment
- To promote and foster equality in society and in male/female relationships
- To restructure institutions so discriminatory practices are eliminated.

PROCESS AND TECHNIQUES

Because many women who seek help do not recognize that the origin of their problems lies in the inferior status of women in society, part of the counseling process begins with education. Counselors emphasize the value of social, political, and economic action as a major part of treatment. Feminists adapt interventions from a wide range of theoretical orientations, usually explaining the possible effects of and the rationale for their use.

- **Gender-role analysis.** Gender-role expectations begin early in life and affect the way individuals behave. In gender-role analysis counselors help clients ferret out messages they have been given by significant others about how they should behave or appear. For example, clients may have internalized messages such as "Be passive" or "Be pretty." These messages are assessed for their positive and negative impacts, and statements or self-statements are identified that clients may want to change. A plan is then developed to implement the desired changes.
- **Gender-role intervention.** In gender-role intervention, counselors conduct a social analysis of the implications of gender roles and other social expectations for clients. This process provides a broader framework within which clients can assess individual psychological problems; it gives clients insight into ways that social issues may be impacting them. For example, social expectations that women should be thin may be linked to difficulties clients are having regarding body image, weight, and self-esteem.
- **Power analysis.** In power analysis, counselors help clients recognize the difference in power between men and women in society. Power refers to the ability to access resources to effect change on a personal and/or external level (Worrell & Remer, 2003). As clients analyze power differences, therapists help them identify alternate kinds of power they may possess and ways to make appropriate changes. For instance, clients may not be able individually to control a chaotic situation, such as verbal or physical abuse. However, they may be able to call in allies to help rectify the situation, or they may leave the environment, and under no circumstances must they internalize the abusive messages.
- **Power intervention.** Power intervention is more spontaneous than other techniques. It involves strengthening or empowering clients by reinforcing their statements or giving them information (Sharf, 2016). Through power intervention clients become more self-sufficient, confident, courageous, and competent. For example, if clients are reinforced for being forthright in giving feedback to people who have acted inappropriately, they will most likely continue that behavior and gain enhanced status in their environments.
- **Assertiveness training.** One of the ways clients may be empowered is by being taught how to be assertive—that is, stating what one wants in a clear and direct way. Assertiveness is different from aggression or passivity. For instance, the assertive statement "I want to go home now" differs significantly from the aggressive statement "I'm leaving you dull, boring losers" or the passive statement "I can't make up my mind whether to go or stay. What do you think I should do?" Like many other forms of behavior, assertiveness can be taught through role-playing and modeling. It is a skill that must be evaluated culturally and exercised in sensitive, sensible, and appropriate ways.
- **Reframing and relabeling.** The techniques of reframing and relabeling are used in a number of therapeutic approaches to help clients see situations from another perspective and thereby attribute a different meaning to certain behaviors. For example, behaviors that might be seen as pathological, such as depression, can be relabeled as coping mechanisms or as reactions to an oppressive

policy or practice within society. In feminist therapy, societal expectations are frequently explored, leading clients to understand themselves better. The result is often "a shift from blaming oneself to looking at society for an explanation" (Sharf, 2016, p. 506).

- **Bibliotherapy and scriptotherapy.** Reading and writing can reinforce therapeutic explorations. Therefore, feminist therapists often encourage their clients to read books or magazines or view appropriate media material, such as films, to assist them in understanding themselves and society better. Journaling or keeping a log of what is being learned or thought or felt can be therapeutic too. Materials either read or written can be the grist for much discussion in counseling sessions.

- **Demystifying therapy/self-disclosure.** When clients do not understand how counseling works, a power differentiation is created, with the professional in charge of the therapeutic process being most powerful. To break down this barrier, feminist therapists are clear, open, and direct in explaining what counseling is and how it works. They inform clients about the parameters of the process and work with them in an egalitarian way. One helpful strategy is **self-disclosure,** in which the counselor shares with the client personal thoughts and feelings that are educative and yet revealing of the counselor as an individual. In this process, an effort is made to normalize, equalize, and liberate the experiences and emotions of the person in therapy.

- **Group work/social action.** Although therapeutic groups—such as support, self-help, and advocacy groups—are not always a part of feminist therapy, they can be useful adjuncts to this approach (Corey, 2017). Such groups connect clients with one another and promote unity among the women involved. These groups may benefit clients who are in therapy or may be a powerful follow-up after counseling ends. Similarly, joining a social action organization may help clients help themselves and others by working to change society's stereotypes of women.

Reflective Question

Assertiveness can change the way people feel about themselves and the way others feel about them. What are the positives in being assertive as opposed to being passive or aggressive? Is there a downside to being assertive?

DIVERSITY AND MULTICULTURAL ISSUES

Diversity and multicultural issues deal with such factors as culture, ethnicity, gender, ability, sexual orientation, socioeconomic status, spirituality, age, and the world of military service. Using these criteria feminist counseling is seen as a multicultural and diverse form of therapy (Bryant-Davis, 2019). Its concepts and strategies apply equally to individuals and groups. However, it has been criticized for not paying enough attention until recently to factors such as class, status, privilege, and power, especially regarding women of color. This lack of attention is best understood historically. Initially, feminist therapy focused mainly on middle-class white women.

Nevertheless, issues related to various forms of discrimination are important topics of discussion within this approach and are becoming more frequent and encompassing (Kendall, 2007; Piran, 2016).

Gender issues are highlighted in feminist therapy, and nonsexist development is stressed. For example, in career development feminist thought focuses on requirements for work instead of stressing traditional work roles by gender. Men as well as women may profit from feminist therapy by becoming more attuned to themselves and to gender-prescribed roles that inhibit their growth and restrict their relationships. Overall, feminist counseling is an intentionally diverse and socially constructive approach to therapy (Brown, 2008, 2018).

EVALUATION OF THE THEORY

Strengths and Contributions

Feminist therapy has paved the way for gender-sensitive counseling practices (Corey, 2017). It has helped therapists from many other theoretical persuasions consider potential bias, especially toward women, in many traditional therapeutic practices. Feminist therapy was originally developed to address the negative effects of societal sexism on the lives of women and later expanded to focus on the impacts of all forms of oppression on people's lives (Remer, 2008). This awareness has made it possible for clinicians to be fairer in their work with individuals, groups, couples, and families.

A second contribution of the feminist approach is its effectiveness "with women who are motivated for change and empowerment" (Austin, 1999, p. 69). Feminist therapy gives women a way of moving beyond passivity and traditionally ascribed roles. It opens up a way for women to explore the inequality of power differentials in gender interactions. Furthermore, it explores power in relationships and society and the ways in which women can become more powerful through assertive means. It also advocates self-acceptance, including one's body, and teaches clients not to devalue or discount themselves because they are female or imperfect.

Another contribution of feminist counseling is its stress on the varied roles men and women may have and the limited flexibility society promotes because of gender-ascribed behaviors. Through its emphasis on social and political realities that create problems for women and men, feminist therapy addresses oppressive factors in the fabric of society and takes the blame off women for many of their difficulties.

In addition, feminist counseling highlights the importance of interpersonal relationships and behaviors such as cooperation and self-disclosure. Feminist therapists demystify the counseling relationship and stress the egalitarian nature of counseling. This approach allows greater focus on the change process itself.

Men too may benefit from feminist counseling practices when they are sensitized to the plight of women and to the limitations men face when they are forced to maintain a masculine role (Levant, 2001). These insights help men realize how gender-role stereotypes negatively influence society.

Finally, feminist therapy is extremely flexible and inclusive. It can be combined with many other ways of working with clients. Few if any counseling theories cannot incorporate feminist principles, ideas, and techniques, thereby broadening their work with diverse client groups in various stages of life, and perhaps stimulating positive social change.

Reflective Question

How are the techniques and strengths of feminist theory similar to and different from those in the behavioral and cognitive-behavioral counseling approaches?

Limitations and Criticisms

The major drawback to feminist therapy is that there is little controlled outcome research on it. "The effectiveness of feminist therapy, both in relative and absolute terms, has not been rigorously evaluated" (Prochaska & Norcross, 2018, p. 393). Therefore, it is impossible to state whether feminist therapy is appropriate for clients with specific conditions and concerns.

Another limitation of feminist therapy is the difficulty of finding adequate training. The Stone Center at Wellesley College is conducting work on what it is like to be female in society. They are also studying the difficulties women in the United States face in therapeutic situations. However, the Stone Center is not a training center for feminist therapy (Sharf, 2016).

Yet another criticism of feminist therapy is that it does not take a neutral stand on issues. Instead, it actively advocates for definite change in the social structure, especially in the area of equality, power in relationships, the right to self-determination, freedom to pursue a career outside the home, and the right to an education. Although nothing is inherently wrong with any of these goals, feminist therapists need to be cautious to avoid pushing an agenda on their clients (Corey, 2017). Some clients who come for counseling are not interested in changing social structures and some may feel pressed to make social changes before they are ready.

As stated before, feminist therapy has received a rather harsh critique in recent years as it focuses on the inequality between men and women without addressing the inequalities between women (Kendall, 2020). This conversation is now taking place but is still a work in progress.

A final criticism of feminist therapy is its lack of agreement on whether the approach is a theory or a philosophical orientation. In recent years, advocates of this approach have asserted that it is a theory (e.g., Crawford, 2018; Enns, 2004). However, as such, it differs significantly from other mainstream theories except for existentialism, which also is criticized for its emphasis on philosophy and its lack of concrete approaches originating from the theory itself.

TREATING LINDA WITH FEMINIST THERAPY

Conceptualization

From a feminist perspective, Linda has not been able to reach her potential because she grew up in a patriarchal culture that limited her growth and development as a person because she is female. Thus, she is stuck in a limiting, gender-stereotyped role in which she is stymied in her attempts to achieve and is devalued as a woman. Sociopolitical and cultural forces have conspired to keep her pigeonholed in taking care of others' needs but not her own. Linda knows in some ways that life is not working for her, but she needs to clarify exactly what she wants.

Treatment Process

As a feminist therapist, you work as an educator, a collaborator, and a partner with Linda. You explore with her the ways in which her strengths and abilities have been discounted or devalued, such as her father's negative stereotyping because of her gender. You work with Linda to define her concerns and goals as concretely as possible. Your goals for her include

- Becoming aware of society's and her own internalized messages regarding women and men.
- Becoming more empowered and developing skills that will help her grow.
- Balancing independence with dependence.
- Becoming self-nurturing.
- Promoting and fostering equality in society.
- Valuing diversity.

To help Linda reach these goals, you conduct a **gender-role analysis** in which Linda focuses on identifying limiting or enabling messages in her life given by significant others. Thereafter, you perform a gender-role intervention, which gives Linda insight into ways that social issues may be affecting her. Next, you repeat the analysis and the intervention focusing on the topic of power. In this process, you help Linda identify the power she has and reinforce herself for becoming more self-sufficient, confident, courageous, and competent.

You also teach Linda assertiveness through role-playing and modeling. In this way she is freed to ask for what she wants without being aggressive or passive. Furthermore, she learns how to reframe and relabel situations so that she does not pathologize herself. In addition, you encourage Linda to read books and magazines or view films that can assist her in understanding herself and the role of women in society. Moreover, you suggest that she keep a log of what she is learning, thinking, and feeling. Finally, you advise her to join a support group with other women to advocate for and promote equality within society. Linda finds that idea intriguing and begins to explore what it means to be a woman in the 21st century and what possibilities are available to her. A bonus from her support group is that she forms new friendships with others with whom she has much in common and learns helpful information about jobs and education.

Reflective Question

What do you think of feminist therapy compared with other therapies covered in this text? What are the strengths of this approach? What are the limitations?

SUMMING UP

A recent phenomenon growing out of the women's movement of the late 1960s and 1970s, feminist theory, and feminist therapy is a multifaceted approach to counseling rather than a well-formulated set of constructs (Enns, 2004). It challenges the attitudes of traditional counseling theories, which often advocate maintaining the status quo of a male-dominated, hierarchical society.

According to feminist theory, gender-role expectations have a profound impact on human development. Because women and men are socialized differently, models of psychological development based on male development fail to recognize that women's identity develops in a context of connectedness and relationship with others (Jordan, 2000; Miller, 1991). Feminist counselors seek to empower women to change the social contexts that suppress them (Austin, 1999), working through gender and power analysis and intervention as well as universal interventions such as bibliotherapy and reframing/relabeling. The result is greater personal and social sensitivity and often social activism.

In feminist therapy, external forces are recognized as the root of women's problems. Clients learn self-appreciation and self-value, and they learn to change their environments rather than adjust to them. They also learn to advocate for social change and to develop egalitarian rather than hierarchical relationships.

CHAPTER 12 RECAP: FEMINIST THERAPY

Major Theorists
Rachel Hare-Mustin, Ellyn Kaschak, E. Kit Childs, Paula Caplan
Reiko Homma-True, Laura S. Brown, Annette Brodsky, Harriett Lerner, Lenore Walker, Nancy Chodorow, Oliva Espín, Carol Travis
Phyllis Chesler, Miriam Greenspan, Hannah Lerman, Jeanne Marecek, Mary Gergen, Carol Enns, Jean Baker Miller

View of Human Nature/Personality
Much diversity of views within this theory
Social constraint and oppression are inflicted on girls and women
People know what is best for themselves; there is a superiority of self-knowledge
Importance of social change if people are going to change

Role of the Counselor
Educator, collaborator, active participant
Diagnosis according to feminist terminology

Goals
Awareness of gender-role socialization and internalized messages, replacement with functional messages
Enhanced self-esteem
Stress on personal empowerment
Focus on developing skills to bring about change in the environment
Emphasizes equality in society and in male/female relationships
Balance of independence and interdependence
Importance of self-nurturance is stressed
Appreciation of all diversity

Process and Techniques
Inferior status of women as basis
Interventions adapted from many orientations
Use of gender-role analysis and intervention
Use of power analysis and intervention
Assertiveness training, relabeling/reframing, bibliotherapy/scriptotherapy
Demystification of therapy, group work

Diversity and Multicultural Issues
Equal application to all people
Focus on issues of discrimination
Emphasis on nonsexist development
Increased awareness of men

Strengths and Contributions
Paves the way for gender-sensitive counseling
Empowers women
Stresses varied gender roles and related inhibitions
Emphasizes interpersonal relationships
Stresses self-acceptance
Is flexible and inclusive

Limitations and Criticisms
Little controlled outcome research
Limited training available
Subjective position on social issues
Lack of agreement on orientation (theory or philosophy)
Lack of attention to factors of race, class, status, privilege, and power
among women

KEY TERMS

assertiveness training   160
bibliotherapy   161
demystifying therapy   161
feminist movement   156
feminist theory   156
gender-role analysis   160
gender-role intervention   160

group work/social action   161
power analysis   160
power intervention   160
reframing and relabeling   160
scriptotherapy   161
self-disclosure   161

LEARNING MORE

A number of periodicals devoted to feminist therapy and theory may prove
helpful in exploring this approach to counseling.

Psychology of Women Quarterly
Sex Roles
Women and Therapy

In addition to journals, several training institutes and professional associations offer clinicians an opportunity to learn more about the lives of women and the best ways to work with them in therapeutic settings.

Stone Center, Wellesley College
106 Central Street
Wellesley, MA 02481 www.wellesley.edu

Psychology of Women (Division 35) American Psychological Association
https://www.apa.org/about/division/div35

Association for Women in Psychology
https://www.awpsych.org/

The Feminist Institute
https://www.thefeministinstitute.org/

National Organization for Women
1000 16th Street NW, Suite 700
Washington, DC 20036 www.now.org

CLASSROOM ACTIVITIES

1. How has feminist theory and therapy improved the lives of women? How has feminist theory and therapy improved the lives of men? What areas in society do you think might be improved if feminist theoretical approaches were applied to them?
2. Visit the website of the National Organization of Women (NOW) or invite a local member of NOW to your class. Discuss current issues impacting women and the strategies employed to address these situations.
3. What did you learn about gender roles growing up? How have they changed? How have they remained the same? Why do you think some individuals are reluctant to make changes in the ways they were taught as a child? What does this reluctance tell you about change and fostering change?

13
Bowen Systems Therapy

■ ■ ■

Estranged, he traveled home
trying to connect to his family.
In concert, he emerged
thoughts and feelings in harmony.
Life became less mysterious.

"Return and Reemergence" © S. T. Gladding

CHAPTER OVERVIEW

From reading this chapter you will learn about

■ The influence and power of families on individuals.
■ What a genogram is and the advantages of creating a genogram.
■ How anxiety and triangles can negatively affect a family and an individual.

As you read, consider

■ How healthy or dysfunctional your family of origin was growing up.
■ How helping a family can also help an individual.
■ How differentiated you are from others in your environment.

Family counseling is a relatively recent approach especially compared to individual therapy theories. This approach grew out of the need to help families become healthier and more functional with the number of family therapy theories mushrooming in number and popularity in the 1950s and 1960s. At its inception, family therapy was considered radical. The family was seen as a living system, which was quite different from more individually oriented ways of working.

One of the oldest and most distinguished theories of working with families is Bowen family therapy. Murray Bowen and Michael Kerr have been its chief architects and advocates. Bowen himself was the major originator of this philosophy. Nonetheless, other authors, such as McGoldrick (2011, 2016; McGoldrick et al., 2020) and Friedman (2011), have popularized many of this theory's concepts.

This chapter covers Bowen family therapy, which can be used with individuals, couples, and families. The next chapter addresses strategic therapy, one that has some of the versatility of the Bowen approach but a different philosophy and methodology. These two therapies, along with solution-focused therapy, represent the innovation and creativity connected with counseling families and the individuals in them.

MAJOR THEORIST: MURRAY BOWEN

Murray Bowen (1913–1990) was the oldest of five children in a tightly knit family that resided for several generations in a small town in Pennsylvania. After going off to college and medical school, Bowen moved away and kept a formal distance from his parents, maintaining family relations on a comfortable but superficial level. Bowen, a psychiatrist, became interested in working with families while he was employed at the Menninger Clinic. As early as 1951, he began to require that mothers of disturbed children live in the same hospital setting as their offspring during treatment (Guerin, 1976). From this experience, he became interested in studying mother-patient symbiosis—that is, the intense bond that develops between a parent and a child that does not allow either to differentiate from the other (Bowen, 1960, 1961).

In 1954 Bowen joined Lyman Wynne at the National Institute of Mental Health (NIMH), where he continued to study the dynamics of families with schizophrenic children. Bowen worked with the research team at NIMH on a pilot project to hospitalize and treat all members of such families. He recognized during this time that the characteristics a schizophrenic family exhibited were similar to symptoms in many dysfunctional families. A few years later Bowen moved to Georgetown University, where he researched family dynamics and developed his therapeutic approach.

For Bowen, therapy and theory cannot be separated without doing a disservice to both. He preferred to think of himself as a theorist, one who stood alone in conceptualizing "the family as a natural system ... which could only be fully understood in terms of the fluid but predictable processes between members" (Wylie, 1991, p. 26). Bowen viewed himself as a scientist in search of universal truths, and his theory "constantly strives to make continuous what other theories dichotomize"—for example, nature/nurture, male/female, physical illness/emotional illness (Friedman, 1991, p. 136).

During his years at Georgetown, especially in the 1970s, Bowen completed his most productive personal and professional work. Personally, he removed himself from the triangulation with his parents by returning home and reacting cognitively and neutrally to a number of emotional issues family members presented to him (Anonymous, 1972). Professionally, he clarified his theory (Bowen, 1978), began the Georgetown Family Center Symposium, expanded the Georgetown Family Center to new, off-campus quarters, and initiated the American Family Therapy Association (AFTA) "in order to restore a serious research effort in family therapy" (Wylie, 1991, p. 77). He died of lung cancer in 1990.

VIEW OF HUMAN NATURE/PERSONALITY

Murray Bowen was influenced by events in his own life, especially his difficulties with his family of origin. His personal situation had a major impact on what he proposed regarding the development of others (Anonymous, 1972; Papero, 1991). Bowen stated that individuals who do not examine and rectify patterns passed down from previous generations are likely to repeat these behaviors in their own families (Kerr, 1988, 2003, 2019). That possibility is particularly likely if family members, especially those of different generations, are either emotionally overinvolved with each other or emotionally cut off from each other. Bowen concerned himself with the family's emotional system and its impact on family members' personalities.

A key element of Bowen family therapy is that "there is a **chronic anxiety** in all of life that comes with the territory of living" (Friedman, 1991, p. 139). This anxiety is both emotional and physical and is shared by all protoplasm. Some individuals are more affected than others "because of the way previous generations in their families have channeled the transmission" of this anxiety to them (Friedman, 1991, p. 140).

If anxiety remains low, few problems exist for individuals or families; the family emotional system is undisturbed. However, when anxiety rises, predictable patterns occur.

To address chronic anxiety and emotional processes in families and society, Bowen emphasizes eight interlocking concepts through which therapists can understand the dynamics within a family:

- Differentiation of self.
- Multigenerational transmission process.
- Nuclear family emotional system.
- Family projection process.
- Triangles.
- Sibling position.
- Societal regression.
- Emotional cutoff (Bowen, 1978; Gilbert, 2004; Kerr, 1981, 2003, 2019).

Differentiation refers to the ability of persons to distinguish themselves from their family of origin on an emotional and an intellectual level and to balance the intrapsychic and interpersonal dimensions of the self (Bowen, 1978; Kerr, 2003; Titelman, 2014). Differentiated people can recover emotional equilibrium quickly after stress passes (Greene et al., 1986). They are **autonomous**, which is the ability to think through a situation clearly. For instance, Peleg-Popko (2004) found family differentiation (specifically, adolescents' relationships with their mothers) to be negatively correlated with levels of test and trait anxiety and positively correlated with cognitive performance.

Undifferentiated or fused is the opposite of differentiation. It implies an emotional dependence on family members, even if living away from them. Undifferentiated people are vulnerable to stress and are much more prone to physical and social illnesses than others (Hooper & Doehler, 2011). In such situations, family members may exhibit dysfunctional behaviors such as bulimia, which are more likely to become chronic when they occur. "Theoretically, at least four factors influence a person's level of differentiation: 1) emotional reactivity, 2) emotional cutoff, 3) fusion with others, and 4) the ability to take an 'I-position'" (Tuason & Friedlander, 2000, p. 27). It is through differentiation that families and the individuals in them can change. People vary in the level of self-differentiation they can achieve at any one time; the concept itself denotes a process (Bowen, 1965).

Reflective Question

Why is differentiation so important for the health and well-being of persons and for society? When have you seen a lack of differentiation negatively affect someone?

Another of Bowen's basic concepts deals with the coping strategies and patterns that tend to be passed from generation to generation, an important phenomenon known as the **multigenerational transmission process**. Families that present a problem have had the forces of several generations shaping and carrying it along. In marriage, people tend to select partners at their own level of differentiation (Bowen, 1976), from which union a **nuclear family emotional** system evolves.

Spouses with equally high levels of identity are able to establish and maintain clear individuality "and at the same time to have an intense, mature, nonthreatening, emotional closeness" (Bowen, 1965, p. 220). Indeed, research shows that couples that are less reactive, cut off, or fused and that are able to relate from an I-position "experience the greatest levels of marital satisfaction" (Skowron, 2000, p. 233). This result is particularly true if the male partner remains emotionally present and available.

On the other hand, spouses with equally low levels of differentiation have difficulty establishing intimacy because they have developed only pseudoselves—that is, pretend selves (Kerr, 1988, p. 43). The pseudoselves fluctuate according to situations and usually result in the fusion of these selves into a "common self with obliteration of ego boundaries between them and loss of individuality to the common self" (Bowen, 1965, p. 221). Couples tend to produce offspring with the same level of differentiation the parents have, a process Bowen describes as **family projection** (Kilpatrick, 1980).

To rid themselves of anxiety, spouses with low self-differentiation keep an emotional distance from each other. When anxiety becomes too great, it is frequently manifested in one of four ways: (1) marital conflict, (2) physical or emotional illness in one spouse, (3) projection of the problem to the children, or (4) a combination of these (David, 1979).

When working with individuals and couples, Bowen family therapists look for **triangles** (Kerr, 2003), which can occur between people or between people and things. A triangle consists of a state of calm between a comfortable twosome and an outsider (Anonymous, 1972); it is "the basic building block of any emotional system and the smallest stable relationship system" (Kilpatrick, 1980, p. 168). The original triangle is between a child and parents. Some triangles are healthy; others are not. In the latter case triangles are a frequent way of dealing with anxiety, allowing tension between two persons to be projected onto another person or object. In stressful situations, anxiety can spread from one central triangle within the family to interlocking triangles outside the family, especially in work and social systems (Kerr, 1988, 2003).

Reflective Question

Where have you observed triangles in your community outside of couple relationships? How prevalent are they? What does that tell you about the health and well-being of where you live?

Bowen therapists also examine **sibling positions** because people can develop fixed personality characteristics based on their functional birth order in the family (Toman, 1961). The more closely a marriage replicates a couple's sibling positions in their families of origin, the better the chance for success. For example, if a youngest son marries an oldest daughter, both have much to gain from the arrangement because the youngest son most likely enjoys being taken care of, and the oldest daughter probably enjoys taking care of someone.

By examining these processes, family members gain insight and understanding into the past and are freed to choose their behavior in the present and future. Similarly, they gain a perspective on how well society is doing. In a society under too much stress (e.g., from population growth or economic decline), **societal regression** occurs because too many toxic forces counter the tendency to achieve differentiation.

ROLE OF THE COUNSELOR

In the Bowen model, the differentiation of the therapist is crucial. Bowen family therapists must maintain a calm presence and be differentiated from their families of origin (Friedman, 1991); objectivity and neutrality are important characteristics of Bowen therapists. To be able to work with families, therapists must first undergo emotional change (Kerr, 1981), or those they work with will not be able to experience healthy shifts.

Having personally resolved family-of-origin concerns, the Bowen therapist is usually involved in coaching on more cognitive levels. Initially, family members—primarily individuals or couples—talk to the therapist or to one another through the therapist so that emotional issues do not cloud communication (Kerr, 2003). According to Bowen, therapists should not encourage people to wallow in emotionalism but should teach them by example to transcend it, behaving with reason and self-control. Therapy should be just like a Socratic dialogue, with the teacher or coach calmly asking questions until the student learns to think independently (Wylie, 1991, p. 27).

Bowen family therapy looks at boundary and differentiation issues from a historical perspective. Therapists instruct individuals to search for clues as to where various family pressures have been expressed and how effectively the family has adapted to stress since its inception, through three previous generations if possible. Individuals might draw a genogram or visit their family of origin to obtain this information. By examining family dynamics, therapists become interpreters with their clients in working through multigenerational patterns of fusion and cutoffs and then resolving areas of difficulty.

Reflective Question

Do you think the process of Bowen therapy could be sped up and be just as effective if it were not a Socratic dialogue?

GOALS

Bowen family therapy promotes differentiation in self/family and intellect/emotion. Therapists help their clients, especially couples, separate their feelings from their intellect and in the process **detriangulate**.

Another primary goal is that family members come to understand intergenerational patterns and gain insight into historical circumstances that have influenced the ways they currently interact (Learner, 1983). Then it is hoped that clients can focus on changing the intergenerational inferences operating with the current family. Therapists can help family members differentiate from each other and become more diverse and fluid in their interactions (Bowen, 1978; Ceja & Gasbarrini, 2018). At the end of treatment individuals should be able to relate on an autonomous, cognitive level, and projective patterns of blame should be changed (Kerr & Bowen, 1988). Nuclear family members should experience greater self-differentiation.

PROCESS AND TECHNIQUES

In Bowen family therapy the chief focus is an individual or couple; the whole family is usually not seen, even though the emphasis is systemic (Kerr, 2003). "A theoretical system that thinks in terms of family, with a therapeutic method that works toward improvement of the family system, is 'family' regardless of the number of people in the sessions" (Kerr, 1981, p. 232). By changing just one person, therapy may directly influence an entire family. Thus the therapist may work "with all involved family members present, with any combination of family members present, or with only one family member present." However, "since the two spouses are the two family members most involved in the family ego mass, the most rapid family change occurs when the spouses are able to work as a team in family psychotherapy" (Bowen, 1965, p. 220).

Bowen family therapy is not technique oriented; rather it is process oriented, with techniques used to help clients when needed. Bowen therapists ask questions about their clients' thoughts and give homework assignments. Among the techniques most often employed are genograms, going home again, detriangulation, person-to-person relationships, differentiation of self, and asking questions.

A genogram is a visual representation of a family tree, depicted in geometric figures, lines, and words (McGoldrick et al., 2020). Genograms include information about family relationships over at least three generations. They help people gather information, hypothesize, and track relationship changes in the context of historic and contemporary events (Dunn & Levitt, 2000). "From this simple diagram, counselors and clients alike are able to view simultaneously family composition, gender, age, ethnicity, dates of birth, marriages, divorces, deaths, and other important family events" (Frame, 2000, p. 69) (see Figure 13.1).

The tangibility and nonthreatening nature of a genogram help clinicians gather a large amount of information in a relatively short period. Furthermore, genograms can increase "mutual trust and tolerance" among all involved in their construction (Sherman, 1993, p. 91). Bowen family therapy "advises people to go 'back, back, back and up, up, up' their family tree to look for patterns, 'recycling,' getting not just information but a feel for the context and milieu that existed during each person's formative years" (White, 1978, pp. 25–26). This process promotes the shift from emotional reactivity to clear cognitions.

Genograms can be color coded to indicate everything from substance abuse (Bacon, 2019) to forms of spirituality (Frame, 2000). Data in genograms are scanned for:

- Repetitive patterns, such as triangles, cutoffs, and coalitions.
- Coincidences, such as the deaths of members or the ages of symptom onset.
- The impact of change and untimely life cycle transitions, such as off-schedule events (e.g., marriage, death, and the birth of children occurring at a different time than is the norm) (McGoldrick, 2011).

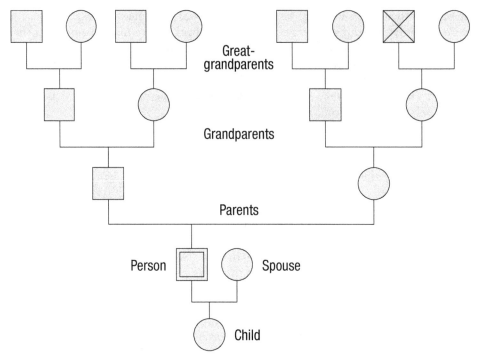

Figure 13.1 Genogram of the Smith family

Source: From *Family Therapy: History, Theory, and Practice* (3rd ed., p. 137) by Samuel T. Gladding. Copyright 2002. Reprinted by permission of Pearson Education.

In **going home again,** the family therapist instructs the individual client or family members to return home to get to know better their family of origin (Bowen, 1976). With this type of information, individuals can differentiate themselves more clearly and can operate more fully within all family contexts of which they are a part. However, before returning home, clients may need to learn and practice how to remain calm (Bowen, 1976).

Detriangulation involves "the process of being in contact and emotionally separate" (Kerr, 1988, p. 55). It operates on at least two levels. On one level individuals resolve their anxiety over family situations and do not project feelings onto anyone else. On a second level Bowen therapists help those individuals separate themselves from the tension that arises in the family, refusing to allow themselves to become targets or scapegoats for others who may be overcome with anxiety. For example, if a usually triangulated person stays rational during times of emotional stress, he or she will seldom become the focus of attention for the others in the triangle (Bowen, 1972). On both levels individuals will be free to voice their concerns and try out new ways of acting.

In **person-to-person relationships** two family members "relate personally to each other about each other; that is, they do not talk about others (triangling) and do not talk about impersonal issues" (Piercy & Sprenkle, 1986, p. 11). For instance, a father may say to his son, "Your actions remind me of myself when I was your age." In return, the son may say, "I really don't know much about you when you were a boy. Please tell me about what you did and how you felt when you were my age." Such a process promotes individuation or autonomy and intimacy.

"**Differentiation of self** has to do with the degree to which a person is able to distinguish between the subjective feeling process and the more objective intellectual (thinking) process" (Gibson & Donigian, 1993, p. 28). This procedure may involve all the preceding techniques plus some confrontation between family members and the therapist. As mentioned earlier, a failure to differentiate results in fusion, in which "people are dominated by their automatic emotional system"; they have "less flexibility, less adaptability, and are more emotionally dependent on those around them" (Sauber et al., 1985, p. 43). Over generations, children most involved in family fusion move toward a lower level of differentiation of self (Bowen, 1972). For example, they may develop eating disorders. In such cases Bowen therapists try to help these individuals (usually young women) increase their self-differentiation through assertiveness training, healthier family boundaries, enhanced cognitive communication skills, and new coping behaviors for stress (Levy & Hadley, 1998).

In each of the techniques in Bowen family theory, a consistent strategy is to ask questions. In fact, **asking questions** is deemed the magic bullet of Bowen therapists. For instance, when major events such as deaths, births, and marriages disturb the equilibrium of a family, emotional shock waves may result (Bowen, 1976). Questions can help individuals involved in Bowen family therapy better understand the reactions of those in their families.

Reflective Question

How comfortable are you asking questions to members of your family? Think of some of the behavioral, cognitive, and cognitive-behavioral strategies you read about earlier.

DIVERSITY AND MULTICULTURAL ISSUES

Bowen therapy is flexible in its applications and can be used in many multicultural and diverse situations (McDowell et al., 2018). For instance, it has been used with homeless who are not mentally ill or addicted to help them break the pattern of behavior leading up to and maintaining homelessness (Hertlein & Killmer, 2004).

However, some Bowen concepts are limited in their applicability to different cultures (Erdem & Safi, 2018). On the positive side, genograms can be diverse in nature and can include worldview and cultural factors that influence the behavior of family members (McGoldrick et al., 2020; Thomas, 1998). In addition, there is evidence that differentiation is applicable across cultures. However, for some groups such as Filipinos and North Americans, "psychological well-being in adulthood may well be affected by factors outside of the family, such as peer relationships, employment, or societal influences" (Tuason & Friedlander, 2000, p. 33).

The Bowen approach is somewhat controversial concerning gender-specific issues. Bowen theory proposes that the genogram is gender neutral in its display of facts and patterns. However, Knudson-Martin (2002) suggests that many women, as well as persons from less individualistic cultures and very spiritual persons, develop a connected self that is significantly different from Bowen's image of separate selves engaged with each other. Knudson-Martin contends that Bowen theory ignores many of the positive aspects of togetherness.

EVALUATION OF THE THEORY

Strengths and Contributions

A strength of Bowen theory is that it calls attention to family history, emphasizing the importance of noticing and dealing with past patterns to enable individuals and families to avoid repeating these behaviors in the future. The **genogram** is a specific tool developed to plot historical linkages and as such is increasingly used by theorists of all persuasions in assessing client families.

Another strength of Bowen family therapy is that it is a well-established and heuristically appealing approach. Its emphasis on theory as well as its practical nature makes it attractive. In addition, the theory and the therapy are extensive and intertwined. The theory is a blueprint for the therapy; the therapy is consistent with and inseparable from the theory. Family therapists are indebted to Bowen for intertwining these two aspects.

A further strength is that Bowen is insightful and detailed in suggesting the course of working with families. Bowen established a center for educating practitioners, ensuring that his approach will continue to be learned and used.

One final contribution is that Bowen family therapy is systemic in nature, controlled in focus, and cognitive in practice, thereby giving clinicians and their clients a concrete way of evaluating progress (Bowen, 1975). Furthermore, unlike many other systemic family approaches, Bowen family therapy can be used extensively with individuals or couples. It is considered "the most comprehensive theory of individual functioning from a family systems perspective" (Skowron & Platt, 2005, p. 281).

Limitations and Criticisms

The Bowen approach is vulnerable to criticism for its failure to validate fully its intergenerational hypothesis (Tuason & Friedlander, 2000). In other words, the ideas behind this approach are intriguing but are not always verified. A related concern is that the theory underlying the approach is its own paradigm (Friedman, 1991). Setting up research questions to refute or verify this approach is a challenge of the highest order.

Another drawback is that Bowen's stress on the importance of the past encourages some families or family members to examine their history rather than deal immediately with present circumstances. Such a process may promote insight but not action.

A third limitation of Bowen theory is the time and, consequently, the financial resources that Bowen family therapy requires of its clients. Most people cannot afford to invest as heavily in this process as is necessary. Thus, the number of people who can benefit from this approach is limited.

A final criticism of the Bowen approach is the complex and convoluted nature of Bowen's writings about the continuity of and connection between theory and therapy (Kaplan, 2000). Reading Bowen is not easy.

Reflective Question

What do you know about your family? What more would you like to know? How can knowledge in and of itself be therapeutic?

TREATING LINDA WITH BOWEN FAMILY SYSTEMS THERAPY

Conceptualization

From a Bowen family systems perspective, Linda is most likely undifferentiated from her family of origin. Therefore she suffers from chronic anxiety and has difficulty relating to others from an I-position. This inability to relate on a deep level has resulted in Linda's developing a pseudoself that fluctuates with situations. She becomes angry when threatened and either lashes out, as in her past jobs, or withdraws, as with her family and her fascination with adventure books and films.

Linda's state of functioning is a result of multigenerational transmissions; she reflects the low level of differentiation in her family. If this condition is not rectified, Linda will most likely start forming triangles to scapegoat people and activities about which she becomes anxious.

Treatment Process

As a Bowen family therapist, you maintain a calm presence in the midst of Linda's anxiety because you have dealt with your own family-of-origin issues. You work cognitively with Linda as a coach, a teacher, and a catalyst, being as objective and neutral as possible. It is not necessary for Linda to bring her family to therapy because you can help her make changes and gain insight that will alter the system dynamics in her family.

Initially, you press Linda for clues on how her family has dealt with stress. You ask her questions. You also have her draw a genogram, a multigenerational family diagram that reveals how past generations in the family have acted and reacted in times of significant turmoil and transition. Your goal in each of these activities is to have Linda draw on historical information to influence the present. If Linda can separate her thoughts from her feelings and herself from her family, she may become more autonomous, differentiated, and healthy.

You also assign Linda homework: She is to go home again and have person-to-person relationships with as many family members as possible. In addition, she is to ask questions of her parents and siblings about relationships in the family. The hope is that she will learn information that will help her detect family patterns and then change her ways of relating.

If successful, Linda will be able to differentiate herself from her family and form deep and lasting bonds with others. The process of therapy takes several months, but in the end Linda is calmer and has begun to think about what her next steps will be vocationally, as well as in the community and in her family.

SUMMING UP

Bowen family therapy is an established approach to working with individuals and families. A psychoanalytically trained psychiatrist, Murray Bowen devised his own approach to working with families, especially couples, based in part on his life experiences and in part on psychoanalytic theory.

Bowen theory emphasizes the importance of unconscious forces in family life. The therapy is systemic, although its primary clients are individuals and couples. It emphasizes the importance of historical intergenerational patterns and uses a cognitive strategy to help couples and family members differentiate and change their ways of thinking. In the process, the therapist acts as a coach, a teacher, and a catalyst.

Overall, this approach emphasizes in-depth exploration of clients' families and concentrates on long-term results. It requires a considerable investment of time and resources. Yet Bowen theory is concrete in outcome and gives its clients a way to recognize dysfunctional patterns transmitted across generations.

CHAPTER 13 RECAP: BOWEN SYSTEMS THERAPY

Major Theorists
Murray Bowen, Michael Kerr, Monica McGoldrick

View of Human Nature/Personality
Impact of a family's emotional system on personalities
Focus on previous generations' transmission of anxiety
Basic concepts: differentiation, multigenerational transmission process, nuclear family emotional system, family projection process, triangles, sibling position, societal regression

Role of the Counselor/Therapist
Is objective and neutral
Has resolved family-of-origin concerns
Teaches, coaches, displays self-control
Instructs individuals to search for clues through construction of genograms

Goals
Promote differentiation
Understand intergenerational patterns
Change troublesome patterns

Process and Techniques
Focus on process
Questions and homework assignments
Use of genograms
Going home again
Detriangulation
Person-to-person relationships
Differentiation of self
Asking questions

Diversity and Multicultural Issues
Genograms pick up cultural traditions and patterns
Differentiation applicable in multiple cultures
Little consideration is given to factors outside the family
Focus is on individuality, not togetherness

Strengths and Contributions
Calls attention to family history, deals with past patterns
Is well-established and heuristic
Has a blueprint for therapy
Has a center for educating practitioners
Is systemic, controlled, and cognitive

Limitations and Criticisms
Has failed to validate intergenerational hypothesis
Stresses the past, sometimes at the expense of the present
Is difficult to refute or verify
Requires substantial time and money
Can be complex and convoluted

KEY TERMS

asking questions 175
autonomous 170
chronic anxiety 169
detriangulate 172
differentiation 170
differentiation of self 175
family projection 171
genograms 176
going home again 174

multigenerational transmission
  process 171
nuclear family emotional
  system 171
person-to-person relationships 174
sibling position 171
societal regression 172
triangles 171
undifferentiated, aka fused 170

LEARNING MORE

A number of periodicals carry articles on the theory, research, and practice of Bowen family therapy. One journal devoted exclusively to this theory/therapy is *Family Systems: A Journal of Natural Systems Thinking in Psychiatry and the Sciences.* It is an interdisciplinary journal published since 1994 by the Georgetown Family Center. The aim of the journal is to advance the understanding of human emotional functioning and behavior based on Bowen theory.

The Georgetown Family Center also has a wealth of information on Bowen family therapy with a variety of clients in audiovisual media including audio and video recordings of each annual symposium since 2005, the Bowen Audio Lectures, and the Kerr Lecture Series. Further information about the therapy, conferences, and publications is available at:

Bowen Center for the Study of the Family
Georgetown Family Center
4400 MacArthur Blvd NW, Suite 103
Washington, DC 20007-2521
800-GFC-6882 or 202-965-4400; https://thebowencenter.org/

CLASSROOM ACTIVITIES

1. Make a genogram of your family for the past three generations. Seek help from family members if you are uncertain of facts or events. Afterward, discuss with a classmate what you learned either about your family or about making genograms. (If this activity is not suitable for you, make a genogram of a well-known historical family and note the patterns you observe.)

2. Evaluate your emotional and cognitive reactions to the following events: a wedding, a funeral, the birth of a baby, studying for a test, the completion of a mundane task like vacuuming, and reading a story about your hometown in a national newspaper. Which experiences generated the most emotion? Which engendered the most thought? What does this simple exercise tell you about the power of affect and cognition in life?

3. What family or work-based triangles are active in your community—for example, mother/child/school, boss/subordinate/product? With a classmate, make a list. After you have completed the list discuss what factors would make people more susceptible to forming triangles and how individuals could detriangulate in the situations you have listed.

14

Strategic Therapy

■ ■ ■

In desperation she did all she could
to keep her lover amused;
She cleaned, cooked, and even lied
but still she was abused.

"Abused" © S. T. Gladding

CHAPTER OVERVIEW

From reading this chapter you will learn about

■ Major dimensions of family life that strategic therapists focus on.
■ Four common procedures strategic therapists use to ensure a successful therapeutic outcome.
■ The advantages of using a directive over other forms of intervention.

As you read, consider

■ The value of telling a family you will only work with them for 10 sessions.
■ The advantages and disadvantages of working on only one problem at a time.
■ The limitations and benefits of a theory that is technique driven.

Strategic therapy is a brief, systematic, optimistic, pragmatic, and evidence-based approach to counseling (Hoyt, 2019; Szapocznik & Hervis, 2020). It can be used in a variety of settings including health and mental health clinics, substance abuse treatment programs, social service agencies, private practices, homes, schools, and churches. Strategic therapy practitioners are indebted to the genius of Milton Erickson, whose work influenced their theoretical founders. Erickson's goal in treatment was change; he believed in utilizing the resources of his clients and designing a "strategy for each specific problem" (Madanes, 1991, p. 396). Erickson then gave directives and indirect suggestions to help his clients assist themselves. He did not care whether people gained insight as long as their actions produced beneficial results. "If Freud was a philosopher-priest from Vienna, Erickson was a samurai warrior from Wisconsin" (Wylie, 1990, p. 28).

Although inspired by Erickson, the ideas and techniques of strategic therapy have been refined primarily in three different centers:

• The Mental Research Institute (MRI) in Menlo Park, California.
• The Family Therapy Training Institute of Miami (FTTIM), Florida.

- The Family Therapy Institute of Washington, D.C, aka the Washington School, 1976–1994, no longer in existence.

The MRI form of strategic therapy is the older of these therapeutic approaches. It is a descendent of the Bateson communications studies group conducted in Palo Alto from 1952 to 1962. Among the most active pioneers of this approach were Paul Watzlawick, John Weakland, Lynn Hoffman, Peggy Penn, and Richard Rabkin. The Family Therapy Training Institute of Miami (FTTIM) is a clinical, research, and training center established by Jose Szapocznik and Olga Hervis. It is known for its community involvement and evidence-based studies. Historically, the Washington School, organized in the mid-1970s and associated with Jay Haley and Cloe Madanes, who were married at the time, was a center that generated numerous ideas and methods about strategic therapy and taught practitioners as well.

The strategic therapy approaches have a history that is both long and distinguished. Jay Haley (1963, 1973) coined the term "strategic therapy" to describe the work of Milton Erickson, who paid extreme attention to the details of the symptoms his clients presented. His focus, like that of most present-day strategic therapists, was to change behavior by manipulating it, not to instill insight.

MAJOR THEORISTS: MILTON ERICKSON AND JAY HALEY

Milton Erickson (1901–1980) was a psychiatrist who specialized in hypnosis. He was the founding president of the American Society for Clinical Hypnosis and a fellow of the American Psychiatric Association and the American Psychological Association. He was especially attuned to the power of the unconscious mind as a creative, often positive, solution-generating entity.

Erickson conducted therapy by paying extreme attention to the details of the symptoms his clients presented, whatever form they might take. For example, he would focus on beliefs, background, history, habits, or anything else that would help him help his clients. Erickson's center of attention, like that of most present-day strategic therapists, was on changing behavior by manipulating it and not on instilling insight into those with whom he worked. Erickson frequently used metaphors and stories as ways of making suggestions to his clients. He discovered his effective methods by trial and error and was largely self-taught.

Erickson, who was color-blind and dyslexic, might not have been as influential as he came to be had he not contracted polio at the age of 17 on his family's farm in Wisconsin. Doctors did not expect him to live because of the severity of his condition. They told his parents as much, and overhearing the conversation, Erickson grew angry and became determined to prove the physicians wrong. He willed himself into a state of autohypnosis and lived through the day on which the doctors had said he would die. Paralyzed except for his hearing and the movement of his eyes, he became a keen observer of people, especially his family. He not only had time to observe, but he also had time to remember as well, and through recall he remembered the movement of his body and eventually gained all of his facilities back.

Later in life, he developed post-polio syndrome and was eventually confined to a wheelchair. The Bateson Group from Palo Alto, California, particularly Gregory Bateson and his wife, Margaret Mead, had consulted with Erickson by this time about trance states that Mead had observed in Bali. Through Bateson, Jay Haley came to know Erickson and essentially made his work widely known by describing it in his book *Uncommon Therapy* (1973). From this point on, Erickson found himself much in demand until the end of his life, giving lectures and teaching his methods to others.

Erickson achieved his objectives in therapy by the following procedures:

- Accepting and emphasizing the positive (i.e., he framed all symptoms and maladaptive behaviors as helpful).
- Using indirect and ambiguously worded directives.
- Encouraging or directing routine behaviors so that resistance is shown through change and not through normal and continuous actions (Haley, 1963).

Jay Haley (1923–2007) was one of the most distinguished and controversial creators in the field of family therapy. He influenced the Bateson group and the MRI group as a founding member of both and set up the Family Therapy Institute of Washington, DC, with Cloe Madanes in 1976. In addition, he served as an effective communicator between people and groups and a strong advocate of family therapy in public and professional settings (Ray, 2007).

Haley's development was unique among family therapists; he learned from and with the three people who had the most influence on the evolution of family therapy—Milton Erickson, Gregory Bateson, and Salvador Minuchin. Haley began his career with Gregory Bateson in 1952. Because Haley had a master's degree in communications, his chief responsibility on Bateson's research team was to take the lead in diagnosing communication patterns in schizophrenic families. Because of that work, Haley became interested in the hypnotherapy communication process of Milton Erickson. Haley learned hypnosis from Erickson in 1953 and later taught and practiced it (Simon, 1982). He also incorporated many of Erickson's ideas into his own concepts about therapy and learned to become a therapist under Erickson's supervision. Haley adopted and modified Erickson's individual emphasis so that it would work with families.

In 1962, after the Bateson team dissolved, Haley joined the Mental Research Institute staff and worked there until 1967. At this time, he stopped doing therapy and became primarily involved in "family research and the observation of therapy" (Simon, 1982, p. 20). He also became the first editor of the initial journal in the field of family therapy, *Family Process*, and held that position from 1962 to 1969. Haley became even more involved in supervision when he moved east to join Salvador Minuchin at the Philadelphia Child Guidance Center in 1967. With Minuchin he organized "the Institute for Family Counseling (IFC), a project training people from the Philadelphia ghetto, who had no formal education beyond high school, to be family therapists" (Simon, 1982, p. 20). This effort further established his prominence.

In 1976, he moved to the Washington, DC, area to establish the Family Therapy Institute with Cloe Madanes. Thereafter he published two of his most influential books, *Problem-Solving Therapy* (1976) and *Leaving Home* (1997). These books spell out the essence of strategic therapy as he viewed it, with an emphasis on power and hierarchy.

Haley is described as having the skills of a power broker and a military strategist and making these skills "respectable therapeutic techniques" (Wylie, 1990, p. 28). Haley retired in 1995 and died in his sleep 12 years later in La Jolla, California. There was no memorial service in Haley's honor; instead, he asked that in his memory students and admirers do something nice with their families (Zeig, 2007).

VIEW OF HUMAN NATURE/PERSONALITY

In general, strategic family therapists concentrate on the following dimensions of family life:

- **Family rules**—the overt and covert rules families use to govern themselves.
- **Family homeostasis**—the tendency of the family to remain in the same pattern of functioning unless challenged to do otherwise.
- **Quid pro quo**—the tendency of family members to treat others in the way they are being treated.
- **Redundancy principle**—a family's repetition of limited behavioral sequences.
- **Punctuation**—the belief that what individuals say in a transaction is caused by what others say.
- **Symmetrical relationships** and **complementary relationships**—relationships that are among equals (symmetrical) and among unequals (complementary).
- **Circular causality**—the idea that events are interconnected and that behaviors are caused by multiple factors.

Reflective Question

How can a change in a family's structure or roles change the family for better or worse? Think of an example.

ROLE OF THE COUNSELOR

As a group, strategic family therapies follow Ericksonian principles, emphasizing short-term treatment of about 10 sessions. Often strategic therapies are characterized as **brief therapy**, referring to the clarity about what needs to be changed rather than to the time required. "A central principle of brief therapy is that one evaluates which solutions have so far been attempted for the patient's problem" (Priebe & Pommerien, 1992, p. 433). Then different solutions are tried that are often the opposite of what has already been attempted (Watzlawick, 1978). "Brief therapists hold in common the belief that therapy must be specifically goal-directed, problem-focused, well-defined, and, first and foremost, aimed at relieving the client's presenting complaint" (Wylie, 1990, p. 29).

The roles of strategic therapists differ among the sub-schools. However, those who work within this methodology believe in being active and flexible with their clients. It is the therapist's responsibility to plan strategies to resolve family problems. Therefore, counselors often proceed quickly and specifically to resolve presenting problems and virtually ignore family histories and personal diagnoses (Wylie, 1990). "They are symptom focused and behaviorally oriented" (Snider, 1992, p. 20).

"The first task of the therapist is to define a presenting problem in such a way that it can be solved" (Madanes, 1991, p. 396). The therapist usually tries to define it as something that the family has voluntary control over and that involves a power struggle. The therapist attempts to help family members make changes that alter family dynamics from a competitive stance, in which there are winners and losers, to a cooperative position, in which everyone wins (Watzlawick, 1983).

Most strategic therapists are overtly active and direct (Gardner et al., 2006). For instance, Haley (1990) believed it was essential to make changes in individuals and families within the first three sessions. Thus, he worked hard at reframing a client's perceptions and the presenting complaints. Haley also strove for a unique and innovative approach in each case, tailored to the family as Erickson would have done, much like a surgeon would plan an operation. "Therapists also use structural interventions such as attempting to unbalance family systems by joining with one or more members on a conflictual point, fortifying generational boundaries, and supporting members at particular times to accomplish a specific objective" (Snider, 1992, p. 20). Families usually have homework assignments between sessions.

Reflective Question

What were the overt rules in your family when you were a child? What were the covert rules? How did they contribute to the functioning of your family?

GOALS

The goals of strategic therapy are to resolve, remove, or ameliorate the problem that the family has agreed to work on (Snider, 1992). In addition, the family must learn, at least indirectly, how to address other problems in a constructive manner. Often, resolving family difficulties involves a multitude of interventions, or steps. Four common procedures help ensure a successful outcome:

- Defining a problem clearly and concisely.
- Investigating all solutions that have previously been tried.
- Defining a clear and concrete change to be achieved.
- Formulating and implementing a strategy for change. (Watzlawick, 1978)

Overall, the emphasis in strategic therapy is on process rather than content. The methods used focus on breaking up vicious cycles of interaction and replacing them with virtuous cycles that highlight alternative ways of acting (Friesen, 1985).

PROCESS AND TECHNIQUES

Strategic therapists are innovative. They believe that it is not helpful to tell people what they are doing wrong or to encourage catharsis (Haley, 1976). If individuals and families are going to change, alterations in behaviors must precede new perceptions and feelings. This goal can be accomplished in an almost endless number of ways.

Each intervention in strategic therapy is tailored to the idiosyncrasies of individuals and problems. This customization makes strategic therapies some of the most technique driven of all approaches to helping. In general, strategic family therapists emphasize reframing, directives, paradoxes, ordeals, pretending, and positioning.

Reframing involves the use of language to induce a cognitive shift within family members and alter the perception of a situation. In reframing, a different interpretation is given to a family's situation or behavior, a circumstance is given new meaning, and therefore, other ways of behaving are explored. Reframing does not change a situation, but "the alteration of meaning invites the possibility of change" (Piercy & Sprenkle, 1986, p. 35). For instance, depression may be conceptualized as irresponsibility or stubbornness. Overall, reframing helps establish rapport between the therapist and the family and breaks down resistance. What was once seen as out-of-control behavior may become voluntary and open to change (see Figure 14.1).

A **directive** is an instruction from a family therapist to a family to behave differently. "The directive is to strategic therapy what the interpretation is to psychoanalysis. It is the basic tool of the approach" (Madanes, 1991, p. 397). Many types of directives can be given, including **nonverbal messages** (e.g., silence, voice tone, and posture), **direct and indirect suggestions** (e.g., "Go fast" or "You may not want to change too quickly"), and assigned behaviors (e.g., when you think you will not sleep, force yourself to stay up all night). The purpose of outside assignments is to help individuals behave differently so that they can have different subjective experiences. Directives also increase the influence of the therapist in the change process and give the therapist information about how family members react to suggested changes. One example of a directive is to tell a family to go slowly in working to bring about change. If they disobey the directive, their resistance to change may dissolve. If they follow the directive, the therapist may gain more influence in their lives.

One of the most controversial and powerful techniques in the strategic approach is **paradox** (Sexton & Montgomery, 1994). Although fine distinctions can be made between them, this process is similar to prescribing the symptom. It gives families permission to do something they are already doing and is intended to lower or eliminate resistance. Jay Haley (1976) is one of the best-known proponents of this technique, which can take many forms, especially the following three.

- In **restraining**, the therapist tells the client family they are incapable of doing anything other than what they are doing. For example, a therapist might say, "In considering change, I am not sure you can do anything other than what you are presently doing."

Figure 14.1 Reframing

Shiri Esh'har for Zebra on Wheels

- In **prescribing,** family members are instructed to enact a troublesome dysfunctional behavior in front of the therapist. For instance, parents may be asked to show how they argue with their 16-year-old about getting a driver's license. They are told to continue the argument as long as it usually lasts and to come up with the same impasses.
- **Redefining** is attributing positive connotations to symptomatic or troublesome actions. The underlying idea is that symptoms have meaning for those who display them, whether such meaning is logical or not. In the case of a school-phobic daughter, the therapist might redefine her behavior as an attempt to keep her parents together by focusing their attention on her.

Ordeals involve helping clients give up symptoms that are troublesome to maintain (Haley, 1984). In this method, the therapist assigns an ordeal, which is a constructive or neutral behavior that must be performed before one can engage in the undesirable behavior. For example, an ordeal might be to exercise before the onset of depression. The ordeal is always healthy but is not an activity the client wants to engage in. The hope is that the client will give up the symptom in order to avoid performing the constructive behavior.

The **pretend technique** is a gentler and less confrontational technique than most of the other procedures used in the strategic approach. Cloe Madanes (1981, 1984) is identified as the creator of this concept. The therapist asks family members to pretend to engage in a troublesome behavior, such as having a fight. The act of **pretending** helps individuals change by experiencing control of a previously involuntary action (see Figure 14.2).

Figure 14.2 The pretend technique
Shiri Esh'har for Zebra on Wheels

Positioning involves acceptance and exaggeration of what clients or family members are saying (Piercy & Sprenkle, 1986). If conducted properly, it helps clients see the absurdity of what they are doing, thereby freeing them to do something else. For example, if a son states that his relationship with his father is difficult, the counselor might respond, "No, it is absolutely hopeless" (Watzlawick, 1983).

Reflective Question

Directives are preferred to many other strategic therapy techniques. They are straightforward ways of changing behaviors. When have you seen directives work in your own life or in the lives of others?

DIVERSITY AND MULTICULTURAL ISSUES

Strategic counseling has been used effectively in many cultures and subcultures (Michael, 2019). For example, Santisteban et al. (2003) found brief strategic therapy to be effective in working with Hispanic youth exhibiting behavioral problems and drug use. Likewise, Soo-Hoo (1999) found brief strategic therapy effective in working with Chinese American families and consistent with their family values. The concept of reframing was an especially effective principle in this work. In addition, Szapocznik and Hervis (2020) have found their form of strategic therapy to be effective with multiple minority populations from a wide range of ethnic, racial, and socioeconomic backgrounds and geographic areas.

In short, strategic family therapists seem to be sensitive to different cultures and are able to work within them. Richeport-Haley (1998) describes a brief strategic therapy approach that can be an alternative to a culture-focused therapy. A **culture-oriented counselor** focuses on understanding cultural premises and then attempts to do therapy within the worldview of the clients. In contrast, the strategic approach emphasizes the structure of the family and offers techniques that can be used whatever the culture.

Strategic therapy is noted for its gender sensitivity as addressed by Cloe Madanes (1990). Many of today's strategic therapy practitioners use pretend techniques, which are much gentler and more gender friendly than paradox or ordeals. Counselors also pay attention to gender-related issues. For example, Madanes has devised a 16-step procedure for working with sex offenders and their victims. This approach is notable for obtaining clear facts, connecting sexuality with spirituality, and persuading the offender to seek forgiveness while kneeling before the victim.

EVALUATION OF THE THEORY

Strengths and Contributions

A major strength of strategic therapy is its flexibility with a variety of clients. This approach has been successfully used with family members who display such dysfunctional behaviors as enmeshment, eating disorders, and substance abuse (Haley, 1980; Stanton et al., 1982).

Another positive characteristic of the strategic approach is that most therapists who use it "now concede that real change is possible at the individual and dyadic level—that the entire system need not always be involved in lower-order change" (Fish, 1988, p. 15). Because significant change can be brought about without having the entire family involved in treatment sessions, the chances of a desirable outcome are increased.

A third contribution of the strategic approach is its focus on innovation and creativity. Strategic therapists trace their lineage to Milton Erickson, who was especially skilled in devising novel ways to help his clients. Strategic clinicians have continued that effort, and through their "introduction of the novel or unexpected, a frame of reference is broken and the structure of reality is rearranged" (Papp, 1984, p. 22).

An additional strength of strategic therapy is its ability to be employed with a number of other therapies (Alexander & Parsons, 1982; Fish, 1988; Haley, 1976; Steinberg et al., 1997). Because many influential therapists have a historical or personal connection with strategic therapy, they continue to be influenced in their thoughts and actions by dialogue and debate with and among strategic therapists.

A final strength of strategic therapy is the research connected with it. Szapocznik and Hervis (2020) have been especially active and diligent in conducting research on the effectiveness of strategic therapy with families, groups, and individuals. Their research has yielded impressive results and they have set up an institute for training therapists in their form of strategic therapy—brief strategic family therapy (BSFT).

Reflective Question

How do you think the multiple techniques of strategic therapy contribute to clients' attitudes of feeling valued and unique?

Limitations and Criticisms

One aspect of strategic therapy that may be considered a limitation is its concentration on one problem. Even though the one-problem approach may help families marshal their resources to deal with an identified difficulty quickly and efficiently (Snider, 1992), many families have more than one presenting problem that needs attention.

A second criticism of strategic therapy is that the approach is seen as too cookbookish and mechanical (Simon, 1984). This charge results from the prescribed methods of treatment by the MRI and Jay Haley, although therapists who embrace this theory do experience considerable flexibility.

An additional limitation of this approach is the skill necessary to implement some of its methods. For instance, the use of paradox can be powerful in the hands of a skilled clinician, but it can be a catastrophe if employed in a naive way (Friesen, 1985). Some strategic approaches demand considerable training before practitioners can implement them properly.

Another drawback of strategic therapy concerns time and emphasis. Therapists within this orientation restrict the number of therapeutic sessions, hoping to motivate families to work. However, the seriousness or extent of problems may not be dealt with adequately (Wylie, 1992). It is hoped that families will learn problem-solving skills by resolving one specific situation, although some families may not achieve this goal.

A final downside of strategic therapy is its lack of collaborative input from clients. Some models, such as those devised by Haley, emphasize power techniques and the expertise of the therapist. All stress the creativity of the therapist to find a solution for the family. Thus the strategic therapist who does not produce the desired results in clients usually takes the blame. This approach is the antithesis of most other forms of therapy.

Reflective Question

The strategic approach involves being in charge of the counseling session and what is done in it. How comfortable are you in such a role?

TREATING LINDA WITH STRATEGIC THERAPY

Conceptualization

From the perspective of strategic therapy, Linda is stuck in a homeostatic pattern of difficult interaction with older authority figures, especially demanding and demeaning men. Linda's husband was apparently much like her father, and she obeyed him even when it meant having an abortion she did not want. Linda's bosses have not been any better in their treatment of Linda, displaying sexist behavior. In many ways, Linda has acted with her husband and her bosses as she did with her father.

Linda began this behavior when she followed the rule in her family that women are inferior. This pattern has led her to function below her abilities and act out in ways that are potentially harmful to her. For example, she pursued a 2-year business degree instead of a 4-year college degree, then started working as a secretary instead of seeking a more challenging career, and recently gave notice on one job before she found another. Linda has consistently set up complementary relationships in which she is unequal. These relationships and her associated actions have left her depressed, discouraged, and trapped in unfulfilling and disheartening situations. She has also followed the redundancy principle of repeating a limited number of behaviors. Because she blames others, especially her family, for where she is today, she avoids them. However, she has not broken out of her self-defeating behavior to create new friends and opportunities.

Treatment Process

As a strategic counselor, you are quite active as you begin your work with Linda. First, you evaluate the effectiveness of solutions Linda has tried so far—for example, obedience, passive-aggressive behavior, and depression. You then help Linda define her problem in such a way that it becomes solvable: "The problem is being passive and not utilizing my abilities."

After the problem is defined, you give Linda a homework assignment. Because she came alone initially, you give her the task of bringing her family into therapy with her the next time. You want her family to collaborate with her to find better ways to experience life, thereby setting up a cooperative and potentially exciting relationship. Your goal is to help Linda formulate and implement a strategy for change in which she can be successful, breaking out of the vicious cycle she has been in and into a virtuous cycle.

When Linda comes in with her family, you are creative in finding a strategy that will work for everyone. You reframe the family's difficulties as members having forgotten to give positive and helpful messages to each other. As with anything forgotten, learning to remember is quite possible. This reframing of the problem from a negative to a positive and from a basis of blame to one of remembering is appealing to all family members. Therefore, you give them the following directive: during their Sunday lunch time, each person is to give to every other family member a sincere and helpful message framed in a positive manner. No one resists the assignment, and you remind them that they can pretend to be sincere if they find that aspect difficult.

The next week the family reports that it carried out the directive. Thus you see no need to use paradox or ordeals. You exaggerate and accept all that the family members say and compliment them on helping one another. You learn that Linda has received feedback that she is capable, smart, and able to do anything she sets her mind to. You notice that family members are sitting closer to one another and are more jovial. As the strategic therapist you are functioning as the expert, using your power as a physician does to bring about healing and growth through powerful interventions. After several more sessions, Linda and her family terminate their treatment with you. They are interacting positively and often with each other.

SUMMING UP

Strategic therapy is among the most popular approaches to working with individuals and families. The Mental Research Institute (MRI) and Jay Haley, following the creative genius of Milton Erickson, formulated it in the 1960s. It is short-term, specific, positive, and designed to change behaviors and thoughts other therapeutic approaches often overlook. As they did originally, strategic family therapists continue to limit to 10 the number of sessions in which they see a family. They work actively on clearly defined problems.

Strategic family therapists are innovative and creative. They use a variety of techniques including reframing, directives, prescribing the symptom, ordeals, pretending, and positioning. This approach is used in diverse and multicultural contexts and, thanks to the work of Cloe Madanes, is gender sensitive. Strategic therapy emphasizes the power and expertise of the therapist.

CHAPTER 14 RECAP: STRATEGIC THERAPY

Major Theorists
Milton Erickson, John Weakland, Jay Haley, Paul Watzlawick
Jose Szapocznik, Olga Hervis, Cloe Madanes

View of Human Nature/Personality
View of dysfunction as attempt to adapt
Developmental framework of the family life cycle
Personalities of individuals and families shaped by various factors—for
    example, family rules and family homeostasis, quid pro quo, circular
    causality

Role of the Counselor
Systemic view of problem behaviors, focus on process rather than content
Resolution of presenting problems, little attention to insight
Action and goal orientation
Brief, limited therapy—10 sessions or fewer

Goals
Resolve problematic behaviors
Generate new functional behaviors
Motivate by limiting number of sessions
Instill skills for resolving future conflicts

Process and Techniques
Innovative intervention tailored to specific situation
Acceptance of presenting problem(s)
Technique-driven
Use of reframing, directives, and paradoxes
Use of ordeals and pretending
Frequent homework assignments

Diversity and Multicultural Issues
Used effectively in many cultures and subcultures
Employed with gender-related concerns

Strengths and Contributions
Pragmatic and flexible
Innovative and creative
Intent on changing perceptions to foster new behaviors
Focused on one problem and limited sessions to enhance motivation
Strong research base, especially Family Therapy Training Institute of Miami

Limitations and Criticisms
May shortchange clients who have multiple problems or who need more
    time
May appear too cookbookish or mechanical
Demands considerable training for certain techniques
May not empower families

KEY TERMS

brief therapy   184
circular causality   184
complementary relationships   184
culture-oriented counselor   188
direct and indirect suggestions   186
family homeostasis   184

family rules   184
nonverbal messages   186
ordeals   187
paradox   186
positioning   187
prescribing   187

LEARNING MORE

A number of periodicals feature articles on the theory, research, and practice of strategic therapy. Most are mainstream family therapy journals.

American Journal of Family Therapy
Contemporary Family Therapy: An International Journal
Family Process
Journal of Family Psychotherapy

Strategic therapy is practiced in multiple settings; its innovative techniques and strategies make it a popular approach in counseling and therapy, especially with families. For more information, contact one of these strategic training institutes:

Mental Research Institute (MRI)
671 Oak Grove Avenue, Suite H
Menlo Park, CA 94025
650-321-3055 http://www.mri.org/https://mri.org

Family Therapy Training Institute of Miami (FTTIM)
1221 Brickell Avenue, 9th Floor
Miami, FL 33131
(305) 859-2121 (toll free)
https://brief-strategic-family-therapy.com/ or info@bsft-av.com

CLASSROOM ACTIVITIES

1. With a classmate, role-play a situation in which one of you presents a problem that is vague. The other person, as the strategic therapist, should then attempt to clarify the problem and put it into a form in which it can be solved.
2. Take four common concerns you have heard before and try to reframe them, such as "saving energy" for "laziness." Talk with the class as a whole about your perceptions of the concerns before and after your reframing.
3. Make up an ordeal you must perform before you can do something you want to do. For example, count to 150 before you get mad or take a shower before you eat an extra dessert. After you have completed the ordeal several times, talk to classmates about how it helped or hindered you.

15

Solution-Focused Therapy

■ ■ ■

She tells her story
of pain and sorrow
it is heavy as a day without a tomorrow.
She speaks again
and highlights new facts
her face is calm
her manner relaxed.
Time has been extended
hope has been awakened.

"Hope and Change" © S. T. Gladding

CHAPTER OVERVIEW

From reading this chapter you will learn about

■ How small changes can make a difference in a person's life.
■ How solution-focused therapists see clients falling into one of three categories: visitors, complainants, or customers.
■ How the miracle question can help motivate clients to see and work toward solutions.

As you read, consider

■ The difference in perceiving someone as stuck as opposed to sick.
■ How change is inevitable in life and how this concept can be used in counseling.
■ Why exceptions to problems may be helpful in resolving them.

One of the most recent theoretical developments in the field of counseling is the creation of solution-focused therapy. This approach grew out of strategic family therapy, particularly the Mental Research Institute (MRI) model. However, it departs from that tradition by concentrating on finding solutions instead of dealing with problems (Sharry et al., 2012).

One of the most experienced and articulate spokespersons for the solution-focused approach was Steve deShazer, who studied with Milton Erickson, and Insoo Kim Berg. This model appeared first in deShazer and Berg's writings and those of their associates at the Brief Family Therapy Center in Milwaukee, Wisconsin (deShazer, 1982, 1985, 1988, 1991; deShazer & Berg, 1992). Current advocates of the solution-focused position include Bill O'Hanlon and his associates (O'Hanlon & Weiner-Davis, 1989; O'Hanlon & Wilk, 1987), Patricia O'Hanlon Hudson (Hudson & O'Hanlon, 1991), Michele Weiner-Davis, Alan Gurman, Eve Lipchik, and Scott Miller. Solution-focused therapy has a Midwestern origin with a world-wide application.

MAJOR THEORISTS: STEVE DESHAZER AND BILL O'HANLON

Although Steve deShazer and William O'Hanlon developed their ideas separately, the various forms of this theory spring from the work of Milton Erickson (1901–1980). Steve deShazer (1940–2005) began his career at the MRI in the mid-1970s. In the late 1970s, he and other individuals in Milwaukee established the Brief Family Therapy Center (Kaplan, 2000). There deShazer first gained attention as a therapist and began to emerge as a major theorist through his writings in the 1980s. Initially, deShazer was considered a strategic family therapist influenced by the work of not only Milton Erickson but also Gregory Bateson and the staff of the MRI. However, beginning in the 1980s and continuing until his death, deShazer's writings and presentations were distinct from the mainstream of the strategic family therapy approach.

DeShazer (1982) identified his theory as brief family therapy, sometimes called just **brief therapy**, and described it as an ecosystemic approach. Whenever possible, he employed a team, collectively known as consultants, which observed a session from behind a one-way mirror and transmited messages to the therapist at a designated break time. Thus a client benefited from multiple inputs.

Bill O'Hanlon (1953–) entered the therapeutic world because of his own life experiences. As an adolescent, he was unhappy and shy; as a college student, he was isolated and uncomfortable in the world. He reports that he felt like "all exposed nerve—no skin—everything hurt" (Krauth, 1995, p. 24). He experimented with drugs and noticed that "the reality we all take for granted could be changed by a couple of micrograms of something introduced into one's body" (Bubenzer & West, 1993, p. 366). He also contemplated suicide but changed his mind when a friend offered him a lifetime of free rent on a Nebraska farm if he would stay alive. That possibility changed his outlook on life and led to his interest in therapeutic work that went beyond repairing damage or dealing with pathology.

After earning a tailor-made master's degree in family therapy from Arizona State University, O'Hanlon went on to receive special tutelage under Milton Erickson in exchange for tending Erickson's garden. Erickson's influence on O'Hanlon was profound and shifted his attention to a focus on solutions. He was also influenced by the MRI's work. In 1980, O'Hanlon became a major proponent of solution-focused therapy, which he now prefers to call **possibility therapy** (Bubenzer & West, 1993; Krauth, 1995). He characterizes his approach as pragmatic and full of Midwestern values.

VIEW OF HUMAN NATURE/PERSONALITY

The view of human nature characteristic of solution-focused therapy is built on the philosophy of **social constructionism**, which is the social or cultural context of people or families. Because culture influences the way individuals view the world, therapy must incorporate the philosophy of **constructivism**, which states that reality is not an objective entity, but a reflection of observation and experience (Maturana & Varela, 1987; Simon et al., 1985).

At the foundation of this approach is the belief that dysfunctional people are often stuck in dealing with their problems (deShazer, 1985). They use unsatisfactory methods to solve their difficulties, relying on patterns that do not work (Bubenzer & West, 1993). Solution-focused therapy is aimed at breaking such repetitive, non-productive behavioral patterns by enabling individuals and families to take a more positive view of troublesome situations and actively participate in doing something different. "It is not necessary to know the cause of the complaint or even very much about the complaint itself in order to resolve it" (Cleveland & Lindsey, 1995, p. 145). The presenting problem is simply the problem for which a solution needs to be worked out (Kaplan, 2000). No extensive analysis is needed.

Another premise of solution-focused therapy is that individuals really want to change. To underscore this idea, deShazer (1984, 1989) considered resistance no longer a valid concept. When clients do not follow therapists' directions, they are actually cooperating by teaching therapists the best way to help them.

A related concept is that only a small amount of change is necessary. An analogy used to illustrate this point notes that a 1-degree error in a plane's path across the United States results in a destination that is considerably off course (deShazer, 1985). Small amounts of change can also encourage people to realize that they can make progress. Even minute change boosts confidence and optimism and creates a ripple effect (Spiegel & Linn, 1969).

Reflective Question

When have you seen a small change make a difference in a person's life? Reflect on what a difference it made.

ROLE OF THE COUNSELOR

Solution-focused therapists construct solutions in collaboration with clients (Kiser et al., 1993). However, one of the therapists' first roles is to determine how active clients will be in the process of change. Clients usually fall into one of three categories: visitors, complainants, or customers. **Visitors** are not involved in the problem and are not part of the solution. **Complainants** complain about situations but can be observant and describe problems even if they are not invested in solving them. **Customers** are not only able to describe a problem and their involvement in it but are also willing to work to solve it. If therapists are working with customers or can help visitors and complainants evolve into customers, appropriate intervention strategies can be developed (Fleming & Rickord, 1997).

A solution-focused therapist becomes a "facilitator of change, one who helps clients access the resources and strengths they already have but are not aware of or are not utilizing" (Cleveland & Lindsey, 1995, p. 145). In this process, practitioners work with clients to change their perspective on a problem, paying special attention to language (West et al., 1997). Positive assumptions about change are constantly conveyed. For example, therapists might ask a presuppositional question such as

"What good thing happened since our last session?" In addition, "by selecting a specific verb tense, or implying the occurrence of a particular event … individuals are … led to believe that a solution will be achieved" (Gale, 1991, p. 43). Likewise, when an improvement occurs, therapists use positive blame and recognition of competence through such questions as "How did you make that happen?" (Fleming & Rickord, 1997).

Solution-focused therapists believe that it is important to fit therapeutic interventions into the context of individual or family behavior. This fit has been articulated by deShazer (1985), who contends that a solution does not have to be as complex as the presenting problem. The example of locks and keys illustrates what he means. Locks may be complex, but opening them does not require a similar complexity of keys. In fact, **skeleton keys** (i.e., standardized therapeutic techniques) can be helpful in dealing with most locks, regardless of complexity (see Figure 15.1).

To obtain a good solution fit, deShazer (1985) used a team whenever possible to begin **mapping** or sketching out a course of successful intervention. However, it is up to clients to define what they wish to achieve; therapists then help them define clear, specific goals that can be conceptualized concretely (deShazer, 1985; O'Hanlon & Weiner-Davis, 1989). In this process, clients and therapists begin to identify solutions—that is, desired behaviors. "Therapy is over when the agreed upon outcome has been reached" (O'Hanlon & Wilk, 1987, p. 109).

Solution-focused therapists encourage individuals and families to make small changes—in both perception and behavior—and to do so rapidly (deShazer, 1985; O'Hanlon & Weiner-Davis, 1989). Once that small change is achieved, regardless of the method used, therapists get out of the way and let the "beneficial difference amplify itself naturally" (Fleming & Rickord, 1997, p. 289). Solution-focused therapists do not distinguish between short-term and long-term problems; some problematic behaviors endure longer than others do because the right solutions have not

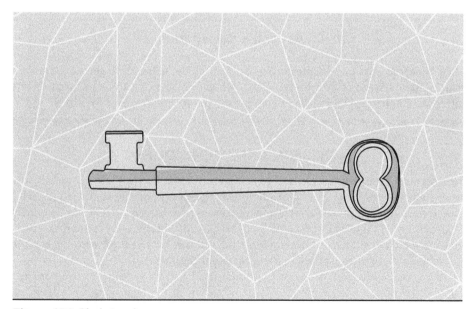

Figure 15.1 Skeleton key
Shiri Esh'har for Zebra on Wheels

been tried. Instead, solution-focused therapists are always challenging their clients to envision a "future that has possibilities of change" (Bubenzer & West, 1993, p. 372), a practice that "provides hope and expands the options for solutions" (Erdman, 2000, p. 100). To increase motivation and expectation, solution-focused therapy, like strategic therapy, emphasizes short-term treatment, between 5 and 10 sessions.

Reflective Question

What do you think of the solution-focused approach's three categories of clients: visitors, complainants, or customers? How useful do you see these categories?

GOALS

Solution-focused therapy encourages clients to seek solutions and tap internal resources. The belief is that all individuals and families have resources and strengths with which to resolve complaints (Cleveland & Lindsey, 1995); the task is simply to get them to use the abilities they already have. Thus, solution-focused therapy encourages, challenges, and sets up expectations for change. Therapists try to help clients unlock their set views, be creative, and generate novel approaches with broad applicability. The concept of pathology, as defined in the *Diagnostic and Statistical Manual of Mental Disorders*, does not play a part in the treatment process.

Identifying what is a problem and what is not a problem is a key component in the solution-focused process (deShazer, 1988). It emphasizes exceptions to generally accepted ways of behaving and viewing situations (O'Hanlon & Wilk, 1987). Solution-focused therapy takes the Ericksonian position that change is inevitable and helps clients reframe their situations positively.

Reflective Question

When have you seen an exception to a problem be the solution to the situation? For instance, people who stutter do not do so when they sing, so some individuals who stutter use singing or singing-like behavior to convey information to others.

PROCESS AND TECHNIQUES

The processes and techniques used in solution-focused therapy are geared to solutions, not problems. They have considerable research support (Franklin et al., 2017). A focus on a detailed personal or family history of problems is believed to be unhelpful (deShazer, 1985; O'Hanlon & Weiner-Davis, 1989) because there are many problems for which the cause is not understood yet can be resolved without such an understanding. Thus causal understanding is unnecessary.

A second subtle but primary technique used in this therapy is to cocreate a problem. Initially, an agreement is made as to which problem is to be solved. For example, both therapist and family must agree that a family's failure to discipline a child properly is the difficulty that needs to be addressed.

A third technique is to ask clients for a hypothetical solution to their situation, often using the **miracle question**, a technique created by Isoo Kim Berg. For example, "If a miracle happened tonight and you woke up tomorrow and the problem was solved, what would you do differently?" (Walter & Peller, 1993, p. 80). Such a question invites clients to suspend their present frame of reference and enter the reality they wish to achieve.

Another novel technique in solution-focused therapy is to focus on exceptions—that is, to look for times when clients' goals may be happening (Krauth, 1995). "In a practical sense, exceptions do not exist in the real world of clients; they must be cooperatively invented or constructed by both the client and the therapist while exploring what happens when the problem does not occur" (Fleming & Rickord, 1997, p. 289). For example, a couple that is quarreling a lot might find that they are peaceful whenever they sit down to eat. By examining the dynamics of situations or at various times, clients may learn something about who they are and how they interact. Moreover, in the process they may become different. "Inventing exceptions to problems deconstructs the client's frame: I am this way, or it always happens that way" (Fleming & Rickord, 1997, p. 289).

Reflective Question

How does the solution-focused idea of exceptions relate to the Gestalt idea of figure/ground?

Solution-focused therapists may also use the technique of **scaling**, in which questions are asked using a scale of 1 (low) to 10 (high) to help clients move toward their goal. This technique helps make problems seem more concrete and tangible (Erford, 2020). For example, a therapist might say, "On a scale of 1 to 10, how far do you think you have come in solving your problem?" If the client chooses 6, the therapist might ask what it would take to reach 7. By answering the question, the client may reach a new understanding about what immediate, realistic, and measurable steps should be taken (Fleming & Rickord, 1997) (see Figure 15.2).

A sixth technique in this approach involves second-order or qualitative change. The goal is to change clients' patterns by intervening in the order of events in clients' lives or altering the frequency and duration of a dysfunction (O'Hanlon, 1987). For example, a couple who has been having long fights at dinner might agree to finish their meal before arguing and then limit their discussion of the difficult topic to 15 minutes. This type of change in the structure and duration of events is likely to alter family dynamics.

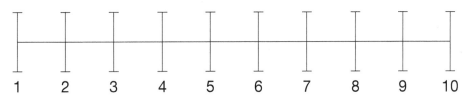

Figure 15.2 Scale from 1 to 10

A seventh intervention is to give clients compliments. For solution-focused therapists, especially deShazer (1982), a compliment is a written message designed to encourage a client's strengths—that is, to support internal motivation. A **compliment** consists of a positive statement with which the client(s) can agree. For example, a therapist might say, "I am impressed with your hard work to bring about change and the way all of you are discussing what needs to happen next." A compliment is always planned as a lead-in to giving clients a task or assignment. It builds a **yes-set**—that is, a tendency to respond affirmatively.

An additional technique is to provide clients with a **clue**, or an intervention that mirrors the clients' usual behavior. It is intended to alert clients to the idea that some behavior is likely to continue (deShazer, 1982). For example, a therapist's intervention might be, "Don't work too hard trying to spend time talking, because conversation is something that regularly occurs in your environment and you can do it naturally." The idea behind a clue is "to build mutual support and momentum for carrying out later interventions" (Sauber et al., 1985, p. 23).

One final strategy, mentioned earlier, is to use procedures that have worked before and that have a universal application. These skeleton keys help clients unlock a variety of problems (deShazer, 1985). Five interventions have been found useful in a number of situations (deShazer & Molnar, 1984):

- "Between now and next time we meet, we (I) want you to observe, so that you can tell us (me) next time, what happens in your (life, marriage, family, or relationship) that you want to continue to happen" (p. 298). Such an assignment encourages clients to look at the stability or steadiness of the problems on which they wish to work.
- "Do something different" (p. 300). This type of request encourages individuals to explore their range of possibilities, rather than to continue to do what they believe is correct. DeShazer gives an example of a woman who complained that her husband, a police detective, was staying out late every night with his friends. The deShazer team suggested that her husband might want her to be more mysterious. Therefore, one night she hired a babysitter, rented a motel room, and stayed out until 5 a.m. Her husband had come in at 2 a.m. Nothing was said, but her husband began staying home at night.
- "Pay attention to what you do when you overcome the temptation or urge to ... perform the symptom or some behavior associated with the complaint" (p. 302). This instruction helps clients realize that symptom behaviors are under their control.
- "A lot of people in your situation would have ... " (p. 302). This type of statement helps clients realize that they may have options other than those they are exercising. With such awareness, they can begin to make needed changes.
- "Write, read, and burn your thoughts" (p. 302). This experience consists of writing about past times and then reading and burning the writings the next day in an attempt to move on (deShazer, 1985) (see Figure 15.3).

Overall, solution-focused interventions help clients view their situations differently. They can also give them hope, thereby assisting them in powerful ways (Bubenzer & West, 1993). In the words of deShazer and Molnar (1984), "It now appears to us that the therapists' ability to see change and to help the clients to do so as well, constitutes a most potent clinical skill" (p. 304).

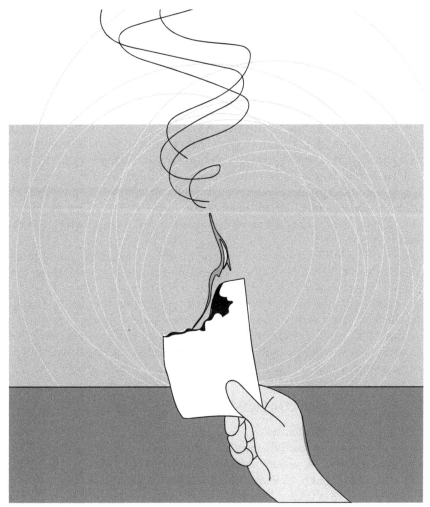

Figure 15.3 Burning thoughts
Shiri Esh'har for Zebra on Wheels

Reflective Question

On a scale from 1 to 10 (the highest number being the most positive), rate how much you are enjoying learning about counseling theories. What would you have to do to get a higher number?

DIVERSITY AND MULTICULTURAL ISSUES

Solution-focused therapy has made strides in recent years to become more sensitive to and appropriate for different cultural groups—for example, Chinese (Cheung, 2001; Yeung, 1999), Muslim Americans (Chaudhry & Li, 2011), American Indians

(Meyer & Cottone, 2013), and African American and Mexican American families (Corcoran, 2000). The practice of solution-focused therapy has been extended to end-of-life and grief counseling too (Simon, 2010). Practitioners of the approach have also sought to integrate it with other cultural views of helping. For instance, Hung-Hsiu-Chang and Ng (2000) compare the phenomenon of change in two different worldviews—I Ching and solution-focused therapy—and attempt to integrate these views for therapeutic usefulness.

Kim (2014) has edited the most extensive collection of research on the appropriateness of solution-focused therapy in different cultural settings. Besides the groups already mentioned, this book examines solution-focused therapy with LBGQ clients, the disabled, immigrants, and the economically poor. In addition to cultural settings, solution-focused therapy has also been associated with wellness, especially with college students (Beauchemin, 2018). Furthermore, Taylor (2019) has produced creative and playful approaches for using solution-focused therapy with children and adolescents.

Solution-focused therapy is also sensitive to trauma issues prevalent in all cultures. O'Hanlon & Bertolino (2002), for example, address sexual abuse and the ways in which solution-focused therapy can help survivors work through their trauma. Another gender-sensitive approach is a "gender solution-focused genogram to help clients identify the beliefs and behaviors related to their presenting problems" (Softas-Nall et al., 1999, p. 179). This special type of genogram may be particularly useful in identifying past gender-role messages that have negatively influenced present behaviors.

EVALUATION OF THE THEORY

Strengths and Contributions

A strength of solution-focused therapy is that it concentrates on and is directed by a client's theory or story. Before any attempt is made to create change, clients' experiences are accepted. Whatever clients bring to therapy is examined from a broad context, but the past is emphasized only when it calls attention to the present. O'Hanlon compares this type of approach with the Rogerian concept of listening attentively to how people are feeling before trying to implement change (Bubenzer & West, 1993).

A second contribution of solution-focused therapy is that therapists assist clients in defining their situations with clarity, precision, and possibility. These therapists emphasize that "the defined problem should be achievable" (Todd, 1992, p. 174). Sometimes success is measured in the elimination of a problem; at other times, clients may change their perception of a situation or discover exceptions to troublesome times. Small changes in behavior are the basis for larger systemic changes, and therapists encourage and reinforce any type of change. Their belief is that once change starts, it will continue. "Solution-focused brief therapy ... asserts that change is inevitable" (Kok & Leskela, 1996, p. 398).

Another positive aspect of solution-focused therapy is that it does not focus on a clinical understanding of a client's situation; instead, the focus is on change. The therapist's job is to produce change by helping clients focus on their solutions to the problems they have reported. Therapists may prompt change by challenging their clients' worldviews, asking appropriate questions, and assigning tasks that help clients unlock their own potential. Grantham and Budnik (2016) have even produced worksheets solution-focused therapists can use with their clients to facilitate the process.

A related strength of solution-focused therapy is that it is empowering as it assists clients in assessing and utilizing their resources. Formula tasks and awareness exercises help people help themselves. Clients "are encouraged to imagine a future without the problem(s) so that they can identify what they will be doing (solutions)" (Kok & Leskela, 1996, p. 398).

Furthermore, the flexibility of solution-focused therapy is exceptional. It can be employed in working with a variety of disorders and situations, such as children and adolescents in a family context (Berg & Steiner, 2003), problem drinkers (Berg & Miller, 1992), and eating disorders (McFarland, 1995).

Limitations and Criticisms

One drawback to solution-focused therapy is that little attention is paid to client history. Sometimes individuals need to resolve issues from their past before they can move into the present or future. However, solution-focused therapy makes no provision for such a need.

A second criticism of solution-focused therapy is that it ends when a behavioral goal is reached (O'Hanlon & Wilk, 1987). If there is no further complaint or objective, there is no further treatment. In this respect, solution-focused therapy is like many forms of behavioral therapy; it concentrates on resolving a concrete objective. Although behavioral accomplishments are important, some clients need additional help changing accompanying thoughts and/or feelings. Again, solution-focused therapy does not provide for such needs.

Another limitation of solution-focused therapy is that some proponents, mainly deShazer and Berg, use a team approach in helping clients. Even though there are generally fewer sessions in such an approach, the expense of this treatment may be great.

TREATING LINDA WITH SOLUTION-FOCUSED THERAPY

Conceptualization

From a solution-focused perspective, Linda is stuck in a pattern of dysfunctional behavior. She really wants to change but does not know how and consequently is angry and depressed with suicidal thoughts. She has found some solace from the pain of her divorce and interpersonal failures in romance novels, television shows, and action movies. When she is engaged in any of these activities, she does not feel as badly, but these escapes are temporary. However, you see these activities as exceptions to her dysfunctional way of interacting with others. Moreover, although you do not dwell on history, you notice that Linda could have gone to a 4-year college and wonder if intelligence is one of her assets.

Treatment Process

As a solution-focused therapist, you want to set up a collaborative working relationship with Linda and challenge her to envision a new future. Linda is a customer who wants to get better and is willing to work. Consequently, you convey to her that change is inevitable and set up expectations for such change, even if it is small. You also remind Linda that you have only 5 to 10 sessions in which to treat her, so it is important to get right to work.

Initially, you work with Linda to cocreate a problem, which turns out to be that she is lonely, feeling helpless, and cut off from meaningful relationships. When you ask Linda the miracle question, you find out that if the problem were resolved, she would have friends in her life, earn a college degree, and be closer to her family. When you ask her to scale her handling of her problem, she puts it at a 3. For that rating to be higher—that is, more positive—Linda says she would be reading fewer books, watching less television, and seeing fewer movies. She would also apply to a college and find a hobby she could engage in with others.

You compliment Linda on her strength and suggest that a lesser person would have caved in to the circumstances. At the same time, you work with her to find all the exceptions to her feeling depressed, such as when she is reading. You work with her as well to find skeleton keys she can use to overcome her situation. One such key is a telephone call to friends to set up times to do things together. Another skeleton key is to call a local community center to locate activities that she would enjoy and that would introduce her to new people. A third skeleton key is to visit a nearby college and inquire about admission. In all of these situations, Linda is likely to be more energized, more optimistic, and less depressed.

After Linda completes her initial homework, you ask her to scale her feelings about her life again. Her score increases to a 6. You then challenge her to envision an even brighter future and let her convey to you the ways that future might come about, such as her becoming more active in social outlet groups, reconnecting with her family in a different way, and applying to college. After this session and one more, you terminate therapy, although Linda can refer herself back if necessary. Before termination, though, you do ask Linda to report back to you about her progress in a couple of months, reemphasizing the fact that change is inevitable and need not be large to make a big difference in her life.

SUMMING UP

In the 1980s and especially in the 1990s, the work of deShazer, Berg, Weiner-Davis, and O'Hanlon brought national attention to solution-focused therapy. This approach concentrates on bringing change to a wider range of client problems. It is short-term, specific, and positive and concentrates on effecting small changes in the process of facilitating larger ones. Although unique, solution-focused therapy was greatly influenced by Milton Erickson.

Solution-focused therapy is concerned with changing present behaviors rather than examining past histories. It stresses that individuals and families have untapped resources that can and should be marshaled in helping them help themselves. This approach is creative in innovative ways that go beyond traditional forms of therapy—for example, it emphasizes that change is inevitable and small change may be very effective in a person's life.

CHAPTER 15 RECAP: SOLUTION-FOCUSED THERAPY

Major Theorists
Steve deShazer, William O'Hanlon
Insoo Kim Berg, Michele Weiner-Davis

View of Human Nature/Personality
Importance of social constructionism
Dysfunctional use of unsatisfactory methods to solve difficulties
Availability of personal resources/strengths
Innate desire to change
Value of small change

Role of the Counselor
Collaborates with client
Assesses client involvement as visitor, complainant, or customer
Fosters a new perspective
Fits intervention to client
Lets small changes grow
Does not distinguish between short-term and long-term problems
May use team approach

Goals
Tap internal client resources and seek solutions
Change client focus from problems to solutions
Reframe situations positively

Process and Techniques
Use of short-term framework
Focus on single problem
Use of miracle question and scaling
Focus on exceptions, change in organization, and structure
Use of compliments, clues, skeleton keys

Diversity and Multicultural Issues
Applicable to different cultural groups
Sensitive to victims of sexual abuse
Appropriate for gender solution-focused genograms

Strengths and Contributions
First accepts clients' stories/experiences
Defines situations carefully
Focuses on change
Helps clients utilize resources
Emphasizes small change, inevitability of change
Is flexible

Limitations and Criticisms
Pays little attention to client history
Ends when behavioral goal is reached
May increase expense with team approach

KEY TERMS

brief therapy (focus on a single
    problem) 195
burning thoughts 200–201
clue 200
complainants 196
compliment 200
constructivism 195
customers 196

exceptions 199
mapping 197
miracle question 199
possibility therapy 195
scaling 199
skeleton keys 197
social constructionism 195
visitors 196

LEARNING MORE

A number of periodicals carry articles on the theory, research, and practice of solution-focused therapy.

American Journal of Family Therapy
Journal of Family Therapy
Journal of Systemic Therapies

Solution-focused therapy is a popular approach to use with a variety of clients. More information is available from the following related organizations and institutes:

Brief Family Therapy Center
P.O. Box 13736
Milwaukee, WI 53213
414-302-0650 http://www.brief-therapy.org/

European Brief Therapy Association http://www.ebta.nu/

CLASSROOM ACTIVITIES

1. Think of a small change you made in the past that made an important difference in your life. Talk with a classmate about that change and other small changes you have seen others make that were beneficial.
2. Look at a behavior that is troublesome to you or somebody else. Then focus on exceptions—that is, times when the behavior is not happening. What do the exceptions tell you about the dynamics of the behavior and the person displaying it?
3. Practice asking the miracle question to friends or relatives who complain they are having a problem. What do you notice about their reactions?

16

Psychodrama

■ ■ ■

Emotions ricochet around the room
fired by an act of self-disclosure
in an atmosphere of trust.
I, struck by the process,
watch as feelings penetrate the minds of members
and touch off new reactions.
Change comes from many directions
triggered by simple words.

"Group Dynamics" © S. T. Gladding

CHAPTER OVERVIEW

From reading this chapter you will learn about

■ The origins and premises of psychodrama.
■ The three phases of psychodrama (warm-up, action, and integration).
■ The main techniques used in psychodrama.

As you read, consider

■ The similarity of psychodrama compared to other theories.
■ The distinct techniques psychodrama uses to bring about change.
■ The populations psychodrama might be a potent theory for.

Drama is pervasive in society. Popular Broadway shows such as *Hamilton* and *Wicked* enact many of our most basic emotions and give us insight into human behavior. The Academy Awards too dramatically give us a glimpse of humanity at its best and worst. Apart from theatre and film, we speak of teenage girls sometimes behaving as "drama queens" and we talk about delinquent adolescent boys as "acting out." Shakespeare's phrase that "all the world's a stage" is confirmed in our observations of others. Actions and words convey dramatically and sometimes humorously the world of humanity. An example of both occurred when a woman who was mad at Abraham Lincoln called him two-faced. The notably humorous but unhandsome Lincoln replied, "Ma'am, if I were two-faced, would I be wearing this one?"

In this chapter, a form of drama—psychodrama—is examined. Psychodrama is one of the oldest and most dynamic theories devised for working with individuals in groups (Fox, 2008; Von Ameln & Becker-Ebe, 2020). It is based on existential and communications theories and is opposite from psychoanalysis in its approach to therapy. A core tenet of psychodrama is Moreno's **theory of spontaneity-creativity**— that is, the best way for an individual to respond creatively to a situation is through spontaneity—a readiness to improvise and respond in the moment.

Psychodrama is applicable in a number of settings and is practiced worldwide (Blajan-Marcus, 1974; Blanc & Boutinaud, 2017; Moreno, 1949; Sang et al., 2018). One of the most productive spin-offs of this approach is the use of role-play with psychoeducational, psychotherapeutic, and growth groups (Blatner, 1996, 2005).

MAJOR THEORISTS: JACOB MORENO (1889–1974) AND ZERKA MORENO (1917–2016)

Psychodrama explores the human psyche through dramatic action. The idea evolved out of Jacob Moreno's creativity, which was fostered by his encounters with children and his love for spontaneity and creativity. Moreno believed spontaneity and creativity theoretically were the underlying contributors to psychological health (Orkibi, 2019). Moreno initially experimented with his theory in the streets of Vienna after World War I with an enactment procedure known as the "Living Newspaper." He spent the rest of his life developing and refining the concepts and practice of psychodrama both in Austria and in the United States (Moreno, 1984; Moreno, 2014; Nolte, 1989). Psychodrama gained notoriety in the United States as a therapeutic intervention at Moreno's psychodrama theater in Beacon, New York, and at St. Elizabeth's Hospital in Washington, DC.

Moreno found that individuals who played nonscripted and unrehearsed parts, as well as members of audiences, experienced an **emotional catharsis** (a release of pent-up feelings) because of participating in or observing dramatic enactment. Shortly thereafter, psychodrama as a formal system was conceptualized, with Moreno stressing the uniqueness of the approach by having group members relive, instead of retelling or analyzing, significant events or conflicts in their lives. He advocated a group approach in an era of intrapersonal emphasis. Psychodrama became an extension of Moreno's personality (Fox, 2008; Moreno, 2014). Therefore, many of his contributions to the field of counseling (e.g., his emphasis on action and his focus on the here and now) have never been properly acknowledged.

Zerka Moreno's life and credentials were quite different from Jacob Moreno's. She was born Zerka Toeman in Amsterdam in 1917 and attended secondary school in the Netherlands and a technical school in London before settling in the United States in 1939. She did not attend college or medical school, yet she was very intelligent. She met Jacob Moreno in 1948 when she sought psychiatric care for a sister. They married shortly thereafter. Zerka, along with Jacob, cofounded the International Association for Group Psychotherapy and the American Society of Group Psychotherapy and Psychodrama. Zerka also authored dozens of books and articles on psychodrama, including her 2012 memoir, *To Dream Again*. She continued to practice psychodrama for more than 30 years after Jacob Moreno's death and clarified many of his ideas.

VIEW OF HUMAN NATURE/PERSONALITY

Psychodrama is predicated on the assumption that people are continually evolving and can become aware of matters pertaining to their lives at any developmental stage. Individuals who are open to themselves begin to realize their strengths as well as their liabilities. Such realizations make them more capable of meeting external demands in creative and purposeful ways.

Psychodrama emphasizes a freeing of individuals from the irrational forces that bind them into dysfunctional behavior patterns. Psychodrama emphasizes action (Carnabucci, 2014). The approach is conducted in a group setting and group members are given an opportunity to act out and experience various aspects of their problem(s). Personal interactions and encounters focus on the here and now, spontaneity and creativity, full expression of feelings, and reality testing (Von Ameln & Becker-Ebe, 2020).

An emphasis of psychodrama is on the holistic interaction of protagonists—that is, clients, in their dramas. Protagonists rework their lives as both players and playwrights (Blatner, 2000). Habitual verbal defenses are circumvented and new realizations occur (Blatner, 2005). For instance, group members might show the group how their interactions with their father affected their view of work. The members would then enact alone or with others early memories that came to mind. The result would be a new awareness by the group members that they could then discuss observations from others of what they noticed in the enactment(s).

Reflective Question

What do you think about acting and actors and the roles they assume? Do you think it changes them over time? Why? Have you ever played a part in a play? How did it affect you?

ROLE OF THE COUNSELOR

The director of a psychodrama is a therapist with training in this discipline. He or she is the leader and as such wears many hats. Moreno (1953, 1964) suggests that the director serves as a producer, a facilitator, an observer, and an analyzer. The director sets norms and models skills that ensure safety and personal control (Brown-Shaw et al., 1999). The director builds his or her skills in three areas:

- Knowledge of methods, principles, and techniques.
- Understanding of personality theory and its relationship to developing an evolving philosophy of life.
- His or her own personality development and maturity. (Blatner, 1996)

In addition to a broad general knowledge of life and human nature, a director is expected to have completed specific coursework in subject areas such as general psychology, group process, communication theory, and nonverbal communications.

The director's function is to conduct such tasks as

- Leading the warm-up experience.
- Encouraging the development of trust and spontaneity.
- Establishing a structure so that protagonists can identify and work on significant issues in their lives.
- Protecting members from abuse by others.
- Bringing some type of closure to group sessions.

Potential directors should have experienced many psychodramas and have received direct supervision from experienced directors. Overall, Corsini (1966) concludes that effective group directors possess three qualities: creativity, courage, and charisma.

Reflective Question

How do you think people's lives might change if they saw themselves as the directors of their lives instead of just players?

GOALS

The desired outcome of psychodrama can be described as catharsis, insight, and emotional resolution (Horvatin & Schreiber, 2006; Moreno, 1964). Yablonsky (1981) states that Moreno's goal in psychodrama is "to develop a 'theatrical cathedral' for the release of the natural human spontaneity and creativity that he believed existed naturally in everyone" (p. 274). Through psychodrama, individuals should be able to experience and work through past, present, or anticipated events that have caused them distress. When they have gained emotional and cognitive insight by acting out their difficulties, they will reach a stage of renewed self-awareness, readjustment, integration, acceptance, control, and prevention.

It is essential that participants in psychodramas be willing to take risks and be open to constructive feedback. One of the desirable spin-offs from psychodrama is the learning that takes place when one is not the main protagonist. A definite spillover effect from this approach is watching a main character reach resolution on important issues.

PROCESS AND TECHNIQUES

The practice of psychodrama is multidimensional. First, physical and personal factors must be considered, such as a stage, a protagonist, actors, a director, and an audience (Blatner, 1996, 2005; Nolte, 2020).

The **stage** is the area where the action takes place. It may be a platform or simply be a part of a room. The stage is wherever the participants want it to be. For instance, Jason may say, "The corner of the room will be my stage this time." Most groups find it beneficial to have the stage in a separate place from where the group meets to remind members that the enactments are different from verbal interchanges (Blatner, 1996).

The **protagonist** is the subject of the psychodrama enactment (Blatner, 2005). He or she may play many parts. For example, in a psychodrama, Laurel as the protagonist played different parts of herself, from sweet and innocent to mean and spiteful. At times, the protagonist may step out of a scene and observe. Regardless, the goal of the protagonist is to express the thoughts, feelings, and issues relevant to the role. A key element to being a protagonist is spontaneity.

Actors play the parts of other important people or objects in the play. They are called "**auxiliaries**," and with prompting from the protagonist, they can play the protagonist's double, an antagonist, or even a piece of furniture or a plant. An auxiliary can play more than one part, such as both the protagonist's best friend and worst enemy.

The **director** guides protagonists in the use of psychodramatic methods to help them explore their problems (Blatner, 1996). The director is roughly equivalent to the group leader in designating what is going to happen next and how.

Finally, the **audience** describes others who are present during the psychodrama. The purpose of the audience is to give feedback regarding what they saw, heard, and felt during the psychodrama. Sometimes the audience becomes involved while the psychodrama is conducted and makes sound effects or comments at the request of the director. For example, the audience might be directed to repeat to Rhonda when she gets angry and makes a mistake, "Keep cool. Use your head. Keep cool. Use your head." In such cases, the audience becomes a chorus.

Reflective Question

When have you experienced life differently or been affected by watching a theatre production or movie? What changed in your life?

The psychodrama process employing these techniques generally goes through three phases: warm-up, action, and integration.

1. **Warm-up phase**—The warm-up phase is characterized by the director making sure he or she is ready to lead the group and that members are ready to be led. This process may involve both verbal and nonverbal activities designed to put everyone in the right frame of mind to conduct the psychodrama and establish trust and an atmosphere of spontaneity (Blatner, 2005; Moreno, 1940). For instance, the director may walk around arranging furniture while speaking to participants. Then he or she may lead the group in some get-acquainted exercises. After these activities, the group may engage in action exercises (e.g., sensory awareness methods, guided imagery), which help members discover common themes within the group as well as focus on individual concerns. Overall, the warm-up is experiential and allows members to process some of the technical procedures they will experience in the actual psychodrama (Howie & Bagnall, 2015; Leveton, 2001). Specific techniques often employed in the warm-up phase are:
   - **Creative imagery**—This warm-up technique consists of inviting psychodrama participants to imagine neutral or pleasant objects and scenes. The idea is to help participants become spontaneous. For instance, Del realizes he can create a picture of a sunrise from a mountaintop although he lives on a coastal plain.
   - **Magic shop**—This warm-up technique is especially useful for protagonists who are ambivalent about their values and goals. It involves a storekeeper (an auxiliary ego) who runs a magic shop filled with special qualities. The qualities are not for sale but may be bartered for (Verhofstadt & Leni, 2000). Thus, if Leroy, the protagonist, wants better relationship skills, he may have to give up irrational anger in exchange.

At the end of the warm-up, the action phase of psychodrama begins.

2. **Action phase**—The action phase of the psychodrama process involves the enactment of protagonists' concerns. The crucial thing in the action stage is that protagonists express repressed emotions and find a new, effective way to act. The director helps each protagonist who chooses to work "set the stage" for a specific scene in the here and now. Group participants are assigned auxiliary ego roles of significant others or things in the protagonist's life. Then the opening scene is enacted after which the protagonist and auxiliary egos are given an opportunity to refine their roles.

The action phase includes more techniques than any other part of the psychodrama. At the heart of psychodrama is the **encounter**, an existentialist concept that involves total physical and psychological contact among individuals on an intense, concrete, and complete basis in the here and now. The encounter can relate to past events, anticipated happenings, or present circumstances, but it always involves taking a moment or a situation in one's life and expanding it in various dimensions (Leveton, 2001).

One dimension the encounter deals with is **surplus reality**—a "psychological experience that transcends the boundaries of physical reality" (Blatner, 2005a, p. 429). These experiences, which include relationships with individuals who have died or were never born, or with God, are often as important to people as actual occurrences. For example, Jodie might still grieve for the child she lost in childbirth. In the encounter, she could express her feelings through dramatically reliving the scene of loss and the ways she might have handled or dealt with the tragedy at that time. Overall, the encounter is the experience of identity and total reciprocity, summed up by Moreno (1914) in the following poetic way:

> A meeting of two: eye to eye, face to face. And when you are near I will tear your eyes out and place them instead of mine, and you will tear my eyes out and will place them instead of yours, and I will look at you with your eyes and you will look at me with mine. (p. 3)

Other main concepts that emphasize Moreno's premise on experiencing one's situation fully in the here and now during the action phase of a psychodrama are spontaneity, situation, sculpting, soliloquy, monodrama, double, mirror, role reversal, tele, catharsis, and insight.

- **Spontaneity** is the response people make that contains "some degree of adequacy to a new situation or a degree of novelty to an old situation" (Moreno, 1945, p. xii). The purpose of spontaneity is to liberate oneself from scripts and stereotypes and gain new perspectives on life. Responding in new creative ways is part of this process. For example, Mildred, instead of panicking when she is given a math test, now begins to sit calmly and study the whole exam before making a response.
- **Situation** is the emphasis on the present, where "natural barriers of time, space, and states of existence are obliterated" (Greenberg, 1974, pp. 16–17). Under these circumstances, individuals can work on past problems, future fears, and current difficulties in a here-and-now atmosphere. For instance, Lucas plans for his high school graduation, college, and an entry-level job by confronting his fear of success and his present lack of self-confidence.

- **Sculpting**—In this exercise, group members use nonverbal methods to arrange other group members into a configuration like that of significant individuals with whom they regularly deal, such as family members or social peers. The positioning involves body posturing. It assists members in seeing and experiencing their perceptions of significant others in a dynamic way. For example, by arranging family members with their backs toward her, Regina realizes how shut out of her family she felt when growing up.

- **Soliloquy**—This technique involves the protagonist giving a monologue about his or her situation as he or she is acting it out. For instance, an individual driving home from work alone may give words to the thoughts that are uppermost on his or her mind, such as "I feel life is unfair." A variation on this activity is the **therapeutic soliloquy technique,** in which private reactions to events in the protagonist's life are verbalized and acted out, usually by other actors. For example, other group members may push and tug at each other, showing Helena her ambivalence about going on to graduate school.

- **Monodrama or autodrama**—In this technique, the protagonist plays all the parts of the enactment; no auxiliary egos are used. The individual may switch chairs or talk to different parts of the self. The monodrama is a core feature of Gestalt therapy too. For instance, Walt becomes the significant thoughts he has about his upcoming marriage and has a dialogue between these expressions in different chairs arranged in a circle.

- **Double and multiple double**—The **double** is an important technique in psychodrama. The group member designated by the director takes on the role of the protagonist's alter ego and helps the protagonist express inner feelings. The double follows the lead of the director but can also make feeling statements to guide the director in case they miss a cue (Monterio-Leitner, 2001).

In cases in which the protagonist has ambivalent feelings, the **multiple double** technique is used. In these situations, two or more actors represent different aspects of the protagonist's personality. The doubles may speak at once or take turns. Through their input, the protagonist should gain an idea of what his or her thoughts and feelings are.

Doubles can emphasize or amplify statements made by the protagonist in a number of ways. Speaking to the protagonist in the first person, doubles may verbalize nonverbal communications, question themselves, interpret what is being said and not said, contradict feelings, make a self-observation, or engage in denial (Blatner, 1996, 2000). For instance, referring to Irene's changing jobs, her double says, "I wonder for whom I am doing this, myself or my children?" An effective double will reach the core of the protagonist's experience, and the protagonist will feel confirmed and understood.

- **Mirror**—In this activity, the protagonist watches from offstage while an auxiliary ego mirrors the protagonist's posture, gesture, and words. This technique is used to help the protagonist see himself or herself more accurately. For instance, Rufus learns through watching Buster mirror him that he is not the clearheaded, decisive individual he imagined himself to be.

- **Role reversal**—In this technique, the protagonist switches roles with another individual on stage and plays that individual's part. For instance, Zelda becomes Mia and acts like her. Zerka Moreno (1998) stated that role reversal encourages the maximum expression of conflict. Hagedorn and Hirshhorn (2009) maintain that role reversal is a core part of psychodrama.

Reflective Question

Although a role reversal may result in conflict, a refusal to do so may deepen prejudice. Think of how you might act if you reversed roles with people you did not agree with. Might your prejudice lessen?

- **Tele** is the total communication of feelings between people, "the cement which holds groups together" (Moreno, 1945, p. xi). It is experienced most when it occurs between two people. At its best, it involves complete interpersonal and reciprocal empathy. In a tele, Mitch and Sandy tell each other which qualities they most admire in the other and how it makes them feel when they think they have expressed one or more of these qualities, such as empathy and poise.
- **Catharsis** is one of the "end products" of spontaneity and tele. Catharsis involves an emotional purging, such as when Delilah screams out about her mother, "All I ever wanted you to do was love me!" Although it is one of the end products of spontaneity and tele, catharsis is "the beginning of reparation and healing" because what was disowned, such as suffering and grief, is now personally accepted, expressed, and integrated (Westwood et al., 2003, p. 123).
- **Insight** is a related concept to catharsis, consisting of immediate new perceptions and understandings about one's problems that occur during or after the experience of catharsis. For instance, in the preceding example, Delilah might say after her cathartic experience, "I never realized I was so angry."

3. **Integration/Sharing phase**—The last phase of a psychodrama—integration/sharing—involves discussion and closure. It is necessary because after the action phase, a protagonist is off balance, vulnerable, and in need of support. During integration and sharing, the director encourages the group to give the protagonist as much personal, supportive, and constructive feedback as possible. Feedback focuses initially on the affective rather than the intellectual aspects of the enactment. Toward the end of the group session, it is appropriate to express some cognitive aspects of what has been experienced (Blatner, 1996; Corey, 2017). At the completion of this phase, an emphasis is placed on understanding and integrating what has been learned so the protagonist can act differently if similar situations arise.

A psychodrama ends with protagonists becoming themselves as they were before the psychodrama began. This transition from acting to becoming oneself again is known as de-roling. When de-roling it is important to go through a ritual such as "One, two, three, I am me." Then, after the protagonist is back to being the person he or she was before the psychodrama, there is time for **group sharing, processing, identification** with elements of the role-play, and **closure.**

Group sharing is simply giving everyone involved in a psychodrama, including the audience, an opportunity to comment on what they saw and heard. **Processing**

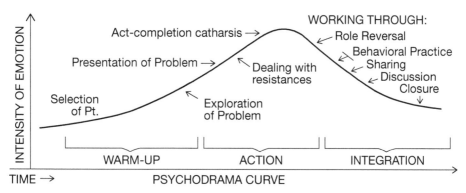

Figure 16.1 Psychodrama curve

is delving deeper into the psychodrama to talk about how participants at all levels were affected by what they experienced. During processing, **identification** and **integration** occur where members of a group state how they could or could not see themselves acting in certain ways or saying specific things and what they have learned from the psychodrama experience. When there is identification and integration, a bond of understanding is created between individuals and ways of understanding self and others become deeper.

Finally, the director moves the group to **closure**. In this phase of the group, the discussion among members transitions from affective responses and behavioral descriptions to becoming cognitive. It results in what is sometimes known as **cognitive capping**—that is, remembering on an intellectual basis what occurred and the lessons learned. By becoming more cognitive, members of the psychodrama group can leave the psychodrama and resume their lives as before but with new knowledge.

The techniques employed in psychodrama as well as the process are dependent on many variables (Nolte, 2020). Among the most important factors that influence both are the situation of the protagonist, the skill of the director, the availability of actors, the size of the audience, the goals of the session, and the phase in which the psychodrama is operating. Special situations will require different skills. Regardless, it is important that techniques be employed in a methodological manner (Holmes & Karp, 1991; Moreno & Moreno, 1959) (see Figure 16.1).

DIVERSITY AND MULTICULTURAL ISSUES

Psychodrama is very much attuned to diversity and multicultural issues. This theoretical approach is applicable in psychoeducational and business settings as well as psychotherapeutic environments. For example, Harvard Law School uses certain aspects of psychodrama to help students practice interpersonal skills they have difficulty performing (Bordone, 2000).

Furthermore, psychodrama can be employed with individuals of all age, educational, and socioeconomic levels. For instance, Amatruda (2006) helped 10–13-year-old elementary school children in a special education program communicate more positively with one another and improve their status with peers by using action techniques and psychodrama methods. Students' negative behaviors in the classroom decreased, their interactions with one another were more positive, and their attitudes toward their own potential improved because of the psychodrama-based conflict resolution and skill-building training.

Other forms of psychodrama have been used in family therapy, addiction treatment, training of theologians, sensitizing of leaders, support of LGBTQ adolescents, and supervision of counselors (Allan, 2015; Gendron, 1980; Wilkins, 1995). A unique use of psychodrama is in middle school to help teachers and counselors demonstrate the concept of roles (Shaffer, 1997) and to describe and prevent bullying behavior. A novel form of psychodrama is a structured "guided autobiography," which is used with older people as an educational and therapeutic exercise (Brown-Shaw et al., 1999).

Reflective Question

Do you think psychodrama is the most effective theory in this book for dealing with diversity? Why or why not?

EVALUATION OF THE THEORY

Strengths and Contributions

Psychodrama groups can be powerful and have much to commend them as ways of working with others. A major strength of psychodrama is its diversity and multicultural inclusiveness. Pyschodrama can be used with individuals from all backgrounds, life stages, and abilities. It is very flexible and useful in a variety of settings (Farmer, 2018).

A second positive aspect of psychodrama is its teaching potential. Group members learn a great deal about themselves through their active participation (Kranz & Lund, 1993). As Zerka Moreno (1983) pointed out, professionals in various mental health specialties can use psychodrama to learn how they interact and resolve matters with difficult clients. Psychodrama gives these professionals a feeling for situations.

A third strength of a psychodrama group is its fostering of creativity and spontaneity within leaders and members (Coven et al., 1997). A major problem that people have is their inability to find resolutions to stressful or harmful situations. Psychodrama promotes new ways to help people find solutions to problems. By acting on a difficulty in the confines of a safe environment, the protagonist gets a feel for how things can be different (Moreno, 1987).

A fourth positive aspect of psychodrama is its integrative and vicarious effect. Psychodrama emphasizes action coupled with emotional release. A by-product of this process is the change in thoughts that accompanies changes in behavior and emotion (Coven et al., 1997). This change is not limited to the protagonist, but can extend to members of the audience. As the psychodrama concludes, a good psychodrama director "shifts the focus to the audience and discusses the impact of their experiences, parts of the psychodrama with which they identified, issues they got in touch with, and what they learned from the psychodrama in general" (Ohlsen et al., 1988, p. 105).

A fifth strength of psychodrama is the input and feedback the audience and actors give the protagonist and each other (Moreno, 1964). Psychodrama promotes interaction and experiential learning among group members. Furthermore, it is an effective form of therapy for many. For instance, Orkibi (2019) in reviewing the research literature on psychodrama found that psychodrama intervention had a significant effect on relapse prevention and rumination. Furthermore, Tarashoeva et al. (2017) found treatment with "psychodrama and pharmacotherapy achieved significantly greater reduction" in clients' "anxiety symptoms, increases in their spontaneity, and an improvement in their quality of life and social functioning," versus clients who received only pharmacotherapy (p. 55).

Limitations and Criticism

A major limitation of psychodrama is the danger of overexposing the protagonist to himself or herself as well as to the audience. A sense of timing and knowledge of what hidden factors need to be exposed are crucial. The ability of a psychodrama director to know when and what to emphasize takes years to develop. First attempts at helping are not as polished as later efforts.

A second area of concern to professional group workers is the quantity and quality of the research underlying psychodrama. Role-playing has the potential to change individual attitudes and behaviors (Mann, 2010), but psychodrama is more than role-playing. While Kipper and Ritchie's (2003) meta-analysis of 25 experientially designed studies showed psychodrama is effective, with role reversal and doubling emerging as the most effective interventions, the infrequency of research publications that validate the clinical observations is a drawback to the use of this theory.

A third limitation of psychodrama relates to the availability of training. There are few training centers for directors. Needed qualities of directors go beyond experience with observing/participating and studying to include intuition and charisma. There is the danger that some psychodrama groups may differ radically from others because of the self-awareness and knowledge of the director. Since 1975, the American Board of Examiners in Psychodrama, Sociometry and Group Psychotherapy has tried to ensure uniformity in professional standards for directors.

A final criticism of psychodrama is that it may focus too much on expression of feelings rather than change in behavior. A lot of emphasis in psychodrama is placed on effect and present experiences. If the group is not carefully constructed, then the emotional part of the theory and the here-and-now emphasis will override the integrative aspect of the approach.

TREATING LINDA WITH PSYCHODRAMA

Conceptualization

Psychodrama is primarily a group-based theory, and Linda has been a person without any meaningful groups in her history. She is psychologically distant from her family, has not socialized with others inside or outside of her work environment, and seems to have had an inferior position with her former husband, father, and even her protective brother. She reads about romance, consumes action videos, and watches ways to make home improvements, all of which are solitary activities.

Yet, despite her lack of friends and lackluster history of interacting with others, Linda harbors some ambition. While presently seeing herself as aimless and depressed, she thinks of getting a 4-year college degree rather than following up on suicidal ideations. In addition, she wants a more challenging career where she is more in charge and not a victim to bosses who seem to exploit her. Her dreams will require her to learn to interact positively and productively in groups.

Treatment Process

Linda seems teachable and open to finding out more about how she can make the needed changes in her life. Yet she is hesitant as well. You spend time initially doing warm-up exercises with her using a number of verbal and nonverbal techniques to establish rapport and build trust so Linda will feel comfortable with you and the group. You then move to have Linda included with a small group of other individuals in a psychodrama where Linda is just an observer as a part of the audience. Your rationale is to help Linda be more comfortable with others, model peer-appropriate behavior, and have Linda experience the power of the psychodrama process. You want Linda to see how group members integrate catharsis and insight into learning to do something differently.

At the next meeting of the group, you ask Linda if she would like to be the protagonist—that is, the client. When she accepts you direct her to start with a soliloquy about her current situation. You encourage catharsis and to facilitate the expression of her feelings you have another member of the psychodrama act as a double expressing Linda's emotions that have been implied but not said. You then direct psychodrama members in the group to sculpt Linda's family and work situations so she can see more clearly what they look like. You follow this exercise up with mirroring, where Linda sees herself from offstage being played by an auxiliary ego who portrays her posture, gesture, and words. This action phase is followed by the integration/sharing phase where Linda consolidates what she has been through and lets the group know what she has learned and the insight she has gleaned.

There is no step-by-step process of what comes next except you try to help Linda take on the role of protagonist in real life as much as possible. This strategy is in order for her to act on her difficulties and experiences and to behave differently in her interactions with others so she can find new ways of feeling and behaving. You direct Linda in role-plays, soliloquies, role reversals, and as many other psychodrama techniques as appropriate in a safe environment with others so she learns more about herself and the ways she acts in multiple situations. In the process, Linda comes to new realizations about herself and behaves differently.

SUMMING UP

Jacob Moreno created psychodrama shortly after World War I. He and his wife, Zerka, believed change occurs best in groups and through behavioral means such as acting. Psychodrama evolved under the Morenos' guidance in Europe, South Africa, and finally in the United States.

In psychodrama, the counselor becomes a director and clients become actors. Before beginning a psychodrama a warm-up phase occurs, followed by the action and integrative/sharing phases. Each of these phases utilizes specific techniques. Change usually occurs in the integrative/sharing phase when clients are most vulnerable and yet most open to cognitively understanding themselves, others, and how acting in certain ways can help them become more of the person they wish to be.

CHAPTER 16 RECAP: PSYCHODRAMA

Major Theorists
Jacob Moreno, Zerka Moreno

View of Human Nature/Personality
Humans are creative, and the job of psychodrama is to help people be more creative and productive in their lives.
Psychodrama emphasizes freeing individuals from the irrational forces that bind them into dysfunctional behavior patterns.

Role of the Counselor
Director—a producer, a facilitator, an observer, and an analyzer
Conducts psychodramas through the warm-up, action, integrative/sharing phases of the process
Encourages the development of trust and spontaneity in self and others
Establishes a structure so that protagonists can identify and work on significant issues in their lives
Protects members from abuse by others
Brings closure to groups and group participants so they come to cognitively understand themselves better and see the constructive actions they can take

Goals
Psychodrama emphasizes action as a way of understanding.
Stress is on personal interaction, and focus is on the here and now, spontaneity and creativity, full expression of feelings, and reality testing.
Protagonists rework their lives as both players and playwrights.

Process and Techniques
Psychodrama goes through three phases: warm-up, action, and integration/sharing. Some major techniques in these phases are
    Creative imagery
    Magic shop
    Spontaneity
    Sculpting
    Soliloquy
    Monodrama or autodrama
    Double and multiple double
    Mirror
    Role reversal
    Tele
    Insight
    Group sharing

Diversity and Multicultural Issues
May be employed with individuals of all age, educational, and socioeconomic levels

May be employed in family therapy, addiction treatment, and the support of LGBTQ adolescents

Strengths and Contributions
Can be used in multiple settings with a wide variety of people
Teaching potential—Group members learn a great deal about themselves through their active participation.
Promotes new ways to help people find solutions to problems
Emphasizes action coupled with emotional release for protagonists and audiences
Promotes interaction and experiential learning among group members

Limitations and Criticisms
Danger of overexposing the protagonist to himself or herself as well as to the audience
Limited quantity and quality of research
Few training centers for directors
May focus too much on expression of feelings rather than change in behavior

KEY TERMS

LEARNING MORE

American Society of Group Psychotherapy and Psychodrama (ASGPP). Website https://asgpp.org/index.php
International Association for Group Psychotherapy (IAGP). Website https://iagp.com/contact/ or http://www.iagp.com/membership
British Psychodrama Association http://www.psychodrama.org.uk/
North American Drama Association https://www.nadta.org/

CLASSROOM ACTIVITIES

1. Explore the differences between drama therapy (https://www.nadta. org/) and psychodrama (https://asgpp.org/). Which do you think is most effective with specific populations? Why?

2. Zerka Moreno, the wife of Jacob Moreno, saw clients and worked as a psychodrama therapist but never attended college. What do you think about someone without a professional degree working as a therapist? What is the place of paraprofessionals in mental health?

3. Sociometric methods are ways of measuring aspects of social relationships, such as social acceptance (i.e., how much an individual is liked by peers) and social status (i.e., a child's social standing in comparison to peers). How do you think psychodrama could be used in modifying individuals' social relationships?

17
Crisis Counseling

■ ■ ■

Moving past the time and through the shadows,
you look for hope in the yet-to-be days.
I want to say, "I'm here. Trust the process."
but the struggle is your own;
So I withdraw and watch you work
while occasionally offering you words
and images of the possible.

"Through Shadows" © S. T. Gladding

CHAPTER OVERVIEW

From reading this chapter you will learn about

■ The multiple definitions of a crisis.
■ The four major types of crises and how they are alike and different from each other.
■ The directed and action-oriented nature of crisis counseling.

As you read, consider

■ When you have been in or seen someone in a crisis, and try to recall what that experience was like.
■ The importance of grieving a loss.
■ The concept of resilience and what part it plays in resolving a crisis.

"Crisis intervention skills are essential tools for clinicians working with clients who are experiencing traumatic life events or are in a state of acute crisis" (Parikh & Morris, 2011, p. 364). During the past two decades, the need for crisis intervention services has increased significantly. One reason more services are needed is the recent upsurge of large-scale violent acts occurring in the United States (Schmidt & Cohen, 2020), as evidenced by:

■ The terrorist attacks on New York City and Washington, DC, in 2001.
■ The 2007 Virginia Tech massacre.
■ The 1999 shootings at Columbine High School.
■ The 1995 bombing of the Alfred P. Murrah Federal Building in Oklahoma City.
■ The 2014 shootings of Sandy Hook elementary school children.
■ The 2020 COVID-19 pandemic.

Violent acts occur "with such frequency and indiscriminateness that no one can consider him- or herself safe" (Myer, 2001, p. 3).

Other natural disasters, including earthquakes, floods, fires, hurricanes, and tornadoes, result in tragic losses of lives and homes. Hurricane Katrina struck the southern coast of the United States in August 2005, causing devastating, long-lasting effects. Likewise, the wildfires in the west in recent summers, especially in California in 2019, left thousands homeless. On an international level, tsunamis, earthquakes, and cyclones have had catastrophic effects on people in Southeast Asia, Japan, Pakistan, and China. Automobile and plane accidents, injury, illness, and disease can also have shattering effects on victims and their families.

Before discussing crisis counseling interventions practitioners can make, it is important to clarify what is meant by the term **crisis**. Many definitions have been proposed, including the following:

- Crisis is a perception or experiencing of an event or situation as an intolerable difficulty that exceeds the person's current resources and coping mechanisms. Unless the person obtains relief, the crisis has the potential to cause severe affective, behavioral, and cognitive malfunctioning (James & Gilliland, 2017).

- Crises are personal difficulties or situations that immobilize people and prevent them from consciously controlling their lives (Belkin, 1984, p. 424).

- Crisis is a state of disorganization in which people face frustration of important life goals or profound disruption of their life cycles and methods of coping with stressors. The term "crisis" usually refers to a person's feelings of fear, shock, and distress about the disruption, not to the disruption itself (Brammer, 1985, p. 94).

- A crisis is a critical phase in a person's life when his or her normal ways of dealing with the world are suddenly interrupted (Lewis et al., 2003, p. 117).

As can be seen from the multiple concepts of crisis, there is no simple or straightforward way to define what a crisis is. However, a crisis consists of three components: an event, a client's perception of the event, and the failure of the client's typical coping methods (Miller, 2012). Although a single event may precipitate a crisis, a combination of personal traits, environmental factors, and interpersonal support systems affects the way the event is perceived and managed. An event that is relatively minor for one individual, such as failing a final examination, may be perceived as a crisis by someone else. In addition, the timing, intensity, and number of other stressors the person is experiencing can affect the complexity of the crisis.

MAJOR THEORISTS: ERICH LINDEMANN AND GERALD CAPLAN

Erich Lindemann (1900–1974) and Gerald Caplan (1917–2008) are considered two of the most prominent pioneers in the field of crisis counseling. Lindemann (1944, 1956) helped practitioners recognize normal grief due to loss and the stages individuals go through in resolving grief. He worked at Massachusetts General Hospital in Boston as the chief of psychiatry and is noted for his extensive study on the effects of traumatic events on survivors and families after the Coconut Grove Night Club fire in 1942 (Satin, 1984). Caplan (1964) expanded Lindemann's concepts to the total field of traumatic events. He viewed crisis as a state resulting from impediments to life's goals that are both situational and developmental. His life is briefly traced here.

Gerald Caplan was born in Liverpool, England. He received a bachelor's degree in anatomy and physiology as well as a medical degree from Victoria University of Manchester. He was trained in London at the Tavistock Clinic by John Bowlby and at the Psychoanalytic Institute by Anna Freud. As the son of a rabbi, Caplan developed a commitment to Zionism that led him to move to Israel in 1948. There he helped establish psychiatric services. A meeting with Erich Lindemann resulted in a faculty position at the Harvard School of Public Health's Community Mental Health Program.

Caplan created the Laboratory of Community Psychiatry in Harvard Medical School, where he remained until 1977, after which he returned to Israel to direct a department of child and adolescent psychiatry. His lifelong mission was to advance a population-oriented approach to mental health that placed prevention at its core. In advocating this view, he developed and refined crisis, mental health, and support intervention techniques that fueled the community mental health movement. He died in Jerusalem following a long struggle with Parkinson's disease.

VIEW OF HUMAN NATURE/PERSONALITY

Loss is an inevitable part of life. Developmentally and situationally, healthy people grow and move on, leaving some things behind, whether intentionally, by accident, or because of growth. **Grieving** is a natural reaction to loss. The extent of the grief and its depth are associated with the value of what has been lost and how. In some cases, the pain may be small because the person was not attached to or invested in the objects left behind, or the person had adequate time to prepare. In other cases, an individual may feel overwhelmed because of the value the person, possession, or position had in his or her life or because of the sudden and/or traumatic way the loss occurred. In such cases, there is a crisis.

Although crises represent highly stressful and disruptive situations, they do not imply mental illness. Many but not all crises are limited in time, usually lasting somewhere between 6 and 8 weeks, after which the major symptoms of distress diminish. However, crises can have long-term physical and psychological outcomes, depending on how the crisis is resolved (Sandoval et al., 2009).

It is important to distinguish between disasters and crises. Disasters may be natural or human caused (Schmidt & Cohen, 2020). Crises are more widespread and can be classified as developmental, situational, existential, and ecosystemic (Duffey & Haberstroh, 2020; James & Gilliland, 2017).

1. *Developmental Crises.* Developmental crises occur during the normal flow of human growth and maturation. As people move through different developmental stages in their lives, they may experience crises during certain changes or shifts. For example, a developmental crisis may occur when the last child leaves home or when a person retires. When the event corresponds to culturally accepted patterns and timetables, it is less likely to be experienced as a crisis than when it does not (e.g., pregnancy after marriage versus teenage pregnancy or voluntary retirement at an appropriate age versus forced early retirement). Developmental crises are considered normal; however, individuals perceive and respond to them in different ways and with varying degrees of success. They may be especially traumatic if the timing of events is not within acceptable norms.

2. *Situational Crises.* A situational crisis occurs when an unexpected, extraordinary event takes place that the person had no way of anticipating or controlling. Examples include automobile accidents, rape, job loss, sudden illness, and death of a loved one. A situational crisis is random, sudden, shocking, intense, and often catastrophic. It is in one of two categories that most people consider a crisis, the other being **ecosystemic**.

Reflective Question

When have you seen someone have a situational crisis? How did they behave? What, if any, action by the person or someone else helped?

---

3. *Existential Crises.* An existential crisis includes "inner conflicts and anxieties that accompany important human issues of purpose, responsibility, independence, freedom, and commitment" (James & Gilliland, 2017, p. 13). At times, existential crises are precipitated by *nonevents*, such as realizing that an individual is never going to have children or make a significant difference in a particular field of work. An existential crisis may occur when realizing at age 50 that you have wasted your life and cannot relive past years, or a spouse/partner of 25 years questions the value of the relationship and seriously considers moving out. A major characteristic of existential crises is they are mostly mental.
4. *Ecosystemic Crises.* Ecosystemic crises are natural or human-caused disasters (Schmidt & Cohen, 2020). They overtake a person or group of people who "find themselves, through no fault or action of their own, inundated in the aftermath of an event that may adversely affect virtually every member of the environment in which they live" (James, 2008, p. 14). In many ways, ecosystemic crises are situational crises that have widespread ramifications. The terrorist attacks of September 11, 2001, the breaking of the levees in New Orleans, and suicide bombings exemplify human-caused ecosystemic crises with wide-reaching effects. Ecosystemic crises caused by natural phenomena include hurricanes, tornadoes, tsunamis, wildfires, and earthquakes.

Reflective Question

What do you see as the similarities between a developmental and an existential crisis?

ROLE OF THE COUNSELOR

Practitioners who work in crises need to be mature individuals with a variety of life experiences with which they have successfully dealt. They need to also have a good command of basic helping skills, high energy, and quick mental reflexes, and yet be poised, calm, creative, and flexible in the midst of highly charged situations.

Counselors are often direct and active in crises (Webber & Mascari, 2018). The role is quite different from that of other forms of counseling. There are **two main components of crisis counseling**: 1) first-order intervention (psychological first aid) and 2) second-order intervention (crisis therapy).

First-order intervention involves "making sure clients are safe, stress-related symptoms are reduced, clients have opportunities to rest and recover physically [when necessary], and clients are connected to resources and social supports they need to survive and recover from the crisis" (Miller, 2012, p. 3). Second-order intervention involves assessing, planning, implementing, and following up to help the client develop new knowledge and skills. Through second-order interventions, clinical practitioners strive to help those who have been in crisis create a new, productive, and mentally healthy life.

Second-order interventions are numerous and may extend in time far beyond the crisis. Schmidt and Cohen (2020) suggest a variety of interventions that may be helpful. These include **brain-based trauma interventions** (e.g., eye movement desensitization and reprocessing, tapping, brainspotting) and **trauma-informed therapies** (e.g., cognitive-behavioral therapy and art, music, and animal-assisted therapies). **Wellness activities** (e.g., yoga, meditation, and cardiovascular exercise) are also part of this process.

Reflective Question

How do you see the two components of crisis counseling (psychological first aid and crisis therapy) relating to each other? Explain.

GOALS

Goals within crisis counseling initially revolve around getting those who are suffering immediate help in a variety of forms (e.g., psychological, financial, legal). "What occurs during the immediate aftermath of the crisis event determines whether or not the crisis will become a disease reservoir that will be transformed into a chronic and long-term state" (James & Gilliland, 2017, p. 5).

At first, counselors use basic crisis theory to help "people in crisis recognize and correct temporary affective, behavioral, and cognitive distortions brought on by traumatic events" (James & Gilliland, 2017, p. 11). This service, **psychological first aid**, is directive in nature. It focuses on the physical safety and comfort of victims while promoting social engagement and helping survivors of a trauma find missing loved ones or attend to issues associated with traumatic grief, guilt, or shame. It is different from grief counseling approaches that try to help individuals find remediation for more ongoing problems. Second, long-term adjustment and health are the focus. Individuals and even communities may require considerable follow-up on the part of crisis counselors or other helping specialists to rebuild and move on in their lives (see Figure 17.1).

Reflective Question

Think of when you have followed up about a project on which you were working. What did you notice in follow-up that you did not observe initially? Do you think the same dynamics apply to crisis counseling? If so, how are they the same and different from your experience of task follow-up?

PROCESS AND TECHNIQUES

Techniques used in crisis counseling vary according to the type of crises mentioned earlier, and the potential for harm. However, according to James (2008), what a crisis practitioner does and when he or she does it is dependent on assessing the individuals experiencing crisis in a continuous and fluid manner.

Assessment may include what Miller (2012) defines as the **BASIC personality profile**—behavioral, affective, somatic, interpersonal, and cognitive. Strengths and weaknesses in these domains are examined. The assets clients have for moving on and healing—for example, **resilience** (the ability to recover from adversity)—are noted. Three essential listening activities that need to be implemented during this time are:

- *Defining continuing or major problems*, especially from the client's viewpoint.
- *Ensuring client and others' safety*, which means minimizing physical and psychological dangers.
- *Providing support*, which means communicating to the client genuine and unconditional caring.

After and sometimes during the middle of listening comes acting strategies, or **in-crisis actions**, which include:

- *Examining alternatives*—that is, recognizing alternatives that are available and realizing some choices are better than others;
- *Making plans* where clients feel a sense of control and autonomy in the process so they do not become dependent; and
- *Obtaining commitment* from the client to take the planned actions.

1 Protecting from further harm

2 Opportunity to talk without pressure

3 Active listening

4 Compassion

5 Addressing and acknowledging concerns

6 Discussing coping strategies

7 Social support

8 Offer to return to talk

9 Referral

Figure 17.1 Component of psychological first aid

Practitioners should follow up with clients after a crisis has settled down enough for clients to have made plans they intent to complete. The emphasis in such cases is to highlight strengths to help clients feel they are in control (Meier & Davis, 2019). If necessary, counselors should further assess whether clients have had delayed reactions to the crisis they have experienced, such as **posttraumatic stress disorder (PTSD)**. If PTSD has occurred more intensive therapeutic interventions, possibly hospitalization, may be needed.

During and even after a crisis, helping specialists need to debrief. Two approaches to debriefing are: **Critical Incident Stress Debriefing (CISD)** and one-on-one crisis counseling (Jordan, 2002). In CISD a seven-stage group approach is used that helps individuals deal with their thoughts and feelings in a controlled environment using two counselors (Roberts, 2005; Stebnicki, 2016). This approach evolves through an emphasis on introduction, facts, thoughts, reactions, symptoms, teaching, and reentry. The CISD group session ranges from 1 to 3 hours and is generally provided 1 to 10 days after an acute crisis and 3 to 4 weeks after a mass disaster (Roberts, 2005). One-to-one counseling uses some of the same techniques as CISD, but the treatment lasts from 15 minutes to 2 hours and for only one to three sessions (Everly et al., 2000). It is less likely to re-traumatize an individual.

Regardless of the approach used, symptoms and reactions require attention. Common emotional responses include denial, anger, anxiety, sadness, confusion, blame, shame, and fear. Common physical symptoms include restlessness, sleep disturbances, eating disturbances, nightmares, flashbacks, heart palpitations, and vomiting. Some of these symptoms immediately follow a critical incident, while others surface over time. If help is not forthcoming or if there is no follow-up, survivors may turn to drugs or alcohol to deal with the trauma and their mental health will suffer.

Reflective Question

Debriefing has been compared to catharsis. How do you think it is similar to and different from catharsis? What makes you think so?

DIVERSITY AND MULTICULTURAL ISSUES

"The plain and simple truth is that we don't know a lot about how culture, crises, and crisis intervention interact. Very little research has been done in the area" (James & Gilliland, 2017, p. 25). What is known is that multicultural helping is enhanced when practitioners use methods and strategies and define goals consistent with the life experiences and the cultural values of clients (Sue et al., 2019). Likewise, it is important to refer survivors of crises to appropriate cultural postcrisis resources, for example referring African American families with children to *An Activity Book for African American Families: Helping Children Cope with Crisis* (2012), rather than a book for another cultural group.

In crisis counseling of clients with gender-sensitive issues, counselors must tailor their approaches to helping to the identity of the person(s) with whom they are working. They must be sensitive to the gender identity of those they serve, realizing some men who are hurting psychologically may be reluctant to talk about their pain. Likewise, some women who are suffering may cry when describing their feelings. The opposite may be true too. Likewise, an openness to LGBTQA needs must be considered and they should be sensitively handled. Adjustment on the part of the helper is called for in these situations and others like them (Goodrich & Luke, 2015).

EVALUATION OF THE THEORY

Strengths and Contributions

Dramatic and traumatic events, from earthquakes to shootings, occur in many people's lives. Crisis counseling is a two-pronged approach to helping individuals deal with the physical or mental devastations associated with these happenings. This type of counseling provides psychological first aid in the immediate aftermath of such situations. Crisis counseling is also involved in helping individuals make long-term plans so they can get on with their lives and not develop posttraumatic stress disorders.

A second strength of crisis counseling is that it is direct and relatively brief. In the midst of a crisis people are often confused and need direction as to what to do, when, where, and how. They are not ready for reflection. They need to focus on survival first. Crisis counseling provides individuals with this specificity.

A third strength of crisis counseling is that it may involve physical help—for example, food and shelter—as well as psychological components—for example, finding someone to talk to. Therefore, human services practitioners along with other helping specialists can provide comfort and safety to people in need on multiple levels. This type of assistance helps individuals calm down and assess themselves and their surroundings so they can begin to see what their needs are.

Limitations and Criticisms

While crisis counseling excels in meeting the immediate needs of individuals, it does not provide for services that last for more than a few weeks. Therefore, victims of crises must follow up with other professionals after a crisis has passed. The process of follow-up with another helper can be frustrating as well as time consuming. Sometimes those who have suffered crises feel they are being handed off from one agency or person to another and in the process they become discouraged.

A second drawback to crisis counseling is not all crises that individuals go through are amenable to crisis counseling. For instance, developmental crises, such as aging, are usually not worked with in this way. Yet these non-physical and sometimes investible types of crises are often as painful and distressing as events that are more outwardly observable.

A final criticism of crisis counseling is the fact that it lacks strong theoretical support. It could be argued that crisis counseling is built on Abraham Maslow's hierarchy of needs with the rationale that more physical needs must be satisfied before higher psychological needs can be met. However, Maslow's theory is seldom mentioned when crisis counseling is discussed and thus some individuals do not consider this approach to be little more than providing comfort and assistance for those who have suffered an injury or a loss.

TREATING LINDA WITH CRISIS COUNSELING

Conceptualization

Linda is facing both a developmental and an existential crisis. The developmental crisis is Linda's transition from being married for seven years to suddenly being single and not used to living on her own. Even when abuse occurs in a relationship, as in Linda's case, it takes time for a person to get used to being free of that behavior and being on his or her own again. Making like-minded friends is also developmental. At this point in her life, Linda is not connected except tangentially to her family. She is drifting and alone.

The existential crisis stems from Linda seeking meaning in her life that she has not found previously. At 32, she has had 7 years of a bad relationship and 12 years of mundane, dead-end jobs with bosses she considers sexist. Linda knows she has potential because of her high school grades. Yet, out of high school, she chose to do less than she was capable of because of family and societal pressures. Her pattern of underachievement has left her feeling depressed and stuck in passive behaviors such as reading romance novels, watching television, and viewing action-packed movies. None of these behaviors has proven satisfying for Linda.

Treatment Process

You realize that the two types of crises Linda is facing are interrelated and that you cannot treat one without handling the other. A first line of outreach is to help Linda understand the stages in divorce and the feelings that go with them. Like other kinds of loss, divorce causes people to go through a process. You essentially want to help Linda learn about the nature of decoupling and reconnecting.

Besides gaining knowledge about what it is like to divorce, Linda needs to make a plan about what to do with her life once her immediate needs have been met. You point out options she has like returning to college for a 4-year degree, moving to another city where there are more singles, becoming involved in a YWCA exercise program, joining a local interest group such as a book club, or looking for a career that requires more of a commitment from her and rewards her better. Linda needs to know what choices she has whether she remains physically where she is now or moves. Once choices are discussed and explored, Linda then has to make decisions on what to do and when.

The process of helping Linda in her existential crisis involves assisting her in discerning where she wants to be and what she wants to become. It is about how she wishes to spend her life and finding activities she finds meaningful. This aspect of working with Linda lasts longer than that involved in the resolution of her developmental crisis.

Overall, crisis counseling with Linda is of an immediate and a long-term nature. It deals with matters that can be resolved quickly and those that are of a more agonizing and uncertain nature. Once Linda gains a perspective on where she is in life, as a divorced, underachieving, hurt person, she can not only plan for becoming a new person but can also take concrete steps in that direction. Your job is to help her feel safe in doing so and reinforce her courage in trying new behaviors that are healthy and fulfilling.

SUMMING UP

A crisis is an event or situation that is so overwhelming that a client does not have the resources or coping abilities to deal with it. A crisis has three components: an event, a client's perception of the event, and the failure of the client's typical coping methods. Crisis counseling was created when professional helpers realized a need to assist victims of man-made or natural disasters in a way not found in other models of helping. This approach to working with others is based on the realization that those who suffer through a crisis have a need for short-term and long-term assistance to get back on their feet and build a new life. **Crisis counseling** is a two-pronged process that offers first- and second-degree interventions that are immediate (psychological first aid) and long term (therapy).

Crises take at least four different forms—developmental, situational, existential, and ecosystemic—with the most noticeable and publicized of crises being situational and ecosystemic. When conducting crisis counseling, practitioners are direct and action oriented, especially at the beginning of their work. This stance is because in many crises, clients are confused, aimless, and in a state of shock as well as grief. Thus, using acting strategies or in-crisis actions of examining alternatives, making plans, and obtaining commitment from a client to take the planned action is essential. Because crisis counseling is so intense, it is important that those who work in this area regularly debrief so they stay healthy and available to others.

CHAPTER 17 RECAP: CRISIS COUNSELING

Major Theorists
Erich Lindemann
Gerald Caplan

View of Human Nature/Personality
Loss and grief are a natural part of life.
When a person feels overwhelmed by loss and does not have adequate coping skills, there is a crisis.
People experience four major types of crises: developmental, situational, existential, and ecosystemic.

Role of the Counselor
Active and often direct in crisis situations, especially physical crisis situations

Work with people in the two stages of crisis:
- First-order intervention (psychological first aid).
- Second-order intervention (crisis therapy).

Goals
Get those who are suffering immediate loss help in a variety of forms: psychological, physical, financial, and legal
Correct temporary affective, behavioral, and cognitive distortions brought on by traumatic events
Find remediation for more ongoing, long-term problems
Help crisis victims recreate themselves in healthy ways

Process and Techniques

Assess what is happening in specific environments and in persons experiencing a crisis. Use three essential listening activities:
- Defining the problem,
- Ensuring client safety, and
- Providing support.

Use acting strategies or in-crisis actions of examining alternatives, making plans, and obtaining commitments from clients to take planned action

Debrief from working with crisis victims to stay healthy

Diversity and Multicultural Issues

There is little research regarding diversity and multicultural issues in crisis counseling.

Practitioners should be sensitive to the diversity and cultural-related issues of those with whom they work.

Strengths and Contributions

This approach is beneficial: brevity, directness, follow-up.

This approach uses modest goals and objectives because of the sudden and/or traumatic nature of crises.

This approach relies on its intensity, which is greater than many other forms of counseling.

This approach utilizes a transitional model of helping.

Limitations and Criticisms

This approach deals with situations of an immediate nature as opposed to those that are more encompassing.

This approach does not go into the same depth in coming to resolution that most counseling approaches do initially.

This approach is more time limited and trauma oriented than most forms of therapeutic interventions.

KEY TERMS

BASIC personality profile   227
brain-based trauma
   interventions   226
crisis   223
crisis counseling   231
critical incident stress debriefing
   (CISD)   228
developmental crises   224
ecosystemic crises   225
examining alternatives   227
existential crises   225

first-order intervention
   (psychological
   first aid)   226
grieving   224
in-crisis actions   227
making plans   227
nonevents   225
obtaining commitment   227
posttraumatic stress disorder
   (PTSD)   228
psychological first aid   226

LEARNING MORE

A number of periodicals carry articles on the theory, research, and practice of crisis counseling.

Illness, Crisis & Loss
Journal of Crisis Intervention and Suicide Prevention

Crisis counseling is a popular approach to use with a variety of clients. More information is available from the following related organizations and institutes:

American Institute of Health Care Professionals
http://www.aihcp.org/mission.htm

Crisis Counseling Assistance and Training Program
http://www.samhsa.gov/dtac/proguide.asp

Trauma and Disaster Mental Health, American Counseling Association
https://www.counseling.org/knowledge-center/mental-health-resources/
    trauma-disaster

CLASSROOM ACTIVITIES

1. Natural ecosystemic crises, such as forest fires or hurricanes, make national news frequently. Since they are so common, why do you think they are reported on so often? How do you think helping practitioners can be of assistance in such situations?
2. Crisis counseling is much more directive and action oriented than many of the helping approaches already presented in this book. Why do you think this approach is helpful to people in crisis? Would a more subtle approach be better for someone in an existential or developmental crisis as opposed to someone in a situational or ecosystemic crisis? Why do you think so?
3. What is your feeling about the usefulness of crisis counseling? Do you think it is a different form of helping than the other theories you have studied in this book? Discuss your reaction to this theory with classmates.

18

Professional Ethics and Codes of Ethics

■ ■ ■

Ethical conduct is sometimes vague
and should not be taken for granted.
Lecturing on it can be a bore
the epitome of pedantic.
It is best displayed in deeds
that meet community needs.

"Ethics" © S. T. Gladding

CHAPTER OVERVIEW

From reading this chapter you will learn about

■ The importance of ethics and ethical codes.
■ Six principles for making ethical decisions.
■ Prevalent forms of unethical behaviors in professional contexts.

As you read, consider

■ The limits of ethical codes.
■ Resources for making ethical decisions.
■ Criteria for judging whether an action is ethical.

Counseling is not value free or neutral (Cohen & Cohen, 2019; Cottone & Tarvydas, 2016; Welfel, 2016). Rather, it is an active profession based on values, which are "orienting beliefs about what is good … and how that good should be achieved" (Bergin, 1985, p. 99). Values are at the core of relationships. All goals "whether they are goals for symptom relief or goals to modify a lifestyle are subtended by value systems" (Bergin, 1992, p. 9). In addition, because counseling is such a complex and multifaceted profession, counselors by necessity must depend on codes of ethics (Remley & Herlihy, 2020).

Counselors who are not clear about their values and ethical responsibilities, as well as those of their clients, can cause harm despite their best intentions (Wilcoxon et al., 2013). Therefore, it is vital for them to be knowledgeable about themselves and the ethics pertaining to their professional responsibilities. The question is how. The answer is through knowing what ethics are, what professional ethical codes include, the limits of ethical codes, how to make ethical decisions, and how to deal with someone who acts unethically (Pope & Vasquez, 2016). This chapter explores these vital aspects of ethics since they are essential to the health and well-being of counseling professionals.

WHAT ARE ETHICS?

Ethics involve "making decisions of a moral nature about people and their interaction in society" (Kitchener, 1986, p. 306). The term is often used synonymously with "morality," and in some cases, the two terms overlap. Both deal with "what is good and bad or the study of human conduct and values" (Van Hoose & Kottler, 1985, p. 2). Yet each has a different meaning.

"Ethics is generally defined as a philosophical discipline that is concerned with human conduct and moral decision making" (Van Hoose & Kottler, 1985, p. 3). Ethics are normative in nature and focus on principles and standards that govern relationships between individuals. "**Professional ethics** are beliefs about behavior and conduct that guide professional practices," such as those between counselors and clients (Calley, 2009, p. 477). Morality differs. It involves judgments and evaluations of actions. Words frequently used with the term "morality" include good, bad, right, wrong, ought, and should (Grant, 1992). Helping professionals have morals, and the theories they employ have embedded within them moral presuppositions about human nature that explicitly and implicitly question first, "what is a person and second, what should a person be or become?" (Christopher, 1996, p. 18).

As a group, mental health professionals are concerned with ethics and values. However, some are better informed or more attuned to these issues. Patterson (1971) has observed that individuals' professional identities are related to their knowledge and practice of ethics. Welfel (2016) states that the effectiveness of professional helpers is connected to their ethical knowledge and behaviors as well. Therefore, ethics are essential.

Reflective Question

How effective can counselors be if they are knowledgeable about professional ethics but are substantially different in their behaviors?

WHY ARE PROFESSIONAL CODES OF ETHICS IMPORTANT?

To address ethical situations, helping professionals have developed codes of ethics based upon an agreed set of values. Professionals in all domains, such as social work, counseling, psychology, and rehabilitation, voluntarily abide by the ethical codes of their disciplines for many reasons. "Among its many purposes, a code of ethical conduct is designed to offer formal statements for ensuring protection of clients' rights while identifying expectations of practitioners" (Wilcoxon, 1987, p. 510). Three other reasons for the existence of ethical codes according to Van Hoose and Kottler (1985) are as follows:

1. **Ethical codes protect a profession from government.** They allow a profession to regulate itself and function autonomously instead of being controlled by legislation.

2. **Ethical codes help control internal disagreements and bickering,** thus promoting stability within a profession.
3. **Ethical codes protect practitioners from the public,** especially in malpractice suits. If professionals behave according to ethical guidelines, the behavior is judged to be in compliance with accepted standards.

In addition, ethical codes help increase public trust in the integrity of a profession and provide clients with some protection from incompetent charlatans (Vacc et al., 2001). Clients can also use codes of ethics as a guide in evaluating questionable treatment.

A **code of ethics** is a major sign that an association has developed into a mature discipline. A code of ethics clarifies the nature of ethical responsibilities. These include

- Informing clients of the nature of helping.
- Supporting the mission of the association.
- Establishing principles that inform best practice.
- Assisting members in constructing a course of action, such as what they should do when they do not have the necessary skills to treat a client.
- Serving as the basis for processing ethical complaints and inquiries (Ponton & Duba, 2009).

Most professional helping associations have several topical headings in their codes of ethics (Pope & Vasquez, 2016). These sections focus on relationships, including professional responsibilities to clients and their welfare and ways to handle troublesome subjects such as fees, bartering, referrals, and termination. Sections covering confidentiality, privileged communication, and privacy in counseling are usually included too. They focus on the exceptions to the right to privacy, records, consultation, and research as well as training and issues related to professional responsibility, such as professional competence. Public responsibility and relationships with other professionals, including colleagues, employers, and employees are also usually included in codes of ethics.

In addition, ethical codes usually cover evaluation, assessment, and interpretation of tests, informed consent, release of information, proper diagnosis of mental disorders, conditions of assessment administration, multicultural and diversity issues, and forensic evaluation. Research and publications and delineating research responsibilities, rights of research participants, and reporting of research results are other sections in most professional codes of ethics.

Reflective Question

What are some ways counselors might use codes of ethics to help them sort out their personal and professional values?

LIMITATIONS OF ETHICAL CODES

Ethical codes are general and idealistic; they seldom answer specific questions. Furthermore, these documents do not address foreseeable professional dilemmas. Rather, they provide guidelines, based on experiences and values, of how professional helpers should behave. In many ways, ethical standards represent the collected wisdom of a particular time.

A number of specific limitations exist in any code of ethics. Here are some of the limitations most frequently mentioned (Corey et al., 2018; Talbutt, 1981):

- **Some issues cannot be resolved by a code of ethics.**
- **Enforcing ethical codes is difficult.**
- **Some ethical issues are not covered in codes** since codes do not address every possible situation.
- **Ethical codes are historical documents.** What may be acceptable practice at one time may later be considered unethical.
- Sometimes **conflicts** arise **between ethical and legal codes.**
- There is often **difficulty in bringing the interest of all parties involved** in an ethical dispute **together systematically.**
- **Ethical codes are not proactive documents** for helping professionals deciding what to do in new situations.

Ethical codes are useful in many ways, but they do have their limitations. Counselors and therapists need to be aware that they will not always find all the guidance they want when consulting these documents. Nevertheless, whenever an ethical issue arises, mental health professionals should first consult ethical codes to see whether the situation is addressed.

MAKING ETHICAL DECISIONS

Ethical decision making is not always easy, yet it is a part of being a professional. It requires virtues such as character, integrity, and moral courage as well as knowledge (Welfel, 2016). Some mental health professionals operate from personal ethical standards without regard to the ethical guidelines developed by professional associations. They usually function well until faced with a dilemma "for which there is no apparent good or best solution" (Swanson, 1983, p. 57). At such times, ethical issues arise and these individuals experience anxiety, doubt, hesitation, and confusion in determining their conduct. Unfortunately, when they act, their behavior may turn out to be unethical because it is not grounded in an ethical code or it is grounded in only part of a code that they have extracted to justify their behavior.

Reflective Question

When have you seen someone try to justify their behavior without referencing values and ethics? What did you think about their actions?

It is in difficult, murky, and personally troubling situations that those in helping professions need to be aware of resources for ethical decision making such as books and articles on ethics as well as experienced colleagues (Welfel, 2016). Such resources are especially important when questions arise over potentially controversial behaviors such as setting or collecting fees, conducting multiple relationships, or working with individuals whose beliefs and styles therapists do not agree with. Ethical reasoning, "the process of determining which ethical principles are involved and then prioritizing them based on the professional requirements and beliefs," is crucial (Lanning, 1992, p. 21).

In making ethical decisions, helping specialists should take actions "based on careful, reflective thought" about responses they think are professionally right in particular situations (Tennyson & Strom, 1986, p. 298). Six ethical principles related to such activities and ethical choices are:

- **Beneficence** (doing good and preventing harm).
- **Nonmaleficence** (not inflicting harm).
- **Autonomy** (respecting freedom of choice and self-determination).
- **Justice** (fairness).
- **Fidelity** (faithfulness or honoring commitments and promises).
- **Veracity** (truthfulness). (Remley & Herlihy, 2019)

All these principles involve conscious decision making throughout the helping process. Of these principles, some experts identify nonmaleficence as the primary ethical responsibility in the field of counseling relationships. Nonmaleficence involves not only the "removal of present harm" but also the "prevention of future harm, and passive avoidance of harm" (Thompson, 1990, p. 105). It is the basis on which professionals respond to clients who may endanger themselves or others and why they respond to colleagues' unethical behavior (Daniluk & Haverkamp, 1993).

Reflective Question

Think of the case of Linda that you have read about in previous chapters. What actions based on ethical principles could you take in helping her?

In addition to these guidelines, Swanson (1983) lists other factors for assessing whether helpers are acting in ethically responsible ways. The first is personal and professional honesty. Counselors and other mental health professionals need to operate openly with themselves and those with whom they work. Hidden agendas or unacknowledged feelings hinder relationships and place everyone involved on shaky ethical ground. One way to overcome personal or professional honesty problems that may get in the way of acting ethically is supervision (Kitchener, 1994).

A second factor is acting in the best interest of clients. This ideal is easier to discuss than to achieve. At times, professional helpers may impose personal values on clients and ignore what they really want (Gladding & Hood, 1974). At other times, they may fail to recognize an emergency and too readily accept that clients' best interests are served by doing nothing.

A third factor is that therapists act without malice or personal gain. Some clients are difficult to like or to deal with, and therapists must take special care with these individuals. Likewise, avoiding relationships with likable clients either on a personal or professional basis is crucial. Errors in judgment are most likely to occur when the professional helper's self-interest becomes a part of the relationship with a client (St. Germaine, 1993).

A final factor is whether a professional helper can justify an action "as the best judgment of what should be done based upon the current state of the profession"

(Swanson, 1983, p. 59). To make such a decision, those who work in mental health environments must keep up with current trends by reading the latest literature, attending in-service workshops and conventions, and becoming actively involved in local, state, and national activities.

In many situations, the proper behavior is not obvious (Wilcoxon et al., 2013). For example, the question of confidentiality in balancing the individual rights of a person with COVID-19 or another contagious disease and society's right to be protected from the spread of these diseases is one with which some professional helpers struggle (Harding et al., 1993). Likewise, multiple ethical dilemmas arise in counseling adult survivors of incest, including those of confidentiality and the consequences of making decisions about reporting abuse (Daniluk & Haverkamp, 1993). Therefore, when they are in doubt about what to do in a given situation, it is crucial for those involved in counseling to consult and talk over situations with colleagues, in addition to using principles, guidelines, casebooks, and professional codes of ethics.

Among the best ways to learn how to make ethical decisions is taking courses and obtaining continuing education credits. Such classes can bring about significant attitudinal changes, including increased knowledge about ethical areas of self-awareness, multiple relationships, impairment, diversity, and multiculturalism (Coll, 1993; Herlihy & Painter, 2018). Because ethical attitudinal changes are related to ethical behavioral changes, courses in ethics on any level are extremely valuable.

Van Hoose and Paradise (1979) conceptualize the **ethical behavior of counselors** in terms of a **five-stage developmental continuum of reasoning**:

- **Punishment orientation.** At this stage, the counseling professional believes external social standards are the basis for judging behavior. If individuals violate a societal rule, they should be punished.
- **Institutional orientation.** Professional helpers who operate at this stage believe in and abide by the rules of the institutions for which they work. They do not question the rules, and they base their decisions on them.
- **Societal orientation.** At this stage, decisions are based on societal standards. If a question arises about whether the needs of society or of an individual should come first, the needs of society are always given priority.
- **Individual orientation.** The individual's needs receive top priority at this stage. Helpers are aware of societal needs and are concerned about the law, but they focus on what is best for the individual.
- **Principle (conscience) orientation.** In this stage, concern for the individual is primary. Ethical decisions are based on internalized ethical standards, not external considerations.

The work of Van Hoose and Paradise is especially important because it explains directly how those in the helping professions reason about ethical issues and indirectly how continuing education may make a difference in the way they think about ethics. It is heuristic (i.e., researchable or open to research) and can form the basis for empirical studies of the promotion of ethical behavior.

Overall ethical behavior and ethical decision making are greatly influenced by the prevalent attitudes in the setting in which one works, by one's colleagues, and by the task being performed (e.g., assessing, diagnosing). Therefore, implementing ethical decisions and actions in counseling sometimes involves substantial personal and professional risk or discomfort (Faiver et al., 2004).

Those who go into professional helping should check thoroughly the general policies and principles of an institution before accepting employment because employment in a specific setting implies employees agree with its policies, principles, and ethics. When individuals find themselves in institutions that misuse their services and do not act in the best interests of their clients, they must either act to change the institution through educational or persuasive means or find other employment.

In making ethical decisions where there are no guidelines, it is critical for professionals to stay abreast of current issues, trends, and even legislation related to the situation they face. In the process, they must take care not to stereotype or otherwise be insensitive to clients. Anticipation of problems and implementation of policies that produce humane and fair results are essential.

UNETHICAL BEHAVIOR

Unethical behavior in the helping professions can take many forms. The temptations common to people everywhere exist for those in counseling. They include "physical intimacy, the titillation of gossip, or the opportunity (if the gamble pays off) to advance one's career" (Welfel & Lipsitz, 1983, p. 328). Some forms of unethical behavior are obvious and willful, such as racism, whereas others are more subtle and unintentional, such as suggesting a therapeutic strategy that has not been thoroughly researched. Regardless, the harmful outcome is the same. The following are some of the most prevalent forms of unethical behaviors in the helping professions (Herlihy & Corey, 2015):

- Violation of confidentiality.
- Exceeding one's level of professional competence.
- Negligent practice.
- Claiming expertise one does not possess.
- Imposing one's values on a client.
- Creating dependency in a client.
- Sexual activity with a client.
- Certain conflicts of interest, such as dual or multiple relationships—where the role of the helper is combined with another relationship either personal or professional and not monitored for appropriateness of boundaries. (Moleski & Kiselica, 2005)
- Questionable financial arrangements, such as charging excessive fees.
- Improper advertising.
- Plagiarism.

Although most helping professionals act ethically, occasional situations arise in which such is not the case. In these circumstances, those who are aware of the situations must take some action. Otherwise, by condoning or ignoring these situations they risk eroding their own sense of moral selfhood and find it easier to condone future ethical breaches, a phenomenon known as the **"slippery slope effect."**

Reflective Question

When have you seen the slippery slope effect displayed in public life, such as dubious financial deals? How could you see the slippery slope effect happening in professional helping relationships?

Herlihy (1996) suggests several steps to take in working through potential ethical dilemmas, especially with impaired professionals. The first is to identify the problem as objectively as possible and the helper's relationship to it. Such a process is best done on paper to clarify thinking.

The second step in the process is to apply the current associational (e.g., psychology, counseling, social work) codes of ethics to the matter. In such cases, clear guidance as to a course of action may emerge (Gladding, 2007). Next, a professional should consider the moral principles of the helping professions discussed earlier in this chapter, such as beneficence, justice, and autonomy. Consultation with a colleague is also an option.

If action is warranted, the colleague in question should first be approached informally. This approach involves confrontation in a caring context, which hopefully will lead to the professional in question seeking help. If it does not, the confronting helper should consider the potential consequences of all other options and then define a course of action. Such a course might include filing an ethical complaint with a national association or licensing board. A complaint may be filed either by the professional who has queried his or her colleague, or by a client who believes he or she has been treated unethically.

In examining courses of action, there should be an evaluation of where each potential action might lead. Criteria for judgment include one's comfort surrounding

- Publicity (i.e., if the actions in this matter were reported in the press).
- Justice (i.e., fairness).
- Moral traces (i.e., lingering feelings of doubt).
- Universality (i.e., is this a course I would recommend others take in this situation?).

Finally, a course of action is chosen and implemented. In such a case, the professional helper must realize that not everyone will agree. Therefore, he or she needs to be prepared to take criticism as well as credit for what has been done.

SUMMING UP

As this chapter has pointed out, the matter of ethics in the helping professions is complex and multidimensional. To act ethically professionals must first know what ethics are and how to distinguish them from concepts such as morality. They also need to know about

- Codes of ethics relevant to helping situations.
- How to make ethical decisions.
- How to deal with someone acting unethically as well as how to evaluate their own actions.

It is fair to say that of all the dimensions involved in helping others, those that pertain to ethics are among the hardest to understand and to implement. The reason is that ethical matters require a higher level of thinking than most other aspects of counseling or assisting others. Theories and techniques, for example, are more straightforward. It is usually not difficult to assess whether a helping professional at any level is accurately behaving in accord with the theory or technique. However, ethics are a constant challenge for professionals because society is constantly changing. For example, during the pandemic of 2020, many counseling sessions were held virtually through Zoom and other social media platforms. The effectiveness of and ethics of offering counseling this way had not been raised or studied much up to this point. When such massive and rapid changes occur, they are more open to interpretation and scrutiny. In these situations, an individual must employ ethical principles in making a decision about what to do because there is no precedent.

However, despite the fact that new circumstances arise that require adjustments to offering counseling services and the use of theories in the process, ethics are vital to the health, well-being, and future of the helping professions (Manning, 2002). It could even be said that ethics are the hub around which all other aspects of helping revolve. If that is the case, understanding ethics will always be relevant and essential, especially as the helping professions, especially those involving counseling, move forward.

CHAPTER 18 RECAP: PROFESSIONAL ETHICS AND CODES OF ETHICS

What Are Ethics?

Ethics involve making decisions of a moral nature about people and their interaction in society.

Professional ethics are beliefs about behavior and conduct that guide professional practices.

The effectiveness of helpers is connected to their ethical knowledge and behaviors.

Why Are Professional Codes of Ethics Important?

A code of ethical conduct is designed to offer formal statements for ensuring protection of clients' rights while identifying the expectations of practitioners.

Ethical codes protect a profession from government and allow it to regulate itself and function autonomously.

Ethical codes help control internal disagreements and bickering and promote stability within a profession.

Ethical codes protect practitioners from the public, especially concerning malpractice suits.

Ethical codes help increase public trust in the integrity of a profession.

Ethical codes clarify the nature of ethical responsibilities.

Limitations of Ethical Codes

Some issues cannot be resolved by a code of ethics.

Enforcing ethical codes is difficult.

Some ethical issues are not covered in codes.

Ethical codes are historical documents.

Sometimes conflicts arise between ethical and legal codes.

There may be difficulty in bringing the interest of all parties involved in an ethical dispute.

Ethical codes are not proactive documents.

Making Ethical Decisions

Six ethical principles related to activities and ethical choices are:

beneficence (doing good and preventing harm)
nonmaleficence (not inflicting harm)
autonomy (respecting freedom of choice and self-determination)
justice (fairness)
fidelity (faithfulness or honoring commitments and promises)
veracity (truthfulness)

Other factors for assessing whether helpers are acting in ethically responsible ways:

personal and professional honesty
acting in the best interest of clients
acting without malice or personal gain

Ethical behavior of counselors is based on a five-stage developmental continuum of reasoning:

punishment orientation
institutional orientation
societal orientation
individual orientation
principle (conscience) orientation

Employment in a specific setting implies employees agree with the hiring institution's policies, principles, and ethics.

Unethical Behavior in Helping Professions Involves

Violation of confidentiality
Exceeding one's level of professional competence
Negligent practice
Claiming expertise one does not possess
Imposing one's values on a client
Creating dependency in a client
Sexual activity with a client
Certain conflicts of interest, such as a dual or multiple relationships
Questionable financial arrangements, such as charging excessive fees
Improper advertising
Plagiarism

Steps to take in working through potential ethical dilemmas, especially with impaired professionals: 1. Identify the problem as objectively as possible. 2. Apply the current associational (e.g., psychology, counseling, social work) codes of ethics to the matter. 3. If action is warranted, the colleague in question should first be approached informally and confronted in a caring context.

Criteria for evaluating where potential action might lead in confronting a colleague about unethical behavior:

publicity (i.e., if the actions in this matter were reported in the press)
justice (i.e., fairness)

moral traces (i.e., lingering feelings of doubt)
universality (i.e., is this a course I would recommend others take in this
 situation?).

KEY TERMS

autonomy 238
beneficence 238
code of ethics 236
codes of ethics limitations 236
criteria for judging a course of action
 in an ethical situation 241
fidelity 238
justice 238
justice (i.e., fairness) 241

moral traces 241
nonmaleficence 238
professional ethics 235
publicity 241
six ethical principles 238
slippery slope effect 240
unethical behavior 240
universality 241
veracity 238

LEARNING MORE

Code of Ethics for:
American Counseling Association
https://www.counseling.org/knowledge-center/ethics

American Psychological Association
https://www.apa.org/ethics/code

National Association of Social Workers
https://www.socialworkers.org/About/Ethics/Code-of-Ethics

CLASSROOM ACTIVITIES

1. Helping professionals are not immune to temptations. Think of a time
   when you were tempted to do something wrong. How did you resist
   doing so? What did you learn? How did you feel afterward?
2. What excuses have you heard from people who acted unethically? Do
   you think there are valid excuses for not acting in an ethical manner? If so,
   which ones are valid? If not, why not?
3. Name three exemplary models of ethical behavior. What made these individuals exemplary?

Epilogue

■ ■ ■

In the preceding chapters, you have read about the importance of theories and have been able to surmise how the most popular theories of today work therapeutically. You have also read about the importance of ethical issues in using theories and about crisis counseling. Beginning counselors sometimes question which theory or theories work best. They may even engage in heated debates about minor issues associated with various theories. The public as well as management groups connected to mental health issues, such as HMOs, frequently also have such discussions. The reason is clinicians, treatment specialists, insurance companies, and the public want assurance about outcomes of treatment. Theories are only as good as their proven evidence-based effectiveness in certain situations or with specific populations.

In recent years, researchers have tended to validate cognitive, behavioral, and cognitive-behavioral theories more than others in their helpfulness. This trend is not surprising, given that these approaches to counseling are probably the most objectively measured. Still, the classic question persists when a new client is seen: "What treatment, by whom, is most effective for this individual with that specific problem (or set of problems) and under which set of circumstances?" (Paul, 1967, p. 111).

It is beyond the scope of this text to give a definitive answer to Paul's pondering, because that would require delving into an almost inexhaustible number of variables related to a client such as family background, traumatic experiences, and physical and psychological issues. Research has verified, though, that a number of psychologically oriented treatments are valuable with some specific disorders (Murdock, 2017; Seligman & Reichenberg, 2014). In addition, a number of emerging theories hold significant promise (Wedding & Corsini, 2019). The relationship, as well as the theoretical approach, in a clinical setting seems to be the key to individuals getting better and moving on with their lives.

THEORIES, CLIENTS, AND YOU

Regardless of the current state of research about theories, it is important to emphasize that knowing and utilizing a theory in counseling is important both singularly and in combination. Theories ground you as a helper by making you aware of what practitioners and researchers have proposed and how their ideas and implementations have worked. However, it must be stressed that individuals respond differently to theories. As stated at the beginning of this text, counselors may even change theories during the course of treatment with the same person. As you have seen in the chapter vignettes, Linda's outcomes are related to the approaches employed with her.

Yet, as crucial as the qualities and backgrounds of theories and clients are, you as the counselor are equally important. Applying theoretical approaches to therapeutic situations is both an art and a science. It involves knowing the research behind what you do and being aware of yourself, others, and the developmental stage of helping in which you are engaged. There are no cookbooks for or shortcuts to thinking, feeling, and acting within the moments you engage in assisting another human being. If you remember this fact, you will likely do well in applying the theories you have learned here and others you may master later. Your sensitivity to the complexity of working with people will have increased, and the helping relationships you establish will be informed by the past as well as the present.

FINAL CONSIDERATIONS

As you have seen from reading how different theories work, many reasons are given as to what various approaches emphasize and what techniques they use. These explanations are based on developmental and situational factors. Thus, the same client may be conceptualized in a number of ways, depending on who is providing services. However, even though theories are unique, they are paradoxically similar in using specialized vocabularies, terms, and procedures. Counselors have their own special language that must be mastered. Backgrounds and personalities of helping specialists enter treatment too, and appropriate ways of responding to and interacting with individuals must be learned so the personhood of helpers does not detract from the theories they know or use.

You will do well to remember that despite some drawbacks and limitations, theories provide guidance about what is occurring in the lives of people and how such issues might best be handled (Austin, 1999). Theories also influence the process of helping—that is, what will be done and how—as well as outcomes, or results. In the end, all theories deal with perception and persuasion (Frank & Frank, 1991). They seek to make life better for the individuals we are privileged to work with. However, how they are used makes a difference. Like a knife, a theory may help heal or it may wound; it depends on who uses it and how.

In developing your comfort level in using theoretical models, you should remember that most theories involve a number of components, such as views on human nature, processes, techniques, diversity issues, strengths, and limitations. No theory is perfect. Indeed, the best theories are always evolving and growing because they are being actively researched and practiced. When everything is taken into consideration, you may find working with people more complicated than you initially imagined, but you may also find it more stimulating, rewarding, and fulfilling than you expected. Theories can help lead the way. Nothing could be more exciting and inviting!

Glossary

■ ■ ■

ABC Model antecedent-behavior-consequence

ABCs of REBT: A signifies an activating experience, **B** represents how the person thinks about the experience, and **C** is the emotional reaction to B.

acceptance and commitment therapy (ACT) a postmodern psychological intervention theory that uses acceptance and mindfulness strategies, together with commitment and behavior change strategies, to increase psychological flexibility—that is, being in the moment

acting "as if" clients are instructed to act as if they are the persons they want to be—for instance, the ideal persons they see in their dreams

action phase a psychodrama process involving the enactment of protagonists' concerns. The crucial thing is that protagonists express repressed emotions and find a new, effective way to act.

actors play the parts of other important people or objects in a psychodrama. They are called **auxiliaries**, and with prompting from the protagonist, they can play the protagonist's double, an antagonist, or even a piece of furniture or a plant.

adult ego state not subdivided or related to a person's age. It is the objective, thinking, data-gathering part of a person. The adult ego state tests reality, much as the ego does in Freud's system.

anal stage the second stage of Freud's stages of psychosexual development. In this stage, children (between the ages of 18 months and 3 years) obtain erotic pleasure from withholding and eliminating feces.

analysis of resistance when clients who resist therapeutic processes, such as being late for appointments, not paying fees, or blocking thoughts during free association, are helped to gain insight into what they are doing as well as other behaviors they are displaying

analysis of transference when clients who experience transference work with their therapist to learn from it and are freed to move on to another developmental stage

anatomy of an emotion feelings are a result of thoughts, not events, and self-talk influences emotions. This process is generally known as **rational emotive education (REE).**

applied behavior analysis (ABA) the successor to operant conditioning. ABA makes use of reinforcement, punishment, extinction, stimulus control, and other procedures derived from laboratory research.

assertiveness learning to state what one wants in a clear and direct way

assertiveness training Training that consists of counterconditioning anxiety and reinforcing assertiveness. Clients are taught that everyone has the right, not the obligation, of self-expression. Clients then learn the differences among aggressive, passive, and assertive actions.

assessment (Adlerian) analyze clients' lifestyles, examine family constellations, early memories, dreams, priorities, and ways of responding

assignment behaviors actions a therapist gives to help individuals behave differently so they can have different subjective experiences

audience describes others who are present during psychodrama

autonomous the ability to think through a situation clearly

basic crisis theory an approach to help people in crisis recognize and correct temporary affective, behavioral, and cognitive distortions brought on by traumatic events

BASIC personality profile behavioral, affective, somatic, interpersonal, and cognitive

bedlam a term describing madness or chaos that originated from the Bethlem Royal Hospital in London, which specialized in treating the mentally ill and was renowned for its disarray and turmoil

behavior (Glasser) thought and action are interrelated with feeling and physiology.

behavior therapy a term used to describe diverse behavioral approaches in counseling

behavioral determinist a behaviorist who emphasizes learning as the primary determinant of human actions

behavioral disputation involves behaving in a way that is the opposite of the client's usual way

behavioral rehearsal practicing a desired behavior until it is performed in the way a client wishes

behaviorists therapists who use behavioral approaches in counseling

bibliotherapy the reading of self-help and other helpful books that give clients insight into themselves and helpful new ways of thinking and behaving

bottom dog (Gestalt therapy) doing what you want to do

brain-based trauma intervention examples eye movement desensitization and reprocessing, tapping, brainspotting

brief therapy (strategic therapies) referring to clarity about what needs to be changed rather than to the time required

catastrophizing mentally distorting an event so that one becomes fearful of it

catching oneself (Adlerian) clients learn to become aware of self-destructive behaviors or thoughts.

cathartic method a way of treating people through talking so they release their pent-up or repressed emotions. Anna O, one of Freud's most famous patients, coined the term "talking cure" for this method of therapy.

cathexis a psychoanalytic term for emotional attachment to an idea, person, or object

chaining a method of teaching a behavior using behavior chains—that is, sequences of individual behaviors that follow one another and when linked together form a terminal behavior

change is inevitable a Milton Erickson position that states change will happen and thus helps clients reframe their situations positively as change happens

child ego state (transactional analysis) the first ego state to develop, it is that part of the personality characterized by childlike behaviors and feelings. Childlike behavior may be described as inquisitive, affectionate, selfish, mean, playful, whiny, and manipulative. The **child ego** state consists of **two subdivisions**—the natural or free child and the adaptive child. The **natural child** is the part of the person that is spontaneous, impulsive, feeling oriented, and often self-centered and pleasure loving. The natural child is also intuitive, creative, and responsive to nonverbal messages. The **adaptive child** is the compliant part of the personality that conforms to the wishes and demands of parental figures.

choice theory asserts that people choose to be the way they are. It replaced control theory as the base of reality therapy in the 1990s.

chronic anxiety a key element of Bowen family therapy, which is the tenet that all of life's anxiety comes with the territory of living. This anxiety is both emotional and physical and is shared by all protoplasm.

circular causality the idea that events are interconnected and that behaviors are caused by multiple factors

client a person, group, or family seeking help from a counselor. The medical equivalent of client is patient.

closure the discussion among members in a psychodrama transitioning from affective responses and behavioral descriptions to becoming cognitive

clue an intervention that mirrors the clients' usual behavior. It is intended to alert clients to the idea that some behavior is likely to continue.

code of ethics a document drawn up by a professional association that offers formal statements for ensuring protection of clients' rights while identifying expectations of practitioners

code of ethics limitations 1) Some issues cannot be resolved by code of ethics. 2) Enforcing ethical codes is difficult. 3) Some issues are not covered by codes. 4) Ethical codes are historical documents. 5) Sometimes there is conflict between ethical and legal codes. 6) Difficulty arises in bringing the interest of all parties involved in an ethical dispute together. 7) Ethical codes are not proactive documents.

cognitions thoughts, beliefs, and internal images

cognitive bypass belief that an experience directly causes feelings instead of thoughts

cognitive capping remembering on an intellectual basis what has occurred and the lessons learned

cognitive counseling theories – cognitive therapy (CT) and **cognitive behavior therapy (CBT)** both focus on mental processes and their influence on mental health.

cognitive disputation involves the use of direct questions, logical reasoning, and persuasion. Direct questions challenge clients to prove that their responses are logical.

cognitive distortions ways of thinking that are not true. These include all-or-nothing thinking (**dichotomous thinking**), selective abstraction, overgeneralization, magnification and minimization of thoughts, personalization, labeling and mislabeling, catastrophizing, mind reading, and negative predictions.

cognitive interventions bringing cognitive distortions into greater awareness—for example, challenging absolutes and all-or-nothing thinking, reattribution, and labeling of distortions

cognitive rehearsals consistently rehearsing healthy thoughts

cognitive restructuring where clients are taught to identify, evaluate, and change self-defeating or irrational thoughts that negatively influence their behavior. This process is accomplished by getting them to vocalize their self-talk and then change it, when necessary, from negative to neutral or positive.

cognitive-behavioral theories blending of behavioral and cognitive strategies to help people make needed changes

cold cognition descriptive and nonevaluative statements, such as "I lost my job"

commonalities that behaviorists share 1) assume that all behavior is learned, 2) learning can be effective in changing maladaptive behavior or acquiring new behavior, 3) reject the idea that the human personality is composed of traits

complementary transaction a term in transactional analysis to describe when both persons are operating either from the same ego state (e.g., child to child, adult to adult) or from complementary ego states (e.g., parent to child, adult to parent)

compliment consists of a positive statement with which the client(s) can agree.

A compliment is always planned as a lead-in to giving clients a task or assignment. It builds a **yes-set**—that is, a tendency to respond affirmatively.

conditional acceptance persons are valued only when they conform to others' wishes

confrontation (Gestalt therapy) when counselors point out to a client incongruent behaviors and feelings, such as smiling when nervous

congruence the condition of being transparent in a therapeutic relationship by giving up roles and facades

conscience (psychoanalytic theory) the part of the superego that induces guilt when persons act against ways they have been taught

conscious mind one of three levels of consciousness according to Freud. The conscious mind is attuned to events in the present, to an awareness of the outside world.

constructivism a philosophy that states that reality is not an objective entity, but a reflection of observation and experience

contingency contracts a contract that spells out behaviors to be performed, changed, or discontinued, the rewards associated with the achievement of these goals, and the conditions under which rewards are to be received

continuous reinforcement reinforcing a behavior every time it occurs

control theory a theory that argues all behavior is generated internally. Thus the only thing that people obtain from the outside world is information. Reality therapy initially tried to use this theory as the underpinning of its ideas.

counterconditioning the process of unlearning and replacing learned association

courage a willingness to take risks without knowing what the consequences may be

covert sensitization eliminates undesirable behavior by associating it with unpleasantness. It is used in treating clients who have problems with smoking, obesity, substance abuse, and sexual deviation.

creative imagery a warm-up technique in psychodrama that consists of inviting participants to imagine neutral or pleasant objects and scenes in order to help participants become spontaneous

crisis a critical phase in people's lives when their normal ways of dealing with the world are suddenly interrupted and they become overwhelmed, disorganized, or immobilized and unable to cope

criteria for judging a course of action in an ethical situation 1) one's comfort level surrounding the situation, 2) publicity (i.e., if the actions in this matter were reported in the press), 3) justice (i.e., fairness), 4) moral traces (i.e., lingering feelings of doubt), and 5) universality (i.e., is this a course I would recommend others take in this situation?)

critical incident stress debriefing (CISD) a seven-stage group approach used to help individuals deal with their thoughts and feelings after a crisis in a controlled environment using two counselors

crossed transaction an inappropriate TA ego state is activated, producing an unexpected response. Crossed transactions hurt, prompting individuals to withdraw from each other or switch topics.

culture-oriented counselor focuses on understanding cultural premises and then attempts to do therapy within the worldview of the clients

de-roling (psychodrama) transition from acting to becoming oneself again

defense mechanisms strategies that protect a person from being overwhelmed by anxiety, through adapting to situations or distorting or denying events

demystifying therapy using clear, open, and direct communication in explaining what counseling is and how it works

denial a defense mechanism where a person does not consciously acknowledge an unpleasant or traumatic event or situation

detriangulate separating feelings from intellect

developmental crises during the normal flow of human growth and maturation people move through different developmental stages and experience certain changes such as aging or retirement. Developmental crises are considered normal.

dialectical behavior theory (DBT) a postmodern behaviorally based treatment to teach people how to live in the moment, develop healthy ways to cope with stress, regulate their emotions, and improve their relationships with others, often used in treating mood disorders

differentiation refers to the ability of persons to distinguish themselves from their family of origin on an emotional and an intellectual level and to balance the intrapsychic and interpersonal dimensions of the self. Four factors influence a person's level of differentiation: 1) emotional reactivity, 2) emotional cutoff, 3) fusion

with others, and 4) the ability to take an I-position.

differentiation of self the degree to which a person is able to distinguish between the subjective feeling process and the more objective intellectual (thinking) process

direct and indirect suggestions messages a therapist gives a family such as "Go fast" or "You may not want to change too quickly"

directive an instruction from a family therapist to a family to behave differently

director the individual who guides protagonists in the use of psychodramatic methods to help them explore their problems

discovering life's meaning according to Viktor Frankl people discover life's meaning in three ways: 1) by doing a deed—that is, by achieving or accomplishing something, 2) by experiencing a value, such as a work of nature, culture, or love, 3) by suffering— that is, by finding a proper attitude toward unalterable fate

displacement a defense mechanism where energy is channeled away from one object to an alternative—that is, to a safe target

dispute irrational thoughts (REBT) questioning a thought in one of three ways—cognitive, imaginal, or behavioral

double (psychodrama) where the group member designated by the director takes on the role of the protagonist's alter ego and helps the protagonist express inner feelings

dream analysis Freud believed that dreams were "the royal road to the unconscious." In dream analysis clients are encouraged to dream and remember dreams. Clinicians are especially sensitive to two aspects of dreams, the manifest content (obvious meaning) and the latent content (hidden but true meaning), and may interpret both.

dream work (Gestalt) clients present dreams and are directed to experience what it is like to be in each part of the dream (dramatized free association) in which individuals become all parts of the dream. In this way, clients get more in touch with the multiple aspects of themselves.

eclectic combining theories or techniques from a wide variety of therapeutic approaches to treat clients instead of using a singular theoretical approach

ecosystemic crises natural or human-caused disasters

educational support groups (Adlerian) groups that help parents understand their children better and plan effective intervention strategies

effective and active techniques (William Glasser) teaching, employing humor, confronting, role-playing, giving feedback, formulating specific plans, and making contracts

ego "the executive of the mind" according to Freud. The ego functions to keep the desires of the id and the superego in check while realistically helping the person interact with the outside world. The ego works according to the **reality principle**, with reality being what exists.

ego ideal the part of the superego that strives for perfection and rewards actions that follow parental and societal dictates

ego psychology a term for Freud's theory that focuses on the ego's normal and pathological development

egogram a chart in TA that shows which ego state a person employs most

elegant REBT concentrates on the beliefs of clients and focuses on their taking responsibility for their own feelings. In the process, clients realize that success in everything is not essential and that catastrophe does not result from every unfulfilled want.

emotional catharsis a release of pent-up feelings

emotional control card (ECC) a wallet-sized ECC that lists four emotionally debilitating categories—anger, self-criticism, anxiety, and depression. Under each category is a list of inappropriate or self-destructive feelings and a parallel list of appropriate or non-defeating feelings. In potentially troubling situations, clients can refer to the cards and change the quality of their feelings about the situation.

empathy the ability to feel what it is like to be the client and to feel with clients and convey this understanding back to them

empowering when clients learn new ways to think and behave and are free to generalize their learning to new situations and end their treatment

empty chair technique (Gestalt) in this procedure clients focus on an empty chair and talk to the various parts of their personality. The technique is a **three-stage model: opposition, merging, and integration**. It is emotionally charged.

encounter an existentialist concept that involves total physical and psychological contact among individuals in a psychodrama on an intense, concrete, and complete basis in the here and now

encouragement (Adlerian) when counselors state their belief that behavior change is possible. It implies faith in a client and is the key to making productive lifestyle choices.

environmental planning where client sets up part of the environment to promote or limit certain behaviors

eros life-giving energy found in the id. Eros is the opposite of thanatos.

essence of normality having a feeling of concern for others according to Alfred Adler

ethical behavior of counselors five-stage developmental continuum of reasoning 1) punishment orientation, 2) institutional orientation, 3) societal orientation, 4) individual orientation, 5) principle (conscience) orientation

ethical principles related to the activities and ethical choices 1) **beneficence** (doing good and preventing harm), 2) **nonmaleficence** (not inflicting harm), 3) **autonomy** (respecting freedom of choice and self-determination), 4) **justice** (fairness), 5) **fidelity** (faithfulness or honoring commitments and promises), 6) **veracity** (truthfulness)

ethics making decisions of a moral nature about people and their interaction in society. The term is often used synonymously with "morality," and in some cases, the two terms overlap.

exaggeration (Gestalt therapy) Clients accentuate their own unwitting movements or gestures, such as using their hands when trying to talk about something difficult they have never shared before. In the process they make the inner meaning of these behaviors apparent.

exceptions looking for times when clients' goals may be happening or that troublesome behaviors may not be happening

exercises ready-made techniques in therapy

existential crisis inner conflicts and anxieties that accompany important human issues of purpose, responsibility, independence, freedom, and commitment

existential vacuum a sense that life has lost all meaning

existentialism a philosophy that addresses what it means to be human, including thoughts, feelings, and anxieties. Three beliefs existentialists hold in common are 1) the importance of anxiety, values, freedom, and responsibility in human life; 2) an emphasis on finding meaning in one's actions; 3) the belief people form their lives by their choices

existentialist goals in therapy have clients 1) shift from an outward to an inward frame of reference, 2) become more sensitive to their existence, 3) realize their unique traits and characteristics, 4) improve their encounters with others, 5) establish a will to meaning, 6) decide about both present and future directions in life

experiments activities that grow out of the interaction between counselors and clients that are not planned. What is learned is often a surprise to both.

extinction the elimination of a behavior by withdrawal of its reinforcement

facilitator an enabler rather than a director, the role a person-centered counselor takes

failure identity (William Glasser) a maladjusted personality characterized by a lack of confidence and a tendency to give up easily

fallible human being a term used in REBT to discourage people from rating themselves as good or bad

false or impossible goals of security trying to please everyone

family homeostasis the tendency of the family to remain in the same pattern of functioning unless challenged to do otherwise

family projection the Bowen family therapy tenet that couples tend to produce offspring with the same level of differentiation the parents have

family rules the overt and covert rules families use to govern themselves

faulty style of life a life that is self-centered and based on mistaken goals and incorrect assumptions associated with feelings of inferiority

faulty values believing in the necessity of being first no matter what needs to be done to achieve that goal

feminist counseling an approach that highlights the importance of interpersonal relationships and behaviors such as cooperation and self-disclosure

feminist movement a movement, especially active in the 1970s, to challenge patriarchal power

feminist theory a theoretical approach that uses women's values and beliefs as its framework

fictions subjective evaluations of oneself and one's environments

figure present needs; **ground** other needs—a Gestalt concept on people's perceptions. When a present need is met, the figure is relegated to the background and becomes the ground.

firstborns according to Adler firstborns are socialized to conform, achieve, behave, and please. They experience the loss of their unique position (i.e., are "dethroned") in the family when a second child is born.

five basic mistakes caused by fictions overgeneralizing, false/impossible goals of security, misperceptions of life and life demands, minimization/denial of one's worth, faulty values

five goals of Adlerian therapy 1) increase social interest, 2) make a lifestyle change, 3) change self-defeating thoughts and behaviors, 4) increase self-understanding, 5) encourage client to see equality among all people

five layers of neurosis (Gestalt therapy) 1) **phony layer** consists of pretending to be something that one is not, 2) **phobic layer** is an attempt to avoid recognizing aspects of oneself that an individual would prefer to deny, 3) **impasse layer** has no sense of direction, 4–5) **implosive and explosive layers** are often grouped together; people at these layers frequently feel vulnerable to feelings. As they peel back the layers of defensiveness built up over the years (implosive layer), they may explode in intense feelings of joy, sorrow, or pain (explosive layer).

five main solution-focused therapy techniques 1) between now and next time we meet, we (I) want you to observe, so that you can tell us (me) next time, what happens in your (life, marriage, family, or relationship) that you want to continue to happen, 2) do something different, 3) pay attention to what you do when you overcome the temptation or urge to perform the symptom or some behavior associated with the complaint, 4) a lot of people in your situation would have … 5) write, read, and burn your thoughts

five ordinal positions are emphasized in Adlerian literature on the family: firstborns, secondborns, middle children, youngest children, and only children

fixated (psychoanalysis) when someone becomes excessively frustrated or overindulged as a child and their level of development is arrested, resulting in their becoming overly dependent on the use of defense mechanisms

fixed-interval schedule a regular time schedule of reinforcement, such as a salary payment every two weeks

fixed-ratio schedule reinforcement based on the number of responses made—for instance, being paid for the number of items produced

flooding (behavioral therapy) where an imagined anxiety-producing scene is presented to a fearful person but it does not have dire consequences as in implosive therapy. Flooding helps desensitize people to stimuli they are anxious about.

focus on consciousness an underlying principle of reality therapy; human beings operate on a conscious level and are not driven by unconscious forces or instincts according to this theory.

four common procedures used to ensure a successful outcome in strategic therapies 1) defining a problem clearly and concisely, 2) investigating all solutions that have previously been tried, 3) defining a clear and concrete change to be achieved, 4) formulating and implementing a strategy for change

four different phases of Adlerian therapy 1) establishing a relationship, 2) performing analysis and assessment, 3) promoting insight, and 4) reorienting

four major methods of understanding and predicting human behavior according to TA 1) **structural analysis** understanding what is happening within the individual, 2) **transactional analysis** describing what happens between two or more people, 3) **game analysis** understanding transactions that lead to bad feelings, 4) **script analysis** understanding an individual's life plan

four specific steps in behavioral counseling 1) define the problem, 2) take a developmental history, 3) establish specific goals, 4) determine the best method for change

four ways of thinking about experiences (REBT) 1) positive, 2) negative, 3) neutral, 4) mixed

free association a psychoanalytic technique used to explore the unconscious of clients who report whatever comes to their minds as soon as it occurs even if silly, irrational, suggestive, or painful. The id speaks while the ego remains silent according to Freud. The material uncovered in this process becomes the stuff of interpretation and analysis.

Freudian slip errors of speech often sexual or aggressive in nature—for example, "I loathe you" instead of "I love you"

fully functioning person (person-centered therapy) an individual with no need to apply defense mechanisms to everyday experiences who is increasingly willing to change and grow, open to experience, trusting of self-perception, and engaged in self-exploration and evaluation

games a term in transactional analysis for ulterior motivated transactions that appear complementary on the surface but end in bad feelings. **First-degree games** in transactional analysis are played in social circles with anyone willing to participate. They generally lead to mild upsets. **Second-degree games** in transactional analysis occur when the players go after bigger stakes, usually in more intimate circles, and end up with bad feelings. **Third-degree games** in transactional analysis usually involve injury; the players end up in jail, the hospital, or the morgue.

gender-role analysis a process in feminist counseling where counselors help clients ferret out messages they have been given by significant others about how they should behave or appear

gender-role intervention a process in feminist counseling where counselors conduct a social analysis of the implications of gender roles and other social expectations for clients

generalization the display of behaviors in environments other than those in which the behaviors were originally learned

genital stage the last of Sigmund Freud's psychosexual stages of development, which begins around age 12 and lasts until about age 18. If all has gone well previously, each gender takes more interest in the other and heterosexual patterns of interaction appear.

genogram a visual representation of a family tree, depicted in geometric figures, lines, and words. Genograms include information about family relationships over at least three generations and help people gather information, hypothesize, and track relationship changes in the context of historic and contemporary events.

gestalt whole figure

Gestalt therapy an experiential and humanistic approach to change associated with Gestalt psychology, a school of thought that stresses the perception of completeness and wholeness and believes people are more than the sum of their parts. It is anti-deterministic.

Gestalt therapy rules 1) **principle of now** always uses the present tense, 2) **"I-and-thou relationship"** always addresses someone directly instead of talking about him or her, 3) **uses the word "I,"** 4) uses **awareness continuum** focus on how and what rather than why, 5) **conversion of questions** convert questions into statements

Gestalt view of human nature trust the inner wisdom of people, much as person-centered counseling does

going home again a Bowen family therapy technique where the family therapist instructs the individual client or family members to return home to get to know better their family of origin

grieving deep sorrow, a natural reaction to loss

group sharing having everyone in psychodrama, including the audience, comment on what they saw and heard

healthy style of life (Adlerian) the belief healthy people focus on society (i.e., social tasks), work, and sexuality, plus two other challenges of life: spirituality and coping with self

heuristic researchable or open to research

homework when clients are assigned to practice tasks outside counseling sessions

hot cognitions heavily laden emotional-demand statements that may reveal varied distortions, such as overgeneralizing, catastrophizing, magnification, and all-or-nothing thinking. These cognitions often lead to dysfunctional behaviors because they are filled with both demands and distortions.

humane theory an early 18th-century theory that advocated those with mental disorders should receive humane treatment, such as time outdoors each day, a nutritious diet, and communication with others

humor (reality/choice therapy) the ability to see the absurdity within a situation and view matters from a different and amusing perspective

I take responsibility (Gestalt therapy) an exercise where clients make statements about perceptions and close each statement with the phrase "and I take responsibility for it." The exercise helps clients integrate and own their perceptions and behaviors.

id a Freudian term for the inherited givens of the personality present at birth. The id is amoral, impulsive, and irrational and works according to the **pleasure principle**—that is, it pursues what it wants because it cannot tolerate tension. The id operates through drives, instincts, and images (such as dreaming, hallucinating, and fantasizing), a thought process known as the **primary process**. The id contains the psychic energy (**libido**) of persons.

ideal self (what people are striving to become) and the **real self** (what people are). The further the ideal self is from the real self, the more alienated and maladjusted persons become.

identification a defense mechanism where a person incorporates the qualities of another, thereby removing any fear that person might have of the other and giving him or her new behavioral skills

identity a psychologically healthy sense of self. Personal identity precedes performance.

implosive therapy desensitizing clients to a situation by having them imagine an anxiety-producing situation that may have dire consequences, without having been taught to relax first (as in **systematic desensitization**)

in-crisis actions consist of 1) examining alternatives—that is, recognizing alternatives that are available and realizing some choices are better than others; 2) making plans—where clients feel a sense of control and autonomy in the process so as not to become dependent; 3) obtaining commitment from the client to take planned actions

individual psychology Alfred Adler's name for his theory, which emphasizes a holistic perspective. Individuals are indivisible.

inelegant REBT focuses on activating events and the distortions clients may have. It does not give clients any coping strategies for dealing with situations. Instead, clients are encouraged to assure themselves that they will do better in the future or that they are good persons.

inferiority complex the tendency for each person to feel initially inferior to others

ing verbs (reality therapy/control therapy) use of "ing" verbs such as "angering" or "bullying" to describe clients' thoughts and actions

insight a related concept to catharsis, consisting of immediate new perceptions and understandings about one's problems that occur during or after the experience of catharsis

integration and sharing the last phase of a psychodrama where a director encourages the group to give the protagonist as much personal, supportive, and constructive feedback as possible

intermittent reinforcement schedule reinforcing a behavior less often once it is learned

interpretation when therapists help clients understand the meaning of past and present personal events, including giving clients explanations and analysis of their thoughts, feelings, and actions. Intepretation, from an Adlerian perspective, often takes the form of intuitive guesses about a client, based on counselors' general knowledge of ordinal positions and family constellations.

interval reinforcement schedule the length of time between reinforcers

intraindividual diversity diverse components of being that exist within individual on an unconscious level

irrational thinking or **irrational Beliefs (iBs)** include (according to Albert Ellis) the invention of upsetting and disturbing thoughts regarding self, others, and life

I-Thou personal quality the quality person-centered counselors look for in a counselor-client relationship

journaling keeping a log of what is being learned, thought, or felt

labeling and **mislabeling** the way people characterize themselves by giving themselves labels

latency between the ages of 6 and 12 children show little manifest interest in sex

levels of empathy (Carkhuff) 1) low, 2) moderately low, 3) interchangeable, 4) moderately high, 5) high

life script positions (transactional analysis) 1) **I'm OK, you're OK** (i.e., a get-on-with position), 2) **I'm OK, you're not OK** (i.e., a get-away-from position), 3) **I'm not OK, you're OK** (i.e., a get-nowhere-with position), 4) **I'm not OK, you're not OK** (i.e., a get-rid-of position)

logotherapy Viktor Frankl's existential theory, third school of Viennese psychotherapy

magic shop a warm-up technique in psychodrama especially useful for protagonists who are ambivalent about their values and goals. It involves a storekeeper (an auxiliary ego) who runs a magic shop filled with special qualities. The qualities are not for sale but may be bartered for.

magnification a cognitive distortion that occurs when an imperfection is exaggerated beyond reality

main assessment instrument in REBT the evaluation of a client's thinking

maintenance a consistent performance of desired actions without depending on anyone else for support

making the rounds (Gestalt therapy) an exercise to get clients to say something they usually do not verbalize. It is particularly effective in a group to help clients become aware of feelings and work through unfinished business.

mapping a sketching out of a course of successful intervention

masculine protest (Adlerian) refers to the attitude in women of wanting to be the best they can be, but in Adler's time men held superior roles to those of women. Adler was concerned for women's rights and equality.

May I feed you a sentence? (Gestalt therapy) Aware of implicit attitudes or messages in what a client is saying, the counselor asks whether the client will repeat a certain sentence that makes the client's thoughts explicit, such as "I am afraid to tell you what I really think because you might reject me." If the counselor is correct about the underlying message, the client will gain insight as the sentence is repeated.

meaning according to Viktor Frankl meaning exists on three levels: a) ultimate meaning (e.g., an order to the universe); b) meaning of the moment; and c) common, day-to-day meaning

messages in transactional analysis 1) Positive messages give children permission to function in multiple ways and do not limit them. 2) Negative messages or injunctions are powerful prohibitions or commands that express disappointment, frustration, anxiety, and unhappiness and may become the basis for destructive scripts.

methods that promote the counselor-client relationship 1) active and passive listening, 2) accurate reflection of thoughts and feelings, 3) clarification, 4) summarization, 5) confrontation, 6) general or open-ended leads

microskills atheoretical helping methods, such as active listening, reflection of feeling and content, immediacy, confrontation, and summarization, that promote relationship formation and exploration of a problem or concern

middle children (Adlerian) in the middle positions of a family these children often feel squeezed in and treated unfairly and do not develop the close, personal types of alliances an oldest or a youngest child may form. However, because of their position, middle children learn a great deal about family politics and the art of negotiation.

mind reading the tendency of some people to guess what others are thinking about them

minimization when a person downplays good points or notable achievements

minimization or denial of one's worth thinking that one will never amount to anything

miniscripts (transactional analysis) focus is on minute-by-minute occurrences. Some of the most common miniscripts are "Be perfect," "Be strong," "Hurry up," "Try harder," "Please someone." These five messages, called **drivers**, allow people to escape their life scripts, but the escape is only temporary.

miracle question a technique created by Isoo Kim Berg that invites clients to suspend their present frame of reference and enter the reality they wish to achieve

mirror a psychodrama activity where the protagonist watches from offstage while an auxiliary ego mirrors the protagonist's posture, gesture, and words. This technique is used to help the protagonist see himself or herself more accurately.

misperceptions of life and life's demands a belief that one never gets any breaks

monodrama or autodrama a psychodrama technique where the protagonist plays all the parts of the enactment; no auxiliary egos are used

morality involves judgments and evaluations of actions

most common techniques in cognitive-behavioral counseling 1) self-instructional training, 2) stress-inoculation training, 3) thought stopping, 4) cognitive restructuring

most prevalent cognitive techniques in cognitive therapy 1) specify (identify) automatic thoughts and correct them, 2) homework, 3) cognitive interventions—for example, challenging absolutes and all-or-nothing thinking, reattribution, and labeling of distortions, 4) cognitive rehearsals, 5) scriptotherapy

multigenerational transmission process the idea in Bowen family therapy that families that present a problem have had the forces of several generations shaping and carrying it along

multiple double a psychodrama technique where two or more actors represent different aspects of the protagonist's personality

necessary and sufficient or core conditions of counseling (Carl Rogers) 1) empathy, 2) positive regard or acceptance, 3) congruence or genuineness

negative family atmosphere a family atmosphere that is authoritarian, rejecting, suppressive, materialistic, overprotective, or pitying

negative predictions beliefs that something bad is going to happen. They may have little basis in fact, but they influence a person's actions just the same.

negative reinforcer an aversive stimulus whose removal is contingent upon performance of a desired action; that removal is reinforcing for the person—for example, nagging

negative scripts (transactional analysis 1) **never scripts:** Individuals never get to do what they want (e.g., "Marriage is bad; never get married"), 2) **until scripts:** Individuals must wait until a certain time to do something they want to do (e.g., "You cannot play until you have all your work done"), 3) **always scripts:** Individuals tell themselves that they must continue doing what they have been doing (e.g., "You should always continue a job once you've started it"), 4) **after scripts:** Individuals expect difficulty after a certain event (e.g., "After age 40 life goes downhill"), 5) **open-ended scripts:** Individuals do not know what they are supposed to do after a given time (e.g., "Be active while you're young")

neurotic individual a person who tries to attend to too many needs at once and therefore does not take care of any one need fully

nonevents events that may have been expected but never occur—for example, having children or making a significant difference in a field of work

nonverbal messages silence, voice tone, and posture

noogenic neurosis (Viktor Frankl) characterized by a feeling that one has nothing to live for

now = experience = awareness = reality the past is no more and the future not yet. Only the now exists in Gestalt therapy.

object in psychodynamic theory, anything that satisfies a need, whether a person or a thing; used interchangeably with the term "other"

object relations theory a psychodynamic theory that proposes children are primarily driven by their need to relate to others, beginning with the mother-infant dyad, and that intrapsychic, interpersonal, and group experiences lay the foundation for the development of individual identity. This theory is the basis for **attachment theory.**

only children Any child born 7 or more years apart from siblings is psychologically an only child. As a group, only children are never dethroned and are at an advantage in receiving a great deal of attention. They may mature early, become high achievers, and develop rich imaginations. Major disadvantages are they may become pampered and selfish and may not be well socialized.

open-ended questions queries that invite a thoughtful response of more than a few words

operant conditioning focuses primarily on how individuals operate in the environment. People learn to discriminate between behaviors that bring rewards and those that do not, which increases behavior that is rewarded and decreases behavior that is either punished or not reinforced.

oral stage the first stage in Sigmund Freud's psychosexual stages of development that occurs during the first year of life. The infant derives pleasure from orally oriented activities such as sucking, biting, and swallowing.

ordeal a constructive or neutral behavior that must be performed before one can engage in the undesirable behavior. Ordeals help clients give up symptoms that are troublesome to maintain.

overcorrection a technique in which clients first restore the environment to its natural state and then make it better

overgeneralization a cognitive distortion where a rule is made based on a few incidences or events

overgeneralizing viewing everything as the same—for example, believing that all Latinx are alike

paradox giving families permission to do something they are already doing. Paradox is intended to lower or eliminate resistance. The best known types of a paradox are 1) **restraining** where the therapist tells the client family that they are incapable of doing anything other than what they are doing, 2) **prescribing** where family members are instructed to enact a troublesome dysfunctional behavior in front of the therapist, 3) **redefining** attributing positive connotations to symptomatic or troublesome actions. The underlying idea is that symptoms have meaning for those who display them, whether such meaning is logical or not.

parent, adult, child the three ego states in transactional analysis

parent ego state incorporates the attitudes and behaviors of parental figures—that is, the dos, shoulds, and oughts. Outwardly, these messages are expressed through critical or nurturing behavior. The **nurturing parent** is the part that comforts, praises, and aids others. The **critical**

parent is the part that finds fault, displays prejudices, disapproves, and prevents others from feeling good about themselves.

peak experiences Abraham Maslow's concept where people feel truly integrated and connected with the universe in a very emotional way

personalization when an event that is unrelated to a person is distorted and made to appear as if it is related

person-centered therapy an anti-deterministic approach that stresses each person can find a personal meaning and purpose in life and is motivated toward self-actualization

person-to-person relationships two family members relate personally to each other about each other—that is, they do not talk about others (triangling) and do not talk about impersonal issues

phallic stage the third stage in Freud's stages of psychosexual development. In this stage, in which the chief zones of pleasure are the genitalia, children (between ages 3 to 5) attempt to resolve their sexual identities by working through their conflictual sexual desires (for boys, the Oedipus complex; for girls, the Electra complex)

phenomenological perspective what is important is a person's perception of reality rather than an event itself

physical or **old brain needs** the need to obtain and use life-sustaining necessities such as food, water, and shelter. Associated behaviors are breathing, digesting, and sweating because the body automatically controls them.

play therapy allows children to communicate through the language of play and then verbally talk about their feelings

positioning acceptance and exaggeration of what clients or family members are saying. If conducted properly, it helps clients see the absurdity of what they are doing, thereby freeing them to do something else.

positive family atmosphere democratic, accepting, open, and social

positive regard love, warmth, care, respect, and acceptance

positive reinforcer valued and pleasurable for the person affected—for example, money and food

possibility therapy Bill O'Hanlon's term for his approach to solution-focused therapy

posttraumatic stress disorder (**PTSD**) delayed reactions to a crisis

power analysis a process in feminist counseling where counselors help clients recognize the difference in power between men and women in society. Power refers to the ability to access resources to effect change on a personal and/or external level.

power intervention involves strengthening or empowering clients by reinforcing their statements or giving them information

preconscious mind a level of consciousness according to Freud between the conscious and unconscious minds and that contains aspects of both. Within the preconscious are hidden memories or forgotten experiences that can be remembered with the proper cues.

pregenital stages the first three of Freud's psychosexual stages of development: oral, anal, phallic

pretend technique a gentle confrontational technique in strategic therapy where family members are asked to pretend to engage in a troublesome behavior

primary emphases of REBT teaching and disputing

primary process thought processes contained within the id consisting of dreams, hallucinations, and fantasies to reduce tension by imagining what it desires

primary psychological needs (reality therapy/control therapy) 1) **belonging** the need for friends, family, and love, 2) **power** the need for self-esteem, recognition, and competition, 3) **freedom** the need to make choices and decisions, 4) **fun** the need for play, laughter, learning, and recreation

primary reinforcer valued intrinsically, such as food

processing delving deeper into a psychodrama to talk about how participants at all levels were affected by what they experienced. During processing **identification** and **integration** occur where members of a group state how they could or could not see themselves acting in certain ways or saying specific things and what they have learned from the psychodrama experience.

professional ethical codes 1) protect a profession from government, 2) help control internal disagreements and bickering and promote stability, 3) protect practitioners from the public, especially in malpractice suits, 4) increase public trust in the integrity of a profession. Professional ethical codes are general and idealistic; they seldom answer specific questions.

professional ethics beliefs about behavior and conduct that guide professional practices, such as those between counselors and clients

projection a defense mechanism where an unwanted emotion or characteristic of a person is attributed to someone else in an effort to deny the emotion or characteristic is part of oneself

protagonist the individual who is the subject of the psychodrama enactment. He or she may play many parts.

pseudoself a pretend self

psychological first aid a directive approach to a crisis where counselor focuses on the physical safety and comfort of victims while promoting social engagement and helping survivors of a trauma find missing loved ones or attend to issues associated with traumatic grief, guilt, or shame

psychopathology (existentialism) a failure to make meaningful choices and maximize one's potential

psychosexual developmental stages Freud's stages of development—oral, anal, phallic and genital. Each stage of development is characterized by the body area providing maximal erotic gratification. There is a latency period between the phallic and genital stages.

psychosocial development Erik Erikson's theory that extends Freud's development emphasis from birth to death and focuses on the achievement of specific life-enhancing tasks. Erikson emphasizes the central role of the ego in life tasks rather than the interplay between the id, the ego, and the superego.

punishment the presentation of an aversive stimulus in order to suppress or eliminate a behavior

push button (**Adlerian**) clients are encouraged to realize they have choices about the stimuli to which they will pay attention and are taught to create the feelings they want by concentrating on their thoughts. The technique is like pushing a button because clients can choose to remember negative or positive experiences.

Q Sort Technique an evaluative method pioneered by Carl Rogers where a client is given 100 cards, each of which contains a self-descriptive sentence and sorts them from most-like-me to least-like-me before, during, and after counseling

quid pro quo the tendency of family members to treat others in the way they are being treated ratio schedule of reinforcement the number of responses between reinforcers

rational emotive behavior therapy songs new words set to common tunes that are humorous and therapeutic

rational emotive education (REE) see anatomy of an emotion

rational emotive imagery (REI) imaginal disputation, a way of practicing correcting your emotional reaction to some real or imagined event

rationalization a defense mechanism that allows a person to find reasonable explanations for unreasonable or unacceptable behaviors in order to make them sound logical and acceptable

reaction formation A defense mechanism where anxiety-producing thoughts, feelings, or impulses are repressed, and their opposites are expressed

reality principle what exists in the outside environment. The principle on which the ego operates. It is the opposite of the pleasure principle.

reality therapy a counseling theory originated by William Glasser in the 1960s that focuses on the present and seeks to help clients change by evaluating what they are doing, making new plans, and then implementing them. Reality therapy is pragmatic and has behavioral overtones.

reality therapy/choice therapy an approach, originally known as reality therapy, that emphasizes choices people can make to change their lives

REBT major goal avoid a more emotional response than is warranted by an event

redundancy principle a family's tendency of repeating a limited number of behavioral sequences

reframing giving a different interpretation to a family's situation or behavior, thus giving a circumstance new meaning. Therefore, other ways of behaving are explored.

regression a defense mechanism where a person returns to an earlier stage of development

reinforcer reward

repression the most basic defense mechanism on which others are built. In it the ego involuntarily excludes from consciousness any unwanted or painful thoughts, feelings, memories, or impulses, but sometimes repressed thoughts slip out in dreams or verbal expressions. Repression is the cornerstone of psychoanalysis.

resilience the ability to recover from adversity

resistance actions that block therapeutic progress such as missing or being late for appointments, not paying fees, persisting in transference, blocking thoughts during free association, or refusing to recall dreams or early memories

responsible behavior (reality therapy/control therapy) allows individuals to take charge of their actions and obtain their goals; it keeps them from interfering with others or getting into trouble.

role-playing a procedure in which clients are asked to act "as if" they are the persons they ideally want to be. Clients practice a number of behaviors to see which work best. Feedback is given and, ideally, insight and empathy emerge from the process.

role reversal a psychodrama technique where the protagonist switches roles with another individual on stage and plays that individual's part

scaling a solution-focused therapy technique in which questions are asked using a scale of 1 (low) to 10 (high) to help clients move toward their goal. This technique helps make problems seem more concrete and tangible

scriptotherapy the process of writing where individuals improve their thoughts by expressing them concretely

sculpting (psychodrama) where group members use nonverbal methods to arrange other group members into a configuration like that of significant individuals with whom they regularly deal, such as family members or social peers. Positioning involves body posturing.

secondary process a Freudian term for rationally thinking through situations and making a reality-based decision. The ego's way of thinking.

secondary reinforcer a reward that acquires its value by being associated with a primary reinforcer—for example, money

secondborns (Adlerian) individuals who are more outgoing, carefree, and creative and less concerned with rules than firstborns. They frequently pursue roles not taken by firstborns.

self-disclosure a process where the counselor shares with the client personal thoughts and feelings that are educative and yet revealing of the counselor as an individual. In this process, an effort is made to normalize, equalize, and liberate the experiences and emotions of the person in therapy.

self-instructional training a cognitive-behavioral procedure where counselors first perform a task or engage in appropriate behaviors while verbalizing aloud through self-talk the reasons behind what they are doing. Clients then do the same task or behavior and give themselves instructions aloud. Next, clients engage in the behaviors while whispering self-instructions and finally perform the behaviors while silently repeating the reasons behind what they are doing.

self-monitoring a behavioral technique composed of two related processes: self-observation and self-recording. **Self-observation** requires that clients notice particular behaviors they exhibit; **self-recording** focuses on keeping track of these behaviors.

self-statements assertions made by people that affect their behaviors in much the same way as statements made by another person

self-talk what people tell themselves

self-theory another term used for person-centered therapy. The self is an outgrowth of what people experience. An awareness of self helps individuals differentiate themselves from others.

seven deadly habits (William Glasser) criticizing, blaming, complaining, nagging, threatening, punishing, and bribing

shame attack exercises (REBT) to help clients learn to behave differently, these exercises usually include an activity that is harmless but dreaded, such as introducing oneself to a stranger or asking for a glass of water in a restaurant without ordering anything else. Clients come to realize that the world does not stop if a mistake is made or if a want remains unfulfilled.

shaping when behavior is learned gradually in steps through successive approximation

sibling positions according to Bowen family therapy individuals develop fixed personality characteristics based on their functional birth order in a family. The more closely a marriage replicates a couple's sibling positions in their families of origin, the better the chance for success.

situation (psychodrama) the emphasis on the present, where natural barriers of time, space, and states of existence are obliterated

situational crisis when an unexpected, extraordinary event occurs that the person had no way of anticipating or controlling—for example, automobile accidents, rape, job loss, sudden illness

six criteria to judge whether a person is choosing a suitable and healthy behavior (reality therapy/choice therapy). 1) behavior is **noncompetitive;** 2) behavior **is easily completed without a great deal of mental effort;** 3) behavior **can be done by oneself;** 4) behavior **has value for the person;** 5) the client believes that **improvements in lifestyle** will result from the behavior; 6) the client **can practice the behavior without being self-critical.**

skeleton keys standardized therapeutic techniques used in solution-focused therapy with the premise that a solution does not have to be as complex as a problem

slippery slope effect by condoning or ignoring, unethical situations counselors risk eroding their own sense of moral selfhood and find it easier to condone future ethical breaches.

small change the idea in solution-focused therapy that only a small amount of change is needed to make an impact on a problematic behavior

social constructionism the social or cultural context of people or families

social-cognitive learning the acquiring of new knowledge and behavior by observing other people and events without engaging in the behavior and without any direct consequences. Synonyms for social-cognitive learning include observational learning, imitation, social modeling, and vicarious learning. Models closest to an observer's age, gender, race, and attitude have the greatest impact. Live models, symbolic models (i.e., those on films and videos), and multiple models (i.e., groups of people) are equally effective in producing behavioral change.

Socratic dialogue a technique used in Bowen family therapy where the counselor takes the position of a teacher or coach and calmly asks questions until the student, in this case the family, learns to think independently

soliloquy a technique that involves the protagonist giving a monologue about his or her situation as he or she is acting it out

specifying (identifying) automatic thoughts (cognitions that occur without effort) and correcting them

spitting in the client's soup (Adlerian) counselors point out certain behaviors to clients, thereby ruining the payoff for the behaviors

splitting a defense mechanism that keeps incompatible feelings separate from oneself

spontaneity the response people make that contains some degree of adequacy to a new situation or a degree of novelty to an old situation. Responding in new creative ways is part of this process.

stage the area where the action takes place in a psychodrama

stimulus-response (S-R) model basically classical conditioning, sometimes called respondent learning. The person need not be an active participant to learn because learning occurs through the association of two stimuli, also known as the conditioning of involuntary responses. Many human emotions, such as phobias, arise because of paired associations.

strategic approach emphasizes the structure of the family and offers techniques that can be used whatever the culture

stress-inoculation training a process where individuals are taught sets of coping skills to help them handle stressful events

striving for perfection (Adlerian) the tendency of people to try to fulfill their own unique potential (completeness)

strokes (transactional analysis) verbal or physical recognition. Strokes result in the accumulation of either good or bad feelings, known as stamps.

style of life (Adlerian) a person's characteristic way of relating to others, viewing the world, behaving, and pursuing long-term goals

style-shift counseling a method of counseling where clinicians in working with a client depart from one theory and adopt another because it is seen as a better fit for the client

sublimation a positive form of displacement when a drive that cannot be expressed directly is channeled into constructive activities

success identity (William Glasser) when needs of acceptance, love, and worth are met

superego Freud's term for the moral branch of the mind, operating according to what is ideal. The superego arises from the moral teachings of a child's parents and functions according to the moral principle, striving for perfection.

superiority complex a person who overcompensates for feelings of inferiority and develops a neurotic fiction (belief) that is unproductive

surplus reality psychological experience that transcends the boundaries of physical reality

syllogisms a deductive form of reasoning (another form of REBT cognitive disputation) consisting of two premises and a conclusion

symmetrical relationships and complementary relationships relationships among equals (symmetrical) and unequals (complementary)

syncretism the lowest level of eclecticism, a sloppy, unsystematic process of putting unrelated clinical concepts together

systematic desensitization designed to help clients overcome anxiety in particular situations. Clients are asked first to describe a situation that causes anxiety and then to rank this situation and related events on a hierarchical scale, from aspects that cause no concern (0) to those that are most troublesome (100). To help clients avoid anxiety and face situations, counselors teach them to relax physically or mentally. Then the hierarchy is reviewed, starting with low-anxiety items. When clients' anxieties begin to mount, they are helped to relax again. The underlying idea is that people cannot feel anxious and relaxed at the same time, a phenomenon called reciprocal inhibition.

talk therapies the idea that speaking to and with clients in a reasonable and logical manner will help them release thoughts and emotions and make needed changes in their lives

task setting (Adlerian) clients initially set short-range, attainable goals and eventually work up to long-term, realistic objectives.

technical eclecticism a type of eclecticism exemplified in the work of Arnold Lazarus and the BASIC ID acronym (behavior, affect, sensation, imagination, cognition, interpersonal, drugs and biology). In this approach, procedures from different theories are selected and used in treatment without necessarily subscribing to the theories that spawned them. The idea is that techniques, not theories, are used in treating individuals.

techniques in transactional analysis besides analysis of structural, transactional, game, and/or script 1) treatment contract emphasizes agreed-upon responsibilities for both counselors and clients, 2) interrogation involves speaking to a client's adult ego state until an adult response is given, 3) specification identifies the ego state that initiated a transaction, 4) confrontation involves pointing out inconsistencies in client behavior or speech, 5) **explanation** teaches the client about some aspect of TA, 6) **illustration** enlightens the client or elaborates on a point, 7) **confirmation** points out recurrence of previously modified behavior, 8) **interpretation** explains to the child ego state of the client the reasons for the client's behavior, 9) **crystallization** involves an adult-to-adult transaction in which the client becomes aware that game playing may be given up.

tele the total communication of feelings between people in a psychodrama

teleological goals future goals, which Adler believes are more powerful in influencing a person than past causes

thanatos Freud's term for death instincts found in the id, often expressed in aggressive or risky behaviors. It is the opposite of eros.

theoretical integrationism a type of eclecticism that requires professional helpers to master at least two theories before attempting any combinations. It assumes a degree of equality between the theories.

theory a group of related laws or relationships used to provide explanations within a discipline such as counseling to explain human thought and behavior, including what causes people to change. A theory provides a model or template that gives practitioners a direction and guidance in working with others. A counseling theory is the why behind the how of helping.

theory of spontaneity-creativity Jacob Moreno's core tenet in psychodrama that the best way for an individual to respond creatively to a situation is through spontaneity—a readiness to improvise and respond in the moment

therapeutic soliloquy technique private reactions to events in the protagonist's life are verbalized and acted out, usually by other actors

thought stopping a process where clients progress from outer to inner control of negative thought patterns. Clients replace self-defeating thoughts with assertive, positive, or neutral ones.

three categories of clients in solution-focused therapy: Visitors are not involved in the problem and are not part of the solution. **Complainants** complain about situations but can be observant and describe problems even if they are not invested in solving them. **Customers** are not only able to describe a problem and

their involvement in it but are also willing to work to solve it.

three components of a crisis an event, a client's perception of the event, and the failure of the client's typical coping methods

three main approaches in contemporary behavioral therapy 1) stimulus-response model, 2) applied behavior analysis, 3) social-cognitive theory

three periods of evolution for person-centered processes and techniques 1) nondirective period (1940–1950), 2) reflective period (1950–1957), 3) experiential period (1957–1980)

time-out a mild aversive technique that separates clients, usually children, from the opportunity to receive positive reinforcement

top dog (Gestalt) thinking what you should do

traditional eclecticism a form of eclecticism where clinicians make an orderly combination of compatible features from diverse theoretical sources into a harmonious whole

transactional analysis main schools of treatment 1) the **classical San Francisco** school (with an emphasis on explanation, diagrams, contracts, and behavioral change), 2) the **cathexis** school (which emphasized confrontation and reparenting), and 3) the **redecision** school (which emphasized the child's compliance with injunctions and the power to make new decisions)

transference denotes a client's response to a clinician as if the clinician were some significant figure in the client's past, usually a parent figure

transtheoretical model (TTM) of change a developmentally based model of change and an alternative to technical eclectic approaches. The model proposes five stages of change—precontemplation, contemplation, preparation, action, and maintenance.

trauma-informed therapies cognitive-behavioral therapy, art, music, and animal-assisted therapies

trephining the drilling of holes in the skull of a person being treated for a mental disorder in prehistoric societies. Ancient people believed that evil spirits possessed individuals who were mentally disturbed.

triangle consists of a state of calm between a comfortable twosome and an outsider. The original triangle is between a child and parent.

two critical periods in children's lives related to identity (reality therapy/control therapy) 1) between the ages of 2 and 5, children learn early socialization skills; 2) between the ages of 5 and 10, children are involved with school, where they gain knowledge and self-concept.

two main components of crisis counseling 1) first-order intervention (psychological first aid) and 2) second-order intervention (crisis therapy)

ulterior transaction where two ego states operate simultaneously and one message disguises the other. Ulterior transactions appear to be complementary and socially acceptable even though they are not.

ultimate human concerns (existentialism) death, freedom, isolation, and meaninglessness

unconscious mind the most powerful and least understood part of the personality according to Freud. Instinctual, repressed, and powerful forces of the personality exist in the unconscious.

underdog another name for bottom dog

undifferentiated or fused the opposite of differentiation. It implies an emotional dependence on family members, even if living away from them. Undifferentiated people are vulnerable to stress and are much more prone to physical and social illnesses than others.

unethical behaviors in helping professions (most prevalent) 1) violation of confidentiality, 2) exceeding one's level of professional competence, 3) negligent practice, 4) claiming expertise one does not possess, 5) imposing one's values on a client, 6) creating dependency in a client, 7) sexual activity with a client, 8) certain conflicts of interest such as dual or multiple relationships, 9) questionable financial arrangements, 10) improper advertising, 11) plagiarism.

unfinished business earlier thoughts, feelings, and reactions that still affect personal functioning and interfere with living life in the present

values orienting beliefs about what is good and how that good should be achieved

variable-interval schedule an irregular time schedule so that reinforcement takes place unpredictably

variable-ratio schedule irregular reinforcement, as a slot machine

viable plan (reality therapy/choice therapy) has eight features and represented by the acronym SAM I2 C3 is 1) Simple—clear, understandable, 2) Attainable—can be accomplished by the client, 3) Measurable—tangible such as recording what was done, when, 4) Immediate—can be started on right away, 5) Involving the clinician in some appropriate way such as giving feedback, 6) Controlled by the client—not under the control of someone else, 7) Committed to be kept by the client realizing change is important, and 8) Consistent in that the client will keep at it and repeated needed changes

victim, persecutor, or rescuer the positions from which people play games in transactional analysis

Viennese Psychoanalytic Society see Wednesday Psychological Society

warm cognition emphasizes preferences and nonpreferences, such as "I lost my job and I really don't want to have to start looking for another one."

warm-up phase (psychodrama) characterized by the director making sure he or she is ready to lead the group and that members are ready to be led

WDEP system (reality therapy/choice theory) a way of helping counselors and clients make progress. In this system, W stands for wants; D involves clients' exploration of the direction of their lives; E stands for evaluation, which is the cornerstone of reality therapy; P stands for plan, which clients make to change behaviors. The plan stresses actions that clients will take, not behaviors that they will eliminate. The best plans are simple, attainable, measurable, immediate, and consistent.

Wednesday Psychological Society a group formally organized in Sigmund Freud's home in 1902 to discuss personality theory. This group became known in 1908 as the Viennese Psychoanalytic Society.

wellness activities yoga, meditation, and cardiovascular exercise

youngest children according to Adler these children receive a great deal of attention from others, who are likely to cater to their needs and may become charmers. They face the danger of becoming spoiled but at the same time may make great strides in achievement because of role models provided by older siblings.

References

Adler, A. (1927). *Understanding human nature*. Fawcett.

Adler, A. (1931). *What life should mean to you*. Little, Brown.

Adler, A. (1956). *The individual psychology of Alfred Adler: A systematic presentation in selections from his writings* (H. L. Ansbacher & R. R. Ansbacher, Eds.). Norton.

Adler, A. (1964). *Social interest: A challenge to mankind*. Capricorn.

Adler, A. (1969). *The practice and theory of individual psychology*. Littlefield, Adams.

Alberti, R. E., & Emmons, M. L. (2017). *Your perfect right: A guide to assertive behavior* (10th ed.). Impact.

Alexander, J., & Parsons, B. (1982). *Functional family therapy*. Brooks/Cole.

Allan, A. B. (2015). *A person-centered psychodrama support group for LGBTQ adolescents in the United States* (Doctoral dissertation, Saint Mary's College of California).

Allen, V. B. (1986). A historical perspective of the AACD ethics committee. *Journal of Counseling and Development, 64*, 293.

Allodi, F. (2012). History of psychoanalysis in Spain and contrasts with the English speaking world. *Actas Espanolas de Psiquiatria, 40*, 1–9.

Amatruda, M. J. (2006). Conflict resolution and social skill development with children. *Journal of Group Psychotherapy Psychodrama and Soiometry, 58*(4), 168–182.

Anonymous. (1972). Differentiation of self in one's family. In J. L. Framo (Ed.), *Family interaction* (pp. 111–173). Springer.

Ansbacher, H. L. (1977). Individual psychology. In R. J. Corsini (Ed.), *Current personality theories* (pp. 45–82). Peacock.

Ansbacher, H. L., & Ansbacher, R. R. (Eds.). (1964). *Superiority and social interest*. Northwestern University Press.

Ansbacher, H. L., & Ansbacher, R. R. (Eds.). (1978). *Cooperation between the sexes*. Anchor.

Antony, M. M., Roemer, L., & Lenton-Brym, A. P. (2020). Behavior therapy: Traditional approaches. In S. B. Messer & N. J. Kaslow (Eds.), *Essential psychotherapies* (4th ed., pp. 111–141). Guilford.

Arnkoff, D. B., & Glass, C. R. (1992). Cognitive therapy and psychotherapy integration. In D. K. Freedheim (Ed.), *History of psychotherapy: A century of change* (pp. 657–694). American Psychological Association.

Assagioli, R. (1965). *Psychosynthesis*. Viking.

Austin, L. (1999). *The counseling primer*. Accelerated Development.

Auvenshine, D., & Noffsinger, A. L. (1984). *Counseling: An introduction for the health and human services*. University Park Press.

Backx, W. (2011). Views on REBT, past, present, and future: Albert Ellis' contribution to the field. *Journal of Rational Emotive and Cognitive-Behavior Therapy, 29*, 263–271.

Bacon, M. (2019). *Family therapy and the treatment of substance use disorders: The family matters model*. Routledge.

Baldwin, C. (1989). Peaceful alternatives: Inner peace. *Journal of Humanistic Education and Development, 28*, 86–92.

Ballou, M., Hill, M., & West, C. (2008). *Feminist theory therapy and practice: A contemporary perspective*. Springer.

Bandura, A. (1969). *Principles of behavior modification*. Holt, Rinehart & Winston.

Bandura, A. (1986). *Social foundations of thought and action: A social cognitive theory*. Prentice Hall.

Bandura, A., & Walters, R. H. (1963). *Social learning and personality development*. Holt, Rinehart & Winston.

Banks, T. (2011). Helping students manage emotions: *Education Psychology in Practice, 27*, 383–394.

Bankart, C. P. (1997). *Talking cures*. Brooks/Cole.

Barkley, R. A. (1991). *Attention-deficit hyperactivity disorder*. Guilford.

Barkley, R. A. (2013). *Defiant children: A clinician's manual for assessment and parent training* (3rd ed.). Guilford.

Barkley, R. A. (2014). *Attention-deficit hyperactivity disorder: A handbook for diagnosis and treatment* (4th ed.). Guilford.

Barnes, G. (1977). Introduction. In G. Barnes (Ed.), *Transactional analysis after Eric Berne: Teachings and practices of three TA schools* (pp. 3–31). Harper & Row.

Barrow, G. (2007). Wonderful world, beautiful people: Reframing transactional analysis as positive psychology. *Transactional Analysis Journal, 37*, 206–209.

Baruth, L. G., & Huber, C. H. (1984). *An introduction to marital theory and therapy*. Brooks/Cole.

Beauchemin, J. D. (2018). Solution-focused wellness: A randomized controlled trial of college students. *Health & Social Work, 43*(2), 94–100.

Beck, A. T. (1976). *Cognitive therapy and emotional disorders*. International Universities Press.

Beck, A. T. (1991). Cognitive therapy: A 30-year retrospective. *American Psychologist, 46*, 368–375.

Beck, A. T., & Alford, B. A. (2009). *Depression: Causes and treatments* (2nd ed.). University of Pennsylvania Press.

Beck, A. T., Rush, A. J., Shaw, B. F., & Emery, G. (1987). *Cognitive therapy of depression*. Guilford.

Beck, A. T., & Weishaar, M. E. (2019). Cognitive therapy. In D. Wedding & R. J. Corsini (Eds.), *Current psychotherapies* (11th ed., pp. 237–272). Cengage.

Beck, J. (2021). *Cognitive behavior therapy: Basics and beyond*. Guilford Press.

Beck, J. S., & Beck, A. (2020). *Cognitive behavior therapy: Basics and beyond* (3rd ed.). Guilford.

Belkin, G. S. (1984). *Introduction to counseling*. WCB/McGraw-Hill.

Bellack, A. S., & Hersen, M. (1998). *Behavioral assessment: A practical handbook*. Allyn & Bacon.

Benjamin, P., & Looby, J. (1998). Defining the nature of spirituality in the context of Maslow's and Rogers's theories. *Counseling and Values, 42*, 92–100.

Berg, I. K., & Miller, S. (1992). *Working with the problem drinker: A solution-focused approach*. Norton.

Berg, I. K., & Steiner, T. (2003). *Children's solution work*. Norton.

Bergin, A. E. (1985). Proposed values for guiding and evaluating counseling and psychotherapy. *Counseling and Values, 29*, 99–115.

Bergin, A. E. (1992). Three contributions of a spiritual perspective to counseling, psychotherapy, and behavior change. In M. T. Burke & J. G. Miranti (Eds.), *Ethical and spiritual values in counseling* (pp. 5–15). American Counseling Association.

Bernard, J. M. (1986). Laura Perls: From ground to figure. *Journal of Counseling and Development, 64*, 367–373.

Berne, E. (1947). *The mind in action*. Simon & Schuster.

Berne, E. (1964). *Games people play*. Grove.

Berne, E. (1966). *Principles of group treatment*. Oxford University Press.

Bhar, S. S., & Beck, A. T. (2009). Treatment integrity of studies that compare short-term psychodynamic psychotherapy with cognitive-behavior therapy. *Clinical Psychology: Science and Practice, 16*, 370–378.

Blackham, G. J., & Silberman, A. (1979). *Modification of child and adolescent behavior*. Wadsworth.

Blajan-Marcus, S. (1974). Psychodrama and its diverse uses. In I. A. Greenberg (Ed.) *Psychodrama: Theory and therapy* (pp. 47–55). Behavioral Publications.

Blanc, A., & Boutinaud, J. (2017). Psychoanalytic psychodrama in France and group elaboration of counter-transference: Therapeutic operators in play therapy. *International Journal of Psychoanalysis, 98*(3), 683–707.

Blatner, A. (1996). *Acting-in: Practical applications of psychodramatic methods*. Springer.

Blatner, A. (2000). *Foundations of psychodrama*. Springer.

Blatner, A. (2005). Perspectives on Moreno, psychodrama, and creativity. *Journal of Creativity in Mental Health, 1*(2), 111–121.

Blatner, A. (2005a). Psychodrama. In R. J. Corsini & D. Wedding (Eds.), *Current psychotherapies* (7th ed., pp. 405–438). Thompson.

Bordone, R. C. (2000). Teaching interpersonal skills for negotiation and for life. *Negotiation Journal, 16*(4), 377–385.

Bowen, M. (1960). A family concept of schizophrenia. In D. Jackson (Ed.), *The etiology of schizophrenia* (pp. 346–372). Basic Books.

Bowen, M. (1961). Family psychotherapy. *American Journal of Orthopsychiatry, 31*, 40–60.

Bowen, M. (1965). Family psychotherapy with schizophrenia in the hospital and in private practice. In I. Boszormenyi-Nagy & J. T. Framo (Eds.), *Intensive family therapy* (pp. 213–243). Harper & Row.

Bowen, M. (1972). Toward the differentiation of self in one's family of origin. In F. D. Andres & J. P. Lorio (Eds.), *Georgetown family symposia* (pp. 70–86). Georgetown University Press.

Bowen, M. (1975). Family therapy after twenty years. In S. Arieti, D. X. Freedman, & J. E. Dyrud (Eds.), *American handbook of psychiatry, V. Treatment* (2nd ed.) (pp. 367–392). Basic Books.

Bowen, M. (1976). Theory in the practice of psychotherapy. In P. J. Guerin (Ed.), *Family therapy: Theory and practice* (pp. 42–90). Gardner Press.

Bowen, M. (1978). *Family therapy in clinical practice*. New York: Jason Aronson.

Boy, A. V., & Pine, G. J. (1982). *Client-centered counseling: A renewal*. Allyn & Bacon.

Boy, A. V., & Pine, G. J. (1983). Counseling: Fundamentals of theoretical renewal. *Counseling and Values, 27*, 248–255.

Braaten, L. J. (1986). Thirty years with Rogers's necessary and sufficient conditions of therapeutic personality change. *Person-Centered Review, 1*, 37–49.

Bradford, K. (2017). Drawing from a deeper well: Contemplative Asian sources of radical existential thought. *Existential Analysis, 28*(1), 118–134.

Bradley, R. W., & Cox, J. A. (2001). Counseling: Evolution of the profession. In D. C. Locke, J. E. Myers, & E. L. Herr (Eds.), *The handbook of counseling* (pp. 27–41). Sage.

Brammer, L.M. (1985). *The helping relationship: Process and skills* (3rd ed.). Prentice Hall.

Brammer, L. M., Abrego, P. J., & Shostrom, E. L. (1993). *Therapeutic counseling and psychotherapy* (6th ed.). Merrill/Prentice Hall.

Bretherton, R., & Orner, R. (2003). Positive psychotherapy in disguise. *Psychologist, 16*, 136–137.

Brown, D. (1997). Implications of cultural values for cross-cultural consultation with families. *Journal of Counseling and Development, 76*, 29–35.

Brown, L. S. (2008). Feminist therapy. In J. S. Lebow (Ed.), *Twenty-first century psychotherapies: Contemporary approaches to theory and practice* (pp. 277–306). Wiley.

Brown, L. S. (2010). *Feminist therapy—Not for women only*. American Psychological Association.

Brown, L. S. (2018). *Theories of psychotherapy series. Feminist therapy* (2nd ed.). American Psychological Association.

Brown-Shaw, M., Westwood, M., & De Vries, B. (1999). Integrating personal reflection and group-based enactments. *Journal of Aging Studies*, *13*(1), 109–119.

Bryant-Davis, T. (Ed.). (2019). *Multicultural feminist therapy: Helping adolescent girls of color to thrive*. American Psychological Association.

Bubenzer, D. L., & West, J. D. (1993). William Hudson O'Hanlon: On seeking possibilities and solutions in therapy. *The Family Journal*, *1*, 365–379.

Buber, M. (1970). *I and Thou*. Charles Scribner's Sons.

Buhler, C., & Allen, M. (1972). *Introduction to humanistic psychology*. Brooks/Cole.

Burger, W. R. (2018). *Human services in contemporary America* (10th ed.). Cengage.

Burns, D. D. (1980). *Feeling good: The new mood therapy*. Signet.

Burns, D. D. (1989). *The feeling good handbook: Using the new mood therapy in everyday life*. Morrow.

Bussey, K., & Bandura, A. (1999). Social cognitive career theory of gender development and differentiation. *Psychological Review*, *106*, 676–713.

Butcher, J., Mineka, S., & Hooley, J. (2013). *Abnormal psychology* (15th ed.). Pearson.

Calley, N. G. (2009). Promoting a contextual perspective in the application of the ACA Code of Ethics: The ethics into action map. *Journal of Counseling & Development*, *87*, 476–482.

Campos, L. K. (2018). Meeting the challenges of a vengeful world with a socially responsible transactional analysis. *Transactional Analysis Journal*, *48*(2), 126–138.

Caplan, G. (1964). *Principles of preventive psychiatry*. Basic Books.

Capuzzi, D., & Black, D. K. (1986). The history of dream analysis and the helping relationship: A synopsis for practitioners. *Journal of Humanistic Education and Development*, *24*, 82–97.

Carkhuff, R. R. (1969a). *Helping and human relations* (Vol. 1). Holt, Rinehart, & Winston.

Carkhuff, R. R. (1969b). *Helping and human relations* (Vol. 2). Holt, Rinehart, & Winston.

Carkhuff, R. R. (1987). *The art of helping* (6th ed.). Human Resource Development Press.

Carlson, J., & Engler-Carlson, M. (2011). Series preface. In R. Wubbolding (Ed.), *Reality therapy* (pp. i–iv). American Psychological Association.

Carlson, J., & Englar-Carlson, M. (2017). *Theories of psychotherapy series. Adlerian psychotherapy*. American Psychological Association.

Carlson, J., Watts, R. E., & Maniacci, M. (2006). *Adlerian therapy: Theory and practice*. American Psychological Association.

Carnabucci, K. (2014). *Show and tell psychodrama: Skills for therapists, coaches, teachers, leaders*. Nusanto.

Cautela, J. R. (1976). The present status of covert modeling. *Journal of Behavior Therapy and Experimental Psychiatry*, *6*, 323–326.

Cavanagh, M. E., & Levitov, J. E. (2002). *The counseling experience* (2nd ed.). Waveland.

Ceja A., & Gasbarrini, M. F. (2018). Multigenerational transmission process in Bowen therapy. In J. Lebow, A. Chambers, & D. Breunlin (Eds.), *Encyclopedia of couple and family therapy*. Springer.

Chandler, C. K., Holden, J. M., & Kolander, C. A. (1992). Counseling for spiritual wellness: Theory and practice. *Journal of Counseling & Development*, *71*, 168–176.

Chaudhry, S., & Li, C. (2011). Is solution-focused brief therapy culturally appropriate for Muslim American counselees? *Journal of Contemporary Psychotherapy*, *41*, 109–113.

Chavez, A., Moore, N., & McDowell, T. (2018). Mexican American immigrant parents striving to raise resilient children: Obstacles, tension points, and resiliency factors. *Journal of Individual Psychology* *74*(1), 4–19.

Cheston, S. E. (2000). A new paradigm for teaching counseling theory and practice. *Counselor Education and Supervision*, *39*, 254–269.

Cheung, S. (2001). Problem-solving and solution-focused therapy for Chinese: Recent developments. *Asian Journal of Counselling*, *8*, 111–128.

Choudhury, T. K., John, K. C., Garrett, R. K., & Stagner, B. H. (2020). Considering psycho-dynamic therapy for older adults. *Psychodynamic Psychiatry*, 48(2), 152–162.

Christopher, J. C. (1996). Counseling's inescapable moral vision. *Journal of Counseling & Development*, 75, 17–25.

Clark, D. A., & Beck, A. T. (2010). *Cognitive therapy of anxiety disorders: Science and practice*. Guilford.

Clark, D. A., & Beck, A. T. (2012). *The anxiety and worry workbook: The cognitive behavioral solution*. Guilford.

Cleveland, P. H., & Lindsey, E. W. (1995). Solution-focused family interventions. In A. C. Kilpatrick & T. P. Holland (Eds.), *Working with families* (pp. 145–160). Allyn & Bacon.

Cohen, E. D. (1987). The use of syllogism in rational-emotive therapy. *Journal of Counseling and Development*, 66, 37–39.

Cohen, E. D., & Cohen, G. S. (2019). *Counseling ethics for the 21st century*. Sage.

Coll, K. (1993). Student attitudinal changes in counseling ethics courses. *Counseling and Values, 27,* 165–170.

Cooper, M., & Mcleod, J. (2011). Person-centered therapy: A pluralistic perspective. *Person-Centered and Experiential Psychotherapies*, 10, 210–223.

Corcoran, J. (2000). Solution-focused family therapy with ethnic minority clients. *Crisis Intervention and Time Limited Treatment*, 6, 5–12.

Corey, G. (2017). *Theory and practice of counseling and psychotherapy* (10th ed.). Cengage.

Corey, G., Corey, M. S., & Corey, C. (2018). *Issues and ethics in the helping professions* (10th ed.). Cengage.

Cormier, S., Nurius, P. S., & Osborn, C. J. (2017). *Interviewing and change strategies for helpers* (8th ed.). Cengage.

Cornell, W. F., de Graaf, A., Newton, T., & Thunnissen, M. (Eds.) (2018). *Into TA: A comprehensive textbook on transactional analysis*. Routledge.

Correia, E. A., Cooper, M., Berdondini, L., & Correia, K. (2017). Characteristic practices of existential psychotherapy: A worldwide survey of practitioners' perspectives. *Humanistic Psychologist*, 45(3), 217–237.

Corsini, R. J. (1966). *Roleplaying in Psychotherapy: A Manual*. Beacon House.

Corsini, R. J. (1988). Adlerian groups. In S. Long (Ed.), *Six group therapies* (pp. 1–43). Plenum.

Corsini, R. J. (2000). Introduction. In R. J. Corsini & D. Wedding (Eds.), *Current psychotherapies* (6th ed., pp. 1–15). Peacock.

Corsini, R. J. (2001). *Handbook of innovative therapy* (2nd ed.). Wiley.

Cottone, R. R., & Tarvydas, V. M. (2016). *Ethics and decision making in counseling and psychotherapy* (4th ed.). Springer.

Coven, A. B., Ellington, D. B., & Van Hull, K. G. (1997). The use of Gestalt psychodrama in group counseling. In. S. T. Gladding (Ed.), *New developments in group counseling* (pp. 17–18). ERIC/CASS.

Covin, A. B. (1977). Using Gestalt psychodrama experiments in rehabilitation counseling. *Personnel and Guidance Journal*, 56, 143–147.

Craighead, L. W., Craighead, W. E., Kazdin, A. E., & Mahoney, M. J. (1994). *Cognitive and behavioral interventions: An empirical approach to mental health problems*. Allyn & Bacon.

Crawford, M. (2018). *Transformations: Women, gender, and psychology* (3rd ed.). McGraw-Hill.

Creed, T. A., Reisweber, J., & Beck, A. T. (2011). *Cognitive therapy for adolescents in school settings*. Guilford.

Cunningham, L. M., & Peters, H. J. (1973). *Counseling theories*. Prentice Hall.

Daniluk, J. C., & Haverkamp, B. E. (1993). Ethical issues in counseling adult survivors of incest. *Journal of Counseling and Development*, 72, 16–22.

Das, A. K. (1998). Frankl and the realm of meaning. *Journal of Humanistic Education and Development*, 36, 199–211.

Datler, W., & Gstach, J. (2001, June 26). *Alfred Adler and his time*. Presentation to the Wake Forest Vienna Theorists class. University of Vienna, Vienna, Austria.

Dattilio, F. M. (2010). *Cognitive-behavioral therapy with couples and families*. Guilford.

David, J. R. (1979). The theology of Murray Bowen or the marital triangle. *Journal of Psychology and Theology, 7*, 259–262.

Deen, S., Turner, M., & Wong, R. (2017). The effects of REBT, and the use of credos, on irrational beliefs and resilience qualities in athletes. *Sport Psychologist, 31*(3), 249–263.

DeRubeis, R. J., Keefe, J. R., & Beck, A. T. (2019). Cognitive therapy. In K. S. Dobson & D. J. A. Dozois (Eds.), *Handbook of cognitive-behavioral therapies* (4th ed., pp. 218–248). Guilford.

deShazer, S. (1982). *Patterns of brief family therapy*. Guilford.

deShazer, S. (1984). The death of resistance. *Family Process, 23*, 11–21.

deShazer, S. (1985). *Keys to solution in brief therapy*. Norton.

deShazer, S. (1988). *Clues: Investigating solutions in brief therapy*. Norton.

deShazer, S. (1989). Resistance revisited. *Contemporary Family Therapy, 11*, 227–233.

deShazer, S. (1991). *Putting differences to work*. Norton.

deShazer, S., & Berg, I. K. (1992). Doing therapy: A post-structural revision. *Journal of Marital and Family Therapy, 18*(1), 71–81.

deShazer, S., & Molnar, A. (1984). Four useful interventions in brief family therapy. *Journal of Marital and Family Therapy 10*, 297–304.

Dinkmeyer, D. (1982a). *Developing understanding of self and others* (DUSOD-1). American Guidance Service.

Dinkmeyer, D. (1982b). *Developing understanding of self and others* (DUSOD-2). American Guidance Service.

Dinkmeyer, D., & Losoncy, L. E. (1996). *The skills of encouragement*. Saint Lucie Press.

Dinkmeyer, D., McKay, G. D., & Dinkmeyer, D., Jr. (1980). *Systematic training for effective teaching* (STET). American Guidance Service.

Dinkmeyer, D., McKay, G. D., & Dinkmeyer, D., Jr. (1997). *The parents handbook: Systematic training for effective parenting* (STEP). American Guidance Service.

Dinkmeyer, D., McKay, G. D., McKay, J. L., & Dinkmeyer, D., Jr. (1998). *Parenting teenagers: Systematic training for effective parenting/Teen* (STEP/Teen). American Guidance Service.

Dinkmeyer, D., & Sperry, L. (2000). *Adlerian counseling and psychotherapy* (3rd ed.). Prentice Hall.

Dobson, K. S., & Dozois, D. J. A. (Ed.). (2019). *Handbook of cognitive-behavioral therapies* (4th ed.). Guilford.

Dodson, K. S., Beck, J. S., & Beck, A. T. (2005). The academy of cognitive therapy: Purpose, history, and future prospects. *Cognitive and Behavioral Practice, 12*, 263–266.

Dollarhide, C. T. (1997). Counseling for meaning in work and life: An integrated approach. *Journal of Humanistic Education and Development, 35*, 178–187.

Dreikurs, R. R. (1950). *Fundamentals of Adlerian psychology*. Alfred Adler Institute.

Dreikurs, R. R. (1967). *Psychodynamics, psychotherapy, and counseling*. Alfred Adler Institute.

Dreikurs, R. R., & Mosak, H. H. (1966). The tasks of life. I: Adler's three tests. *Individual Psychologist, 4*, 18–22.

Dreikurs, R. R., & Soltz, V. (1964). *Children: The challenge*. Hawthorne.

Dryden, W. (1989). Albert Ellis: An efficient and passionate life. *Journal of Counseling and Development, 67*, 539–546.

Dryden, W. (1994). Reason and emotion in psychotherapy: Thirty years on. *Journal of Rational Emotive and Cognitive Behavior Therapy, 12*, 83–89.

Dryden, W. (2010). Elegance in REBT: Reflections on Ellis' and Dryden's sessions with Jane. *Journal of Rational-Emotive & Cognitive Behavior Therapy, 28*, 157–163.

Dryden, W., & Bernard, M. E. (Eds.). (2019). *REBT with diverse client problems and populations*. Springer.

Duffey, T., & Haberstroh, S. (Eds.). (2020). *Introduction to crisis and trauma counseling.* Wiley.

Dunn, A. B., & Levitt, M. M. (2000). The genogram: From diagnostics to mutual collaboration. *The Family Journal: Counseling and Therapy for Couples and Families, 8,* 236–244.

Du Plock, S. (2019). An innocent abroad? An example of brief student counselling. *Existential Analysis, 30*(2), 316–327.

Dusay, J. M. (1977). The evolution of transactional analysis. In G. Barnes (Ed.), *Transactional analysis after Eric Berne: Teachings and practices of three TA schools* (pp. 32–52). Harper & Row.

Dusay, J. M., & Dusay, K. M. (1989). Transactional analysis. In R. J. Corsini & D. Wedding (Eds.), *Current psychotherapies* (4th ed., pp. 405–453). Peacock.

Eckstein, D., & Kaufman, J. A. (2012). The role of birth order in personality: An enduring intellectual legacy of Alfred Adler. *Journal of Individual Psychology, 68,* 60–61.

Eisenberg, M. (1992). Compassionate math. *Journal of Humanistic Education and Development, 30,* 157–166.

Ellis, A. (1962). *Reason and emotion in psychotherapy.* Stuart.

Ellis, A. (1977). The basic clinical theory of rational-emotive therapy. In A. Ellis and R. Grieger (Eds.), *Handbook of rational-emotive therapy* (pp. 3–34). Springer.

Ellis, A. (1980). Foreword. In S. R. Walen, R. DiGiuseppe, & R. L. Wessler, *A practitioner's guide to rational-emotive therapy* (pp. vii–xii). Oxford University Press.

Ellis, A. (1984). Rational-emotive therapy (RET) and pastoral counseling: A reply to Richard Wessler. *Personnel and Guidance Journal, 62,* 266–267.

Ellis, A. (1986). An emotional control card for inappropriate and appropriate emotions in using rational-emotive imagery. *Journal of Counseling and Development, 65,* 205–206.

Ellis, A. (1988). *How to stubbornly refuse to make yourself miserable about anything: Yes, anything!* Stuart.

Ellis, A. (1993). Changing rational emotive therapy (RET) to rational emotive behavior therapy (REBT). *Behavior Therapist, 16,* 257–258.

Ellis, A. (1995). Changing rational-emotive therapy (RET) to rational emotive behavioral therapy (REBT). *Journal of Rational Emotive and Cognitive Behavioral Therapy, 13,* 85–89.

Ellis, A. (1996a). *Better, deeper, and more enduring brief therapy: The rational emotive behavior therapy approach.* Brunner/Mazel.

Ellis, A. (1996b). The humanism of rational emotive behavior therapy and other cognitive behavior therapies. *Journal of Humanistic Education and Development, 35,* 69–88.

Ellis, A. (2002). *Overcoming resistance: A rational emotive behavior therapy integrated approach* (2nd ed.). Springer.

Ellis, A. (2019). The evolution of Albert Ellis and rational emotive behavior therapy. In A. Ellis (Ed.), *The evolution of psychotherapy* (pp. 69–82). Routledge.

Ellis, A., & Ellis, D. J. (2011). *Rational emotive behavior therapy.* American Psychological Association.

Ellis, A., & Ellis, D. J. (2019). Rational-emotive behavior therapy. In D. Wedding & R. Corsini (Eds.), *Current psychotherapies* (11th ed., pp. 157–197). Cengage.

Ellis, A., & Harper, R. A. (1975). *A new guide to rational living.* Wilshire.

Elms, A. C. (1981). Skinner's dark year and Walden Two. *American Psychologist, 36,* 470–479.

English, H. B., & English, A. C. (1956). *A comprehensive dictionary of psychological and psychoanalytical terms.* Longman Green.

Enns, C. Z. (1993). Twenty years of feminist counseling and therapy. *Counseling Psychologist, 21,* 3–87.

Enns, C. Z. (2004). *Feminist theories and feminist psychotherapies: Origins, themes, and variations* (2nd ed.). Haworth.

Enns, C. Z., & Hackett, G. (1993). A comparison of feminist and nonfeminist women's and men's reactions to nonsexist and feminist counseling: A replication and extension. *Journal of Counseling and Development, 71,* 499–509.

Epp, L. R. (1998). The courage to be an existential counselor: An interview with Clemmont E. Vontress. *Journal of Mental Health Counseling, 20*, 1–12.

Erchul, W. P. (2009). Gerald Kaplan. *American Psychologist, 64*, 563.

Erdem, G., & Safi, O. A. (2018). The cultural lens approach to Bowen family systems theory: Contributions of family change theory. *Journal of Family Theory Review, 10*, 469–483.

Erdman, P. (2000). Bringing a symbol: An experiential exercise for systematic change. In R. E. Watts (Ed.), *Techniques in marriage and family counseling* (pp. 99–102). American Counseling Association.

Erford, B. T. (2020). *45 techniques every counselor should know* (3rd ed.). Pearson.

Erford, B. T., Hays, D. G., & Crockett, S. (2020). *Mastering the National Counselor Examination and the Counselor Preparation Comprehensive Examination* (3rd ed.). Pearson.

Ergüner-Tekinalp, B., Johnson-Migalski, L., & Belangee, S. E. (2018). Diversity and social justice: Applying theory and adapting practices. *Journal of Individual Psychology 74*(1), 1–3.

Erikson, E. H. (1963). *Childhood and society* (2nd ed.). Norton.

Erikson, E. H., & Erikson, J. M. (1997). *The life cycle completed* (Extended version). Norton.

Erskine, R. G. (2009). The culture of transactional analysis: Theory, methods, and evolving patterns. *Transactional Analysis Journal, 39*, 14–21.

Eunice Kennedy Shriver National Institute of Child Health and Human Development, NIH, DHHS. (2012). *An Activity Book for African American Families: Helping Children Cope with Crisis* (03-5362B). US Government Printing Office.

Evans, D. (1982). What are you doing? An interview with William Glasser. *Personnel and Guidance Journal, 60*, 460–464.

Everly, G. S., Lating, J. M., & Mitchell, J. T. (2000). Innovations in group crisis intervention: Critical incident stress debriefing (CISD) and critical incident stress management (CISM). *Crisis intervention handbook: Assessment, treatment, and research*, 77–97.

Exner, J. E., Jr., & Erdberg, P. (2005). *The Rorschach: A comprehensive system* (4th ed.). Wiley.

Eysenck, H. J. (1960). *Behavior therapy and the neuroses*. Pergamon.

Fagan, J. (1970). The task of the therapist. In J. Fagan & I. L. Shepherd (Eds.), *Gestalt therapy now* (pp. 88–106). Science and Behavior Books.

Fagan, J., & Shepherd, I. L. (1970). Theory of Gestalt therapy. In J. Fagan & I. L. Shepherd (Eds.), *Gestalt therapy now* (pp. 1–7). Science and Behavior Books.

Faiver, C., Eisengart, S., & Colonna, R. (2004). *The counselor intern's handbook* (3rd ed.). Brooks/Cole.

Farmer, C. (2018). *Psychodrama and systemic therapy*. Routledge.

Fish, J. M. (1988, July/August). Reconciling the irreconcilable. *Family Therapy Networker, 12*, 15.

Fleming, J. S., & Rickord, B. (1997). Solution-focused brief therapy: One answer to managed mental health care. *Family Journal, 5*, 286–294.

Fox, J. (2008). *The Essential Moreno: Writings on Psychodrama, Group Method, and Spontaneity, by J. L. Moreno*. Tusitala.

Fowler, R. D. (1990, October). B. F. Skinner: Farewell, with admiration and affection. *APA Monitor, 21*(10), 2.

Frame, M. W. (2000). Constructing religious/spiritual genograms. In R. E. Watts (Ed.), *Techniques in marriage and family counseling* (pp. 69–74). American Counseling Association.

Frank, J. D., & Frank, J. B. (1991). *Persuasion and healing: A comparative study of psychotherapy*. Johns Hopkins Press.

Frankl, V. (1959). The spiritual dimension in existential analysis and logotherapy. *Journal of Individual Psychology, 15*, 157–165.

Frankl, V. (1967). *Psychotherapy and existentialism: Selected papers on logotherapy*. Washington Square Press.

Frankl, V. (1969a). *Psychotherapy and existentialism: Selected papers on logotherapy.* Simon & Schuster.

Frankl, V. (1969b). *The will to meaning: Foundations and applications of logotherapy.* New American Library.

Frankl, V. (1985, 2006). *Man's search for meaning.* Simon & Schuster/Beacon Press.

Franklin, C., Bolton, K. W., & Guz, S. (2019). Solution-focused brief family therapy. In B. H. Fiese, M. Celano, K. Deater-Deckard, E. N. Jouriles, & M. A. Whisman (Eds.), *APA handbooks in psychology. APA handbook of contemporary family psychology: Family therapy and training* (pp. 139–153). American Psychological Association.

Franklin, C., Zhang, A., Froerer, A., & Johnson, S. (2017). Solution focused brief therapy: A systematic review and meta-summary of process research. *Journal of Marital and Family Therapy, 43*(1), 16–30.

Freud, A. (1936). *The ego and the mechanisms of defense* (J. Strachey, Trans.). International Universities Press.

Freud, S. (1900/1955). *The interpretation of dreams* (J. Strachey, Trans.). Hogarth.

Freud, S. (1923/1933). *New introductory lectures on psychoanalysis* (W. J. H. Sprott, Trans.). Norton.

Freud, S. (1923/1947). *The ego and the id* (J. Strachey, Trans.). Hogarth.

Freud, S. (1925/1959). An autobiographical study. In J. Strachey (Ed. & Trans.), *The standard edition of the complete psychological works of Sigmund Freud* (Vol. 20, pp. 7–74). Hogarth.

Frew, J. (2016). Gestalt therapy: Creatively adjusting in an increasingly diverse world. *Gestalt Review, 20*(2), 106–128.

Friedman, E. H. (1991). Bowen theory and therapy. In A. S. Gurman & D. P. Kniskern (Eds.), *Handbook of family therapy* (Vol. II, pp. 134–170). Brunner/Mazel.

Friedman, E. H. (2011). *Generation to generation: Family process in church and synagogue.* Guilford.

Friesen, J. D. (1985). *Structural-strategic marriage and family therapy.* Gardner.

Fulmer, R. (2018). The evolution of the psychodynamic approach and system. *International Journal of Psychological Studies, 10*(1).

Fursland, A., Byrne, S., Watson, H., La Puma, M., Allen, K., & Byrne, S. (2012). Enhanced cognitive behavior therapy: A single treatment for all eating disorders. *Journal of Counseling and Development, 90,* 319–329.

Gale, J. E. (1991). *Conversion analysis of therapeutic discourse: The pursuit of a therapeutic agenda.* Ablex.

Gardner, B. C., Burr, B. K., & Wiedower, S. E. (2006). Reconceptualizing strategic family therapy: Insights from a dynamic systems perspective. *Contemporary Family Therapy: An International Journal, 28,* 339–352.

Gazda, G. M. (1973). *Human relations development: A manual for education.* Allyn & Bacon.

Gelso, C. J., & Carter, J. A. (1985). The relationship in counseling and psychotherapy: Components, consequences, and theoretical antecedents. *Counseling Psychologist, 13,* 155–243.

Gendron, J. M. (1980). *Moreno—the roots and the branches: A bibliography of psychodrama, 1972–1980, and sociometry, 1970–1980.* Beacon House.

Gibson, J. M., & Donigian, J. (1993). Use of Bowen theory. *Journal of Addictions and Offender Counseling, 14,* 25–35.

Gilbert, R. M. (2004). *The eight concepts of Bowen theory.* Leading Systems Press.

Gilligan, C. (1982). *In a different voice: Psychological theory and women's development.* Harvard University Press.

Gillihan, S. J. (2018). *Cognitive-behavioral therapy made simple.* Althea Press.

Gladding, S. T. (1990). Let us not grow weary of theory. *Journal for Specialists in Group Work, 15,* 194.

Gladding, S. T. (2007). *A guide to ethical conduct for the helping professions* (2nd ed.). Pearson.

Gladding, S. T., & Alderson, K. (2019). *Choosing the right counselor for you.* American Counseling Association.

Gladding, S. T., & Hood, W. D. (1974). Five cents, please. *School Counselor, 21,* 40–43.

Glasser, W. (1961). *Mental health or mental illness?* Harper & Row.

Glasser, W. (1965). *Reality therapy: A new approach to psychiatry.* Harper & Row.

Glasser, W. (1969). *Schools without failure.* Harper & Row.

Glasser, W. (1972). *The identity society.* Harper & Row.

Glasser, W. (1976). *Positive addiction.* Harper & Row.

Glasser, W. (1980). Reality therapy: An explanation of the steps of reality therapy. In W. Glasser (Ed.), *What are you doing? How people are helped through reality therapy* (pp. 44–60). Harper & Row.

Glasser, W. (1981). *Stations of the mind.* Harper & Row.

Glasser, W. (1984). *Control theory: A new explanation of how we control our lives.* Harper & Row.

Glasser, W. (1986). *Control theory in the classroom.* Harper & Row.

Glasser, W. (1988). Reality therapy. Workshop presented at the Alabama Association for Counseling and Development, Fall Conference, November, Birmingham.

Glasser, W. (1998). *Choice theory.* HarperCollins.

Glasser, W. (2000). *Counseling with choice theory.* HarperCollins.

Glasser, W. (2005). *Defining mental health as a public health problem.* Chatsworth, CA.

Glasser, W., & Wubbolding, R. (1995). Reality therapy. In R. Corsini & D. Wedding (Eds.), *Current psychotherapies* (5th ed., pp. 293–321). Peacock.

Glassgold, J., & Iasenza, S. (2004). *Lesbians, feminism, and psychoanalysis: The second wave.* Routledge.

Glauser, A. S., & Bozarth, J. D. (2001). Person-centered counseling: The culture within. *Journal of Counseling and Development, 79,* 142–147.

Glinnwater, J. T. (2000). Gestalt therapy: Treatment of the affective self. *Gestalt Journal, 23,* 81–97.

Gold, L. (1979). Adler's theory of dreams: An holistic approach to interpretation. In B. B. Wolman (Ed.), *Handbook of dreams: Research, theories, and applications* (pp. 319–341). Van Nostrand Reinhold.

Goldiamond, I. (1976). Self-reinforcement. *Journal of Applied Behavior Analysis, 9,* 509–514.

Goldstein, A. (1973). Behavior therapy. In R. Corsini (Ed.), *Current psychotherapies* (pp. 207–249). Peacock.

Goodrich, K., & Luke, M. (2015). *Group counseling with LGBTQI persons across the life span.* Wiley.

Goodyear, R. K. (1987). In memory of Carl Ransom Rogers. *Journal of Counseling and Development, 65,* 523–524.

Goulding, M., & Goulding, R. (1997). *Changing lives through redecision therapy* (Rev. ed.). Grove/Atlantic.

Grant, B. (1992). The moral nature of psychotherapy. In M. T. Burke & J. G. Miranti (Eds.), *Ethical and spiritual values in counseling* (pp. 27–35). American Counseling Association.

Grantham, P., & Budnik, J. (2016). *Practical applications of solution focused therapy: Worksheets to use with clients.* CreateSpace Independent Publishing Platform.

Greenberg, I. A. (1974). Moreno: Psychodrama and group process. In I. A. Greenberg (Ed.). *Psychodrama: Theory and therapy* (pp. 11–28). Behavioral Publications.

Greene, G. J., Hamilton, N., & Rolling, M. (1986). Differentiation of self and psychiatric diagnosis: An empirical study. *Family Therapy, 8,* 187–194.

Grummon, D. L. (1972). Client-centered therapy. In B. Stefflre & W. H. Grant (Eds.), *Theories of counseling* (2nd ed.) (pp. 73–135). McGraw-Hill.

Guerin, P. J. (1976). Family therapy: The first twenty-five years. In P. J. Guerin (Ed.), *Family therapy: Theory and practice* (pp. 2–22). Gardner.

Hackney, H., & Bernard, J. M. (2017). *Professional counseling: A process guide to helping* (8th ed.). Pearson.

Haddock, L. R., & Diambra, J. F. (2018). Person-centered and existential approaches to counseling and psychotherapy. In B. Erford (Ed.), *Group work: Processes & applications* (2nd ed., 371–389). Routledge.

Hagedorn, W. B., & Hirshhorn, M. A. (2009). When talking won't work: Implementing experiential group activities with addicted clients. *Journal for Specialists in Group Work, 34*(1), 43–67.

Haley, J. (1963). *Strategies of psychotherapy.* Grune & Statton.

Haley, J. (1973). *Uncommon therapy.* Norton.

Haley, J. (1976). *Problem-solving therapy.* Jossey-Bass.

Haley, J. (1980). *Leaving home: The therapy of disturbed young people.* McGraw-Hill.

Haley, J. (1984). *Ordeal therapy.* Jossey-Bass.

Haley, J. (1990a). Interminable therapy. In J. Zeig & S. Gilligan (Eds.), *Brief therapy: Myths, methods, and metaphors.* Brunner/Mazel.

Haley, J. (1990b). *Strategies of psychotherapy* (2nd ed.). Triangle Press.

Haley, J. (1997). *Leaving home: The therapy of disturbed young people* (2nd ed.). McGraw-Hill.

Hall, C. S. (1954). *A primer of Freudian psychology.* New American Library.

Hall, C. S., Lindzey, L., & Campbell, J. B. (1998). *Theories of personality* (4th ed.). Wiley.

Hall, W. J., Ruiz Rosado, B., & Chapman, M. V. (2019). Findings from a feasibility study of an adapted cognitive behavioral therapy group intervention to reduce depression among LGBTQ (lesbian, gay, bisexual, transgender, or queer) young people. *Journal of Clinical Medicine, 8*(7), 949.

Hansen, J. C., Stevic, R. R., & Warner, R. W. (1986). *Counseling: Theory and process* (4th ed.). Allyn & Bacon.

Hansen, J. T. (2010). Counseling and psychoanalysis: Advancing the value of diversity. *Journal of Multicultural Counseling and Development, 28*, 16–26.

Harding, A. K., Gray, L. A., & Neal, M. (1993). Confidentiality limits with clients who have HIV: A review of ethical and legal guidelines and professional policies. *Journal of Counseling and Development, 71*, 297–304.

Harman, R. L. (1975). A Gestalt point of view on facilitating growth in counseling. *Personnel and Guidance Journal, 53*, 363–366.

Harman, R. L. (1977). Beyond techniques. *Counselor Education and Supervision, 17*, 157–158.

Harman, R. L. (1997). *Gestalt therapy techniques: Working with groups, couples, and sexually dysfunctional men.* Aronson.

Harper, R. A. (1959). *Psychoanalysis and psychotherapy: 36 systems.* Prentice Hall.

Harris, T. (1967). *I'm OK, You're OK.* Harper & Row.

Hart, J. (1970). The development of client-centered therapy. In J. T. Hart & T. M. Tomlinson (Eds.), *New directions in client centered therapy* (pp. 3–22). Houghton Mifflin.

Haskins, N. H., & Appling, B. (2017). Relational-cultural theory and reality therapy: A culturally responsive integrative framework. *Journal of Counseling & Development, 95*(1), 87–99.

Hatcher, C., & Himelsteint, P. (Eds.). (1997). *The handbook of Gestalt therapy.* Aronson.

Henderson, D. A., & Thompson, C. (2016). *Counseling children* (9th ed.). Cengage.

Heppner, P. P., Rogers, M. E., & Lee, L. A. (1990). Carl Rogers: Reflections on his life. In P. P. Heppner (Ed.), *Pioneers in counseling and development* (pp. 54–59). American Counseling Association.

Herlihy, B. (1996). When a colleague is impaired: The individual counselor's response. *Journal of Humanistic Education and Development, 34*, 118–127.

Herlihy, B., & Corey, G. (2015). *ACA ethical standards casebook* (7th ed.). American Counseling Association.

Herlihy, B., & Painter, E. (2018). Multicultural ethical issues counseling. In C. C. Lee (Ed.), *Multicultural issues in counseling: New approaches to diversity* (pp. 255–272). American Counseling Association.

Herlihy, B., & Park, C. N. (2016). Feminist theory. In D. Capuzzi & M. D. Stauffer (Eds.), *Counseling and psychotherapy* (6th ed., 367–390). American Counseling Association.

Hertlein, K. M., & Killmer, J. M. (2004). Toward differentiated decision-making: Family systems theory with the homeless clinical population. *American Journal of Family Therapy*, *32*, 255–270.

Hickey, M., & Doyle, K. A. (2018). Rational emotive behavior therapy. In A. Vernon & K. A. Doyle (Eds.), *Cognitive behavior therapies: A guidebook for practitioners* (pp. 109–142). American Counseling Association.

Hoffman, E. (1990). Abraham Maslow's legacy for counseling. *Journal of Humanistic Education and Development*, *29*, 2–9.

Hoffman, L., Granger, N., & Mansilla, M. (2016). Multiculturalism and meaning in existential and positive psychology. In P. Russo-Netzer, S. E. Schulenberg, & A. Batthyany (Eds.), *Clinical Perspectives on Meaning* (pp. 111–130). Springer, Cham.

Holden, J. (1993a). *Behavioral consequences on behavior*. Unpublished manuscript, University of North Texas, Denton.

Holden, J. (1993b). *Cognitive counseling* [Videotape]. ACES/Chi Sigma Iota.

Holden, J. (1993c). *Respondent learning*. Unpublished manuscript.

Holden, J. (1993d). *Learning module: Cognitive counseling*. Author.

Holmes, P., & Karp, M. (1991). Inspiration and technique. In P. Holmes & M. Karp (Eds.), *Psychodrama: Inspiration and Technique* (pp. 1–6). Routledge.

Hooper, L. M., & Doehler, K. (2011). The mediating and moderating effects of differentiation of self on body mass index and depressive symptomatology among an American college sample. *Counselling Psychology Quarterly*, *24*, 71–82.

Horney, K. (1967). On the genesis of the castration complex in women. In K. Horney (Ed.), *Feminine psychology* (pp. 37–53). Norton.

Horvatin, T., & Schrieber, E. (Eds.). (2006). *The quintessential Zerka: Writings by Zerka Toeman Moreno on psychodrama, sociometry, and group psychotherapy*. Routledge.

Hosford, R. E. (1980). The Cubberley conference and the evolution of observational learning strategies. *Personnel and Guidance Journal*, *58*, 467–472.

Howie, P. C., & Bagnall, R. (2015). The transmogrification of warm-up: From drama to psychodrama. *The Arts in Psychotherapy*, *44*, 35–44.

Hoyt, M. F. (2019). Strategic therapies: Roots and branches. *Journal of Systemic Therapies*, *38*, 1, 30–43.

Hudson, P. O., & O'Hanlon, W. H. (1991). *Rewriting love stories: Brief marital therapy*. Norton.

Hung-Hsiu-Chang, T., & Ng, K. S. (2000). I Ching, solution-focused therapy and change: A clinical integrative framework. *Family Therapy*, *27*, 47–57.

Ivey, A. E., D'Andrea, M., & Ivey, M. B. (2012). *Theories of counseling and psychotherapy* (7th ed.). Sage.

Ivey, A. E., & Goncalves, O. F. (1988). Developmental therapy: Integrating developmental processes into the clinical practice. *Journal of Counseling and Development*, *66*, 406–413.

Ivey, A. E., Ivey, M. B., & Zalaquett, C. P. (2018). *Intentional interviewing and counseling: Facilitating client development in a multicultural society* (9th ed.). Cengage.

Jackson, M. L. (1987). Cross-cultural counseling at the crossroads: A dialogue with Clemmont E. Vontress. *Journal of Counseling and Development*, *66*, 20–23.

James, M., & Jongeward, D. (1971). *Born to win: Transactional analysis with Gestalt experiments*. Addison-Wesley.

James, R. K. (2008). *Crisis intervention strategies* (6th ed.). Brooks Cole.

James, R. K., & Gilliland, B. E. (2003). *Theories and strategies in counseling and psychotherapy* (5th ed.). Boston: Allyn & Bacon.

James, R. K., & Gilliland, B. E. (2017). *Crisis intervention strategies* (8th ed.). Cengage.

Johnson, N. (1980). Must the RET therapist be like Albert Ellis? *Personnel and Guidance Journal*, *59*, 49–51.

Johnson, S. A. (2013). Using REBT in Jewish, Christian, and Muslim couples counseling in the United States. *Journal of Rational-Emotive & Cognitive-Behavior Therapy, 31*(2), 84–92.

Jones, E. (1953). *The life and work of Sigmund Freud* (Vol. 1). Basic Books.

Jones, E. (1955). *The life and work of Sigmund Freud* (Vol. 2). Basic Books.

Jones, E. (1957). *The life and work of Sigmund Freud* (Vol. 3). Basic Books.

Jones, M. C. (1924). The elimination of children's fears. *Journal of Experimental Psychology, 7*, 383–390.

Jones, R. M. (1979). Freudian and post-Freudian theories of dreams. In B. B. Wolman (Ed.), *Handbook of dreams: Research, theories, and applications* (pp. 271–297). Litton.

Jones-Smith, E. (2021). *Theories of counseling and psychotherapy: An integrated approach* (3rd ed.). Sage.

Jordan, J. V. (1997). *Women's growth in diversity: More writings from the Stone Center.* Guilford.

Jordan, J. V. (2000). A relational-cultural model: Healing through mutual empathy. *Bulletin of the Menninger Clinic, 65*, 92–103.

Jordan, K. (2002). Providing crisis counseling to New Yorkers after the terrorist attack on the World Trade Center. *The Family Journal, 10*(2), 139–144.

Kaplan, D. M. (2000). Who are our giants? *Family Digest, 12*(4), 1, 6.

Kaplan, D. M., Tarvydas, V. M., & Gladding, S. T. (2014). 20/20: A vision for the future of counseling: The new consensus definition of counseling. *Journal of Counseling & Development, 92*(3), 366–372.

Karpman, S. (1968). Script drama analysis. *Transactional Analysis Bulletin, 26*, 16–22.

Karpman, S. (2014). *A game free life.* Drama Triangle.

Keller, M. N., & Noone, R. J. (Eds.). (2020). *Handbook of Bowen family systems theory and research methods: A systems model for family research.* Routledge.

Kelly, E. W., Jr., & Sweeney, T. J. (1979). Typical faulty goals of adolescents: A base for counseling. *School Counselor, 26*, 236–246.

Kelly, K. R. (1988). Defending eclecticism: The utility of informed choice. *Journal of Mental Health Counseling, 10*, 210–213.

Kemp, C. G. (1976). Existential counseling. In G. S. Belkin (Ed.), *Counseling directions in theory and practice.* Kendall/Hunt.

Kempler, W. (1973). Gestalt therapy. In R. Corsini (Ed.), *Current psychotherapies* (pp. 251–286). Peacock.

Kendall, P. C. (2007). *Cognitive-behavioral therapy for impulsive children: Therapist manual* (3rd ed.). Workbook.

Kern, C. W., & Watts, R. E. (1993). Adlerian counseling. *Texas Counseling Association Journal, 21*, 85–95.

Kerr, M. (1981). Family systems theory and therapy. In A. S. Gurman & D. P. Kniskern (Eds.), *Handbook of family therapy.* Brunner/Mazel.

Kerr, M. (1988). Chronic anxiety and defining a self. *Atlantic Monthly, 262*, 35–37, 40–44, 46–58.

Kerr, M. (2003, August 9). *Process of differentiation.* Paper presented at the 111th Annual Convention of the American Psychological Association, Toronto, Canada.

Kerr, M. (2019). *Bowen theory's secrets.* W. W. Norton.

Kerr, M., & Bowen, M. (1988). *Family evaluation: An approach based on Bowen theory.* Norton.

Kilpatrick, A. C. (1980). The Bowen family intervention theory: An analysis for social workers. *Family Therapy, 7*, 167–178.

Kim, J. (Ed.). (2014). *Solution-focused brief therapy: A multicultural perspective.* Sage.

Kindall, M. (2020). *Hood feminism.* Viking.

Kipper, D. A. (1986). *Psychotherapy through clinical role playing.* Brunner/Mazel.

Kipper, D. A., & Ritchie, T. D. (2003). The effectiveness of psychodramatic techniques: A meta-analysis. *Group Dynamics: Theory, Research, and Practice, 7*(1), 13–25.

Kirschenbaum, H. (2004). Carl Rogers's life and work: An assessment on the 100th anniversary of his birth. *Journal of Counseling and Development, 82*, 116–124.

Kirschenbaum, H. (2007). *The life and work of Carl Rogers*. American Counseling Association.

Kirschenbaum, H. (2012). What is "person-centered"? A posthumous conversation with Carl Rogers on the development of the person-centered approach. *Person-Centered and Experiential Psychotherapies, 11*, 14–30.

Kiser, D. J., Piercy, F. P., & Lipchik, E. (1993). The integration of emotion in solution-focused therapy. *Journal of Marital and Family Therapy, 19*, 233–242.

Kitchener, K. S. (1986). Teaching applied ethics in counselor education: An integration of psychological processes and philosophical analysis. *Journal of Counseling and Development, 64*, 306–310.

Kitchener, K. S. (1994). Doing good well: The wisdom behind ethical supervision. *Counseling and Human Development*, 1–8.

Klingler, L., & Gray, N. D. (2015). Reality therapy/choice theory today: An interview with Dr. Robert E. Wubbolding. *Canadian Journal of Counselling and Psychotherapy, 49*(2), 185–197.

Knight, R. M., & C. Johnson, M. (2014). Using a behavioral treatment package for sleep problems in children with autism spectrum disorders. *Child & Family Behavior Therapy, 36*(3), 204–221.

Knight, Z. G. (2013). Black client, white therapist: Working with race in psychoanalytic psychotherapy in South Africa. *International Journal of Psychoanalysis, 94*(1), 17–31.

Knudson-Martin, C. (2002). Expanding Bowen's legacy to family therapy: A response to Horne and Hicks. *Journal of Marital and Family Therapy, 28*, 115–118.

Kocet, M. M. (2006). Ethical challenges in a complex world: Highlights of the 2005 ACA Code of Ethics. *Journal of Counseling and Development, 84*, 228–234.

Kohut, H. (1971). *The analysis of the self*. International Universities Press.

Kohut, H. (1984). *How does psychoanalysis cure?* University of Chicago Press.

Kok, C. J., & Leskela, J. (1996). Solution-focused therapy in a psychiatric hospital. *Journal of Marital and Family Therapy, 22*, 397–406.

Kottman, T., & Meany-Walen, K. (2016). *Partners in play: An Adlerian approach to play therapy*. Wiley.

Kottman, T., & Warlick, J. (1990). Adlerian play therapy. *Journal of Humanistic Education and Development, 28*, 125–132.

Kranz, P. L., & Lund, N. (1993). A reflective analysis through the vision and voices of an undergraduate psychology class. *Journal of Group Psychotherapy, Psychodrama, and Sociometry, 46*, 32–39.

Krasner, L., & Ullmann, L. P. (1973). *Behavior influence and personality: The social matrix of human action*. Holt, Rinehart & Winston.

Krauth, L. D. (1995, December). Strength-based therapies. *Family Therapy News, 26*, 24.

Krumboltz, J. D. (1966). Behavioral goals of counseling. *Journal of Counseling Psychology, 13*, 153–159.

Krumboltz, J. D. (1992, December). *Challenging troublesome career beliefs*. CAPS Digest, EDO-CG-92-4.

Krumboltz, J. D., & Thoresen, C. E. (1976). *Counseling methods*. Holt, Rinehart & Winston.

Lanning, W. (1992, December). Ethical codes and responsible decision-making. *ACA Guidepost, 35*, 21.

Lazarus, A. A. (1967). In support of technical eclecticism. *Psychological Reports, 21*, 415–416.

Lazarus, A. A. (1985). Behavior rehearsal. In A. S. Bellack & M. Hersen (Eds.), *Dictionary of behavior therapy techniques* (p. 22). Pergamon.

Lazarus, A. A. (2000). Multimodal therapy. In R. J. Corsini & D. Wedding (Eds.), *Current psychotherapies* (5th ed., pp. 340–374). Peacock.

Lazarus, A. A. (2009). Multimodal behavior therapy. In W. T. O'Donohue, & J. E. Fisher (Eds.), *General principles and empirically supported techniques of cognitive behavior therapy* (pp. 440–444). Wiley.

Lazarus, A. A., & Beutler, L. E. (1993). On technical eclecticism. *Journal of Counseling and Development, 71*, 381–385.

Learner, S. (1983). *Constructing the multigenerational family genogram: Exploring a problem in context* [Videotape]. Menninger Video Productions.

Lemberger-Truelove, T. (2018). Belonging, striving, and style of life among black women in the Southwestern United States. *Journal of Individual Psychology 74(1)*, 75–95.

Lerner, H. (2014). *The dance of anger: A woman's guide to changing the patterns of intimate relationships*. Harper/Collins.

Lerner, H. (2017). Harriet Lerner: A feminist voice from the wheat fields. *Women & Therapy, 40*, 396–405.

Levant, R. E. (2001). Men and masculinity. In J. Worell (Ed.), *Encyclopedia of women and gender* (Vol. 2, pp. 717–728). Academic Press.

Leveton, E. (2001). *A clinician's guide to psychodrama*. Springer.

Levine, T. B-Y. (Eds.). (2012). *Gestalt therapy: Advances in theory and practice*. Routledge.

Levinson, D. J., Darrow, C. N., Klein, E. B., Levinson, M. H., & McKee, B. (1978). *The seasons of a man's life*. Knopf.

Levitsky, A., & Perls, F. S. (1970). The rules and games of Gestalt therapy. In J. Fagan & I. L. Shepherd (Eds.), *Gestalt therapy now* (pp. 140–149). Science and Behavior Books.

Levy, P. A., & Hadley, B. J. (1998). Family-of-origin relationships and self-differentiation among university students with bulimic-type behavior. *Family Journal: Counseling and Therapy for Couples and Families, 6*, 19–23.

Lindemann, E. (1944). Symptomatology and management of acute grief. *American Journal of Psychiatry, 101*, 141–148.

Lindemann, E. (1956). The meaning of crisis in individual and family. *Teachers College Record, 57*, 310.

Lowe, R. N. (1982). Adlerian/Dreikursian family counseling. In A. M. Horne & M. M. Ohlsen (Eds.), *Family counseling and therapy* (pp. 329–359). Peacock.

Luborksy, E. B., O'Reilly-Landry, & Arlow, J. A. (2011). Psychoanalysis. In R. J. Corsini & D. Wedding (Eds.), *Current psychotherapies* (9th ed., 15–66). Brooks/Cole.

Luke, M. (2018). Person-centered counseling. In S. Degges-White & N. L. Davis (Eds.), *Integrating the expressive arts into counseling practice* (2nd ed., pp. 155–186). Springer.

Maass, V. S. (2021). *Feminist psychology: History, practice, research and the future*. Praeger.

Mackay, B. (2002). Effects of Gestalt therapy two-chair dialogue on divorce decision making. *Gestalt Review, 6*, 220–235.

Madanes, C. (1981). *Strategic family therapy*. Jossey-Bass.

Madanes, C. (1984). *Behind the one-way mirror: Advances in the practice of strategic therapy*. Jossey-Bass.

Madanes, C. (1990). *Sex, love, and violence*. Norton.

Madanes, C. (1991). Strategic family therapy. In A. S. Gurman & D. P. Kniskern (Eds.), *Handbook of family therapy* (Vol. 2, pp. 396–416). Brunner/Mazel.

Maglio, A-S. T., Butterfield, L. D., & Borgen, W. A. (2005). Existential considerations for contemporary career counseling. *Journal of Employment Counseling, 42*, 75–92.

Mahoney, M. J. (1995). *Cognitive and constructive psychotherapies: Theory, research, and practice*. Springer.

Maniacci, M. P., & Sackett-Maniacci, L. (2019). Adlerian psychotherapy. In D. Wedding & R. J. Corsini (Eds.), *Current psychotherapies* (11th ed., pp. 59–100). Cengage.

Mann, D. (2010). *Gestalt therapy: 100 key points and techniques*. Routledge.

Manning, S. S. (2002). *Ethical leadership in human services: A multi-dimensional approach*. Pearson.

Marino, G. (2019). *The existentialist's survival guide*. Harper.

Maslow, A. H. (1998). *Toward a psychology of being* (3rd ed.). Wiley.

Mason, C. P., & Duba, J. D. (2009). Introducing choice theory principles and the choice theory career rating scale for children and adolescents in ASCA national model school counseling programs. *Kentucky Counseling Association Journal, 28(1)*, 51–56.

Masquelie, G. (2006). *Gestalt therapy: Living creatively today.* Gestalt Press Books.

Maturana, H., & Varela, F. (1987). *The tree of knowledge.* New Science Library.

Maultsby, M. C., Jr. (1984). *Rational behavior therapy.* Prentice Hall.

May, R. (1939). *The art of counseling.* Abingdon-Cokesbury.

May, R. (1967). Part three: Psychotherapy. In R. May (Ed.), *Psychology and the human dilemma* (pp. 87–160). Van Nostrand.

May, R. (Ed.). (1969a). *Existential psychology* (2nd ed.). Random House.

May, R. (1969b). *Love and will.* Norton.

May, R. (1975). *The courage to create.* Bantam.

May, R. (1977). *The meaning of anxiety* (Rev. ed.). Norton.

May, R. (1985). *My quest for beauty.* Norton.

May, R., Angel, E., & Ellenberger, H. (Eds.). (1958). *Existence.* Simon & Schuster.

McAdams, C. R., Avadhanam, R., Foster, V. A., Harris, P. N., Javaheri, A., Kim, S., ... & Williams, A. E. (2016). The viability of structural family therapy in the twenty-first century: An analysis of key indicators. *Contemporary Family Therapy, 38*(3), 255–261.

McBride, M. C., & Martin, G. E. (1990). A framework for eclecticism: The importance of theory to mental health counseling. *Journal of Mental Health Counseling, 12,* 495–505.

McDowell, T., Knudson-Martin, C., & Bermudez, J. M. (2018). *Socioculturally attuned family therapy: Guidelines for equitable theory and practice.* Routledge.

McFarland, B. (1995). *Brief therapy and eating disorders: A practical guide to solution-focused work with clients.* Jossey-Bass.

McGoldrick, M. (2011). *The genogram journey: Reconnecting with your family.* Norton.

McGoldrick, M. (2016). *The genogram casebook.* W. W. Norton.

McGoldrick, M., Gerson, R., & Petry, S. (2020). *Genograms: Assessment & treatment* (4th ed.). W. W. Norton.

McIllroy, J. H. (1979). Career as lifestyle: An existential view. *Personnel and Guidance Journal, 57,* 351–354.

Meichenbaum, D. (1977). *Cognitive-behavior modification: An integrated approach.* Plenum.

Meichenbaum, D. (1985). *Stress inoculation training.* Pergamon.

Meichenbaum, D. (1986). Cognitive behavior modification. In F. H. Kanfer & A. P. Goldstein (Eds.), *Helping people change: A textbook of methods* (pp. 346–380). Pergamon.

Meichenbaum, D. (1995). Cognitive-behavioral therapy in historical perspective. In B. M. Bongar & L. E. Beutler (Eds.), *Comprehensive textbook of psychotherapy: Theory and practice* (Vol. 1, pp. 140–158). Oxford University Press.

Meichenbaum, D. (1997). The evolution of a cognitive-behavior therapist. In J. K. Zeig (Ed.), *The evolution of psychotherapy: The third conference* (pp. 95–104). Brunner/Mazel.

Meier, S. T., & Davis, S. R. (2019). *The elements of counseling* (8th ed.). Waveland.

Melnick, J. (2003). Making the learning last. *Gestalt Review, 7,* 1–4.

Meyer, D. D., & Cottone, R. R. (2013). Solution-focused therapy as a culturally acknowledging approach with American Indians. *Journal of Multicultural Counseling and Development, 41,* 47–55.

Miars, R. D. (2002). Existential authenticity: A foundational value for counseling. *Counseling and Values, 46,* 218–226.

Michael, F. H. (2019). Strategic therapies: Roots and branches. *Journal of Systemic Therapies: 38,* 30–43.

Miller, G. (2012). *Fundamentals of crisis counseling.* Wiley.

Miller, J. B. (1986). *Toward a new psychology of women* (2nd ed.). Beacon.

Miller, J. B. (1991). The development of women's sense of self. In J. V. Jordan, A. G. Kaplan, J. B. Miller, I. P. Stiver, & J. L. Surrey (Eds.), *Women's growth in connection* (pp. 11–26). Guilford.

Miller, M. J. (1996). Client-centered reflections on career decision making. *Journal of Employment Counseling, 33,* 43–46.

Miller, M. V. (2008). What lies beyond the field? *International Gestalt Journal, 31,* 133–144.

Miller, R., & Taylor, D. D. (2016). Does Adlerian theory stand the test of time? Examining individual psychology from a neuroscience perspective. *Journal of Humanistic Counseling*, *55*(2), 111–128.

Moleski, S. M., & Kiselica, M. S. (2005). Dual relationships: A continuum ranging from the destructive to the therapeutic. *Journal of Counseling and Development*, *83*, 3–11.

Monette, D. R., Sullivan, T. J., DeJong, C. R. (2011). *Applied social research: A tool for the human services* (8th ed.). Brooks/Cole.

Monterio-Leitner, J. (2001). *Psychodrama: When and why to use doubling.* Presentation at the annual convention of the American Counseling Association, San Antonio, TX.

Moodley, R., & Walcott, R. (Eds.). (2010). *Counseling across and beyond cultures: Exploring the work of Clemmont E. Vontress in clinical settings.* University of Toronto Press.

Moreno, J. L. (1914). *Einladung zu einer Begegnung.* Anzuenggruber.

Moreno, J. L. (1940). Mental catharsis and the psychodrama. *Sociometry*, *3*(3), 209–244.

Moreno, J. L. (Ed.). (1945). *Group psychotherapy: A symposium.* Beacon House.

Moreno, J. L. (1949). Origins and foundations of interpersonal theory, sociometry and microsociology. *Sociometry*, *12*(1/3), 235–254.

Moreno, J. L. (1953). *Who shall survive?* Beacon House.

Moreno, J. L. (1964). *Psychodrama: Volume 1* (rev. ed.). Beacon House.

Moreno, J. L. (1984). Reflections on my method of group psychotherapy and psychodrama. In H. Greenwald (Ed.), *Active psychotherapy* (pp. 130–143). Aronson.

Moreno, J. L., & Moreno, Z. T. (1959). *Psychodrama: Foundations of psychotherapy.* Beacon House.

Moreno, Z. T. (1983). Psychodrama. In H. I. Kaplan & B. J. Sadock (Eds.), *Comprehensive group* (2nd ed.). Williams & Wilkins.

Moreno, Z. T. (1987). Psychodrama, role theory, and the concept of the social atom. In J. K. Zeig (Ed.), *The evolution of psychotherapy* (pp. 341–366). Brunner/Mazel.

Moreno, Z. T. (1998). *The handbook of psychodrama.* Psychology Press.

Moreno, Z. T. (2014). Drawing the personal perceptual socio-cultural atom: An exercise in sharpening and stretching tele function. *Journal of Psychodrama, Sociometry, and Group Psychotherapy*, *62*(1), 29–34.

Morris, K. T., & Kanitz, M. (1975). *Rational-emotive therapy.* Houghton Mifflin.

Murdock, N. L. (2017). *Theories of counseling and psychotherapy* (4th ed.). Pearson.

Murphy, N. (2018). Embracing vulnerability in the midst of danger: Therapy in a high secure prison. *Existential Analysis*, *29*(2), 174–188.

Myer, R. (2001). *Assessment for crisis intervention: A triage assessment model.* Brooks/Cole.

Neukrug, E. S. (2017a). *Counseling theory and practice* (2nd ed.). Cognella.

Neukrug, E. S. (2017b). *Theory, practice and trends in human services* (6th ed.). Cengage.

Newhorn, P. (1978). Albert Ellis. *Human Behavior*, *7*, 30–35.

Newman, C. F., & Beck, A. T. (2009). Cognitive therapy. In H. I. Kaplan & B. J. Sadock (Eds.), *Comprehensive textbook of psychiatry, Vol II* (9th ed., pp. 2857–2872). Lippincott Williams & Wilkins.

Nolte, J. (1989). Remembering J. L. Moreno. *Journal of Group Psychotherapy, Psychodrama, & Sociometry*, *42*, 129–137.

Nolte, J. (2020). *J. L. Moreno and the psychodramatic method.* Routledge.

Nwachuku, U., & Ivey, A. (1991). Culture-specific counseling: An alternative model. *Journal of Counseling & Development*, *70*, 106–111.

Nye, R. D. (2000). *Three psychologies: Perspectives from Freud, Skinner, and Rogers* (6th ed.). Brooks/Cole.

Nystul, M. S. (2019). *Introduction to counseling: An art and science perspective* (6th ed.). Cognella.

O'Hanlon, B., & Bertolino, B. (2002). *Even from a broken web: Brief, respectful solution-oriented therapy for sexual abuse and trauma.* Norton.

O'Hanlon, W. H. (1987). *Taproots: Underlying principles of Milton Erickson's therapy and hypnosis.* Norton.

O'Hanlon, W. H., & Weiner-Davis, M. (1989). *In search of solutions: A new direction in psychotherapy*. Norton.

O'Hanlon, W. H., & Wilk, J. (1987). *Shifting contexts: The generation of effective psychotherapy*. Guilford Press.

Ohlsen, M. M., Horne, A. M., & Lawe, C. F. (1988). *Group counseling* (3rd ed.). Holt, Rhinehart, & Winston.

O'Kelly, M., & Gilson, K. (2019). REBT with Women. In W. Dryden & M. E. Bernard (Eds.), *REBT with diverse client problems and populations* (pp. 303–321). Springer.

Okun, B. F. (1990). *Seeking connections in psychotherapy*. Jossey-Bass.

Okun, B. F., & Kantrowitz, R. E. (2015). *Effective helping* (8th ed.). Cengage.

Olson, M. H., & Hergenhahn, B. R. (2011). *An introduction to theories of personality* (8th ed.). Prentice Hall.

Onedera, J. D., & Greenwalt, B. (2007). Choice theory: An interview with Dr. William Glasser. *The Family Journal, 15*(1), 79–86.

Orkibi, H. (2019). Positive psychodrama: A framework for practice and research. *The Arts in Psychotherapy, 66*, 101603.

Pantalone, D. W., Iwamasa, G. Y., & Martell, C. R. (2010). Cognitive-behavioral therapy with diverse populations. In K. S. Dobson (Ed.), *Handbook of cognitive-behavioral therapies* (pp. 445–464). Springer.

Papero, D. V. (1990). *Bowen family systems theory*. Allyn & Bacon.

Papero, D. V. (1991). The Bowen theory. In A. M. Horne & J. L. Passmore (Eds.), *Family counseling and theory* (2nd ed., pp. 47–76). Peacock.

Papp, P. (1984, September/October). The creative leap. *Family Therapy Networker, 8*, 20–29.

Parikh, S. J. T., & Morris, C. A. W. (2011). Integrating crisis theory and individual psychology: An application and case study. *Journal of Individual Psychology, 67*, 364–379.

Parloff, M. (1976, February 21). Shopping for the right therapy. *Saturday Review*, pp. 14–16.

Partenheimer, D. (1990). Teaching literature toward a humanistic society. *Journal of Humanistic Education and Development, 29*, 40–44.

Passons, W. R. (1975). *Gestalt approaches to counseling*. Holt, Rinehart, & Winston.

Patterson, C. H. (1971). Are ethics different in different settings? *Personnel and Guidance Journal, 50*, 254–259.

Patterson, C. H. (1985). *The therapeutic relationship*. Brooks/Cole.

Paul, G. L. (1967). Strategy of outcome research in psychotherapy. *Journal of Consulting Psychology, 31*, 109–118.

Peleg-Popko, O. (2004). Differentiation and test anxiety in adolescents. *Journal of Adolescence, 27*, 645–662.

Penfield, W. (1952). Memory mechanisms. *Archives of Neurology and Psychiatry, 67*, 178–198.

Penfield, W., & Jasper, H. (1954). *Epilepsy and the functional anatomy of the human brain*. Little, Brown.

Pennebaker, J. W., & Smyth, J. M. (2016). *Opening up by writing it down: How expressive writing improves health and eases emotional pain* (3rd ed.). Guilford.

Perls, F. (1969). *Gestalt therapy verbatim*. Lafayette, CA: Real People Press.

Perls, F. (1970). Four lectures. In J. Fagan & I. L. Shepherd (Eds.), *Gestalt therapy now* (pp. 14–38). Science and Behavior Books.

Perls, F. (1972). *In and out of the garbage pail*. Bantam.

Perls, F. (1976). *The Gestalt approaches and eye witnesses to therapy*. Bantam.

Perls, F., Hefferline, R. F., & Goodman, P. (1951). *Gestalt therapy*. New York: Dell.

Perry, M. A., & Furukawa, M. J. (1980). Modeling methods. In F. H. Kanfer & A. P. Goldstein (Eds.), *Helping people change* (pp. 131–171). Pergamon.

Petrocelli, J. V. (2002). Processes and stages of change: Counseling with the transtheoretical model of change. *Journal of Counseling and Development, 80*, 22–30.

Piercy, F. P., & Sprenkle, D. H. (1986). *Family therapy sourcebook*. Guilford.

Piran, N. (2016). Embodied paths in aging: Body journeys towards enhanced agency and self-attunement. *Women & Therapy, 39*, 186–201.

Pitts, C., & Kawahara, D. M. (2017). Radical visionaries—feminist psychotherapists: 1970–1975. *Women & Therapy, 40*(3–4), 256–259.

Pitts, C., & Kawahara, D. M. (Eds.). (2018). *Radical visionaries—feminist psychotherapists: 1970–1975.* Routledge.

Polster, E., & Polster, M. (1973). *Gestalt therapy integrated: Contours of theory and practice.* Brunner/Mazel.

Ponton, R. F., & Duba, J. D. (2009). The ACA Code of Ethics: Articulating counseling's professional covenant. *Journal of Counseling & Development, 87*, 117–121.

Pope, K. S., & Vasquez, M. J. (2016). *Ethics in psychotherapy and counseling: A practical guide.* Wiley.

Powell, J. (1976). *Fully human, fully alive.* Argos.

Powers, Y. O., & Kalodner, C. R. (2016). Cognitive-behavioral theories. In D. Capuzzi & M. Stauffer (Eds.), *Counseling & psychotherapy* (6th ed., 227–252). American Counseling Association.

Priebe, S., & Pommerien, W. (1992). The therapeutic system as viewed by depressive inpatients and outcome: An expanded study. *Family Process, 31*, 433–439.

Prochaska, J. O., & DiClemente, C. C. (1992). The transtheoretical approach. In J. C. Norcross & M. R. Goldfried (Eds.), *Handbook of psychotherapy integration* (pp. 300–334). Basic Books.

Prochaska, J. O., & Norcross, J. C. (2018). *Systems of psychotherapy: A transtheoretical analysis* (9th ed.). Guilford.

Purkey, W. W., & Schmidt, J. J. (1987). *The inviting relationship.* Prentice Hall.

Purswell, K. E. (2019). Humanistic learning theory in counselor education. *Professional Counselor, 9*(4), 358–368.

Quinn, A. (2013). A person-centered approach to multicultural counseling competence. *Journal of Humanistic Psychology, 53*(2), 202–251.

Rabinowitz, F. E., Good, G., & Cozad, L. (1989). Rollo May: A man of meaning and myth. *Journal of Counseling and Development, 67*, 436–441.

Rapport, Z. (2019). 131 metaphors to learn and teach choice theory and reality therapy. *International Journal of Choice Theory and Reality Therapy, 39*(1), 27–40.

Raskin, N. J., Rogers, C. R., Witty, M. (2019). Person-centered therapy. In D. Wedding & R. J. Corsini (Eds.), *Current psychotherapies* (11th ed., pp. 101–157). Cengage.

Ray, W. A. (2007). Jay Haley—A memorial. *Journal of Marital and Family Therapy, 33*, 291–292.

Reck, Mark I. (2009). *The Gestalt of multiculturalism: An analysis of Gestalt therapy theory in light of ethnic diversity with a focus on Organismic self-regulation* (Doctoral dissertation, Pacific University). Retrieved from: https://commons.pacificu.edu/spp/74

Reeves, C. (1977). *The psychology of Rollo May.* Jossey-Bass.

Remer, P. (2008). Empowerment feminist therapy. In K. Jordan (Ed.), *The quick theory reference guide: A resource for expert and novice mental health professionals* (pp. 167–181). Nova Science Publishers.

Remley, T. P., Jr., & Herlihy, B. (2020). *Ethical, legal, and professional issues in counseling* (6th ed.). Pearson.

Rescorla, R. A. (1988). Pavlovian conditioning: It's not what you think it is. *American Psychologist, 43*, 151–160.

Richeport-Haley, M. (1998). Ethnicity in family therapy: A comparison of brief strategic therapy and culture-focused therapy. *American Journal of Family Therapy, 26*, 77–90.

Rimm, D. C., & Cunningham, H. M. (1985). Behavior therapies. In S. J. Lynn & J. P. Garske (Eds.), *Contemporary psychotherapies: Models and methods* (pp. 221–259). Prentice Hall.

Robert, A. R. (2005). *Crisis intervention handbook: Assessment, treat, and research* (3rd ed.). Oxford.

Rogers, C. R. (1942). *Counseling and psychotherapy*. Houghton Mifflin.

Rogers, C. R. (1951). *Client-centered therapy*. Houghton Mifflin.

Rogers, C. R. (1955). Persons or science? A philosophical question. *American Psychologist, 10*, 267–278.

Rogers, C. R. (1957). The necessary and sufficient conditions of therapeutic personality change. *Journal of Consulting Psychology, 21*, 95–103.

Rogers, C. R. (1959). A theory of therapy, personality, and interpersonal relationships, as developed in the client-centered framework. In S. Koch (Ed.), *Psychology: A study of science* (Vol. 3, pp. 184–256). McGraw-Hill.

Rogers, C. R. (1961). *On becoming a person*. Houghton Mifflin.

Rogers, C. R. (1965). Client-centered therapy: Part I. In E. Shostrom (Producer), *Three approaches to psychotherapy* [film]. Psychological Films.

Rogers, C. R. (1967a). Autobiography. In E. G. Boring & G. Lindzey (Eds.), *A history of psychology in autobiography* (Vol. 5, pp. 341–384). Appleton.

Rogers, C. R. (1967b). The conditions of change from a client-centered viewpoint. In B. Berenson & R. Carkhuff (Eds.), *Sources of gain in counseling and psychotherapy* (pp. 71–86). Holt, Rinehart, & Winston.

Rogers, C. R. (1969). *Freedom to learn*. Prentice Hall.

Rogers, C. R. (1970). *Carl Rogers on encounter groups*. Harper & Row.

Rogers, C. R. (1974). In retrospect: Forty-six years. *American Psychologist, 29*, 115–123.

Rogers, C. R. (1975). Empathic: An unappreciated way of being. *Counseling Psychologist, 5*, 2–10.

Rogers, C. R. (1977). *Carl Rogers on personal power: Inner strength and its revolutionary impact*. Delacorte.

Rogers, C. R. (1980). *A way of being*. Houghton Mifflin.

Rogers, C. R. (1986). Rogers, Kohut, and Erickson: A personal perspective on some similarities and differences. *Person-Centered Review, 1*, 125–140.

Rogers, C. R. (1987). The underlying theory: Drawn from experience with individuals and groups. *Counseling and Values, 32*, 38–46.

Rogers, N., Tudor, K., Tudor, L. E., & Keemar, K. (2012). Person-centered expressive arts therapy: A theoretical encounter. *Person-Centered and Experiential Psychotherapies, 11*, 31–47.

Rose, S. D. (1993). Behavior therapy in groups. In H. I. Kaplan & B. J. Sadock (Eds.), *Comprehensive group psychotherapy* (3rd ed.). Williams & Wilkins.

Roy, T. (2014). *William Glasser: Champion of choice*. Zeig, Tucker, & Theisen.

Sandoval, J., Scott, A. N., & Padilla, I. (2009). Crisis counseling: An overview. *Psychology in the schools, 46*, 246–256.

Sang, Z. Q., Huang, H. M., Benko, A., & Wu, Y. (2018). The spread and development of psychodrama in Mainland China. *Frontiers in psychology, 9*, 1368.

Santisteban, D. A., Coatsworth, J. D., Perez-Vidal, A., Kurtines, W. M., Schwartz, S. J., LaPerriere, A., & Szapocznik, J. (2003). Efficacy of brief strategic family therapy in modifying Hispanic adolescent behavior problems and substance use. *Journal of Family Psychology, 17*, 121–133.

Satin, D. G. (1984). Erich Lindemann as humanist, scientist, and change agent. *American Journal of Community Psychology 12*(5), 519–527.

Sauber, S. R., L'Abate, L., & Weeks, G. R. (1985). *Family therapy: Basic concepts and terms*. Aspen.

Schmidt, R. W., & Cohen, S. L. (2020). *Disaster mental health community planning*. Routledge.

Schwarz, J. E. (Ed.). (2017). *Counseling women across the lifespan*. Springer.

Schultze, G., & Miller, C. (2004). The search for meaning and career development. *Career Development International, 9*, 142–152.

Schuyler, D. (2003). *Cognitive therapy: A practical guide* (Revised). Norton.

Seligman, L. (2004). *Diagnosis and treatment planning in counseling* (3rd ed.). Springer.

Seligman, L., & Reichenberg, L. W. (2014). *Theories of counseling and psychotherapy* (4th ed.). Pearson.

Seligman, M. E. P. (2003, August 8). *Positive psychology: Applications to work, love, and sports.* Paper presented at the 111th annual convention of the American Psychological Association, Toronto, Canada.

Sexton, T. L., & Montgomery, D. (1994). Ethical and therapeutic acceptability: A study of paradoxical techniques. *Family Journal: Counseling and Therapy for Couples and Families, 2,* 215–228.

Shaffer, W. (1997). Psychodrama techniques in the middle school or meanwhile back at Elsinore Castle. In S. T. Gladding (Ed.), *New developments in group counseling* (pp. 33–36). ERIC/CASS.

Sharf, R. S. (2016). *Theories of psychotherapy and counseling* (6th ed.). Cengage.

Sharry, J., Madden, B., Darmody, M. (2012). *Becoming a solution detective: A strengths-based guide to brief therapy* (2nd ed.). Routledge.

Shea, M., & Leong, F. T. L. (2013). Working with a Chinese immigrant with severe mental illness: An integrative approach of cognitive-behavioral therapy and multicultural case conceptualization. In S. Poyrazli & C. E. Thompson (Eds.), *International case studies in mental health* (pp. 205–223). Sage.

Sherman, R. (1993). The intimacy genogram. *Family Journal: Counseling and Therapy for Couples and Families, 1,* 91–93.

Shertzer, B., & Stone, S. C. (1974). *Fundamentals of counseling.* Houghton Mifflin.

Simkin, J. S. (1975). An introduction to Gestalt therapy. In F. D. Stephenson (Ed.), *Gestalt therapy primer* (pp. 3–12). Thomas.

Simon, F., Stierlin, H., & Wynne, L. (1985). *The language of family therapy.* Family Process Press.

Simon, G. M. (1989). An alternative defense of eclecticism: Responding to Kelly and Ginter. *Journal of Mental Health Counseling, 2,* 280–288.

Simon, J. K. (2010). *Solution focused practice in end-of-life and grief counseling.* Springer.

Simon, R. (1982, September/October). Behind the one-way mirror: An interview with Jay Haley. *Family Therapy Networker, 6,* 18–25, 28–29, 58–59.

Simon, R. (1984, November/December). Stranger in a strange land: An interview with Salvador Minuchin. *Family Therapy Networker, 8,* 20–31.

Simon, R. (1986, September/October). Behind the one-way kaleidoscope: An interview with Cloe Madanes. *Family Therapy Networker, 10,* 19–29, 64–67.

Simon, R. (1987, September/October). Good-bye paradox, hello invariant prescription: An interview with Mara Selvini Palazzoli. *Family Therapy Networker, 11,* 16–33.

Singer, E. (1970). *Key concepts in psychotherapy* (2nd ed.). Basic Books.

Skinner, B. F. (1938). *The behavior of organisms: An experimental analysis.* Prentice Hall.

Skinner, B. F. (1948). *Walden two.* Macmillan.

Skinner, B. F. (1953). *Science and human behavior.* Macmillan.

Skinner, B. F. (1967). Autobiography. In E. G. Boring & G. Lindzey (Eds.), *A history of psychology in autobiography* (Vol. 5, pp. 387–413). Appleton-Century-Croft.

Skinner, B. F. (1971). *Beyond freedom and dignity.* Knopf.

Skinner, B. F. (1974). *About behaviorism.* Knopf.

Skinner, B. F. (1976). *Particulars of my life.* McGraw-Hill.

Skinner, B. F., & Vaughan, M. E. (1983). *Enjoy old age.* Norton.

Sklare, G., Taylor, J., & Hyland, S. (1985). An emotional control card for rational-emotive imagery. *Journal of Counseling and Development, 64,* 145–146.

Skowron, E. A. (2000). The role of differentiation of self in marital adjustment. *Journal of Counseling Psychology, 47,* 229–237.

Skowron, E. A., & Platt, L. F. (2005). Differentiation of self and child abuse potential in young adulthood. *Family Journal: Counseling and Therapy for Couples and Families, 13,* 281–290.

Slavik, S. (1991). Early memories as a guide to client movement through life. *Canadian Journal of Counselling, 25,* 331–337.

Slipp, S. (1988). *The technique and practice of object relations family therapy.* Aronson.

Snider, M. (1992). *Process family therapy.* Allyn & Bacon.

Softas-Nall, B. C., Baldo, T. D., & Tiedemann, T. R. (1999). A gender-based, solution-focused genogram case: He and she across the generations. *Family Journal, 7,* 177–180.

Sokol, L., & Fox, M. (2019). *The comprehensive clinician's guide to cognitive behavioral therapy.* PESI Publishing & Media.

Sollod, R. N., Monte, C. F., & Wilson, J. P. (2009). *Beneath the mask: An introduction to theories of personality* (8th ed.). Wiley.

Sommers-Flanagan, J., & Sommers-Flanagan, R. (2018). *Counseling and psychotherapy theories in context and practice: Skills, strategies, and techniques* (3rd ed.). Wiley.

Soo-Hoo, T. (1999). Brief strategic family therapy with Chinese Americans. *American Journal of Family Therapy, 27,* 163–179.

Spangenberg, J. J. (2003). The cross-cultural relevance of person-centered counseling in postapartheid South Africa. *Journal of Counseling and Development, 81,* 48–54.

Spiegel, H., & Linn, L. (1969). The "ripple effect" following adjunct hypnosis in analytic psychotherapy. *American Journal of Psychiatry, 126,* 53–58.

St. Germaine, J. (1993). Dual relationships: What's wrong with them? *American Counselor, 2,* 25–30.

Stanton, D., Todd, T., & Associates. (1982). *The family therapy of drug abuse and addiction.* Guilford.

Statton, J. E., & Wilborn, B. (1991). Adlerian counseling and the early recollections of children. *Individual Psychology, 47,* 338–347.

Stebnicki, M. A. (Ed.). (2016). *Disaster mental health counseling: Responding to trauma in a multicultural context.* Springer.

Steinberg, E. B., Sayger, T. V., & Szykula, S. A. (1997). The effects of strategic and behavioral family therapies on child behavior and depression. *Contemporary Family Therapy, 19,* 537–551.

Stevens, M. J., Pfost, K. S., & Wessels, A. B. (1987). The relationship of purpose in life to coping strategies and time since the death of a significant other. *Journal of Counseling and Development, 65,* 424–426.

Steward, I., & Joines, V. S. (2011). TA tomorrow. *Transactional Analysis Journal, 41,* 221–229.

Steward, I., & Joines, V. S. (2012). *TA Today: A new introduction to Transactional Analysis* (2nd ed.). Lifespace.

Sue, D. W., Sue, D., Neville, H. A., & Smith, L. (2019). *Counseling the culturally diverse: Theory and practice* (8th ed.). Wiley.

Swanson, C. D. (1983). Ethics and the counselor. In J. A. Brown & R. H. Pate, Jr. (Eds.), *Being a counselor* (pp. 47–65). Brooks/Cole.

Sweeney, T. J. (2019). *Adlerian counseling* (6th ed.). Routledge.

Szapocznik, J., & Hervis, O. E. (2020). *Brief strategic family therapy.* American Psychological Association.

Talbutt, L. C. (1981). Ethical standards: Assets and limitations. *Personnel and Guidance Journal, 60,* 110–112.

Tarashoeva, G., Marinova-Djambazova, P., & Kojuharov, H. (2017). Effectiveness of psychodrama therapy in patients with panic disorders: Final results. *International Journal of Psychotherapy, 21*(2), 55–66.

Taylor, E. R. (2019). *Solution-focused therapy with children and adolescents.* Routledge.

Tennyson, W. W., & Strom, S. M. (1986). Beyond professional standards: Developing responsibleness. *Journal of Counseling and Development, 64,* 298–302.

Thomas, A. J. (1998). Understanding culture and worldview in family systems: Use of the multicultural genogram. *Family Journal: Counseling and Therapy for Couples and Families, 6,* 24–32.

Thompson, A. (1990). *Guide to ethical practice in psychotherapy.* Wiley.

Thoresen, C. E. (1969). The counselor as an applied behavioral scientist. *Personnel and Guidance Journal, 47,* 841–848.

Thoresen, C. E., & Coates, T. J. (1980). What does it mean to be a behavior therapist? In C. E. Thoresen (Ed.), *The behavior therapist* (pp. 1–41). Brooks/Cole.

Titelman, P. (2014). *Differentiation of self.* Routledge.

Todd, T. (1992). Brief family therapy. In R. L. Smith & P. Stevens-Smith (Eds.), *Family counseling and therapy* (pp. 162–175). ERIC/CAPS.

Toman, W. (1961). *Family constellation: Its effects on personality and social behavior.* Springer.

Tuason, M. T., & Friedlander, M. L. (2000). Do parents' differentiation levels predict those of their adult children? And other tests of Bowen theory in a Philippine sample. *Journal of Counseling Psychology, 47,* 27–35.

Turkington, C. (1985). Analysts sued for barring non-MDs. *APA Monitor, 16*(5), 2.

Tyrangiel, H. (2011). On Skype with Eric Berne: What did he say after he said hello? *Transactional Analysis Journal, 41,* 16–22.

Vacc, N. A., Juhnke, G. A., & Nilsen, K. A. (2001). Community mental health service providers' code of ethics and the standards for educational and psychological testing. *Journal of Counseling and Development, 79,* 217–224.

Vaihinger, H. (1911). *The philosophy of "as if."* Harcourt, Brace, & World.

Van Deurzen, E., & Adams, M. (2016). *Skills in existential counselling & psychotherapy* (2nd ed.). Sage.

Van Hoose, W. H., & Kottler, J. (1985). *Ethical and legal issues in counseling and psychotherapy* (2nd ed.). Jossey-Bass.

Van Hoose, W. H., & Paradise, L. V. (1979). *Ethics in counseling and psychotherapy.* Carroll.

Verhofstadt, D., & Leni, M. F. (2000). The "magic shop" technique in psychodrama: An existential-dialectical view. *International Journal of Action Methods: Psychodrama, Skill Training, and Role Playing, 53,* 3–15.

Vernon, A. (1996). Counseling children and adolescents: Rational emotive behavior therapy and humanism. *Journal of Humanistic Education and Development, 35,* 120–127.

Volnovich, J. C. (2017). Trauma and contemporary forms of subjectivity: Contributions of Argentine psychoanalysis. *American Journal of Psychoanalysis, 77*(1), 7–22.

Von Ameln, F., & Becker-Ebe, J. (2020). *Fundamentals of psychodrama.* Springer.

Vontress, C. (1979). Cross-cultural counseling: An existential approach. *Personnel and Guidance Journal, 58,* 117–122.

Vontress, C. E., Johnson, J. A., & Epp, L. R. (1999). *Cross-cultural counseling: A casebook.* American Counseling Association.

Walen, S. R., DiGiuseppe, R., & Dryden, W. (1992). *A practitioner's guide to rational-emotive therapy.* Oxford University Press.

Wallace, W. A. (1986). *Theories of counseling and psychotherapy: A basic-issues approach.* Allyn & Bacon.

Walsh, W. M., & McGraw, A. (1996). *Essentials of family therapy.* Love.

Walter, J., & Peller, J. (1993). Solution-focused brief therapy. *Family Journal, 1,* 80–81.

Watkins, C. E., Jr. (1985). Early recollections as a projective technique in counseling: An Adlerian view. *AMHCA Journal, 7,* 32–40.

Watson, J. B. (1913). Psychology as a behaviorist views it. *Psychological Review, 20,* 158–177.

Watson, J. B. (1925). *Behaviorism.* Norton.

Watson, J. B., & Raynor, R. (1920). Conditioned emotional reactions. *Journal of Experimental Psychology, 3,* 1–14.

Watts, R. E. (1996a). Social interest and the core conditions: Could it be that Adler influenced Rogers? *Journal of Humanistic Education and Development, 34,* 165–170.

Watts, R. E. (1996b). Some contemporary rational emotive behavior therapy songs. *Journal of Humanistic Education and Development, 35,* 117–119.

Watts, R. E. (2018). Adlerian therapy and the need for outcome efficacy research. *Journal of Individual Psychology*, 74(3), 277–280.

Watzlawick, P. (1978). *The language of change*. Basic Books.

Watzlawick, P. (1983). *The situation is hopeless but not serious*. Norton.

Webber, J. M., & Mascari, J. B. (Eds.). (2018). *Disaster mental health counseling: A guide to preparing and responding* (4th ed.). American Counseling Association Foundation.

Wedding, D., & Corsini, R. J. (Eds.). (2019). *Current psychotherapies* (11th ed.). Cengage.

Weinrach, S. G. (1980). Unconventional therapist: Albert Ellis. *Personnel and Guidance Journal*, 59, 152–160.

Weinrach, S. G. (1988). Cognitive therapist: A dialogue with Aaron Beck. *Journal of Counseling and Development*, 67, 159–164.

Welfel, E. R. (2016). *Ethics in counseling and psychotherapy* (6th ed.). Cengage.

Welfel, E. R., & Lipsitz, N. E. (1983). Wanted: A comprehensive approach to ethics research and education. *Counselor Education and Supervision*, 22, 320–332.

West, J. D., Bubenzer, D. L., Smith, J. M., & Hamm, T. L. (1997). Insoo Kim Berg and solution-focused therapy. *Family Journal*, 5, 346–354.

Westwood, M. J., Keats, P. A., & Wilensky, P. (2003). Therapeutic enactment: Integrating individual and group counseling models for change. *Journal for Specialists in Group Work*, 28(2), 122–138.

White, H. (1978). Exercises in understanding your family. In *Your family is good for you*. Random House.

Whiteley, J. M. (1987). The person-centered approach to peace. *Counseling and Values*, 32, 5–8.

Widdowson, M. (2010). *Transactional analysis: 100 key points and techniques*. Routledge.

Widdowson, M. (2018). The importance of research in transactional analysis for transactional analysts. *Transactional Analysis Journal*, 48(1), 33–42.

Wilbur, M. P., Roberts-Wilbur, J., & Morris, J. R. (1990). A humanistic alternative for counseling alcoholics. *Journal of Humanistic Education and Development*, 28, 146–165.

Wilcoxon, S. A. (1987). Ethical standards: A study of application and utility. *Journal of Counseling and Development*, 65, 510–511.

Wilcoxon, S. A., Remley, T. P., Jr., & Gladding, S. T. (2013). *Ethical, legal and professional issues in the practice of marriage and family therapy* (5th ed. revised). Merrill/Prentice Hall.

Wilde, J. (1996). The efficacy of short-term rational-emotive education with fourth-grade students. *Elementary School Guidance & Counseling*, 31, 131–138.

Wilkins, P. (1995). A creative therapies model for the group supervision of counselors. *British Journal of Guidance and Counselling*, 23, 245–257.

Wilks, D. (2003). A historical review of counseling theory development in relation to definitions of free will and determinism. *Journal of Counseling and Development*, 81, 278–284.

Wilson, C. J., & Cottone, R. R. (2013). Using cognitive behavior therapy in clinical work with African American children and adolescents: A review of the literature. *Journal of Multicultural Counseling and Development*, 41(3), 130–143.

Wilson, G. T. (2011). Behavior therapy. In R. J. Corsini & D. Wedding (Eds.), *Current psychotherapies* (9th ed., pp. 235–275). Brooks/Cole.

Winkler, K. J. (1986). Scholars prescribe Freud's "talking cure" for problems. *Chronicle of Higher Education*, 33(8), 4–6l.

Wiryosutomo, H. W., Hanum, F., & Partini, S. (2019). History of development and concept of person-centered counseling in cultural diversity. *International Journal of Educational Research Review*, 4(1), 56–64.

Wolpe, J. (1958). *Psychotherapy by reciprocal inhibition building*. Stanford University Press.

Worrell, J., & Remer, P. (2003). *Feminist perspectives in therapy* (2nd ed.). Wiley.

Wubbolding, R. E. (1975). Practicing reality therapy. *Personnel and Guidance Journal*, 53, 164–165.

Wubbolding, R. E. (1988). *Using reality therapy*. HarperCollins.

Wubbolding, R. E. (1991). *Understanding reality therapy.* HarperCollins.

Wubbolding, R. E. (1994). The early years of control theory: Forerunners Marcus Aurelius & Norbert Wiener. *Journal of Reality Therapy, 13,* 51–54.

Wubbolding, R. E. (1996). *Basic concepts of reality therapy.* Institute for Control Theory, Reality Therapy and Quality Management.

Wubbolding, R. E. (1998). *Cycle of managing, supervising, counseling, and coaching using reality therapy.* Center for Reality Therapy.

Wubbolding, R. E. (2000). *Reality therapy for the 21st century.* Brunner-Routledge.

Wubbolding, R. E. (2007). Reality therapy theory. In D. Capuzzi & D. Gross (Eds.), *Counseling and psychotherapy: Theories and interventions* (4th ed., pp. 289–312). Pearson.

Wubbolding, R. E. (2011). *Reality therapy.* American Psychological Association.

Wubbolding, R. E. (2013). *Reality therapy for the 21st century.* Routledge.

Wubbolding, R. E. (2015). The voice of William Glasser: Accessing the continuing evolution of reality therapy. *Journal of Mental Health Counseling, 37*(3), 189–205.

Wubbolding, R. E. (2017). *Reality therapy and self-evaluation: The key to client change.* American Counseling Association.

Wubbolding, R. E., & Brickell, J. (2017). *Counselling with reality therapy.* Taylor & Francis.

Wylie, M. S. (1990, March/April). Brief therapy on the couch. *Family Therapy Networker, 14,* 26–35, 66.

Wylie, M. S. (1991, March/April). Family therapy's neglected prophet. *Family Therapy Networker, 15,* 24–37, 77.

Wylie, M. S. (1992, January/February). The evolution of a revolution. *Family Therapy Networker, 16,* 17–29, 98–99.

Yablonsky, L. (1981). *Psychodrama: Resolving emotional problems through role-playing.* Gardner Press.

Yalom, I. D. (1980). *Existential psychotherapy.* Basic Books.

Yalom, I. D., & Josselson, R. (2011). Existential psychotherapy. In R. J. Corsini & D. Wedding (Eds.), *Current psychotherapies* (9th ed., pp. 310–341). Brooks/Cole.

Yee, T. T. L. (2018). Culturally responsive adlerian counseling for East Asian clients. *Journal of Individual Psychology 74*(4), 388–403.

Yeung, F. K. C. (1999). The adaptation of solution-focused therapy in Chinese culture: A linguistic perspective. *Transcultural-Psychiatry, 36,* 477–489.

Yontef, G., Jacobs, L., & Bowman (2019). Gestalt therapy. In D. Wedding & R. J. Corsini (Eds.), *Current psychotherapies* (11th ed., pp. 309–348). Brooks/Cole.

Young, R. A. (1988). Ordinary explanations and career theories. *Journal of Counseling and Development, 66,* 336–339.

Zalaquett, C., Ivey, A., & Ivey, M. B. (2019). *Essential theories of counseling and psychotherapy: Everyday practice in our diverse world.* Cognella Academic Publishing.

Zeig, J. K. (2007). A tribute to Jay Haley (1923–2007). *American Journal of Clinical Hypnosis, 50,* 5–9.

Zerbetto, R., & Tantam, D. (2001). The survey of European psychotherapy training 3: What psychotherapy is available in Europe? *European Journal of Psychotherapy, Counselling and Health, 4,* 397–405.

Ziff, K. K. (2012). *Asylum on the hill: History of a healing landscape.* Ohio University Press.

Zimbardo, P. G., & Leippe, M. R. (1991). *The psychology of attitude change and social influence.* Temple University Press.

Zinker, J. (1978). *Creative process in Gestalt therapy.* Random House.

Zyromski, B., Dollarhide, C. T., Aras, Y., Geiger, S., Oehrtman, J. P., & Clarke, H. (2018). Beyond complex trauma: An existential view of adverse childhood experiences. *Journal of Humanistic Counseling, 57*(3), 156–172.

Index

■ ■ ■

Page numbers in italics refer to figures and tables.

K

Karpman triangle, *146*, 146–47
Kerr, Michael, 168
key terms
    on psychoanalysis and psychodynamic
        theories, 30–31
    on theories, 13
Kierkegaard, Søren, 47, 48
Kim, J., 202
Klein, Melanie, 19, 29
Kohut, Heinz, 29
Kottler, J., 235–36

L

labeling and mislabeling, 117
language, 246
latency, 19
Lazarus, Arnold, 8–9
Leaving Home (Haley), 183
Lerner, Harriet, 157–58
levels of consciousness, 16
Levinson, D. J., 27
Levitov, J. E., 9
libido, 17
life cycle transitions, 173, 180
lifestyle tasks require courage, *37*
Lincoln, Abraham, 207
Linda's case, 10–11. *See also specific topics*
Lindemann, Erich, 223–24
listening activities, 227
logo (search for meaning), 49
logotherapy, 49, 53, 55
Love and Will (May), 49
love/belonging, 8

M

Madanes, Cloe, 182, 183, 188, 191
magic shop, 211
magnification, 117
maintenance, 9, *9*
making the rounds exercise, 78
manifest content, 24
Man's Search for Meaning (Frankl), 49
marriage, 10
Martin, G. E., 8
Maslow, Abraham, 7–8, *8*, 49, 229
May, Rollo, 48–49, 57
May I feed you a sentence? exercise, 78
McBride, M. C., 8
McGoldrick, M., 168
Mead, Margaret, 182
meaning, 50
The Meaning of Anxiety (May), 48
Meichenbaum, Donald, 116–17. *See also*
    cognitive and cognitive-behavioral
    therapies
mental illness, 92

Mental Research Institute (MRI), 181–82,
    183, 194–95
Metaphor 34, 92
microskills, 7
middle children, 36
mind reading, 118
minimization, 37, 117
ministry, 59
Minuchin, Salvador, 183
mirror, 213, 218
mislabeling, 117
misperceptions of life and life's demands, 37
modern theories, 6–7
monodrama, 213
moralism, 92
morality, 235
moral principle, 18
Moreno, Jacob, 208. *See also* psychodrama
Moreno, Zerka, 208, 213–14, 216, 220
motivation, 123–24
MRI. *See* Mental Research Institute
multigenerational transmission process,
    170–71, 177–78
multiple double, 213

N

National Institute of Mental Health
    (NIMH), 169
natural child, *142*, 142–43
natural disasters. *See* crisis counseling
Nazi concentration camps, 59
Nazi Germany, 16, 49, 59, 72
negative family atmosphere, 36
negative predictions, 118
neurosis, five layers of, 76
never scripts, 147
*New Introductory Lectures on
    Psychoanalysis* (Freud, S.), 16
Ng, K. S., 202
NIMH. *See* National Institute of Mental
    Health
9/11, 222, 225
noncompetitive, 88
nonevents, 225
nonmaleficence, 238
nonverbal messages, 186
noogenic neurosis, 50
Norcross, J. C., 4–5
now, principle of, 75–76, 81
nurturing parent, 143

O

object relations theory, 19–20
objects, 19
Oedipus complex, 18–19
O'Hanlon, Bill, 195, 202
Okun, B. F., 7
On Becoming a Person (Rogers), 59–60

About the Author

■ ■ ■

Samuel T. Gladding is a professor in the Department of Counseling at Wake Forest University in Winston-Salem, North Carolina. He has been a practicing counselor in both public and private agencies since the 1970s. His leadership in the field of counseling includes service as president of the American Counseling Association (ACA), the American Association of State Counseling Boards (AASCB), the Association for Counselor Education and Supervision (ACES), the Association for Specialists in Group Work (ASGW), the International Association of Marriage and Family Counselors (IAMFC), and Chi Sigma Iota (CSI) (the international counseling honor society).

Gladding is the former editor of the *Journal for Specialists in Group Work* and a fellow in both the ACA and the ASGW. He has been a prolific author of scholar-refereed articles, and in 1999 he was included in the top 1% of contributors to the *Journal of Counseling and Development* for the 15-year period 1978–1993. Gladding's most recent books include: *Becoming a Counselor: The Light, the Bright, and the Serious* (2021), *The Creative Arts in Counseling* (6th ed., 2021), *Group Work: A Counseling Specialty* (8th ed., 2020), *A Concise Guide to Opioid Addiction for Counselors* (with Kevin Alderson, 2020), *Choosing the Right Counselor for You* (with Kevin Alderson, 2019), *Counseling: A Comprehensive Profession* (8th ed., 2019), *Family Therapy: History, Theory, & Process* (7th ed., 2018), *The Counseling Dictionary* (4th ed., 2018), and *Clinical Mental Health Counseling* (with Debbie Newsome) (5th ed., 2017).

Gladding's previous academic appointments have been at the University of Alabama at Birmingham (UAB) and Fairfield University (Connecticut). Prior to those appointments he worked as the director of children's services in a rural mental health center and as a community college psychology instructor, both in Rockingham County, North Carolina. Gladding received his degrees from Wake Forest (BA, MA, Ed.), Yale (MA), and the University of North Carolina–Greensboro (PhD). He is a National Certified Counselor, a Certified Clinical Mental Health Counselor, and a Licensed Clinical Mental Health Counselor (North Carolina). Gladding is a former member of the Alabama Board of Examiners in Counseling and the North Carolina Board of Licensed Clinical Mental Health Counselors.

Dr. Gladding is married to the former Claire Tillson and is the father of three adult children. In addition to counseling, he enjoys walking, swimming, reading, humor, and interacting with his family and his therapy dog, Lexie.

CPSIA information can be obtained
at www.ICGtesting.com
Printed in the USA
BVHW081210300621
610414BV00004B/5